Praise for *Making Mergers Work: The Strategic Importance of People*

"*Making Mergers Work* is essential reading for leaders of all stripes, for it shows both 'why' people-related issues are important at each stage of the M&A life cycle, as well as 'what' to pay attention to. The issues it addresses are crucial to the long-term success of any deal, and no organization can afford to ignore them."
—Wayne F. Cascio, Ph.D.
Professor of Management, Graduate School of Business Administration,
University of Colorado, Denver

"I want to know what the human issues will be and who the opinion makers in a target organization are before a deal is closed. That way, we can create an insightful merger plan and know with whom we need to communicate when the inevitable conversion issues arise. *Making Mergers Work: The Strategic Importance of People* provides an excellent resource for understanding and successfully addressing the human issues in any M&A deal."
—David E. Rainbolt
President and CEO, BancFirst

"*Making Mergers Work* is long overdue. It focuses on the critical people issues in mergers and acquisitions. While there has been an extensive amount of research on deal-making, in the end, success comes down to the contributions and value created by the people. Towers Perrin and the SHRM Foundation should be applauded for this pioneering effort."
—Kathryn D. McKee, SPHR, CCP
Senior Vice President and Region Head (retired), Human Resources,
Standard Chartered Bank, North America

"*Making Mergers Work: The Strategic Importance of People* is an outstanding book which should be required reading not only for Human Resource professionals but for any management team contemplating or involved in a merger or acquisition. The appendices themselves are worth more than the price of the book. The importance of HR being involved through the whole acquisition process is clearly documented as value-added."
—James L. Wilkerson
Senior Vice President, Human Resources and Administration, ABB Vetco Gray Inc.

MAKING
MERGERS
WORK

MAKING MERGERS WORK

The Strategic Importance of People

A Towers Perrin/SHRM Foundation Publication

This publication is designed to provide accurate and authoritative information regarding the subject matter covered. It is sold with the understanding that neither the publisher nor the author is engaged in rendering legal or other professional service. If legal advice or other expert assistance is required, the services of a competent, licensed professional should be sought.

This book is published by the Society for Human Resource Management (SHRM®) and funded by the SHRM Foundation. The interpretations, conclusions, and recommendations in this book are those of the authors and do not necessarily represent those of SHRM or the SHRM Foundation.

© 2002 Towers, Perrin, Foster, & Crosby, Inc. All rights reserved.

This publication may not be reproduced, stored in a retrieval system, or transmitted in whole or in part, in any form or by any means, electronic, mechanical, photocopying, recording, or otherwise, without the prior written permission of the Society for Human Resource Management or the SHRM Foundation, both at 1800 Duke Street, Alexandria, VA 22314.

Towers Perrin is one of the world's largest management and human resources consulting firms. It helps organizations improve performance and manage their investments in people, advising them on human resource strategy and management, change and culture, total rewards, including compensation and benefits, HR technology, and administration and communication, both Web and print-based. The firm has over 9,000 employees and 78 offices in 74 cities worldwide.

The Society for Human Resource Management (SHRM) is the leading voice of the human resource profession, representing more than 165,000 professional and student members throughout the world. Visit SHRM Online at www.shrm.org.

As the R&D arm of the profession, the SHRM Foundation expands the body of human resource knowledge through its support of leading-edge research, practical publications, and education initiatives. Visit SHRM Foundation online at www.shrm.org/foundation.

To order additional copies of *Making Mergers Work* please call the SHRMStore at 1-800-444-5006, option #1, or order online at http://www.shrm.org/shrmstore. For bulk order discount information, please email to shrmstore@shrm.org.

ISBN 1-58644-008-X
Printed in the United States of America.
10 9 8 7 6 5 4 3 2 1

FIRST EDITION, October 2001

Contents

Acknowledgments vii
Jeffrey A. Schmidt

Foreword ix
Louis R. Forbringer

Section I	NEW PERSPECTIVE ON M&A
Chapter 1	The Strategic Importance of People .... 3 *Jeffrey A. Schmidt*
Chapter 2	Business Perspective on Mergers and Acquisitions .... 23 *Jeffrey A. Schmidt*

Section II	THE M&A LIFE CYCLE
Chapter 3	The Pre-Deal Stage .... 47 *François Lafaix*
Chapter 4	The Due Diligence Stage .... 75 *Andrew F. Giffin*
Chapter 5	Integration Planning Stage .... 99 *Brent L. Rice*
Chapter 6	Implementation Stage .... 127 *Mary Cianni*

Section III — THE NEW HR EMERGES

Chapter 7	Transforming the HR Organization . . . . 155 *Mary Cianni*	
Chapter 8	Planning the Integration of Rewards . . . . 171 *Kenneth T. Ransby and John M. Burns*	
Chapter 9	HR Technology Integration Strategy . . . . 199 *Alfred J. Walker*	

Section IV — THE NEXT M&A WAVE

Chapter 10	M&A in the New Millennium . . . . 217 *Thomas O. Davenport*	

Appendices

Appendix A	The Global Transaction . . . . 237 *Jeffrey A. Schmidt*	
Appendix B	Major Risks to Implementation . . . . 241 *Jeffrey A. Schmidt*	
Appendix C	More About Due Diligence . . . . 245 *Andrew F. Giffin*	
Appendix D	Executive Compensation Issues . . . . 257 *John R. Ellerman and Richard N. Ericson*	
Appendix E	Functional Integration: Marketing and Sales . . . . 269 *John D. Southwell*	
Appendix F	Benefits Alignment . . . . 283 *Samira A. Kaderali*	

ABOUT THE AUTHORS 291
INDEX 295

Acknowledgments

We at Towers Perrin would like to thank the SHRM Foundation for inviting us to be its partner on this groundbreaking mergers and acquisitions (M&A) research project. M&A is arguably one of the most significant and challenging business issues of our era.

The SHRM Foundation is the nonprofit affiliate of the Society for Human Resource Management (SHRM), the world's largest society of HR professionals with over 165,000 members. It supports leading-edge research on the critical issues affecting the workplace and the HR profession.

We appreciate this opportunity to conduct new research and to share our expertise regarding M&A with the HR professional community and with senior business executives and the investment community at large.

On a personal note, I would like to thank each of the lead authors for contributing chapters to this book. Each contributor is profiled at the end of the appendices. A number of other colleagues were pivotal to completing this book. I extend my personal appreciation to Kathryn Abernathy, leader of Towers Perrin's M&A initiative, for her ongoing sponsorship and steadfast support. Nancy Connors, senior editor, was invaluable in organizing, drafting, and editing the manuscript. Mary Rabault and Laura Brown organized, managed, and kept the project moving despite our authors' numerous commitments and client obligations. Mary retired before we completed the manuscript, but without her brilliant ideas and ability to get things done we would probably still be writing.

A number of Towers Perrin consultants and staff provided invaluable support to the lead authors of each chapter by providing information, writing chapter sections, or reviewing drafts. Our thanks to Lynn Adamson, Brian Beatty, John Beedham, Holly Bennet, Craig Berkowitch, Jack Borbely, Marco Boschetti, Angela Daigle, Steve Davies, Stephanie Eller, Ron Fontanetta, Julie Gebauer, Frank Giampietro, Kevin Hively, Dan

Holland, Peter Jessel, Claudine Kapel, Thaddeus King, Larry Lonergan, Eileen Meehan, Madeleine Payamps, Sarah Smith, W. David Thompson, Amy Unckless, and Charlie Watts.

Jessica Saban-Francis did a superb job working with me to develop, administer, and, most important, evaluate the results of the Towers Perrin/SHRM Foundation survey of HR executives. She was ably assisted by Isaac Mbiti, Jeff Allen, Glen Rehagen, and Ken Oehler. I am especially grateful to my incredibly talented secretary, Rose Tashiro, who patiently toiled over countless hours of drafting, redrafting, and proofreading the manuscript. Bill Montgomery, my friend and colleague, was especially helpful in reviewing the manuscript and working many hours with Nancy Connors and me to "get it right." Thanks also to Karen Allen for her legal review and sharp editorial eye. I also thank Eric Burrows, Mary Duhon, Sharon Clark, Joe Conway, Stanley Davis, and Rachael Astrachan who helped us in many ways to promote this book and are continuing to make sure it is a success.

The enthusiasm and dedication of Marty Walsh, executive director, SHRM Foundation, is greatly appreciated by everyone at Towers Perrin. He was the catalyst and champion for our efforts throughout the many months we labored over the manuscript. Our thanks also go to Lou Forbringer, former president of the SHRM Foundation, who first raised the idea of undertaking this book project within SHRM and who was instrumental in getting the project launched. We also appreciate the generous involvement of Don Howard, an outstanding SHRM volunteer leader, and Patrick Wright, Ph.D., SHRM Foundation Board member, for sharing their insights and considerable experience in finalizing the manuscript.

My personal thanks go as well to Ken Ranftle, a former chairman of SHRM and the recently retired managing director for Human Resources at Towers Perrin, who first brought the idea of this project to me. He reviewed the manuscript and suggested sharpening key areas of our argument. I am grateful to my colleagues John Lynch, Mark Mactas, and Bruce Pittinger, who had the confidence to sponsor this project within our company's Management Committee and who provided the financial support and encouragement needed to keep the project going.

Finally, I would like to thank my family and the families of all the contributing authors at Towers Perrin. Writing this book has required their inspiration, encouragement, understanding, and patience over many months. Without them, the daunting task of tackling as broad and important a subject as we have covered in this book—while at the same time fulfilling our obligations as practicing consultants and balancing our family responsibilities—would have proved to be too great a burden to shoulder.

This book stands as a testament to the unshakable belief that people do matter. This belief is the bedrock on which Towers Perrin and the SHRM Foundation are built.

Jeffrey A. Schmidt
September 2001

Foreword

Just as couples enter into marriages full of hope and good cheer, businesses enter into mergers, acquisitions, joint ventures, and partnerships full of optimism and plans for a rosy future.

To take the metaphor one step further, future brides and grooms are often blinded by love to red flags signaling their partner's faults or misdeeds. Similarly, eager acquiring companies tend to overlook or ignore messy people issues that might get in their way as they try to merge disparate cultures.

The sad irony is that it's usually people who cause both marriages and mergers to fail. Although it's common knowledge that half of all marriages end in divorce, less well known is that more than three-quarters of all mergers and acquisitions (M&As) don't live up to expectations. Perhaps there were unrealistic goals. Or there was a clash of cultures (one was autocratic while the other was laissez-faire). Or maybe both sides wanted the primary leadership role.

Whatever the case, in both personal and business mergers, practical, concrete steps can be taken to greatly increase the likelihood of success. Unfortunately, most companies don't take these steps early enough.

And why should they? After all, the purpose of a merger is to increase shareholder value, so shouldn't senior management focus first and foremost on finance and business issues? Executives face a seemingly endless list of pressing questions, including what the merger will cost, how much the acquirer can expect to gain from it, where the synergies will come from, how to increase market share or eliminate manufacturing redundancies, how to combine research and development, how to streamline management, and so on.

Given this laundry list of critical concerns, the so-called soft issues—managing the vast change that will occur in both organizations, retaining key talent, and getting the best of both organizations' cultures—are far from executives' minds. Yet these are the very issues that, poorly handled—or not handled at all—cause mergers to fail.

It is this book's contention that these issues can be addressed and resolved by bringing the human resources (HR) function into the M&A process at the very beginning. Research conducted for *Making Mergers Work: The Strategic Importance of People* shows that 77 percent of HR directors say they have only some or no involvement in the pre-deal phase, and 43 percent have only some or no involvement in the due diligence stage.

Yet HR directors are anxious to get involved in the process. A few years ago, as the incoming president of the SHRM Foundation Board, I interviewed more than 20 HR executives about their greatest concerns. Not surprisingly, how to help mergers and acquisitions succeed led the list.

At that time, the books available on the M&A process either addressed the financial aspects or simply focused on HR's role. But HR executives wanted one book that could do both: give them a clear understanding of the entire merger process so they could add the greatest value, and provide senior management with extensive details on the roles HR should play from pre-deal through implementation.

We asked Towers Perrin consultants to write this book because of their expertise in working with companies on all facets of a merger, with special emphasis on the human issues. In the past 10 years alone, Towers Perrin has helped numerous clients with mergers, acquisitions, joint ventures, and other types of partnerships. Much of what the firm's consultants have gleaned from their experience is laid out in this book. It not only follows the M&A process from start to finish, it also includes examples of why certain mergers succeed and others don't.

In addition, this book includes the results of an extensive survey of HR executives that Towers Perrin and the SHRM Foundation undertook in 2000. The purpose of the survey was to learn what role the HR function currently plays in mergers and acquisitions and how that role can be recast so that HR can best help senior executives resolve the people issues they will face.

The book should be of great use to HR executives. It will also help business and government leaders, senior executives, academics, and business journalists understand and appreciate the importance of HR in any merger or acquisition.

Whether they succeed or fail, M&As are expensive. They cost time, money, and enormous amounts of corporate and individual energy. Failed mergers hurt more than the bottom line. They can disrupt the company's effectiveness, send morale on a downward spiral, and result in the loss of valuable people.

On the other hand, careful planning and implementation, realistic expectations, and consistent, well-conceived communication with employees can lead to success. And the synergies that grow from an effective merger can do more for the combined company's fortunes than decades of internal growth.

The risks inherent in a merger or acquisition are high and the benefits often uncertain. But the good news is that *Making Mergers Work* can help reduce the risk.

On behalf of the SHRM Foundation, our thanks to Jeff Schmidt and his team of expert authors at Towers Perrin for creating this important book for the HR profession.

Louis R. Forbringer, Ph.D., SPHR
Former President, SHRM Foundation
September 2001

SECTION I
New Perspective on M&A

CHAPTER ONE

The Strategic Importance of People

Jeffrey A. Schmidt

*"It's easy to do a deal. It's tough
to do a deal that works."*

Jerre Stead
Former Chairman, NCR

Mergers and acquisitions (M&As)—from high-tech companies to traditional manufacturing and services businesses—have captured headlines for a decade. Many companies expect a merger or acquisition to provide the scale of operations, resources and capabilities, financial strength, and broad market reach necessary for growth and long-run competitiveness. And yet, study after study concludes that even well-conceived deals often fall short of their promised benefits.

It is not simply bad strategy nor paying too much to complete a deal that causes failures. Rather, when M&As fail, it's frequently because of people or related issues. Key managers and scarce talent leave unexpectedly. Valuable operating synergies evaporate because cultural differences between the companies are not understood or are simply ignored. Cuts in pay or benefits programs create ill will, which reduces productivity. Management doesn't communicate its business rationale or its goals for the new company, and employees flounder in the ensuing confusion. The list goes on and on.

The seeds of success (or failure) are sowed well before the merger or acquisition is made public. Acquirers that fail to do the homework in formulating strategy and in due diligence almost always make mistakes in selecting partners and negotiating deals. For example, they don't consider cultural issues early in discussions. They don't address the ways in which the two companies' managements will work harmoniously. Too little attention is paid to identifying and keeping high-performing, high-potential employees. These mistakes will eventually come back to haunt the new company and its management.

Beyond such mistakes, once a deal is consummated virtually everything pales in comparison to the strategic importance of people management. Indeed, the consequences of a deal that flops are huge for shareholders, employees, customers, and communities alike. The implication is clear: Strategic people management is as crucial to a successful merger or acquisition as a sound strategy and fair valuation.

Over the past few years, a stream of new studies has added to the extensive literature on the successes (or failures) of M&A, particularly the giant combinations. Most of these recent studies expand upon earlier work that shows the majority of deals underperform—some in spectacular fashion—relative to the synergies and benefits their architects had promised and to the average performance of peer groups or the stock market as a whole. Each new study asks again the obvious question: With such a high failure rate, why do chief executive officers (CEOs) and boards of directors continue to pursue M&As?

The overwhelming evidence provided by M&A studies supports two incontrovertible answers. First, companies pursue M&As fearlessly—sometimes for good reasons and sometimes for bad ones—and will probably continue to do so. Second, M&As are risky strategic initiatives with people and cultural aspects that, if not handled well, can doom the deal. In short, M&As require exceptional wisdom, insight, sensitivity, perseverance, and planning to succeed. Good old-fashioned luck also helps, especially when it comes in the form of a strong equities market.

This book provides a fresh perspective on the factors that make a merger or acquisition successful. It provides new insights into understanding and successfully managing the people challenges and gives human resource (HR) professionals the ideas, background information, and practical tools for playing a strategic role at every stage of the M&A process. Armed with this knowledge, HR professionals can, and should, become a strategic business partner in this process.

M&A Life Cycle

The M&A life cycle *(Exhibit 1.1)* comprises the following stages:
- Pre-deal
- Due diligence
- Integration planning
- Implementation

The life cycle process applies to all types of M&As, but how each stage in the process plays out and its relative importance will depend on the type of deal being contemplated.

Pre-Deal Stage

In this initial stage, which can take anywhere from a few weeks to several years, acquirers search for compatible targets or merger partners and will typically complete the following activities:
- Develop a growth strategy defining the role of mergers and acquisitions
- Set criteria for candidate screening, evaluation, and selection
- Identify, gather information about, and assess potential candidates
- Decide which candidate offers the best fit for a deal
- Develop an action plan for executing the deal

Chapter Three presents an in-depth discussion of the pre-deal stage.

Exhibit 1.1 M&A Life Cycle Process

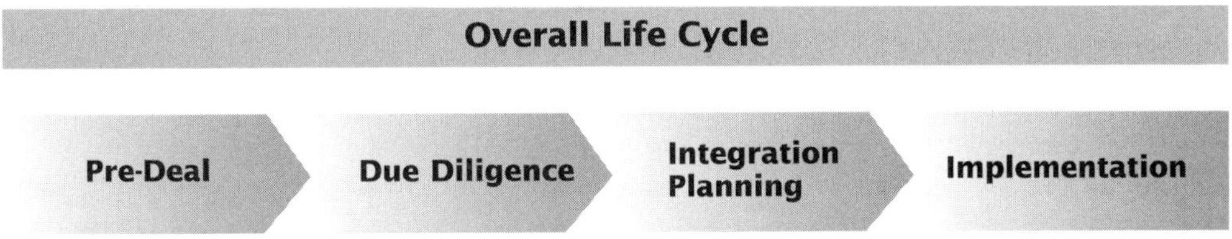

Overall Life Cycle

Pre-Deal	Due Diligence	Integration Planning	Implementation
▪ Finding compatible business ventures and partners	▪ Ensuring the deal is sound and establishing the value proposition	▪ Defining the blueprint for all aspects of the merged entities	▪ Executing the merger integration plan for the new enterprise ▪ Measuring and reporting progress

Source: Towers Perrin analysis.

Due Diligence

During the due diligence stage, which takes place largely after an offer to merge or acquire has been made, companies must ensure that the proposed deal is sound from strategic, economic, and implementation perspectives. This is a critical juncture in the life cycle of the deal. In fact, many transactions fail to proceed beyond this period of intense scrutiny. For example, it may be discovered that the proposed acquisition does not meet the acquirer's needs or standards, or the acquiree may make it clear that it will resist a takeover.

Chapter Four discusses the due diligence stage in depth. Appendix C provides additional details for developing due diligence work plans.

Integration Planning

During the integration planning stage, successful acquirers or merger partners create the comprehensive plan for all aspects of integrating their businesses and organizations. This stage generally takes place within 30 to 100 days of the decision to proceed and may begin even during due diligence if both sides are reasonably confident that the deal will go through. Still, if regulatory approvals are pending, great care must be given to direct contacts and exchange of information or data.

Chapter Five discusses the integration planning stage in depth.

Implementation

This final stage of the M&A life cycle builds on the planning that has gone before. Implementation can take from months to years, depending on the size and complexity of the companies involved and the lead times for major systems and operations integration activities.

Maintaining business continuity and momentum during the implementation stage is the single most important factor in the ultimate success of an M&A, and doing so requires a well-planned, disciplined, and speedy implementation process.

Chapters Six, Seven, Eight, and Nine discuss these and other implementation activities.

Research on the Strategic Role of People

Towers Perrin and the SHRM Foundation conducted a survey in mid-2000 to gain fresh insights into how HR professionals currently add value to a merger or acquisition and to determine ways they can play a more pivotal role in the future. Significantly, two-thirds of the 440 senior HR professionals who responded have been involved in three or more mergers, acquisitions, or joint ventures over the past five years. Over two-thirds of the companies represented have 1,000 or more employees, and almost half (46%) have annual revenues of US$1 billion or more. Although participants are primarily from North America, the respondent group also includes individuals from Europe, Latin America, and Asia Pacific.

The survey concludes that HR has significantly less involvement in the earliest strategic stages of a merger or acquisition (pre-deal and due diligence) than during the later stages (integration planning and implementation). It also shows that in the early stages of a merger or acquisition, HR can positively influence decisions that ultimately will determine success or failure—such as decisions regarding the fit of the two organizations to be joined or whether the two companies' managements and cultures will be compatible. Finally, the research indicates companies that succeed in M&As are likely to have HR professionals with strategic competencies that lead to higher levels of meaningful involvement across the full range of M&A activities.

The balance of this chapter provides an in-depth look at our survey findings, sheds light on HR's current level of involvement in M&As, and demonstrates how earlier HR involvement in strategic people, organizational, and cultural issues could have a significant impact on a deal's ultimate success. Our findings also pinpoint critical distinctions between successful and unsuccessful mergers, as well as the capabilities HR professionals need to get a seat at the deal table. These topics are then further developed throughout the book, which examines each stage of a merger or acquisition and discusses the role the HR function must play at each stage and the competencies its professionals need to do so.

A Closer Look at Our Findings: Great Expectations, Disappointing Results

Companies undertake mergers and acquisitions for myriad reasons, as *Exhibit 1.2* shows. Among survey participants, growing market share was the single most common M&A objective (82%), followed by becoming a leader in industry consolidation (68%). Yet only half of respondents were able to fully achieve those goals. In addition, fewer

Exhibit 1.2 Expected and Achieved M&A Synergies

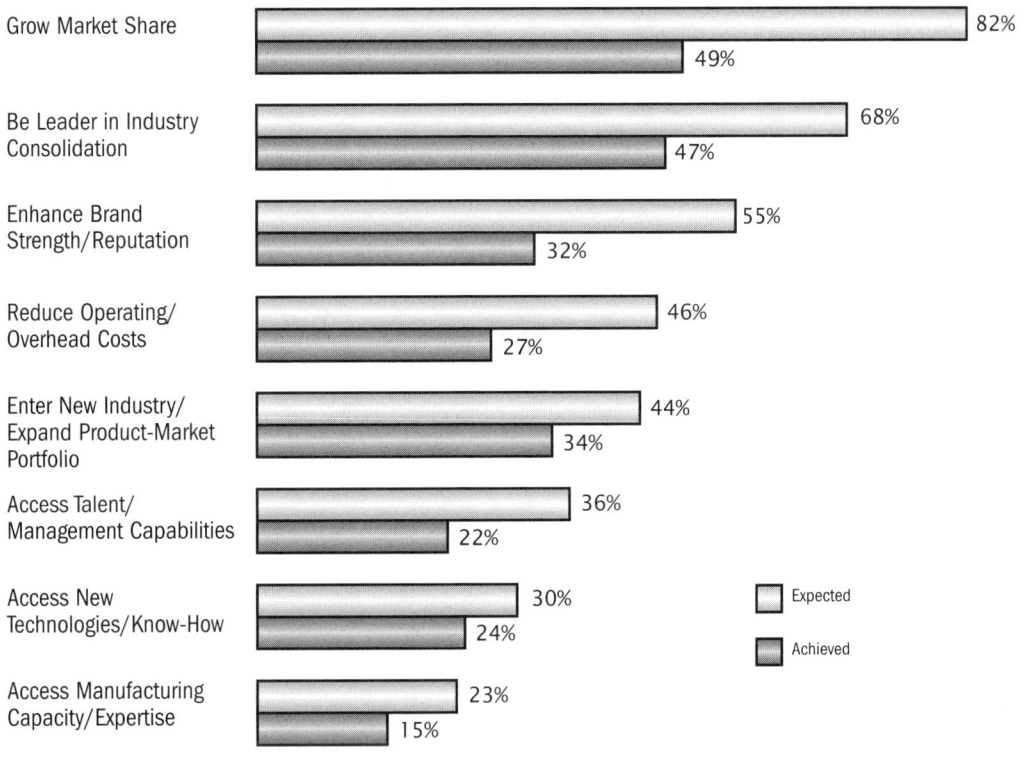

Note: Percentages indicate the respondents that highly expect or substantially achieved (4 or 5 on a 5-point scale) M&A synergies.

Source: Towers Perrin/SHRM Foundation Survey of over 440 HR executives worldwide.

than one-third (32%) were able to enhance the strength of their brand image—the third most important goal of M&A activity.

For comparison purposes, we separated respondents into companies whose mergers and acquisitions were successful (successful companies) and those whose M&As were unsuccessful (unsuccessful companies). By our definition, successful companies were those that said they achieved three or more of the synergies they identified as important or most important. Unsuccessful companies achieved fewer than three of their important or most important synergies *(Exhibit 1.3)*.

Major Obstacles to Achieving Success Stem from People Issues

According to survey respondents, the top seven obstacles to achieving M&A success are the inability to sustain financial performance, loss of productivity, incompatible cultures, loss of key talent, clash of management styles/egos, inability to manage/

Exhibit 1.3 Expected and Achieved M&A Synergies

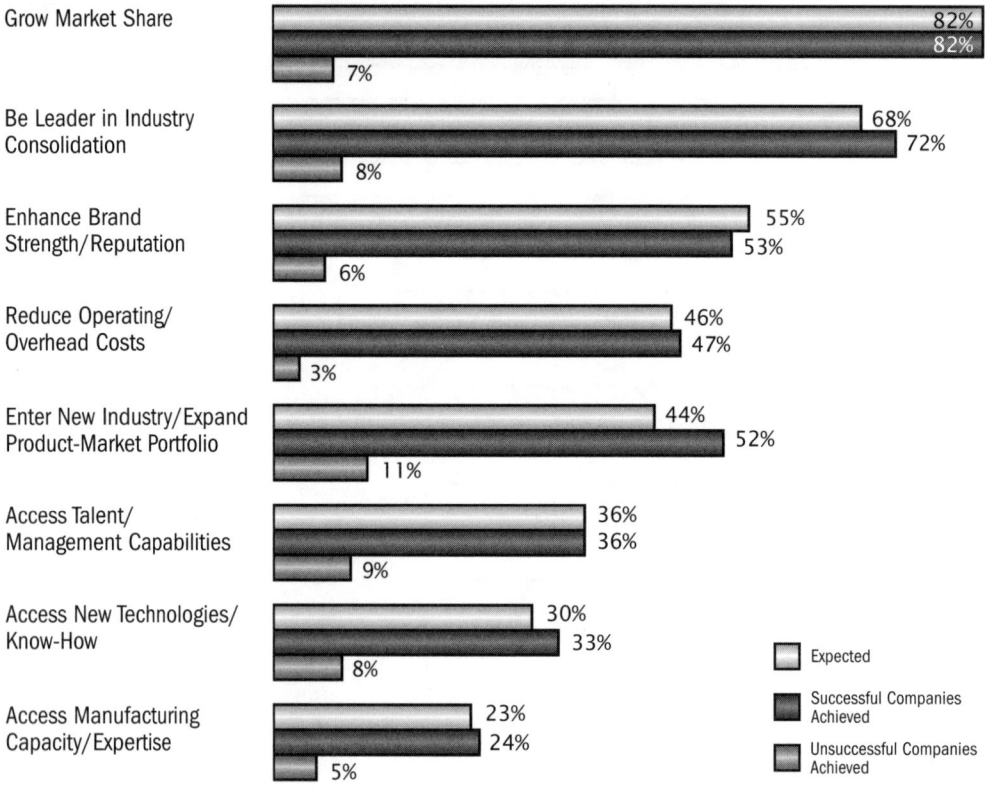

Note: Percentages indicate the respondents that highly expect or substantially achieved (4 or 5 on a 5-point scale) M&A synergies.

Source: Towers Perrin/SHRM Foundation Survey of over 440 HR executives worldwide.

implement change, and objectives/synergies not well understood. All of these obstacles are either directly or indirectly related to the strategic management of people. Of these, cultural differences between companies may be the single highest barrier to success. Our research shows more than half of the survey respondents identified culture issues as a major obstacle to achieving expected synergies in a merger or acquisition, while roughly a third reported success in addressing these issues. That's a huge gap. *Exhibit 1.4* shows more survey results.

Just what is corporate culture? Simply stated, a company's culture is the values, norms, and behaviors that characterize the company and its work environment. It encompasses the way people behave (especially how they work with each other), how they are held accountable, and the way they're rewarded. Culture also includes the way communication flows through the organization. In a nutshell, it's the modus operandi:

Exhibit 1.4 Most Significant Obstacles to Successful M&As

Obstacles

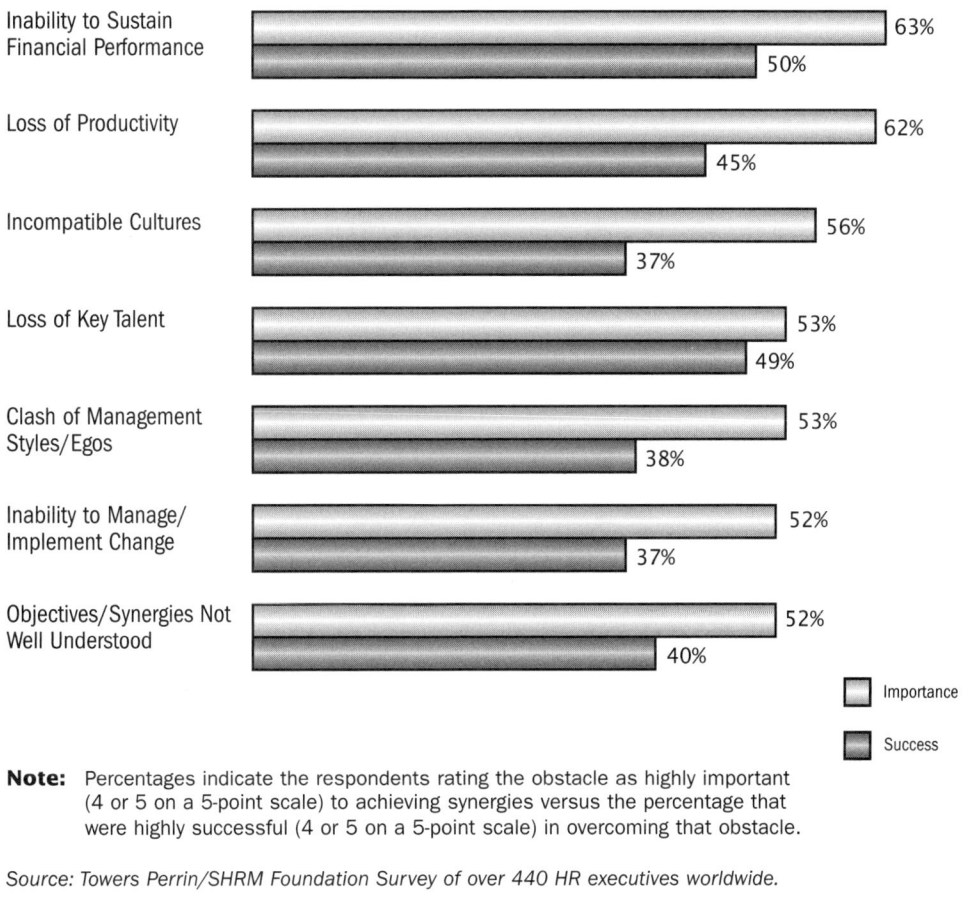

Note: Percentages indicate the respondents rating the obstacle as highly important (4 or 5 on a 5-point scale) to achieving synergies versus the percentage that were highly successful (4 or 5 on a 5-point scale) in overcoming that obstacle.

Source: Towers Perrin/SHRM Foundation Survey of over 440 HR executives worldwide.

"the way business is done and what it's like to work here." The following chart lists some of the significant cultural factors that are embedded in virtually every organization.

Demystifying Culture—Examples of Cultural Attributes

- Management style
- Decision-making process
- Degree of customer commitment
- Entrepreneurial spirit
- Innovation, creativity, and speed to market
- Value of teamwork and collaboration
- Accessibility of leadership
- Performance accountability system
- Total rewards philosophy
- Power relationships

The Strategic Importance of People ■ 9

Exhibit 1.5   Attitudes Toward Cultural Integration

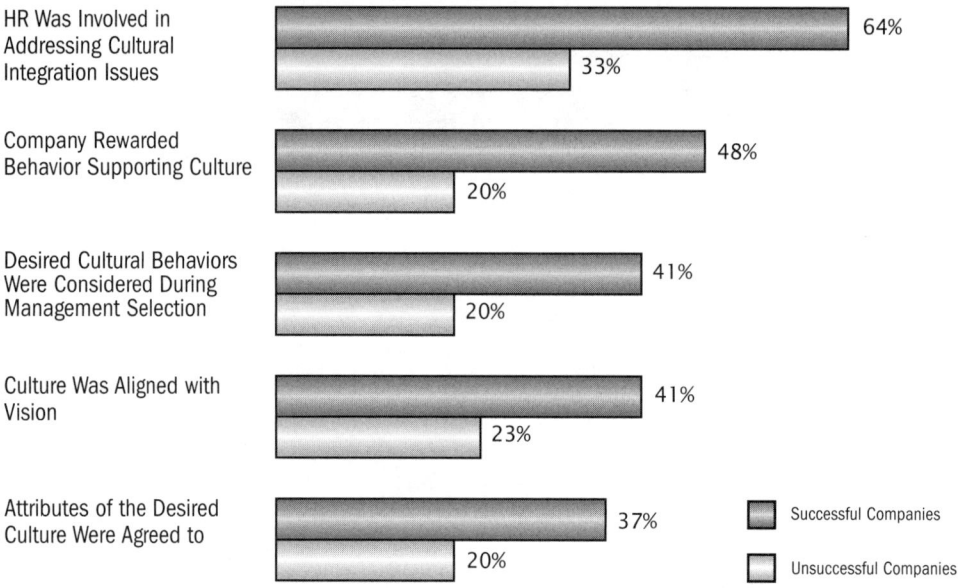

Note: Percentages indicate the respondents that highly agree (4 or 5 on a 5-point scale) with each proposition.

Source: Towers Perrin/SHRM Foundation Survey of over 440 HR executives worldwide.

Although there is no one "right" culture, vastly different or conflicting corporate culture issues can lead to problems in M&As if they're not addressed early. Take, for example, the recent merger between a swift-paced pharmaceutical company with an entrepreneurial, customer-focused culture and a staid chemical company with a more conservative, deliberate style. As a result of runaway employee conflicts that resulted from these vastly disparate cultures, the newly merged company faced a mass exodus of key talent that began during the integration planning stage, before the deal was even closed.

We believe that a key to success is the ability of the two combining organizations to understand each other's cultures by measuring them with specific tools and techniques, and then addressing potential issues early on. Notably, our research confirms that HR's early involvement in cultural integration could help to make the difference between success and failure.

The Towers Perrin/SHRM Foundation survey results underscore both the importance and the difficulty of integrating two cultures. When we compare responses from successful and unsuccessful companies, significant gaps emerge in every aspect of cultural integration—from considering desired behaviors for the new company's culture during management selection, to agreeing about the important attributes of the desired culture for the new company *(Exhibit 1.5)*. These attributes are extremely important

Exhibit 1.6 Overcoming the Obstacles to Successful M&As

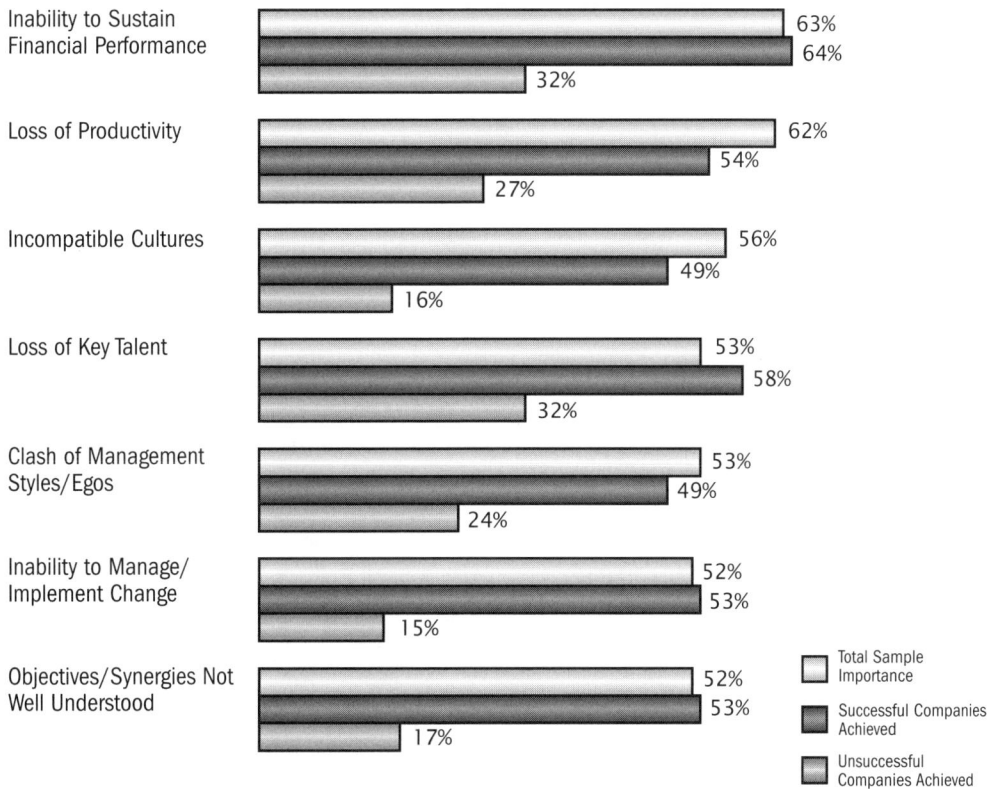

Note: Percentages indicate the respondents rating the obstacle as highly important (4 or 5 on a 5-point scale) to achieving synergies versus the percentage that were highly successful (4 or 5 on a 5-point scale) in overcoming that obstacle.

Source: Towers Perrin/SHRM Foundation Survey of over 440 HR executives worldwide.

because they influence the design of key HR programs, including those for management development and succession.

Comparison of responses from successful and unsuccessful companies reveals gaps between the importance of an obstacle and the ability to overcome it. The gaps are negligible for successful companies for good reason—namely, the ability to overcome these obstacles predicts successful implementation of M&As. By the same token, the opposite is true for unsuccessful companies *(Exhibit 1.6)*. In sum, successful companies have made more accurate assessments of anticipated M&A synergies, and they're capable of overcoming potential obstacles to capturing them.

For all of these reasons and more, HR must have a seat at the planning table—that is, be involved at the beginning stages of the deal—to provide management with critical insights into how the merger or acquisition will affect the newly formed company's people. It is critical for HR to develop strategies that will recommit and engage the

Exhibit 1.7 HR Involvement in M&As

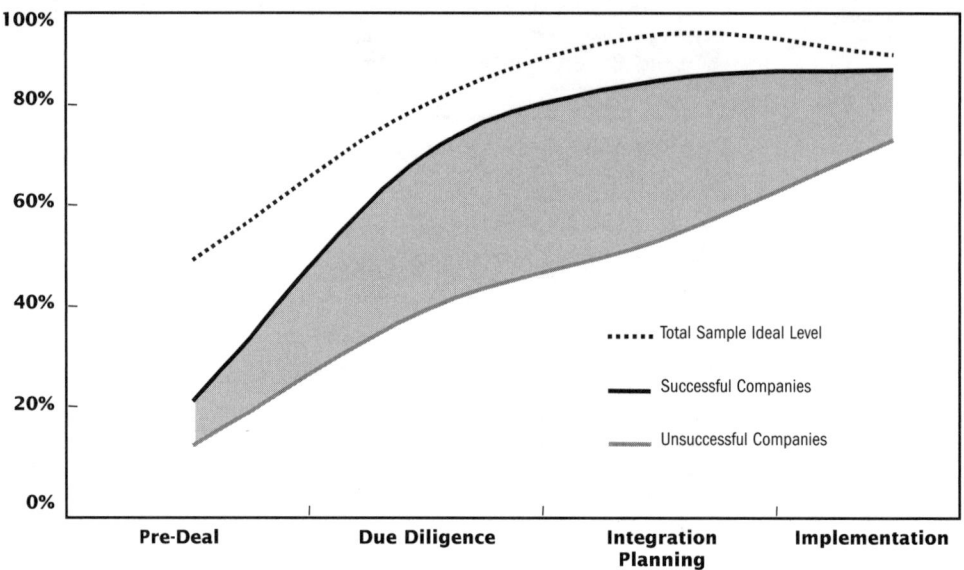

Note: Figures represent the percentage of respondents with high levels of involvement (4 or 5 on a 5-point scale) in each stage.

Source: Towers Perrin/SHRM Foundation Survey of over 440 HR executives worldwide.

employees who will make the new company a success and to help managers implement them. As one savvy vice president of HR put it, "HR is the grease between individual employees affected by the merger and the people making the merger happen."

HR Involvement in the M&A Process: Too Little, Too Late

Survey participants reported relatively little HR involvement in the first two critical stages of a merger or acquisition (pre-deal and due diligence) in which the viability and risks of a merger or acquisition are assessed. HR is significantly more involved during integration planning and implementation, where aligning HR programs and addressing staffing issues are among the key concerns *(Exhibit 1.7)*. Looked at another way, HR has typically participated in the M&A process through its traditional roles and expertise as technical specialists in the people arena rather than as a strategic business partner and trusted advisor within the senior management team. The HR involvement gap at every stage is larger for unsuccessful companies, further supporting the premise that such involvement is crucial to M&A success.

When we compare successful and unsuccessful companies, both types of organizations start out at nearly the same low level of HR pre-deal involvement. But as the deal builds momentum in the due diligence and integration planning stages, and to some extent in the implementation stage, significant differences appear.

Exhibit 1.8 Value and HR Involvement in Pre-Deal Activities

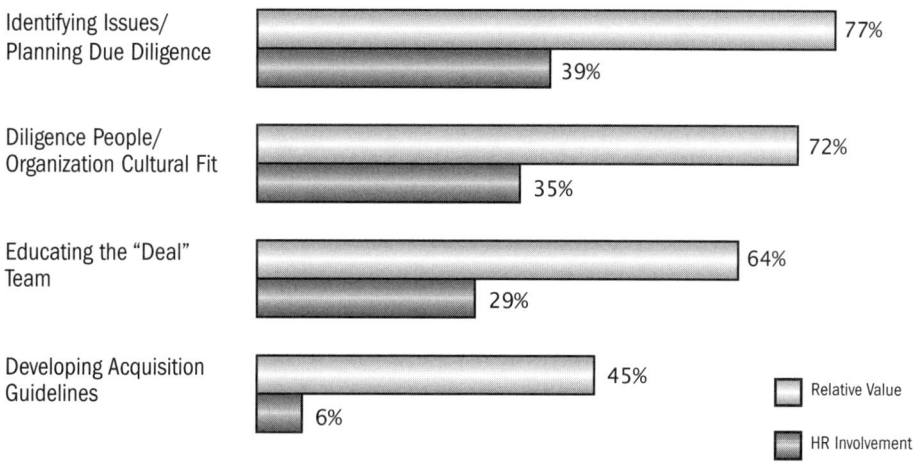

Note: Figures indicate the percentage of respondents rating the activity as highly valuable (4 or 5 on a 5-point scale) and a high level of involvement (4 or 5 on a 5-point scale).

Source: Towers Perrin/SHRM Foundation Survey of over 440 HR executives worldwide.

Pre-Deal

Survey participants rated pre-deal activities to be as important as those of any other stage, yet HR has the lowest involvement in this part of a merger or acquisition. In fact, 7 in 10 HR professionals said they understand the value of identifying issues, assessing people, determining organizational and cultural fit, and educating the "deal team" about the related risks of the potential combination; however, only 4 in 10 said they are substantially involved at this stage *(Exhibit 1.8)*.

It's not surprising why people, organization, and culture issues are frequently overlooked—often with significant consequences—at this stage. HR professionals usually have little involvement, and the usual members of the deal team are not trained to spot or assess such issues. For example, a consumer goods company acquired a competitor to leverage its distribution capability. The pre-deal team heard rumors of retention problems at the acquired company but failed to explore the dimensions, causes, or implications of the problem. Had HR been included on the deal team, these issues probably would have been raised as a red flag. Instead, the deal was made, retention problems escalated, and the new company's distribution synergy was compromised.

Due Diligence

Simply stated, the purpose of due diligence is to determine whether the acquirer is paying the right price for the right target company. The due diligence process must pinpoint

Exhibit 1.9 Agreement with Proposition

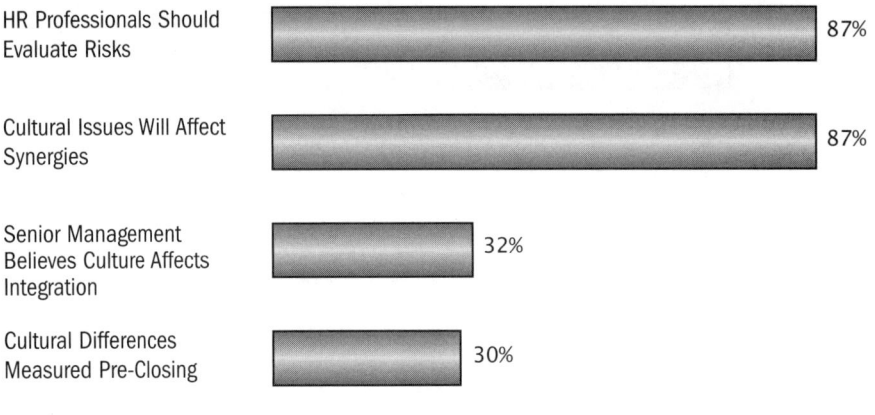

Note: Figures indicate a high level of agreement (4 or 5 on a 5-point scale).

Source: Towers Perrin/SHRM Foundation Survey of over 440 HR executives worldwide.

issues that could raise potential problems. That's a formidable challenge, given the limited time and resources usually available. Even with an exhaustive process, deal wreckers can come from almost anywhere—even areas thought of as only marginally important at first glance. That means the due diligence team must have real subject matter experts to avoid making serious mistakes. HR should be on this team. Noted one senior vice president of a mid-sized software company, "Involving HR earlier could have saved the company $10 million because the deal makers missed an unfunded executive pension program, which turned out to be a major liability. To avoid making the same mistake in the future, HR is now involved in all pre-deal M&A activities."

Performing a cultural assessment is an important task for HR in the due diligence stage. As a senior vice president of a transportation company explained, "Due diligence is the key period for assessing the culture of the companies, including how much bureaucracy they have, how they make decisions, etc. In fact, combining two companies with disparate cultures can only dilute organizational effectiveness." That said, culture is not usually assessed at this stage. This is not because HR doesn't recognize the importance of assessing cultural fit and the associated implementation risks *(Exhibit 1.9)*; rather, only one-third have been able to convince senior management of the role these issues play in the success of the integration process. "Culture is not on the map with senior management," an HR vice president observed. "During our last merger, HR was very disciplined about collecting and analyzing perceptions, reports, interviews, and so forth, but it all ended up at the bottom of our CEO's desk drawer. As I see it, cultural assessments are useful only if senior management understands and prioritizes cultural and behavioral issues."

Oddly enough, HR tends to overlook long-term people performance issues during due diligence. Instead, the research shows HR focuses on three areas: benefits (89%),

Exhibit 1.10 Integration Planning: Value of Activities and HR Involvement

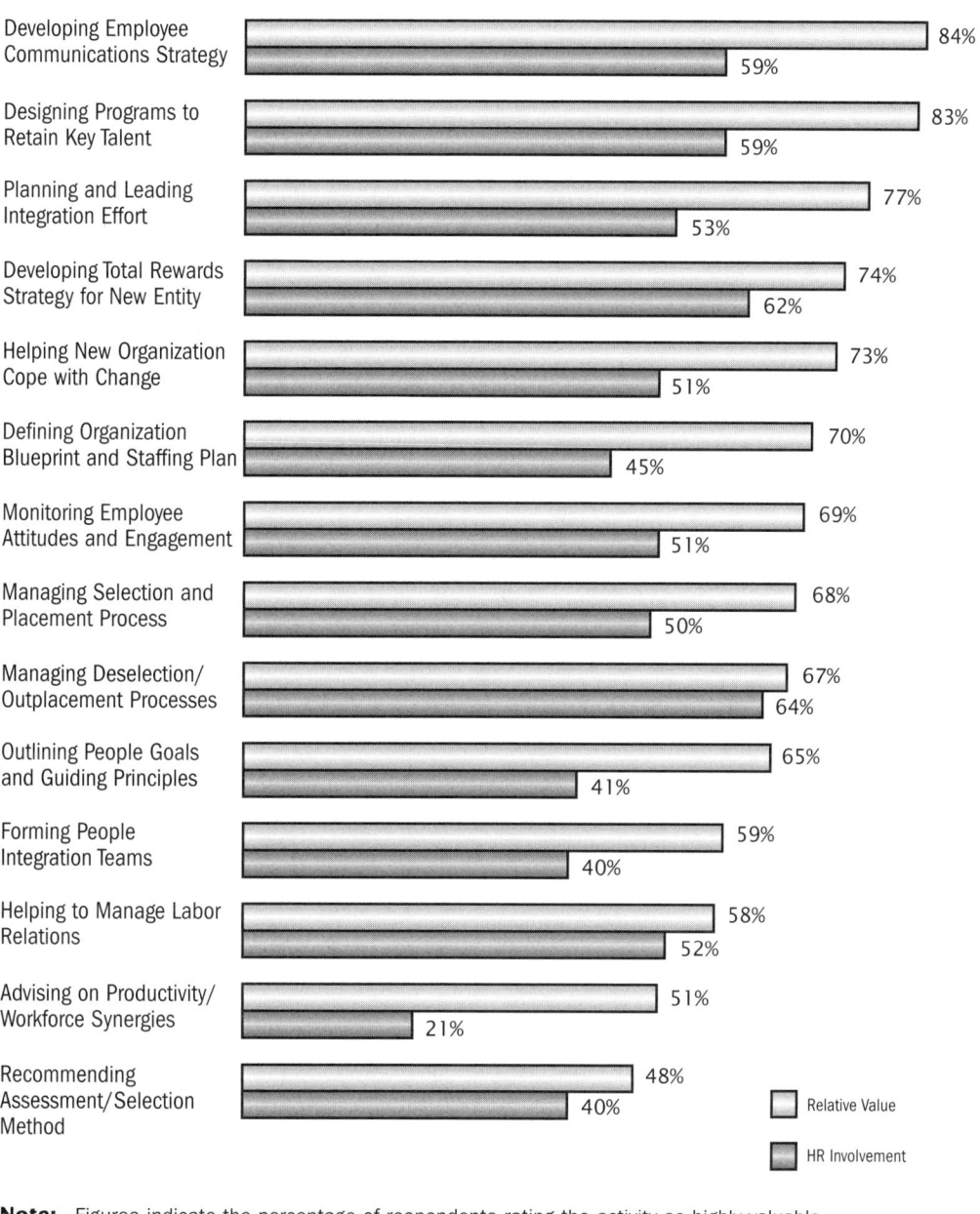

Note: Figures indicate the percentage of respondents rating the activity as highly valuable (4 or 5 on a 5-point scale) and a high level of involvement (4 or 5 on a 5-point scale).

Source: Towers Perrin/SHRM Foundation Survey of over 440 HR executives worldwide.

executive compensation (86%), and employee pay (82%). Much less attention is given to long-term people issues, such as learning and development (23%), organization design and development (47%), and recruitment and retention (40%).

Integration Planning

HR usually begins its full participation in the M&A process during the integration planning stage. Typically, HR is involved for the most part in the more tactical areas, such as planning the placement/outplacement process. Overall, significant gaps exist between the relative value HR could contribute and actual HR involvement in a broad range of strategic activities—from developing an employee communications strategy and designing programs that help to retain key talent, to planning how productivity improvements or other workforce synergies should be captured *(Exhibit 1.10)*.

Implementation

When the two companies actually combine their businesses and organizations during the implementation stage, HR is involved in activities such as the following:
- Aligning HR policies, programs, and practices with business requirements
- Monitoring the progress of people-related synergies and ensuring that workforce momentum is sustained
- Ensuring incentive programs (e.g., bonuses, stock options) are designed to reward executives and key employees for achieving the goals of the merger

Although HR plays a broad and important role during the implementation stage, only one-third of the survey participants had taken part in key cultural support activities. In fact, for the M&A in which they'd been involved, only one-third agreed that the new company's leaders

- Recognize and reward behaviors that support the new culture
- Consider cultural behaviors in selecting management for the new entity
- Align culture with the vision and business strategy of the combined organization
- Identify the desired culture and gain agreement from senior managers and opinion leaders of both organizations

The Communication Gap

Once a deal is completed, the new company's management is under great pressure to achieve the deal's promised synergies as quickly as possible. But achieving these synergies requires that the new company's people commit themselves to the vision and objectives of the new company. And unfortunately, too often the very act of integrating two organizations undermines such commitment. In fact, if employee concerns about the deal or how it affects them personally are not dealt with quickly and satisfactorily, the concerns can mushroom to the point of undermining the new company's ability to capture synergies or other benefits.

Not surprisingly, M&As breed uncertainty, fear, and rumors in the workplace. When push comes to shove, people want to know whether they will still have a job in the "promising new company" they keep hearing about. And if they do manage to hold on to their job, will their pay, benefits, and work environment be enhanced or compromised? Equally important, will the new company invest in their careers and offer

Exhibit 1.11 Elements of M&A Communications Plan

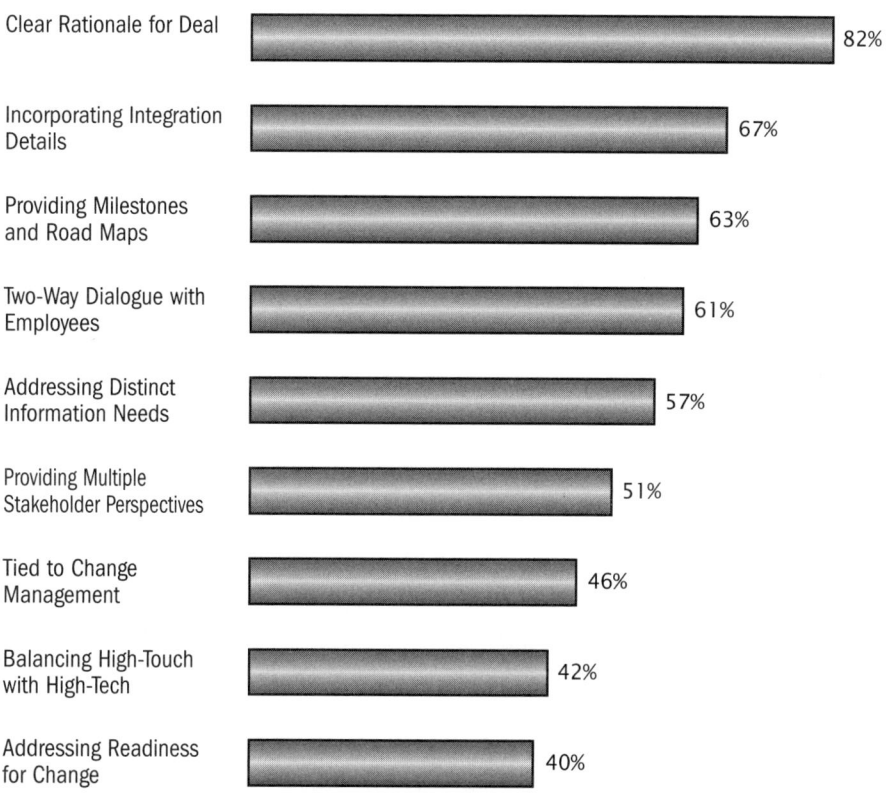

Note: Figures indicate the percentage of respondents that placed a high level of importance (4 or 5 on a 5-point scale) to each element.

Source: Towers Perrin/SHRM Foundation Survey of over 440 HR executives worldwide.

advancement opportunities? To address these issues, a straightforward communications strategy—set in motion early on—is critical.

HR should provide the leadership and expertise the new company's management needs to communicate clearly with employees and other stakeholders. As one HR vice president put it, "Communications is critical. We need to do a better job of helping people understand, 'What about me? My desk? My colleagues? My work?' If you don't answer these questions, the issues will grind people [productivity] to a halt."

Our research confirms that HR professionals are keenly aware of the importance of a communications plan that clearly lays out management's rationale for the deal, the long-range vision and business objectives of the new company, the yardsticks for measuring success, and how all stakeholders are expected to share in the benefits generated by the new company *(Exhibit 1.11).*

It is interesting to note that the Towers Perrin/SHRM Foundation survey shows that slightly more than half of all respondents from successful companies prepared a

Exhibit 1.12 Communications Planning

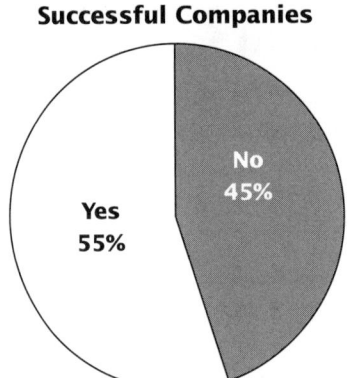
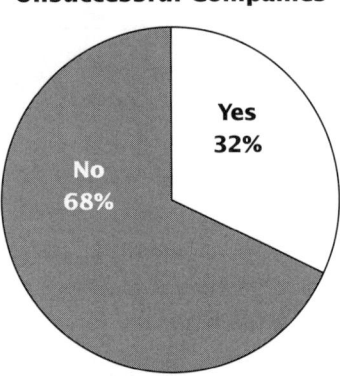

Note: Figures represent percentage of respondents that did or did not implement a communications plan during the M&A.

Source: Towers Perrin/SHRM Foundation Survey of over 440 HR executives worldwide.

communications plan, while just one-third from unsuccessful organizations did so *(Exhibit 1.12).*

Winning Communication Plans Sow the Seeds of Success

Comprehensive, straightforward, concise, and timely communications can help to build commitment and teamwork among employees and an understanding of the reasons for the deal and how major integration decisions will affect them *(Exhibit 1.13).* Noted an HR vice president in the telecommunications industry who played a leading role in a recent successful acquisition, "The new company's leaders don't need spit and polish, just sound communication skills."

The "Right" Role for HR

As awareness of the importance of people issues in M&A activities grows among CEOs and other senior management, HR professionals see the need to take a more strategic role. In fact, a majority of the survey group (65%) agrees that being a strategic partner—fully involved with important decision-making and overall management through all stages of the M&A process—is the "right" role for HR in M&A *(Exhibit 1.14).*

Getting a Seat at the Table: The Skills HR Needs to Succeed

As any seasoned HR professional knows, it's one thing to want to become a strategic partner in M&A and quite another to convince the CEO and other senior management that HR can add value, particularly at the earliest pre-deal and due diligence stages. Survey participants recognize they must master specific skills and capabilities. For instance, a very high percentage of survey participants are convinced that HR leaders

Exhibit 1.13 Results of Communication and Change Management Efforts

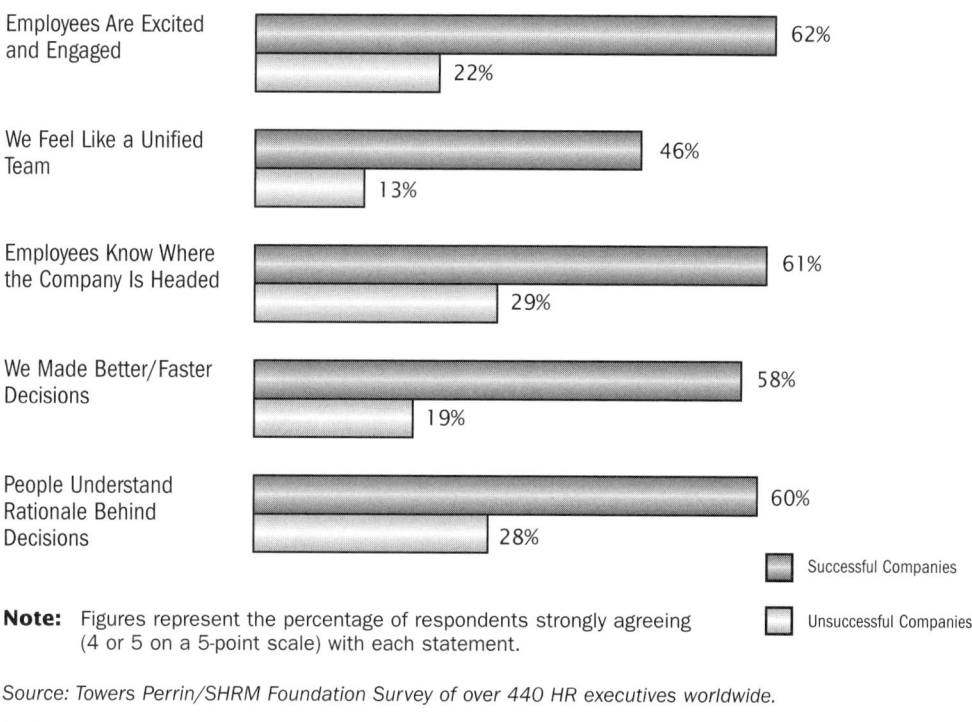

	Successful Companies	Unsuccessful Companies
Employees Are Excited and Engaged	62%	22%
We Feel Like a Unified Team	46%	13%
Employees Know Where the Company Is Headed	61%	29%
We Made Better/Faster Decisions	58%	19%
People Understand Rationale Behind Decisions	60%	28%

Note: Figures represent the percentage of respondents strongly agreeing (4 or 5 on a 5-point scale) with each statement.

Source: Towers Perrin/SHRM Foundation Survey of over 440 HR executives worldwide.

Exhibit 1.14 What Is the Right Role for HR?

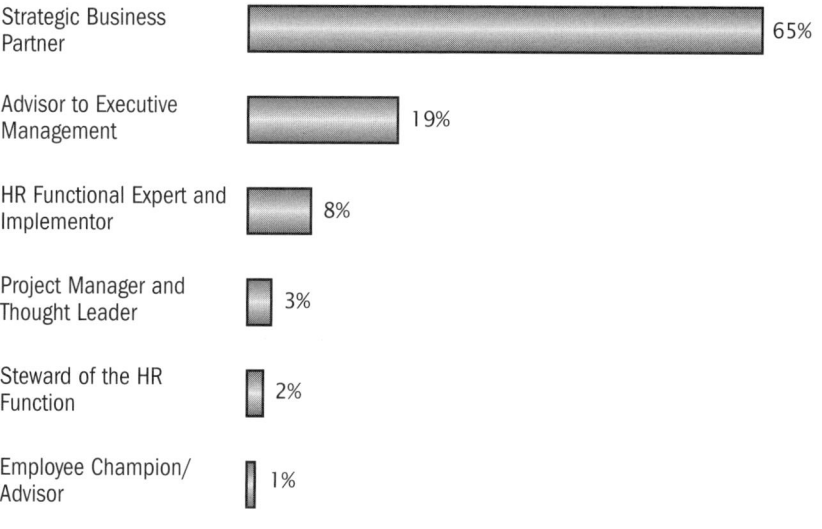

Role	Percentage
Strategic Business Partner	65%
Advisor to Executive Management	19%
HR Functional Expert and Implementor	8%
Project Manager and Thought Leader	3%
Steward of the HR Function	2%
Employee Champion/Advisor	1%

Note: Figures represent the percentage of HR professionals ranking the role as the most ideal.

Source: Towers Perrin/SHRM Foundation Survey of over 440 HR executives worldwide.

Exhibit 1.15 Importance and Current Level of Capability

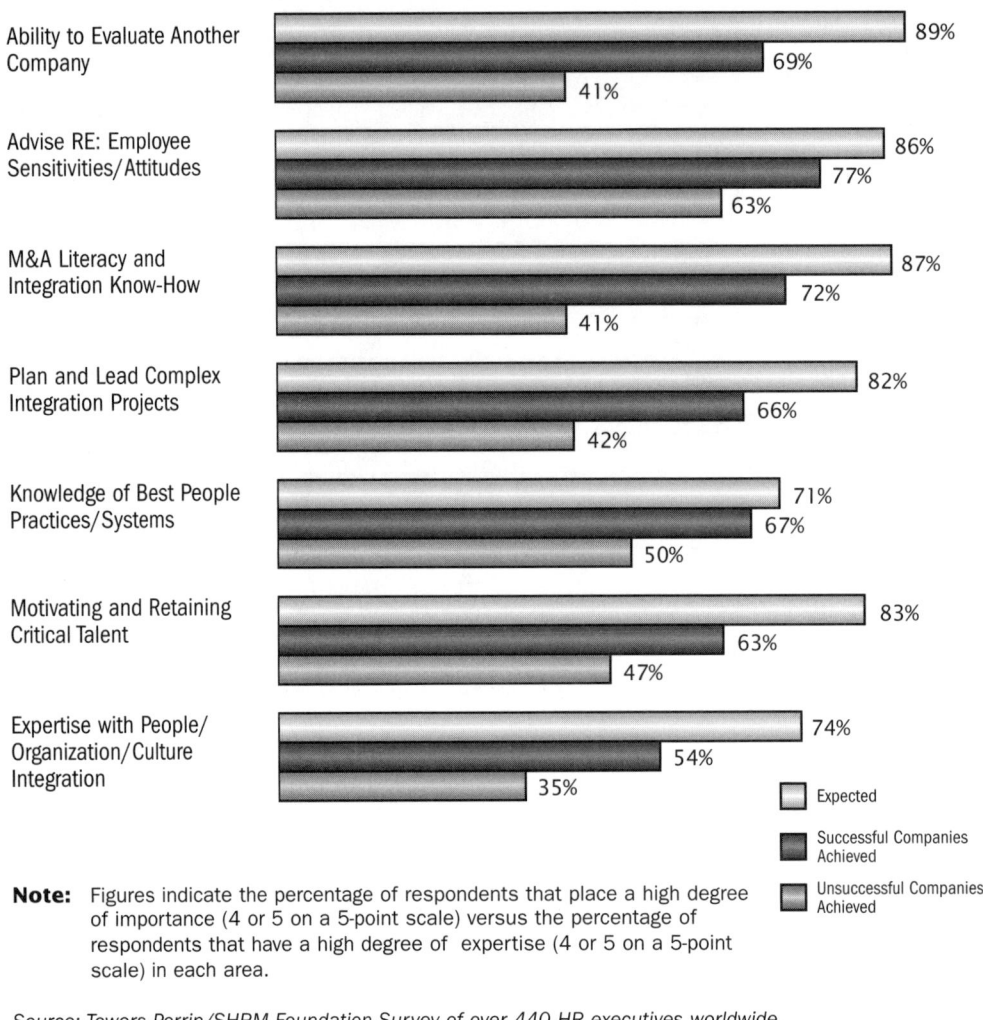

Note: Figures indicate the percentage of respondents that place a high degree of importance (4 or 5 on a 5-point scale) versus the percentage of respondents that have a high degree of expertise (4 or 5 on a 5-point scale) in each area.

Source: Towers Perrin/SHRM Foundation Survey of over 440 HR executives worldwide.

need to understand the general economics of deal making, as well as the associated business and people-related issues. However, they also recognize that significant gaps exist in their current level of knowledge and competence regarding these issues. The largest gaps entail the following:

- M&A literacy and integration know-how
- Ability to evaluate another company
- Ability to lead complex projects

Notably, our survey results reveal that successful companies have much smaller gaps in these critical areas *(Exhibit 1.15)*.

Looked at another way, HR professionals at successful companies have greater M&A competencies than do those at unsuccessful companies. Significantly, these are the very same competencies needed to play a more strategic role throughout the entire M&A process.

Summary

To become full-fledged business advisors, HR professionals must know more about the M&A process overall and how to capture a deal's expected value by identifying and managing key people issues. Armed with this knowledge, HR professionals have a greater chance of gaining a seat at the table with their counterparts in finance, operations, legal, and other functions at the early, strategic stages of the M&A process. Once there, HR can participate fully in key decision-making and management activities throughout the entire M&A process. As one HR vice president aptly put it, "As long as HR can prove its value in being deeply involved with the M&A process, it will be."

A merger or acquisition has a profound impact on the people of both companies, from senior leadership on down. Managing this impact is a crucial dimension of managing a successful transition to a unified leadership, business model, and organization. For some people, the deal marks a beginning of something new and exciting; for others, it is the end of long-standing personal relationships and career ambitions. For employees of an acquired company, the new work environment is also unexplored territory fraught with uncertainty as well as promise. Recognizing and responding compassionately and sensitively to the emotional impact of the deal on each employee will set the tone for the long-term success or failure of the new company.

The research we conducted for this book sheds light on the causes for past failures of mergers and acquisitions. A key finding—supported by other research and our consulting experience—shows that successful M&As depend on the effective management of people issues. Clearly, for this to happen, the HR function must step forward to serve as a powerful catalyst and expert resource for M&A transactions and integrations. CEOs and other senior leaders of the new companies created by M&As must also value the critical importance of people to the success of the deals they make. As one senior vice president of HR—a seasoned veteran of many mergers and acquisitions—put it, "The opportunity cost of failed people solutions is failure of the deal."

Companies formed through M&As need to create enough new long-term value to compensate for their acquisition premiums and the other costs involved in doing and implementing their deals. The capabilities needed to create this new value are all tied to skilled and committed people. Products, markets, technologies, and physical assets are important, but they are inert and create value only if acted upon by the people who make up the capabilities and resources of the new company. So, in the end, successful M&As are about people, first and foremost. ∎

CHAPTER TWO

Business Perspective on Mergers and Acquisitions

Jeffrey A. Schmidt

"Mergers are like any business deal. Some work out and some don't."

William Smithburg
Former Chief Executive Officer, Quaker Oats Co.

To add value to the merger and acquisition (M&A) process—to help their companies avoid poorly conceived deals and implement sound ones successfully—human resource (HR) professionals must have a clear understanding of the business factors that drive M&As. This chapter provides a brief introduction to M&As, with an emphasis on the economics of success in today's M&A environment. Topics include the following:

- Historical perspective
- M&A industry trends
- The results of M&A activity
- Factors influencing M&A results
- Brief overview of M&A economics
- HR and M&A success
- Integration philosophies
- Features of successful integration

Historical Perspective

M&As come in waves. Since the mid-1990s, the current wave has reached record levels in both the number of deals and their value. In fact, the transaction value of worldwide M&As peaked in 1999, and the number of deals was greatest in 2000 (as shown in *Exhibit 2.1*), although the average value of deals fell by about 20 percent from 1999 to 2000.

In part, this recent record activity reflects the large premiums companies have been willing to pay to complete M&As. Buyers and merger partners assume the integrated company resulting from their deals will be more competitive and will create greater shareholder value than the separately owned and operated companies.

Exhibit 2.1 Worldwide Mergers and Acquisitions

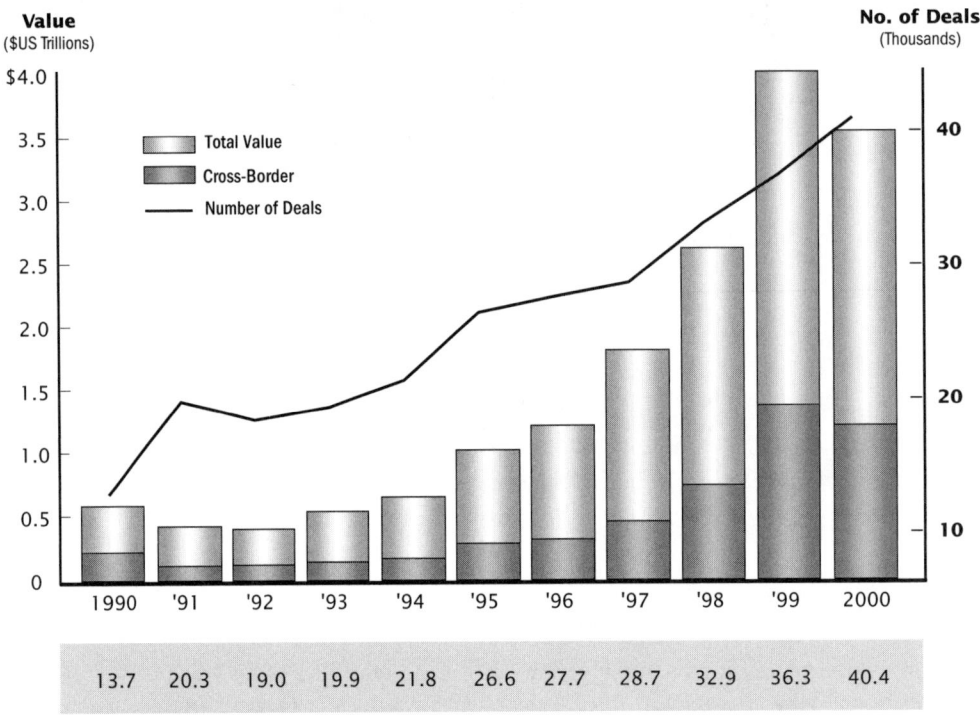

Note: Value is the cash and equity paid, plus debt assumed, to complete the transaction, rounded to the nearest billion.

Source: Securities Data Company.

As reflected in *Exhibit 2.2*, the earliest M&A wave dates back to the late 19th century when oil, steel, tobacco, and other basic industries were consolidated in the creation of oligopolies. Another significant wave occurred in the 1920s when financial promoters consolidated a range of industries including utilities, communications, and automobile production.

In the 1960s, M&As formed large conglomerates. Modern Portfolio Theory—an investment approach that focuses on constructing risk-weighted portfolios of businesses—drove this trend. Advocates of this theory argued that investors could reduce their earnings risk by owning shares in conglomerates whose portfolios of businesses spanned multiple industries in which economic cycles tended to offset each other. But the theory foundered as these conglomerates largely failed to outperform the overall stock market index, and investors realized they could easily diversify their own stock portfolios without owning shares in conglomerates.

By the mid-1970s, conglomerate portfolio theory was out of favor, and M&A activity moved into a period of deconglomeration that ran through the better part of the next

Exhibit 2.2 The Waves of M&A Activities

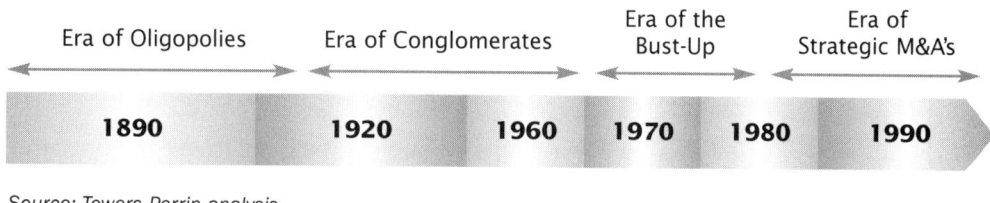

Source: Towers Perrin analysis.

decade. By then, investment analysts and portfolio managers were placing a relatively low market price multiple on conglomerates' earnings. Seizing the opportunity to realize the inherent value of these assets, private equity and leveraged buyout funds became vehicles for acquiring and breaking up the conglomerates. In effect, Wall Street wisdom had come full circle. Now the conglomerate was worth less than the sum of its parts. Hostile takeovers, often financed by junk bonds, became an effective way of breaking up the performance laggards and unlocking value.

Current M&A Wave

The climb in the stock market value over the past decade set the stage for the current M&A wave. Today, companies engage in strategic M&As that are intended to

- strengthen their competitive position by building new capabilities or adding new resources to existing businesses;
- increase sales volume by getting access to new markets or products with the potential for strong growth and by capturing a larger share of existing markets; and
- capitalize on opportunities for reducing manufacturing, distribution, direct labor, and overhead costs—often by adding new technologies, eliminating redundancies, or achieving economies of scale.

These strategic intentions are all evident in large M&As. For example, in the AOL-Time Warner merger, the two partners believe they can achieve high growth by leveraging content and distribution synergies and cross-promoting each other's media products, while significantly cutting their combined $30 billion in annual expenses.

The recent surge in strategic M&As has produced record numbers of deals and values. The surge responds to several powerful technological, demographic, and economic trends.

Technology. We live in a world in which customers are connected with providers of goods and services via expanding and increasingly interconnected information and telecommunications technologies. Combined with the easing of trade barriers and with significant overcapacity in many industries, the increased availability and use of technology fosters ongoing industry consolidation and integration of global markets. To succeed in the new economy, technology and dot-com companies—and mature companies that want to compete with them—must capture shares of highly fragmented and crowded markets. These companies need rapid access to new technical capabilities and innovations to enable them to quickly gain shares in such markets.

Demographics. Given the aging populations in much of the industrialized world, traditional domestic markets frequently offer limited opportunity for demand growth. Too many competitors fighting for the available growth opportunities compounds the prospects for slower growth, which encourages industry consolidation. Competitive forces squeeze many companies that find themselves caught between increasingly large customers and large competitors. For them, it may be necessary to merge or sell out in order to survive in the long run.

Economics. Even more important than these trends is the supremacy of the shareholder value ethos in today's capital markets. Large and small publicly traded companies are often under tremendous pressure to raise earnings through M&As, especially if their organic growth momentum stalls. In addition to combining revenues, they can raise their earnings through the efficiencies gained by consolidating physical assets, operations, and workforces. The cost savings that result can also be significant—at least in the short run.

M&A Industry Trends

The influence of these trends can be seen in a number of key industries, as shown in *Exhibit 2.3*. The following highlights mergers and acquisitions in a few industries.

Financial Services

Technological change, overcrowded markets, and deregulation of the financial services industry have intensified competition and created favorable conditions for industry consolidation. The two goals these combinations hope to achieve are, first, the ability to provide customers with broader service offerings and, second, significant cost savings because of larger scale. These forces have spawned financial service superpowers; banks, brokerage firms, and insurance companies continue to combine into single entities with hundreds of billions of dollars in assets. Among these are NationsBank/Barnett/Bank of America, Citicorp/Travelers/Associates First Capital Group, Firstar/U.S. Bancorp, Bank One/First USA/First Chicago, and First Union/Corestates.

Global Energy

Utility deregulation has fueled consolidation in the electric power industry. Electric and gas utilities have pursued mergers or strategic alliances to achieve greater operating efficiencies and, in turn, build their financial strength. As deregulation changes the rules

Exhibit 2.3 Value of M&A for Selected Industries

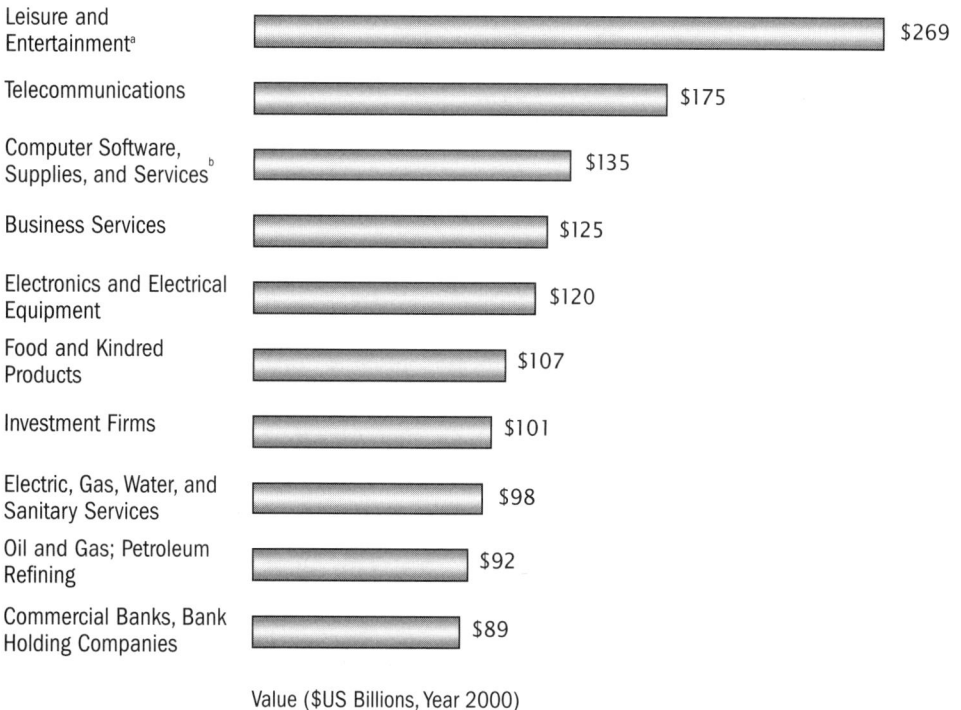

Notes: a) The value of the leisure and entertainment industry is the summation of the motion picture production and distribution industry value and the radio and television broadcasting stations industry value.
b) The value of the computer software, supplies, and services industry is the summation of the prepackaged software industry value and the computer and office equipment industry value.

Source: Securities Data Company; The Economist; Towers Perrin analysis.

---

of competition, utility companies are looking for growth opportunities in other countries. The synergies that deal makers look for include the following:

- Capital expenditure savings derived from adding electricity-generating capacity without the cost of new construction
- Access to a broader customer base and to markets with growing populations and power consumption, enabling increases in top-line revenue
- Cost savings from economies of scale in business and administrative processes (e.g., customer service, billing, and support services)
- Control of power-generating assets to support high-volume power-trading operations

Many of the same reasons, especially cost savings, underpin consolidation in the oil and gas sectors of the worldwide energy business. Global oil and gas entities taking part in recent mega-mergers include Exxon/Mobil, Chevron/Texaco, and BP/Amoco/

ARCO/Castrol. Long-run pressures for earnings growth are likely to cause additional M&As, with the better-performing companies continuing to digest the laggards. Divestitures by the energy giants of nonstrategic assets, such as producing oil and gas properties or processing plants, should also stoke further acquisitions. An example is Phillips Petroleum's acquisition of ARCO's assets in Alaska.

Technology

Technology industries have been a hotbed of M&A activity. A case in point is Cisco Systems. Over the past 10 years, Cisco Systems has engineered approximately 60 acquisitions to enhance its capabilities and drive its 30 percent annual growth. In its most recent fiscal year (ended July 31, 2000), Cisco made 24 acquisitions and planned to make another 25 to 30 in the current fiscal year, though the recent drop in the stock market caused management to reconsider this plan.

Given the rapid pace of change in both technology itself and technology markets, the leading companies are covering their bets by acquiring other technology and service companies. In so doing, they will benefit, regardless of which technological trends end up dominating their markets. And given the risks and the time it normally takes to build a new technology and customer base, serial acquisitions can provide a faster path to market leadership.

The technology industry was favored with high price-earnings (PE) ratios during the bull market of the late 1990s, allowing companies to pay for acquisitions with stock and thus avoid taking on large debts. Even with the drop in share values of NASDAQ-listed companies, M&As for stock can be a good way to secure assets cheaply and to build strong market positions quickly. Acquisitions, as well as joint ventures or alliances, can even help large technology companies such as IBM strengthen their competitive positions.

Global M&A

In the race to access new markets, cut manufacturing and logistics costs, and gain competitive advantage, the number of cross-border M&A transactions has escalated. With the advent of the European Monetary Union, European firms have set records recently for cross-border deals. European firms have also had strong interest in buying their way into the U.S. market, which they believe has stronger growth prospects than can be found at home.

In Canada, 44 percent of all M&As in 2000 involved a U.S. seller or acquirer. And for U.S. companies, 10-year highs were also reached in total acquisitions of foreign businesses and total sales to foreign firms. Activity in Latin American and Asian countries will undoubtedly grow as their economies continue to expand. In fact, the value of M&As in Asia (excluding Japan) reached a record high in 2000, reflecting a growing trend toward consolidation.

This cross-border activity covers many industries, as evidenced by such recent deals as those listed in *Exhibit 2.4*.

Exhibit 2.4 Cross-Border Activity

Companies	Value of Deal
Vodafone (U.K.) and Mannesmann (Germany)	US$203 billion
BP (U.K.) and Amoco/ARCO (U.S.)	US$75 billion
Daimler (Germany) and Chrysler (U.S.)	US$40 billion
Vivendi (France) and Seagram (Canada)	US$40 billion
Bestfoods (U.S.) and Unilever (U.K.)	US$25 billion
Deutsche Bank (Germany) and Bankers Trust (U.S.)	US$9 billion
Lafarge (France) and Blue Circle (U.K.)	US$6 billion
Alcan Aluminium (Canada) and Algroup (Switzerland)	US$5 billion
Cadbury (U.K.) and Snapple (U.S.)	US$1 billion

Note: Value is the cash and equity paid, plus debt assumed, to complete the transaction, rounded to the nearest billion.

Source: Securities Data Company.

Large cross-border deals involve many distinct challenges, including language and cultural differences and regulatory obstacles. (Appendix A contains an in-depth discussion of the implications of cross-border M&As.) These differences can be profound, as the DaimlerChrysler merger amply demonstrates. *Exhibit 2.5* shows the stark reversal of fortune for this merger. DaimlerChrysler began as a "merger of equals," described by many as the forming of the "WELT AG," which means a truly global company in terms of culture, markets, and production. But ebullient optimism about the prospects for the new combined company have given way to headlines about restated expectations, management departures, and layoffs. In the long run, the DaimlerChrysler deal may yield benefits to vindicate its architects and financial advisors, but only time will tell. For now, however, the stakeholders in both companies are paying a heavy price to capture those benefits.

Primary Drivers of These Trends

The recent trend of very large mergers and acquisitions has been favored by several general conditions, including the following:

- A bull market for equities, with many stocks valued well above their long-run averages, providing relatively cheap equity as a primary vehicle for funding acquisitions. The downturn in the S&P 500 and other major stock market indices over the past 12 months may put the brakes on runaway deal making in the near term. But, as William Smithburg, former chief executive officer (CEO) of the Quaker Oats Company, said in a recent *Chicago Tribune* interview, "M&A is here to stay."

- A period of rapid change (e.g., globalization, deregulation, technology shifts), market liberalization, active institutional investing, intense pressure to meet

Exhibit 2.5 DaimlerChrysler Headlines and Timelines

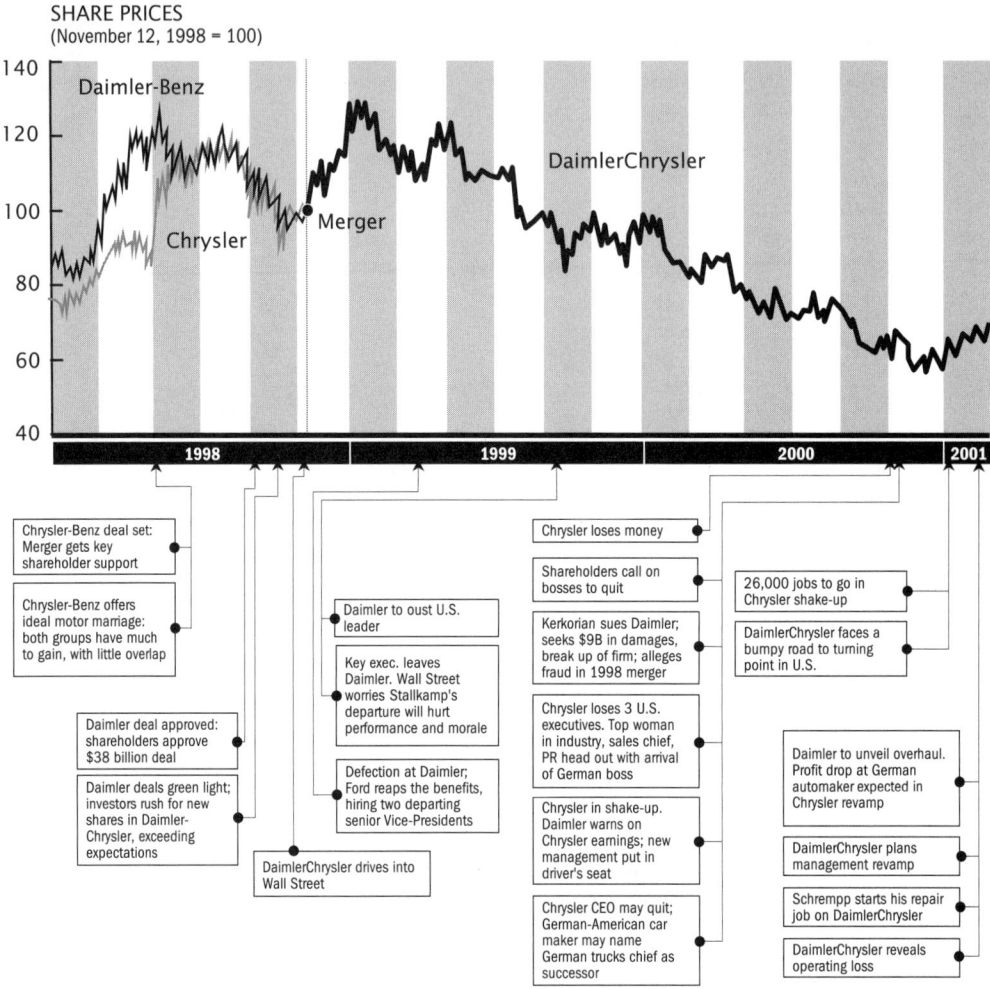

Sources: Financial Times; CNNFN; "Schrempp's Repair Job," The Economist, 3/2001; Towers Perrin analysis.

peer group performance benchmarks, and other factors favoring industry consolidation
- Limited opportunities for organic growth in current markets, despite generally strong economic conditions (until recently) because of the difficulty of increasing market share or generating greater revenues by raising prices
- Belief that achieving greater scale or expanded capabilities and resources via a merger or acquisition will be rewarded with a higher PE ratio and increased market capitalization
- Changes in the climate for large deals such as a favorable regulatory environment and public attitudes

Exhibit 2.6 Results of Selected Acquisitions in Selected Industries

Note: Sample encompasses 24 acquiring companies and 53 acquisitions in information technology, communications, and engineering industries.

Sources: "Capturing the Real Value in High-Tech Acquisitions," Harvard Business Review (September/October 1999), Saiket Chaudturi and Benhaom Tabrizi; Towers Perrin analysis.

The Results of M&A Activity

Many companies are successful in acquiring products, assets, or technologies, but acquiring or merging with publicly traded companies is entirely different. The acid test for successful M&As is predicated on economic theory, which, in its simplest terms, demands that such deals increase wealth for the owners of the companies involved. Many deals, however, fail to meet this test. In fact, regardless of how success is measured—whether compared with promised benefits or with the performance of industry peers—the results of M&A have on average been unexceptional. And these average results are influenced by a few very successful M&As among a much larger number that either fell short of their promised benefits or failed outright.

M&A research covering the past several decades strongly supports the conclusion that most deals have had either a modestly positive or worse impact on earnings and have not created sufficient economic value—at least for the acquiring firms' shareholders. For example, *Exhibit 2.6* shows the results of one representative study published in the *Harvard Business Review*, which found only 21 percent of acquisitions in several industries could be viewed as clear successes.

In a 1995 *Business Week*/Mercer Management Consulting study of 150 deals across different industries, each worth over $500 million, only 17 percent created substantial positive returns, relative to benchmark industry indexes for the acquiring firms' shareholders, while 30 percent substantially eroded shareholder value. Similarly, a 2001 *Chicago Tribune*/A.T. Kearney study of 52 deals completed between 1990 and 2000, each

Exhibit 2.7 Results of Mergers and Acquisitions in Multiple Industries

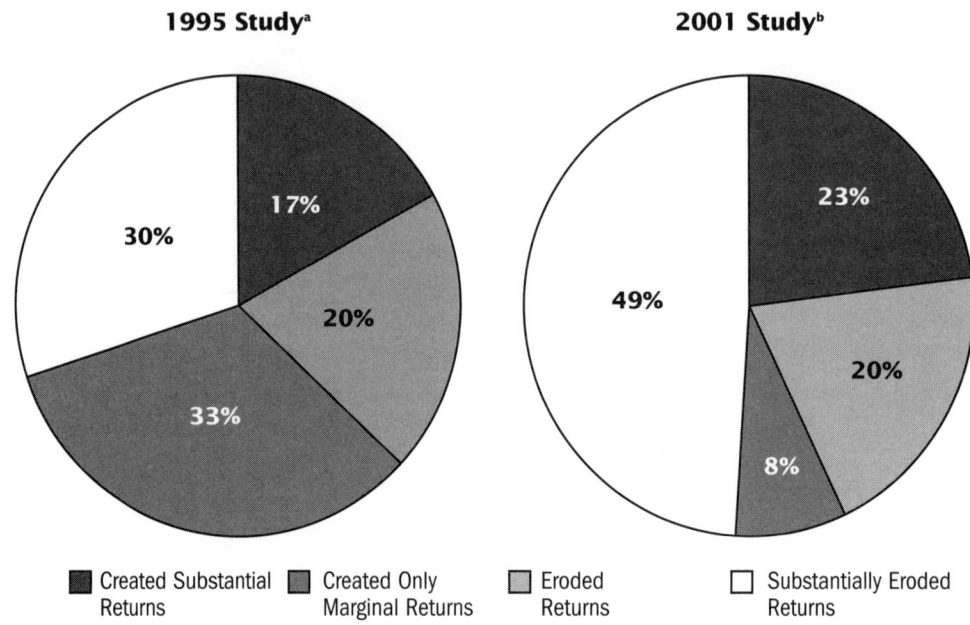

■ Created Substantial Returns ■ Created Only Marginal Returns ■ Eroded Returns □ Substantially Eroded Returns

Notes: a) Based on total stock returns from three months before announcement to three years after announcement and relative to industry indexes: *Business Week*/Mercer Management Consulting analysis.
b) Substantial returns were greater than 10% relative to industry indexes. Based on total stock returns from three months prior to the announcement to two years after the deal was completed relative to industry indexes: *Chicago Tribune*/A.T. Kearney analysis.

Sources: a) Business Week, "The Case Against Mergers" (October 30, 1995), Phillip Zweig; Judy Perlman Kline; Stephanie Anderson Forest; Keven Gudridge; Towers Perrin analysis.
b) Chicago Tribune; "The Big Deals: Promises Unfulfilled" (March 18, 2001); Janet Kidd Stewart; Towers Perrin analysis.

---

valued at over $1 billion, found that only 31 percent created positive returns relative to benchmark indexes for the acquiring firms' shareholders, while 49 percent substantially eroded shareholder value *(Exhibit 2.7)*.

The Towers Perrin/SHRM Foundation survey of HR executives reached the same conclusion: Too many mergers and acquisitions fail to meet expectations.

Although methodologies and results from individual studies vary, we conclude that on average, only one merger or acquisition in five achieves what these studies consider to be a clear success, and at least half fall well short of expectations. However, some research shows that organic growth investments, joint ventures, strategic alliances, and consortiums are on average no more successful than M&As.

Nonetheless, the larger the deal, the more complex and problematic the integration process will be—and the more elusive success will be. Some M&A experts argue that the scale economies used to justify large deals are offset by diseconomies in management

Exhibit 2.8 Top Ten Pitfalls in M&As

Pitfalls Ranked by Negative Impact on M&As
1. Incompatible cultures
2. Inability to manage targets
3. Inability to implement change
4. Nonexistent or overestimated synergies
5. Lack of anticipation of foreseeable events
6. A clash of management styles
7. Overly high acquisition premium
8. Unhealthy acquisition target
9. Need to spin off or liquidate too much
10. Incompatible marketing systems

Sources: Bureau of Business Research at American International College, Springfield, MA. Survey reported in CFO Magazine, April 1996.

---

that result from such deals. In any case, with bigger and more complex deals being done today, it's fair to say that M&A risks have never been greater. Senior managements with acquisitive tendencies who ignore the difficult challenges of integrating and running acquisitions do so at considerable risk to themselves and their shareholders. A sound strategy and shrewd pricing alone are not sufficient to produce a good deal. In the final analysis, the proof is in the integration.

That's why the odds of being successful favor companies that go into deals with a sense of purpose and urgency. For one thing, they are more likely to be attentive to the risks of implementing those deals and to approach integration activities with a degree of commitment that others often fail to muster. More important, they get to the crucial task of stabilizing the workforce as quickly as possible. This immediate response stems the loss of business momentum that often characterizes the early days of many M&As.

Our experience suggests that M&As done largely to reduce costs or strengthen an existing business have a better chance of success, at least in the short run, than those done primarily to grow revenue (e.g., by developing new products or technologies). Typically, deals done to leverage cost efficiency are takeovers in which one company is clearly in charge and leads the integration process. The cost savings, however, may come from significant job losses that can leave a bitter long-term legacy for the new company to overcome. Balancing revenue growth and cost savings may therefore yield the best results of all—especially if both companies had performed well before the deal and share many strengths.

Factors Influencing M&A Results

Because synergies fund the costs of M&As, the inability to achieve desired synergies is the definition of failure. A survey of *Forbes* 500 chief financial officers reveals that the top 10 pitfalls in achieving synergies are mostly due to people or to people-related organizational and cultural issues, as presented in *Exhibit 2.8*.

The Towers Perrin/SHRM Foundation research provides a somewhat different ranking but supports the same overall conclusion about the critical importance of these issues to successful M&As. (See Appendix B.)

The challenges and obstacles to successful implementation of M&As are—either directly or indirectly—people and organizational performance issues. That fact underscores the crucial importance of getting these issues right.

In that vein, research and experience demonstrate that companies significantly improve their chances of success by avoiding the following "Seven Deadly Sins" of implementing M&As:

- Turmoil: Lack of clear strategy before the fact or an ill-conceived plan for integrating management, organization and people systems, and operations
- Alienation: Forced amalgamation that disregards the distinctive, positive cultural attributes of the company being merged with or acquired
- Punishment: Short-sighted changes in rewards strategies and programs that disrupt what had been positive and productive work environments before the deal
- Dissolution: Key employees who become frustrated with turmoil and ambiguity during the integration process and conclude the timing is right to depart for greener pastures
- Dissuasion: A lack of attention to employee stress and morale, or to established mores and protocols, in announcing major changes
- Disappointment: Failing to deliver on commitments and communicating in a way that is perceived not to be complete, hopeful, or entirely honest
- Discontinuity: Sharp decline in production output, sales, customer service, and net income or other key measures of business performance during the first 100 days, often due to key staff being tied up in endless merger meetings

Of course, this is not the complete list of challenges that integrators will face. For example, procrastination—due to ineffectual leadership or issue avoidance—is another common problem. Except for serial acquirers such as GE Capital or Cisco Systems—for whom implementation has developed into a core management competency—it's easy to succumb to the "Seven Deadly Sins." We describe throughout this book how to avoid these mistakes by embracing the best practices of successful integrators.

Brief Overview of M&A Economics

Today's deals often involve premiums that far exceed what investors think these acquired companies are worth on their own. But here's the paradox: The success of a deal tends to be inversely related to the size of the premium. This is because the larger the premium, the greater the synergies that must be captured for the deal to yield sufficient value. Too often, the greater the synergies required, the more optimistic—and less realistic—is management's expectation of delivering the necessary performance. *Exhibit 2.9* shows some differences between growth requirements pre-deal and after a deal.

For many public companies, as much as 60 percent of their stock reflects investor expectations about their future earnings growth. If a premium of, say, 30 to 40 percent

Exhibit 2.9 The Economic Calculus of a Representative Deal

Organic Growth (Pre-Deal)

| Embedded Growth Expectations | Up to 60% of Current Stock Price |

Economic Model

| Pre-Deal Growth Initiatives and Planned Efficiencies |

Merger or Acquisition (Post-Deal)

| Acquisition Premium | From 30-40% of Pre-Announcement Stock Price |
| Transaction Costs | From 2-5% of Pre-Announcement Stock Price |

| Synergies and Other Benefits Required to Yield a Positive Net Present Value (NPV)[a] |

Note: a) Based on tax effects, divestitures/asset sales, and weighted average cost-of-capital.

Source: Towers Perrin analysis.

---

is paid to complete a deal, the future value realized must go 30 to 40 percent beyond the market's implicit growth expectation for the target company—because that growth expectation had already been reflected in the company's stock price. Essentially, the acquirer is making a huge bet on the synergies that must be captured during integration if it is willing to pay that much more than investors think the target company is worth on a stand-alone basis. Aside from the acquisition premium, transaction costs must also be considered in this calculus. These could range up to 5 percent of the target company's preannouncement value.

Stated another way, an acquiring company faces significant financial risk due to
- a high acquisition premium or simply paying too much;
- large transaction costs involved in closing and implementing a deal;
- the difficulty of accurately assessing synergies and the even greater difficulty of capturing them; and
- the harmful effects of deep cost-cutting, imprudent layoffs, and unanticipated divestitures precipitated by all of the above.

The bottom line is that M&A can be a very expensive way to grow a company.

If the deal is to make economic sense, the incremental value from synergies and other benefits must yield a positive net present value (NPV) in light of the premium paid and transaction costs incurred. Conversely, if a merger or acquisition does not develop and achieve significant cost synergy or other benefits, the deal will sooner or

Exhibit 2.10 Examples of M&A Synergies

	Representative Synergies
Revenue Enhancements ■ Acquiring company ■ Acquired company	■ New product offerings or customer/market segments ■ Integrated product development (leverage the other company's R&D) ■ Enhanced service/speed-to-market ■ Less pressure on product/service pricing
Achievable Cost Savings ■ Acquiring company ■ Acquired company	■ New, more efficient technologies ■ Lower-wage locations for operations ■ Elimination of redundancies ■ Increased utilization of capacities ■ Volume benefits for variable-cost items
Process Improvements	■ Reengineering or e-engineering ■ Transfer of best practices
Financial Engineering	■ Lower cost of capital ■ Debt refinancing
Tax Benefits	■ Tax rate advantages ■ Other tax benefits
IMPROVED PERFORMANCE	

Source: Towers Perrin analysis.

later be judged an economic failure. Accordingly, making an acquisition on the basis of the most optimistic assumptions of potential synergies is a first and unmistakable warning of problems down the road.

Some of the major types of synergies and representative examples are shown in *Exhibit 2.10*. These synergies must be identified and quantified with reasonable precision before the deal is closed. They should also be a major part of the baseline used for tracking progress, particularly with respect to realizing the expected value from the merger or acquisition, and should be incorporated explicitly into executive incentive plans. (See Appendix D.)

HR and M&A Success

In the face of the high failure rate for M&As, both companies must work together to get the integration process right. This can happen only when the people who will comprise the new organization understand and accept the deal's goals and believe that the deal is in their best interest and that of the combined organization.

Herein lies one of the key opportunities for the HR community. Although HR professionals are usually not involved in pricing acquisitions, they, along with other members of the management team, are expected to find a way to capture the synergies that will enable the new company to earn a positive NPV.

The persistent inability of companies to fully realize the expected revenue growth and earnings improvements points to a glaring void in the M&A process. Specifically, management does not have enough information about how the deal will affect its target's greatest source of value—its people—and does not plan adequately for the issues that affect employees in both organizations. Human resources professionals should increase their knowledge of the four stages of the M&A process, and then—working directly with senior management—play a strategic role in the entire process, with a particular emphasis on people, organization, and cultural issues.

Strategic partnering is, of course, a two-way street. HR professionals can empower themselves only if the CEO and other senior leadership of the new company listen to their advice—that is, if they understand and value the importance of the people, organizational, and cultural dimensions of M&A. In the final analysis, HR professionals can step up as strategic business advisors only when CEOs and other senior leaders give the same weight to people issues as they do to the deal's potential economics and understand that the positive resolution of people issues directly affects the deal's economics.

Integration Philosophies

Along a continuum of philosophies for integrating acquired or merged corporate entities, four are widely used today, as will be illustrated later. No single philosophy fits all M&A situations. Rather, the "right" philosophy depends on the strategy and specific objectives to be achieved from successful implementation and the time and cost that management of the new company is willing to invest in the integration process. For instance, if the main purpose of the deal is to acquire knowledge capital such as proprietary technologies tied to specific groups of scientists or engineers, the integration approach would logically be different than for a product line extension in a company's own industry. In selecting the right approach, the new company's management must be clear about the capabilities and resources it wants to preserve and how to link them to create the desired synergies. *Exhibit 2.11* shows the types of integration philosophies, which are further detailed below.

Limited Integration

In its simplest terms, this method involves creating a place for the acquired corporation within the acquiring company's reporting structure. The acquiring company views the acquisition as an addition to its existing business portfolio. Consequently, the acquired company usually retains its management team and operational and administrative practices, and employees and their work environment are virtually unaffected. This

Exhibit 2.11 Types of Integration Philosophies

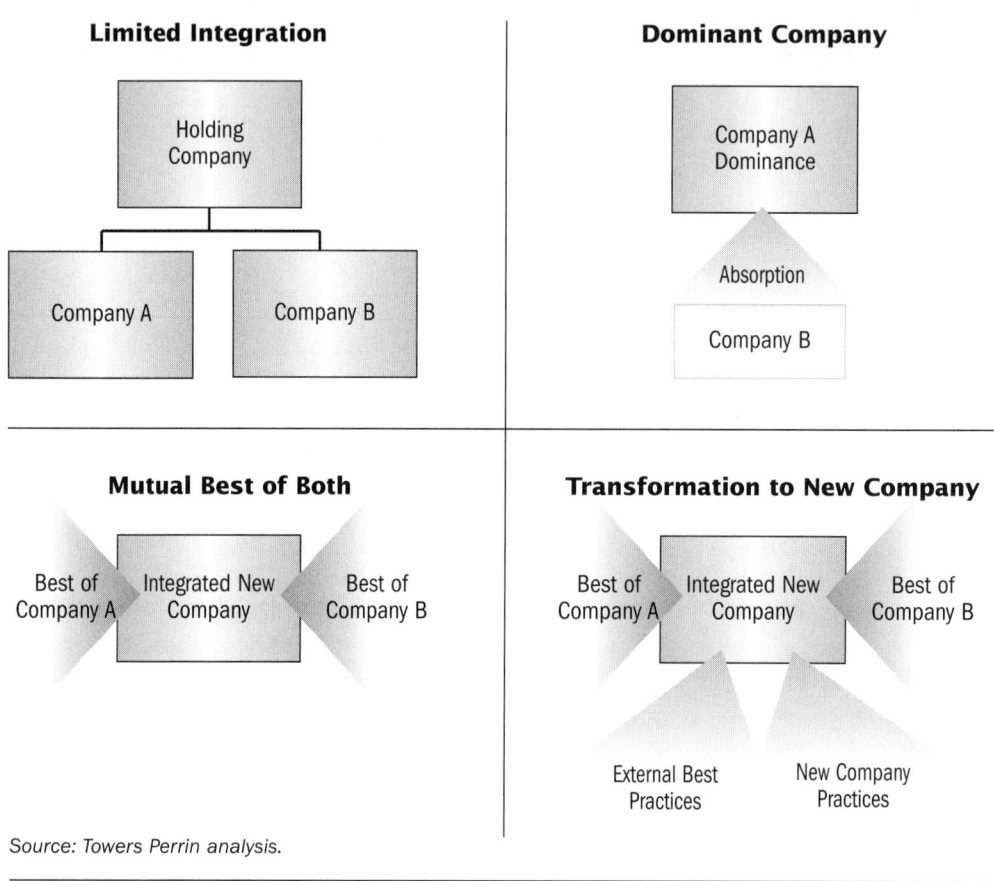

Source: Towers Perrin analysis.

embodies a "light touch" integration philosophy characteristic of holding companies and of highly diversified businesses. Berkshire Hathaway exemplifies this philosophy with its M&A transactions.

Dominant Company

In this approach, the new entity becomes completely subordinate to the acquiring company. Absorption means one company conforms to the management system, organizational structure, business processes, and operating philosophy of the acquiring company (or dominant company in a merger). Absorption is often preferred by intra-industry M&As, largely motivated by cost savings, in which competing companies are consolidated into a single, larger organization. Given the formidable odds against successful integration in general, absorption is often the quickest and surest path to integrating an acquisition, even with the near-term loss of some good people in the process. Recent examples include BP's acquisitions of Amoco Corporation and ARCO, and Daimler's acquisition of Chrysler.

Mutual Best of Both

With this approach, the two companies set out with a fresh view of how to manage, organize, and operate the new entity. This task is accomplished systematically via a thorough and objective examination of the approaches used by the two companies—their structures, systems, processes, cultures, and technologies. The purpose in this approach is to select the best practices from each company and incorporate them into a blueprint for the new entity. Deals in which the main rationale is to strengthen market position or increase market share often take this approach. The successful Wells Fargo combination with Crocker Bank in the mid-1980s is an example. In other situations, however, this approach to integration has failed miserably as both parties get bogged down in endless arguments over whose practices are best. (The term "merger of equals" is often used as a euphemism for certain "dominant firm" acquisitions and is sometimes used inappropriately to describe the Mutual Best of Both integration philosophy.)

Transformation to a New Company

Transformation extends beyond Mutual Best of Both by reviewing—and sometimes incorporating—selected features from the business models or processes of other prominent and highly regarded companies. M&As designed to incorporate leading-edge technologies and world-class sales or other functional capabilities tend to follow this track. This approach is based on the belief that the new company will be more innovative, competitive, and exciting than those companies from which it is formed or after which it may be patterned.

Features of Successful Integration

Some common features of the integration approaches previously described are previewed in this section and covered more fully in later chapters.

Taking a Risk Management Perspective

As noted earlier, an M&A can be an expensive and risky way to grow. Accordingly, as a strategic partner to the company's deal-making team, HR should adopt a risk management perspective. This requires understanding both of broad types of risk involved (see the following list) and the best practices for managing them proactively. HR will tend to focus on organizational risks, but an understanding of the other risk categories allows HR to contribute to management discussions about issues throughout the M&A process.

- Competitive Risks: dubious strategic foundation; competitor poaching of key talent, customers, and distributors; dissolution of strategic supplier alliances
- Economic Risks: premium paid to close the deal is too high, leading to a need to spin off or liquidate too much; overoptimism regarding potential synergies, especially regarding opportunities for cost savings and sales volume growth

- Organizational Risks: unanticipated problems and hidden flaws in integrating workforces, cultures, and organizations; management inattention to important cultural differences; inability to manage the combined entity at the higher performance level needed to make the deal's economics work; adverse consequences from reversal of long-standing HR policies and practices

Our research found 10 major risks (summarized in Appendix B) that have impeded implementation of M&A. HR professionals must understand these risks and how they affect the M&A process. In particular, they must be equipped to identify and help manage their distinct people, organizational, and cultural dimensions.

Organization Design and Management Selection

Whatever philosophy guides the integration process, the members of the new management team and the design of the macro-organization structure for the combined company should be chosen before a deal closes. These questions may even be part of the bid talks between companies. In any case, early decisions on these topics allow each company's management to inform employees as soon as possible about how the new organization will be created and staffed.

It is also important, particularly for retention of management and professional talent, that people feel the new company's leadership team is selected fairly. Ideally, the process should be transparent and objective, and it must comply with pertinent legal standards. Many companies include evaluation by peers, subordinates, and seniors. In the most successful mergers and acquisitions, key jobs are also distributed among the managers from both entities. This requires a sound method for matching capabilities to job specifications. Allocating jobs based on relative equity contributions to the new company or other arbitrary criteria is expedient, but it does not demonstrate to employees that management is committed to making selection decisions in an objective, even-handed manner.

Managing the Integration Process

The Towers Perrin/SHRM Foundation survey of HR executives worldwide indicates that 59 percent believe the top priority for implementing successful M&As is to define the integration philosophy, process, and timeline as early as possible. They emphasize that managing the integration process successfully requires a coherent, prioritized, and understandable plan. The major components should be the following:

- Strategy clarification (an explicit statement of the long-term vision and strategic intent; the business model, corporate identity, and competitive positioning; the values and organizational capabilities; and the integration philosophy to be followed)
- Project management structure (decision-making authorities and process, roles, and accountabilities; means for conflict resolution; performance measurement and progress reporting)

- A master schedule for addressing global issues, functional integration, stakeholder management, contingencies, and so on
- Communications strategy and plan for key stakeholders (customers, investors, employees, and others)
- Team mobilization arrangements (membership, charters, training, logistics, etc.)
- Change program design ("as is/to be" pictures, intermediate and end states at key milestones, change process, etc.)

Throughout the integration process—and particularly during the first 100 days—unforeseen problems will inevitably develop, and management must be ready and able to resolve them. To handle these problems expeditiously and to keep them from undermining financial performance, successful companies separate the day-to-day management of the current businesses from the day-to-day management of the integration process.

Strategy Clarification

Deal makers and integration managers must be clear on the competitive realities and business challenges facing the new entity. Top management should articulate the rationale for the deal in a way that makes as much sense for employees as for shareholders. Employees must understand and buy into the new company's direction as set forth by its senior management team.

Everyone from top management to hourly employees should therefore understand the unified company's long-term vision and business objectives and the reasons for creating a new business model, organization structure, people systems, and work environment. Strategy clarification is the foundation for a well-engineered and effective integration process with a clear plan for achieving synergies and other benefits. As such, it is an essential step for ensuring that a deal is an unqualified success.

Organizing for Integration

To help ensure that people issues are addressed successfully, HR should spearhead project management for the integration planning and implementation stages. HR should be the principal advisor for people and organizational matters and contribute to the analysis of enterprisewide issues such as establishing standards for global integration.

A sound approach to implementing a merger or acquisition involves the establishment of a steering team composed of senior and support executives of the combined entity. The steering team is vital in directing and coordinating activities throughout the integration planning and implementation processes. A representative of HR should be a member of the steering team.

In addition to the steering team, a core multidisciplinary team should serve as a dedicated, full-time analytical resource and focus for managing and coordinating global and functional integration teams. An HR professional should participate as a full member of the core team and advise on matters such as the most appropriate means of determining accountability and tracking progress.

Master Schedule

It is critical to develop and communicate a master schedule for building the unified company, as well as to develop a detailed map of discrete tasks, activities, and deadlines for the integration process. In addition, because many integration activities are concurrent, a project tracking system must be developed to continuously assess progress and to warn of critical activities that fall behind schedule.

In brief, successful integration places a high value on dedicated resources and fundamental project management disciplines, such as

- aligning project management with integration philosophy;
- setting and adhering to tight time frames;
- intensively managing transitions;
- making timely decisions and favoring action over elaborate analysis;
- defining end states at key milestones;
- establishing progress targets; and
- providing a project tracking system.

The first 100 days after closing a deal are often the most critical, given the uncertainty among managers, employees, and other stakeholders. Successful integrators make speedy decisions during this period, taking action instead of belaboring formal processes and undue analysis.

Recognizing this urgency, HR must develop a people strategy for the unified company while managing the day-to-day integration activities of its own function. By addressing people matters quickly and communicating frequently, HR can help to reduce the uncertainty, stress, and anxiety that cause unplanned turnover during the typically chaotic integration period.

Stakeholder Expectations

Performance measurement is a key success factor in M&As. Specifically, companies should measure how well they create value for their stakeholders—including, at a minimum, their investors, customers, and employees.

Among the measures that should be tracked for assessing stakeholder performance are synergy capture, employee engagement, customer satisfaction/perceptions, change readiness/barriers to change, and leadership and communication effectiveness. These measures should have baselines and targets for thresholds and outstanding performance. They should also be linked to one another through an integrated performance scorecard and should be incorporated into executive incentive plans.

Change Program

Beyond project management and functional integration, HR must lead in partnership with line management in defining the change program. The first step is to assess the baseline situation in the current organizations, then to define the "to be" model of the new organization's functioning and culture. Profiling important cultural differences and deciding which elements of each company's culture to retain or discard is a pivotal step in managing change.

Companies that achieve the most efficient transitions find ways to manage change while maintaining their current business momentum. They exercise the appropriate amount of management control and have the ability to learn quickly from their experience. They also attend to the most important issues first: continuity of business performance, employee retention and morale, and customer satisfaction.

Communication Plan

It is hard to overstate the importance of effective communication to successful implementation of M&As. The distinct information needs of all stakeholders must be understood, monitored, and addressed throughout the integration process. Key stakeholders must understand how changes will be implemented and have a sense of how they will be affected.

Understanding stakeholder perspectives is critical to the long-run success of any merger or acquisition. By addressing communications requirements from the perspectives of employees and other stakeholders, management will help to ensure that all stakeholders remain productive and committed to the success of the new company.

Because the various stakeholders have distinct perspectives, it's important to know how they think about post-integration success. As an example, employees in one merger defined success in the following terms:

- Though jobs may be lost, those that remain ought to be challenging and rewarding.
- Where practical, those who are displaced should be offered new positions in the new company.
- New approaches should be taken to promote on merit and to sweep away mediocre managers and other weak performers.
- The merger or acquisition should not be used as a cover for reducing pay and benefits or for demanding longer and longer work hours.
- The positive aspects of the work environment and learning and development opportunities should remain unaffected or, even better, improve.
- Management should communicate openly and honestly throughout the integration process and should handle displaced employees compassionately and generously.
- Morale and productivity should quickly recover after the new organization is restructured and restaffed.

Still, employees tend to be skeptical about what they hear in the rumor-charged environment of a merger or acquisition. Managers must ensure, therefore, that all communications—those that go to all employees, those that go to specific groups, and those that are personal—are open, honest, and set the right tone. People need to know where they stand and what they can expect in the post-integration work environment. They also want to know as soon as possible how and by whom important decisions will be made and the outcomes of those decisions.

What people really want to know is whether the rosy future they're hearing about for the new company includes them. These employee concerns, if not addressed quickly or satisfactorily, can have serious repercussions. So, it's no surprise that our research shows that companies with successful communications tend to achieve the best results in terms of financial improvement, productivity enhancement, and shareholder returns.

Linking M&A to Incentive Pay

In a successful merger or acquisition, capturing synergies is linked to performance incentives. Senior managers should not be rewarded for simply completing the transaction. If their incentives are tied to successful implementation, managers are more likely to focus on the right things throughout all of the stages in the M&A process—and to achieve the necessary synergies.

To tie incentives to M&A, HR must understand the nature of the intended synergies—for example, revenue growth through higher sales volume and increased efficiencies—and then custom design a measurement system that tracks achievement over a pre-deal baseline. If synergies relate to top-line revenue growth, one can look at the growth of the legacy businesses before the closing, then examine the incremental growth rate actually achieved. To measure people synergies such as higher productivity growth, it is critical to first reflect on the nature and drivers of that synergy and then determine the appropriate measurement criteria.

Linking rewards to M&A performance leads to wider and stronger accountability for successful outcomes. Of course, a mechanism must be in place for measuring that performance and for reporting ongoing progress. To that end, CEOs of successful companies build deal success measures into an integrated stakeholder scorecard. ∎

SECTION II
The M&A Life Cycle

CHAPTER THREE

The Pre-Deal Stage

François Lafaix

"The plain fact is that acquiring is much faster than building."
Alex Mandl
Chief Executive Officer, Teligent

Why Merge or Acquire?

While a company may have many reasons to merge with or acquire another, the ultimate purpose should be to increase shareholder value.

Shareholder value is a company's market capitalization (for a publicly traded company) or its value should it be sold to another entity (for a private company). The financial community equates shareholder value with the sum of a company's future cash flows after discounting to account for risks associated with the uncertainty of those future cash flows.

Cash flows are the difference between cash income (which includes revenues from operations as well as from financial activities and other sources) and cash outlays (payments to employees, suppliers, and government bodies and all other costs).

The primary ways to increase shareholder value are by growing revenues, lowering costs, or decreasing business or financial risk so that the company's discount rate is lowered. Most companies seek to increase shareholder value by using more than one of these levers at a time. Often, one lever will be emphasized over the others. For example, a company may pursue a high-risk activity such as the development and launch of a new product if projected revenue growth is likely to increase to a level that more than offsets the corresponding cost increase and compensates adequately for the incremental risks involved.

It is possible to influence shareholder value by corporatewide actions. Adjusting the debt-to-equity ratio of a company, for instance, will influence the cost of capital. Similarly, corporations can restructure their debt or discontinue certain operations that influence shareholder value. Yet the levers for influencing shareholder value are, by and large, employed at the business-unit level. Cost-control goals, for example, can be set at the corporate level, but the managers of individual business units must decide how to meet these goals in ways that make the most sense for their individual functions.

Similarly, revenue growth targets have to be translated into products sold by operating divisions to the right customer segments.

Successful strategies for increasing shareholder value are prone to imitation by competitors. This imitation tends to equalize returns. In other words, if competitors duplicate the levers that a company uses to create shareholder value, then the value created for the first company will disappear or be reduced significantly. The airlines' mileage programs are an example. When American Airlines introduced its AAdvantage program, it was seen as a way to build customer loyalty and increase revenues in the long run. The trade-off was an increase in administrative costs (to manage the program) and slightly reduced near-term revenues (keeping in mind that awards are often used for seats that would not have sold otherwise—first class, for example, or off-peak travel). When competitors began offering similar programs, many of the benefits were negated, but the reduced revenues and increased administrative costs remained.

Some strategies are more difficult for competitors to duplicate. When options are limited within an industry, moves by one company can even constrain the actions of its competitors. JDS Uniphase Corporation's $41 billion acquisition of rival optical telecommunications supplier SDL Incorporated in early 2001 gave the merged company about two-thirds of the global merchant market for optical networking components and a 90 percent share in some specific market segments. Investors might also expect this combination to benefit from scale economies and from a deep understanding of the market, which should translate into above-average profitability.

Sources of Competitive Advantage

Creating lasting shareholder value requires establishing a competitive advantage—preferably, a long-lasting advantage that is difficult to copy. Preferred access to scarce or finite resources is the classic source of competitive advantage, including

- Markets
- Distribution channels
- Raw materials
- Financial capital
- Tangible assets (such as plants and manufacturing equipment)
- People (qualified staff and managers with skills and experience)
- Experience (companies with the highest accumulated experience tend to have, on average, the best cost and quality value proposition, especially when the information gained through experience is not shared with competitors)
- Other intangible assets such as unique technology, proprietary know-how, and brand strength

In fragmented industries, large size can result in lower production costs and in higher price realization because customers are willing to pay a premium for a better-established brand. These "economies of scale" are often the underlying reason for consolidation in mature industries such as the airline or oil and gas industries. There is, unfortunately, a point beyond which the benefits of consolidation erode and where diseconomies of scale begin to appear. For example, concentrated manufacturing presents significant risks, as illustrated by recent incidents at a Ford parts plant called River Rouge. An explosion there in 1999 caused domino-effect production disruptions at several Ford plants that depend on the gigantic River Rouge plant for parts. Moreover, as Microsoft has learned, companies with significant market power tend to attract close government scrutiny to ensure they do not leverage their scale unlawfully.

Time ("first-mover advantage") is another important source of competitive advantage. Although a time advantage will erode, in many situations being first to market can provide a company with a powerful competitive edge. For example, it gives a company the opportunity to set or influence product standards or customer requirements or desires. But competing on time means that a company must be constantly ahead of competitors on the innovation curve, which also involves risks. The market might not be ready for a new technology, for example, or late entrants might render the product of the first entrant obsolete. The competitive dynamic between Apple Computers and the WinTel PC platform illustrates the dangers associated with this approach.

Intangible assets are proving to be another—perhaps even the ultimate—source of competitive advantage. The following are examples:

- A company's organizational capability and culture can be a source of competitive advantage if it helps to strike deals with suppliers, customers, and employees that are not readily available to other companies.
- A company whose culture emphasizes management stability can often secure the necessary commitments and accountabilities from its managers for following through on long-term investments.
- A company with a tradition of social responsibility might also be able to attract investors willing to support the company and its share price even in the event of a stock market downturn or other setback.
- Intangible barriers that make it difficult for new entrants to compete effectively include exclusivity of distribution channels, accumulated experience, the need for high up-front investment, and government regulations.

As Hiroyuki Itami and Thomas Roehl point out in their 1991 book, *Mobilizing Invisible Assets* (Harvard University Press), intangible assets such as corporate culture or knowledge and expertise are often the most effective sustainable sources of competitive advantage—primarily because such advantages are difficult to imitate. Such attributes can also facilitate mergers and acquisitions (M&A) transactions. An extreme illustration of this comes from Taiwan, where a very strong network of personal connections (or *Guanxi*) is critical for business success. As Howard Davis says in his 1992 article, "The Benefits of 'Guanxi': The Value of Relationships in Developing the Chinese Market," in *Industrial Marketing Management*, "Things can get done without *Guanxi* if one invests enormous personal energy, is willing to offend even close friends and trusted associates, and is prepared to see such Pyrrhic victories melt away … On the other hand, with *Guanxi*, everything seems possible."

In that sense, it can be said that people, individually or collectively, represent the main source of sustainable competitive advantage. So it comes as no surprise that people are key to the success or failure of any strategic activity, including M&As.

The Make or Buy Decision

An M&A should be thought of as a strategic tool for increasing shareholder value. Before pursuing a deal, due consideration should be given to other means of creating value such as internal growth or various types of partnerships. Given the significant risks inherent in a merger or acquisition, companies should not gamble on one unless the odds are heavily in their favor. In other words, strategically managed companies live by the maxim, "When in doubt, don't close the deal."

Pros and Cons of an M&A Strategy

Once a strategy for increasing shareholder value has been formulated, management can either use the company's internal capabilities to implement the strategy or can seek access to external capabilities developed by other companies.

Using internal capabilities, or organic growth, is not always the best choice. It can be costly, risky, and inefficient—especially if the new capabilities can be bought at reasonable cost. Internal development of capabilities takes time and resources that may be in short supply or that could be put to more efficient use. What's more, developing internal capabilities faster than overall market growth can result in industrywide overcapacity and—potentially—in unprofitable price-cutting battles.

Combined capabilities can add to shareholder value if they prevent competitors from gaining access to the capabilities needed to grow their businesses. When, for example, limited resources exist within an industry, gaining exclusive or near-exclusive access to them through an acquisition or merger can result in significant competitive advantage. Conversely, missing such an opportunity can put a company at a disadvantage because competitors may gladly seize the same opportunity. Daimler's acquisition of Chrysler, for example, was thought at the time of announcement to have reduced the chances for other European automotive manufacturers such as BMW or Volkswagen AG to enter the North American market.

In some cases, it is possible to gain access to external capabilities through alliances or joint ventures. It's important to note, moreover, that having a minority equity participation in a company that owns critical resources can lead to similar benefits without the trouble, risk, and cost of an acquisition or merger. But in some situations, an out-and-out merger or acquisition is the best way to gain capabilities. For instance, companies that are not willing to sell or license an exclusive resource may be candidates for acquisition.

The relative advantages and disadvantages of organic growth and M&A strategies are summarized in *Exhibits 3.1* and *3.2*.

Notwithstanding the associated risks, pursuing a merger or acquisition can provide significant advantages over other methods for increasing shareholder value.

Exhibit 3.1 M&A Strategy

Pros	Cons
■ Speed of strategy implementation ■ Quick access to complementary assets ■ Removal of actual/potential competitors ■ Significant increase of corporate resources	■ Cost of acquisition (premiums over market value) ■ Dealing with unnecessary adjunct businesses ■ Organizational clashes that weaken business performance

Source: Towers Perrin analysis.

Exhibit 3.2 Internal Growth Strategy

Pros	Cons
■ Manageable incremental risk ■ Compatible with culture and existing management/organizational capabilities ■ Encouraging entrepreneurship and accountability ■ Funded with internal investment	■ Slow to implement, especially large-scale investment programs ■ Need for building new resources or capabilities ■ May add to industry capacity (leading to pricing pressures) ■ Entry cost can be difficult to recoup (in case of failure)

Source: Towers Perrin analysis.

Specifically, a merger or acquisition can create synergies by enabling management to combine the capabilities of two entities and then optimize the results. Synergy can occur at many levels. For example, the combined entity can gain superior bargaining power with suppliers, vendors, and customers. Technologies can also mesh to develop new products and speed them to market, economies of scale can result in lower manufacturing and distribution costs, redundant or surplus resources can be eliminated, cultures can complement each other, and so forth.

The Importance of Synergy

Synergies create shareholder value only if the company formed through merger or acquisition actually outperforms the legacy companies—and that becomes a critical consideration when choosing a merger or acquisition partner, a subject addressed later in this chapter.

Potential synergies are difficult to quantify before implementation. For that reason, they are often either underestimated or overestimated. Adequate planning and disciplined execution to take advantage of synergies is critical (see Chapter Six, which addresses M&A implementation), and management should expect unforeseen challenges to crop up, as was discussed in Chapter One.

The Seller's Perspective

The buyer isn't the only beneficiary of an acquisition. Sometimes, more value for existing shareholders can be created by selling a company rather than by continuing to operate it as a stand-alone entity. Some management teams recognize that their company is no longer viable in isolation and proactively seek partners that complement their market position, skills, and resources. This is always a difficult decision because it can generate a sense of failure in the organization. Still, a proactive approach increases the likelihood of success within a larger company and also allows enough time for management to establish processes and structures to facilitate the integration. The venerable J.P. Morgan commercial and investment banking firm agreed to be acquired by Chase Manhattan when, as more and more financial services conglomerates formed, it became clear that the days of the independent bank were numbered.

The Financial/Opportunistic Rationales

In eras and industries where investment capital is readily available, an acquisition could increase shareholder value without being dependent on an explicit business strategy. Tapping the capital markets signals that a company has growth plans, and investors then put a higher valuation on a company's shares. However, experience shows that deals without a compelling rationale (strategic logic) often prove to be costly mistakes, and the financial community can penalize the acquirer's shareholders by making sell recommendations.

Until recently, the announcement of an impending acquisition often led to a temporary drop in the acquirer's stock value, reflecting in many cases the stock market's concerns that the acquirer was overpaying or that the combined entity would not be able to deliver on projected synergies. Although the New Economy has provided instances where the acquirer's market value has soared on the announcement of a purchase, in the long run it still holds true that shareholder value must correlate with a company's future earnings. In fact, as Internet companies are shifting away from establishing brands and mind-share back toward old-fashioned profitability, M&A investments are again reflecting conventional economic logic.

Although a company's valuation can appear to be high based on its tangible assets alone, investors recognize that intangible assets, such as brand strength and human structural capital, can dominate a company's valuation. Obviously, in the case of many high-growth tech and service companies, most of the assets are intangible and, thus, by definition, "off balance sheet."

Baruch Lev, Philip Bardes Professor of Accounting and Finance at the NYU/Leonard Stern School of Business, has shown that his measure of earnings from intangible assets, Knowledge Earnings, and its associated quantity, Knowledge Capital, are superior to measures such as economic profit, accounting returns, or operating cash flows for explaining market valuations. Knowledge Earnings are defined as the residual value of normalized earnings (to compensate for day-to-day market fluctuations) less earnings attributable to physical assets (assuming a 7 percent rate of return on gross book value) and financial assets (assuming a 4.5 percent rate of return). Knowledge Capital represents the present value of all future Knowledge Earnings, discounted at a rate commensurate with the average growth rate for three knowledge-rich industries—biotech, software, and pharmaceuticals.

Market timing and investor psychology can play a major role in building support for M&A decisions. When the financial community values certain industries and economic sectors above others, it makes capital relatively cheap for some companies, allowing them to acquire other companies in industries that have not appreciated as much. America Online's (AOL's) acquisition of Time Warner is a case in point. AOL's high share price at the time of its offer made Time Warner a relatively cheap acquisition and provided a windfall for Time Warner shareholders at the same time.

Finally, it should be noted that some acquisitions are made for entirely the wrong reasons—for example, management ego and hubris. Such acquisitions have below-average benefits for shareholders, as chronicled in *Barbarians at the Gate: The Fall of RJR Nabisco*, the 1991 Harper & Row bestseller by Brian Burrough and John Helyar.

From Strategy to a Deal

Once a company has decided that a merger or acquisition is the best method for achieving its strategic goals, it must find the most attractive partner, perform research, and analyze this partner to be certain no discernible deal-breakers are present. Then, if the research justifies it, an offer can be made. Depending on discussions between the two companies, the deal can be accepted, accepted with modifications, or rejected. If the deal is ultimately accepted, the two parties will proceed with due diligence. (See Chapter Four.) If it is rejected, the acquiring company then must decide whether to back off or proceed with a hostile takeover.

Let's look in greater detail at each of the steps preceding due diligence.

Setting the Selection Criteria

In most cases, the executives in charge of business development—in collaboration with top management—establish an initial screen, develop a list of candidates, and process them through the screen. The criteria for screening candidates varies from company to company, but most start with basic financial requirements.

To establish a financial hurdle, some companies focus on internal rate of return (IRR), payback period, net present value, or a combination of measures. The actual value of the financial hurdle often depends on the weighted average cost of capital (WACC) of the acquirer. WACC is determined by taking into account the relative importance of debt and equity in financing the firm (financial leverage) and fair remuneration for both debt and equity, given the level of risk associated with the acquirer's businesses.

Financial hurdles are straightforward because they can be easily quantified. Nonetheless, they rely on assumptions that are necessarily subjective and uncertain. When looking at cross-border deals, for example, there is no way to forecast exchange

Exhibit 3.3 Screening Criteria for Partner Considered Alone

Corporate Structure	■ Ownership structure ■ Key shareholders ■ Board membership
Business Strategy	■ Strategic intent ■ Success with announced strategy ■ Market positioning (market shares by segment)
Financial Performance	■ Current revenues, costs, and profitability ■ Revenues, costs, and profitability trends ■ Current valuation and stock performance history ■ Recent stock performance relative to competition
Tangible Assets	■ Value and nature of plant, property, and equipment (PP&E) ■ Value and nature of cash and other liquid assets ■ Working capital requirements
Intangible Assets	■ Patents and other intellectual property ■ Human capital, including critical people or group of people of value to target or to acquirer ■ Management team: key people and personalities ■ Culture fit ■ Brand equity and customer relationships ■ Corporate image/reputation

Source: Towers Perrin analysis.

---

rates accurately. Similarly, the quantification of the risks associated with a particular transaction can vary widely, depending on the methods and assumptions used.

Exhibits 3.3 and *3.4* show representative criteria for screening potential acquisition targets or merger partners on stand-alone and combined bases. Not all criteria apply to all potential M&A situations. The relative weight of the various criteria should also vary depending on the desired objectives.

Effective screening must look beyond the financials, and this is where human resources (HR) practitioners can play a key role. Many deals fail to capture the expected synergies due to incompatible cultures, the loss of key talent, or clashes of management style. In a study of merger results ("Cultural Difference and Stockholder Value in Related Mergers: Brand Equity and Human Capital," *Strategic Management Journal*, 13 [1992], pages 319–334), Sayan Chatterjee et al. suggest that cultural fit has a profound effect on firm performance post-merger. They argue that "the management of a buying firm should pay at least as much attention to issues of cultural fit during the pre-merger search as they do to issues of strategic fit." These issues, like the financial ones, can also be screened during the pre-deal stage, and HR can help develop appropriate criteria and analyses for examining them.

Exhibit 3.4   Screening Criteria for Combined Entity

Deal Options
- Deal structure (acquisition, merger, joint venture, etc.)
- Relative size of the entities to be combined
- Sources of funding for deal (cash, equity swap, etc.)
- Accounting mechanism for transaction
- Resources available for integration (in-house, within target)

Opportunities for Synergies
- Opportunities for revenue enhancement
- Complementary geographic presence, distribution channels, product offering, etc.
- Opportunities for direct/overhead cost reduction
- Tax implications and benefits of deal (e.g., tax-loss carry-forwards)
- Financial engineering (e.g., amortization of goodwill)

Transaction Price Range
- Price range of similar deals
- Standard industry ratios, such as sales or earnings multiples
- Estimate of synergies and other benefits compared with deal premium over current market value
- Associated transaction costs

Risks
- Existing liabilities and pending legal actions
- Golden parachutes and other change of control protection mechanisms (stock option triggers, golden shares, etc.)
- Reactions of antitrust watchdogs, or governmental entities[a]
- Industry reaction to the deal (current customers, suppliers, distributors, and competitors of acquirer and of potential partner)
- Reactions to deal within acquirer and its partner (e.g., increased turnover, impact on motivation, and signaling effect on existing workforce, broken promises, or expectations)

Note: a) Most readers are familiar with the role that the Federal Trade Commission plays in U.S. industries where deals can result in excessive market concentration. Other government agencies can also play a critical role; some countries prevent foreign ownership in certain industries (e.g., the airline industry in the United States). Governments also regulate activities in some sectors (licensing of radio spectra, etc.).

Source: Towers Perrin analysis.

HR can also help the deal team determine which cultures are compatible with the company's own and which are not. When a poisonous combination is detected early in the pre-deal stage, management can save a lot of trouble by giving that company a wide berth. This doesn't mean, however, that companies should acquire or merge only with those targets with very similar organizations and cultures. Injecting a reasonable dose of entrepreneurial culture into a risk-averse organization, for instance, can help ensure a company's long-term survival. In other words, a merger or acquisition can be an excellent way to institute fundamental changes, including changes to culture and accountability mechanisms.

Setting precise cultural requirements is virtually impossible, but understanding what is likely to work is critically important. When a merger of two banks took place a few years ago, how administrative people were to be assigned became a flash point for major controversy. The more team-based, collaborative bank pooled its administrative support employees and assigned them to work teams as needed. For executives and professionals at the more hierarchical bank, however, having a personal secretary conveyed social status in the organization, and the idea of sharing such administrative support was anathema. Advance warning of the potential for this cultural conflict could have saved the merged organization time, frustration, and, ultimately, the loss of some key talent, both managerial/professional and administrative.

Loss of talent is unfortunately a frequent result of a merger or acquisition. With careful pre-deal planning, the impact of such losses can be minimized, no matter what their causes. As a first step, HR should help identify the key talents needed (either by name, job function, or competencies) for implementing the strategy of the combined organization and should recommend what steps should be taken to retain them. For instance, deciding early in the pre-deal screening process that an acquisition prospect with a strong sales force in South America is important for a global expansion strategy will help prioritize retention programs and send a strong message to the current sales team.

Identifying and Selecting Potential Partners

It's rare for a company with a strategy to merge or acquire other companies to start searching for potential partners without any knowledge of the available candidates, unless, perhaps, it is entering a new and unknown geographic market. Usually, management's industry knowledge and experience are used to build the initial list of potential merger or acquisition candidates. The deal team can then expand on this initial list through its own directed search and analysis.

A large number of M&As are triggered by an opportunity offered to a company's management team, usually as a result of networking between executives of both parties or of searches by investment bankers or business consultants. In these cases, as with planned searches, it is beneficial to widen the hunt before proceeding to be certain the opportunistic merger is the best possible one available.

Focusing solely on the deal being offered could keep a company from pursuing more attractive deals that could be located with a reasonable amount of additional study. For example, BMW's acquisition of Rover wasted corporate resources. Rover's turnaround required so much of BMW management's attention that BMW failed to react quickly to the DaimlerChrysler merger or the ensuing wave of industry consolidation. Had BMW considered other options beyond the opportunity to rescue Rover from bankruptcy, it might have been better able to take advantage of the recent wave of consolidation in the automotive industry.

Another important reason for conducting a broad search of potential merger or acquisition candidates is that if two companies are too much alike, the opportunities for synergies will be limited mostly to scale effects and rationalizations (organization, process, and systems). These may be insufficient to justify the premium paid over market to close the deal. Moreover, in an industry with new and vibrant technologies, the acquisition candidates should go beyond direct competitors to include companies with important alternative technologies.

The identification of potential partners typically relies on research into the target company's industry size and growth rate (historical and projected), its competitors and their relative market shares, and each competitor's strategy (market focus, existing partnerships, etc.). In some companies, the corporate business development function conducts this analysis, although in many companies, the business divisions that will house the acquisition are also involved. Depending on the specifics, and usually at the discretion of the executives who champion the possible deal, experts from various functions such as sales and marketing, manufacturing, or research and development will conduct part of the effort.

The research to identify and prequalify targets requires a wide range of information and intelligence sources, including former employees currently working for the acquirer, publicly available information such as financial reports, or purchased intelligence such as off-the-shelf market research or tailor-made consulting studies.

Refining the Analysis

Once the initial prospect list is established, the listed companies must be analyzed in detail in order to prioritize the subsequent research and to select the most promising candidates. This selection process occurs iteratively, with increasing levels of detail and analysis. Initial screening can be done at a very broad level in a matter of days, often using a simple spreadsheet analysis and readily available data.

It is not necessary for a company to wait until the due diligence stage, however, before conducting further research on potential partners. Most companies leave a significant public footprint in the form of analyst reports, public filings, newspaper and magazine articles, and so on. By going to these sources and others, including court records, an acquirer can make a reasonably well-informed valuation of its potential partners.

In fact, the acquirer may already have some of this information at hand. Most companies routinely collect information on their competitors, suppliers, and vendors. This information is sometimes kept in a central file, but it is more common for it to be dispersed and uncataloged. Internal information sources should be mined. For example, the sales force might be able to identify the best salespeople at a target company or may know that the target, particularly if it is a competitor, is experiencing customer difficulties (missed shipments, poor performance of final product, etc.). HR staff might have access to union contracts in force at other companies in its industry. Former employees of the target now employed by the acquirer may be able to help assess cultural compatibility or provide some insights about the target's pay structure and the underlying accountability system, among other issues.

This type of internally generated information usually needs to be supplemented with external research. A good starting point is to search Securities and Exchange Commission filings, analyst reports, press releases, technical papers and patents, industry reports, and the Internet. Although much of this research can be conducted online, it is also important to look for more obscure information sources such as trade and technology journals or local newspapers near the target company's major plants. Another key source of information is public filings. In the United States, for example, the Freedom of Information Act can be used to get detailed information on many companies. Provided the right procedure is followed, information such as Environmental Protection Agency filings and Occupational Safety and Health Administration reports can be secured.

Executive search firms can sometimes provide background on the executives of a target company. Customers, suppliers, and vendors of capital equipment are often willing (and sometimes eager) to share insights on the relative strengths and weaknesses of the various industry players. Employees who routinely interact with counterparts at the target company or with that company's customers or suppliers can access information through informal conversation. In other cases, a dedicated internal team or independent consultants can conduct more formal interviews with these kinds of sources. It is not usually necessary to disclose the ultimate goal of these screening interviews. If protecting the identity of the acquirer and its intentions is critical, third parties can provide a shield of anonymity. Conducting such interviews before the due diligence stage allows the acquirer to gather data on more than one company at a time. In addition, interviews can also help identify candidates other than the target. That said, careful thought must be given to the questions asked and the way these interviews are conducted. Even if these interviews take place before the target is approached, misrepresentations can have legal implications.

Compiling and digesting publicly available information on possible M&A targets requires a well-organized approach to help ensure the optimum value for the time and money invested in the effort. Nonetheless, conducting research early can be very cost effective and may be a competitive necessity. It is likely that competitors are doing such research and are discovering in the process which mergers or acquisitions are most attractive to them.

Taken individually, the available sources of information will not show a complete picture of an acquisition or merger target at this pre-deal juncture. Savvy analysis of the available data will, however, provide a reasonably comprehensive profile of the most attractive partners. To keep down pre-deal research costs, an acquirer may initially focus only on the most promising partner and research other candidates only if the top candidate is eliminated during the review process. In any case, armed with this information, management is then prepared to further narrow its field of candidates.

Exhibit 3.5 summarizes the kinds of information and data that can be used during the screening process.

Exhibit 3.5 Accessible Data/Information and Associated Analyses

Corporate Structure
- Legal, financial, and operating structures
- Composition and structure of board of directors
- List of key shareholders

Business Strategy
- Observed changes in strategy (profile) over a given time frame
- Announced current strategy (major elements and action steps)
- Importance of and positioning in each relevant industry segment
- Economics by segment
- Key customers and how they tend to behave

Financial Performance
- Historical profit and loss (yearly, for at least three years)
- Historical stock performance (market value-added, price/earnings ratio)
- Pro forma profit and loss (typically five years) with detailed assumptions leading to results

Tangible Assets
- Plant layout and key pieces of equipment (including some manufacturing capacity estimate)

Intangible Assets
- Net financial assets
- List of patents, intellectual capital, and other critical know-how
- Importance of these patents and intellectual capital to the success of the potential partnership
- Senior management profiles, summary biographies
- Compensation of senior officers, including granted stock options
- Role, expectations, opportunities inside and outside of target; potential motivation factors
- Compensation philosophy (range and structure)
- Culture profile
- Corporate image
- Brands owned and strength thereof

Synergies
- Potential sources of synergies
- Financial impact of synergies identified, and sensitivity analysis
- Critical steps and resources required to realize synergies
- Assessment of risk and degree of difficulty in capturing synergies

Risk Associated with Target
- Major liabilities pending (e.g., lawsuits, financial weakness)
- Likely reaction of FTC or other government watchdogs
- Likely reaction of customers, competitors, and suppliers (which could take the form of a scenario analysis using game theory concepts)
- Likely reaction within acquirer and within target to announcement of deal
- Critical people who may be likely to leave
- Likely workforce reaction
- Promises the acquirer will have to break with its own staff

Source: Towers Perrin analysis.

Investment analysts provide *pro forma* financial statements for publicly traded companies. However, it is important to go beyond these statements to understand how the numbers were derived. The acquirer must understand the major assumptions in the pro forma statements, what aspects are likely to change the outcome, how sensitive the outcome is to these parameters, and so on. This often requires building a financial model of the target company. This model can be instrumental in valuing the target and in quantifying the synergies identified later on.

The closer a company gets to preparing an offer (and to closing it), the greater the pressure to ignore or downplay information that might compromise a deal. Warren Buffet, Chairman of Berkshire Hathaway, said, "The thrill of the chase blind(s) the pursuer to the consequence of the catch." In fact, what seems at first to be an attractive deal may not withstand the scrutiny of a detailed review. Sound pre-deal research and rigorous analyses are crucial to achieving success with an M&A, but they are valid exercises only to the degree that management heeds their findings.

It is a mistake to think that the deal breakers are limited to the financials. In some cases, a detailed analysis might reveal that a potential partner is missing a distinct organizational capability necessary for capturing synergies—its share of a given market might be smaller than expected, for example. Other problems such as profound cultural differences or people-related risks might also put a deal into question.

Preparing the Offer

In preparing an offer, most companies focus on the financials and, more specifically, on the transaction price (current valuation plus premium). Price is certainly an important part of a deal, but other issues are also significant.

Successful M&As start with a clear vision of what the combined entity—the new company—should aspire to, what it should look like, and how successful outcomes will be measured both in the short and long run. Vision shapes how an acquirer (or the lead company in a merger) should approach the target in order to avoid false expectations during negotiations. By the same token, defining up-front who will lead the combined entity and who will create the integration philosophy are *sine qua non* conditions for a sound agreement to combine managements, organizations, operations, and workforces.

The approach used in implementing a merger or acquisition varies from company to company. Some have policies that limit the matters open for discussion. (The extreme would be a company that establishes one single approach for all M&A activities.) Such policies usually grow out of information gained from good and bad experiences and an analysis of what has worked best in the past. The choice among the various remaining options is often dictated by the specifics of the deal being reviewed and is typically made by the deal team.

In fact, the Towers Perrin/SHRM Foundation research shows that defining the integration philosophy, process, and timeline as early as possible should be the top priority if a successful combination is to be achieved. More than half (59 percent) of the 440-plus executives surveyed rank this as the first or second priority for M&A success.

The legal and financial structure of the deal should also be considered at this pre-deal stage. Many financing mechanisms are available, and the best one depends, in part, on tax regulations and the acquirer's anticipated percentage of ownership of the combined entity. The financing mechanisms range from a purchase of shares of the target to an asset purchase to a stock swap (in the latter case, stock is the currency of the transaction, rather than cash).

When the target acquisition is a spin-off, the pre-deal analysis takes on heightened importance. For example, one company discovered that a spin-off described as a high-tech business was at risk of becoming nothing more than a contract manufacturer because most of the technology expertise and customer access would have stayed with the divesting parent.

Once a compelling business case has been made for a merger or acquisition, it is time to think about a transaction price. Companies have many ways to set a price range, and most use a combination of techniques. Typically, the range reflects on the prices of comparable transactions (a multiple of earnings, sales, or market capitalization). Which multiple is used depends largely on the industry, the time at which the acquisition is taking place, and the current preferences of the financial community (i.e., the market conditions).

In fast-growing industries, such as those spawned by the Internet, it can be difficult to estimate a price range. The target company may have little or no revenue—or may even be planning losses for the next few years—due to its ambitious growth plans. While the chances of not meeting these growth plans may be significant, the target might present a unique opportunity (for a traditional company to enter a Web-based market, for example) that can only be realized through an acquisition or a merger.

In recent M&As, particularly those involving Internet companies, deal makers have set price ranges by analyzing somewhat comparable transactions. Comparable transactions can be defined according to the number of years since incorporation, the number of employees, the size of the potential market, the business model, the alliances already concluded with external parties, and similar factors. But these M&As are risky even with a sound pricing approach. For example, after a period during which transaction prices and valuations for business-to-consumer companies climbed to astronomical heights, many of these companies' share prices plummeted in the stock market correction of 2000–2001.

Economics of an M&A

For the target to sell, the lead partner in a merger or buyer in an acquisition has to offer a market premium—a price above the current share price. In the recent wave of mergers, this premium has averaged 20 to 40 percent, but significant variations exist, depending on the prospects of the combined entity. The premium must be justified by the expected synergies after deducting the estimated costs of the integration effort and disturbances associated with the combination of businesses, organizations, workforces, and assets. These deductions reflect the transaction costs of the deal. As discussed in

Chapter Two, the higher the premium, the less likely it is for a deal to be successful as defined by shareholder value metrics.

This simple economic reality is easy to forget in the heat of closing a deal, particularly if an auction or bidding is involved. Unfortunately, the psychological need to emerge victorious often comes at a sky-high cost to the winner in the form of impossibly high premium and transaction costs. Game theorists call this the winner's curse. In many cases, the premium paid by the winner is pushed even higher because the second-highest bidder also has unrealistic assumptions about the value of potential synergies from the combination and sets its offer price too high. As a result, the so-called winner is forced to top a price that is already above what is reasonable.

As noted in Chapter Two, overwhelming evidence shows that too many M&As fail to generate enough shareholder value. To generate sufficient value, the transaction price for a deal should be less than the value of all the future cash flows of the company to be integrated (considered as a stand-alone), plus the value of all the future cash flows that stem from synergies that can be realized only through the combination.

Unfortunately, companies often fail to achieve this objective and end up overpaying for their deals, as M&A expert Mark Sirower points out in his 1997 book *The Synergy Trap* (Free Press). Even setting aside the issue of premium over stand-alone valuation, the acquirer has to make sure that the acquisition does not destroy value.

This is no trivial matter. M&A are by their very nature disruptive and often cause a loss of business momentum and productivity and weakened financial performance for both companies involved.

Negotiating the Deal

Once management is reasonably certain that combining with another company makes sense and is likely to succeed in both competitive and economic terms, it must state its intention to enter into a relationship with its target.

Today, the vast majority of deals start out amicably. Senior executives from the offering company often approach their counterparts at the target company to test the waters for a negotiation. This can be done straightforwardly or as a long and covert courtship. In the aforementioned proposed merger between JDS Uniphase Corporation and SDL Incorporated, Donald Scifres, SDL's chief executive, said he had suggested the merger to longtime business acquaintance Jozef Straus, his JDS Uniphase counterpart.

Many deals are concluded between companies that have known each other for a long time because they have contractual agreements or common ventures or alliances. In fact, knowing the other partner well makes it easier to address the target company's concerns and issues and increases the chances that the deal proposal is well received from the outset.

After initial discussions, companies usually enter into a nondisclosure agreement (NDA) so they can exchange confidential information. The NDA is the first step toward gaining increasingly greater degrees of understanding and commitment to the deal on the part of both companies.

As with most negotiations, the M&A deal-making process is iterative. The acquiring company typically provides a rough description of what the combined company could look like and what the transaction may be worth. The other party may voice some objections or suggest a different structure for the deal, which will most likely force the acquirer to reconsider its offer. Negotiations continue until the deal becomes acceptable to both parties or is abandoned.

The managers involved in these rounds will vary between the companies. An ad hoc team, specialists from corporate development, or a mix of both conduct most negotiations. The various functions such as legal, finance, or HR can be directly involved in the negotiation team or, more typically, used behind the scenes as subject matter experts when required. Sometimes external parties such as investment bankers, specialized M&A lawyers, and consultants may take part in the negotiations. In large potential transactions, the chief financial officer or chief executive officer often becomes personally involved in negotiations when an agreement is near.

At this stage, companies—especially acquirers—have already invested significant resources in completing the deal. In all likelihood, the deal has been discussed both inside and outside both organizations, and sometimes the intent to purchase or merge has already been made public. Under these circumstances, it is psychologically difficult to terminate negotiations. This phenomenon of "escalation of commitment" is one of the major pitfalls of the latter part of the negotiation process. Often, the same circumstances that would have ruled out a specific target company during the initial screening process or even during the offer preparation will be ignored in the heat of negotiations. Some M&A experts believe that the best way to avoid this pitfall is to actively consider more than one target at a time. Although this may be a viable approach in certain cases, pursuing multiple deals concurrently can put an additional strain on senior management's time and on company resources.

Obviously, not all negotiations result in a mutual decision to go forward. Walking away from a potential deal might be the best decision if the business case and economic rationale are not sound enough to generate confidence that significant value will be created for shareholders. It is never too late to acknowledge a mistake, as Ford and Fiat did when they announced that merger talks between them would end. The stated reason: cultural issues linked to both companies' reluctance to forego the upper hand in the potential merger.

If a potential acquisition target or merger partner is not persuaded to go forward with a deal, the company that wants to proceed has one final option—a hostile takeover. In this scenario, the executives of the target company may learn that their company is subject to a takeover attempt by reading the newspaper or by realizing that another company has stealthily acquired 5 percent, 10 percent, or more of its stock. While hostile takeover is usually not the preferred approach to an acquisition, it might be the only way to close the deal.

A hostile takeover is defined as one that meets with negative reactions from the target's management, who may respond by raising every hurdle to bring up the bid price or thwart the takeover. Indeed, the price of closing the deal can increase significantly if the target looks for a "white knight" to rescue it. Because in most jurisdictions the target's board of directors has a fiduciary obligation to its shareholders to accept the deal that most benefits them, a bidding war may ensue between the hostile bidder and the white knight.

Even if the target company's board agrees to the deal, the likelihood of an economic failure remains high. A hostile takeover has the potential for unrealistic acquisition premiums, management losses, customer alienation, and a host of other ills that can lead to failure. Too often, the only winners are the shareholders of the target company, who benefit from a high acquisition premium.

Signing the Letter of Intent

After the final issues between both parties have been ironed out, they sign a letter of intent (LOI). The LOI commits both parties to seek an agreement in good faith, nothing more. Additional clauses usually prohibit management of the target company from starting negotiations with other parties—at least for a limited period of time. Sometimes the LOI prohibits the target from making irreversible decisions (e.g., major asset sales) that could materially affect the valuation without an agreement beforehand from the other party. The LOI also sets the stage for the due diligence process and often limits the duration of that process. It is typical for an LOI to include the estimated transaction price, deal structure, transaction timetable, required conditions for the deal to be closed, and exit clauses. The LOI is often accompanied by a more stringent NDA.

Gearing Up for the Next Steps

Due diligence is the next step in the M&A life cycle process. The final closing does not take place until the due diligence stage is completed and until the deal has received approval from the pertinent regulatory authorities and from the board of the acquired company (or of both parties in the case of a merger) if the transaction is large enough.

Because the due diligence period is often short, preparation must begin before the clock starts ticking. The due diligence team should be selected well before the LOI is signed, and the team members must be ready to begin work immediately afterward.

A due diligence team should include corporate and operating division members and representatives from each of these areas: accounting/finance, contracts, human resources, insurance and risk management, treasury, environmental health and safety, legal, internal audit, real estate, security, and tax. However, the nature of a given acquisition should dictate the ideal composition of the team. External resources required during the due diligence, such as an environmental consulting team, might also need advance notice that a deal is coming.

Some of the tools used in due diligence can be prepared before the LOI is signed. For example, many companies use checklists to make sure that all potentially relevant issues will be examined. These can be prepared ahead of time. However, because each deal is unique, the checklists should be tailored to the specific circumstances of the merger or acquisition.

In a merger or acquisition, speed of integration is essential for ensuring economic success. The sooner the synergies take effect, the easier it is to justify a deal financially. The longer the period between closing the deal and the anticipated increase in cash flows that arise from it, the greater the level of cash flow discounting. Therefore, companies involved in an M&A must take all reasonable steps to realize expected synergies quickly. To compensate for a delay in realizing synergies, a company has to increase cash flows beyond what was originally forecasted. (Typically, overall cash flows need to increase by 15 percent for each year of delay.)

Planning early for integration, even during the pre-deal stage, is certainly a best practice and an important means for ensuring speedy and successful implementation of a deal. One important aspect is how the deal will be communicated. Events occur so quickly in most M&A situations that being prepared is key to an effective integration process. From the very beginning, employees will be influenced by how swiftly and how frequently news and information is shared with them.

The Origin of Successful M&As

As discussed in Chapter One, people and related organizational and cultural issues play a crucial role in M&A failures. Other types of pitfalls, such as the overestimation of potential synergies and inability to implement change, also have a people component.

Although the pre-deal is only the first stage in the M&A process, many of the people and related pitfalls that confound later implementation can be detected at this stage. Doing so helps to ensure that a solution is found or that a deal with little chance of success is dropped before too much management time and too many resources are devoted to it.

Unfortunately, in the intense, high-stakes atmosphere that frequently surrounds large M&As, it is easy to let long-term, nonfinancial issues get pushed aside. This is especially true in the pre-deal phase, when management is likely to defer people decisions to a later stage. This is a grave error, especially when the deal is made to secure capabilities in product development, engineering, research, or customer management capabilities that reside in the people at the core of the target company—not in the material assets the company owns. *Exhibit 3.6* shows the gap between survey respondents' assessment of the importance of HR roles in the pre-deal stage and their actual involvement in these roles.

The bottom line is that HR has the experience in identifying and understanding issues in several key areas in the pre-deal phase that can affect success. The HR staff must, therefore, be ready to support M&A activities even before potential deals are in play.

As one HR executive said, "Increasingly, the importance of people and talent is becoming apparent in M&A activity. The role of the vice president of HR is to champion the idea that an organization's people strengths are important and to bring that perspective to executives and deals as they happen. The only way to get involved from the beginning of a deal is to be working with a management team that understands the importance of talent."

Exhibit 3.6 The Undervalued Role of HR in Pre-Deal

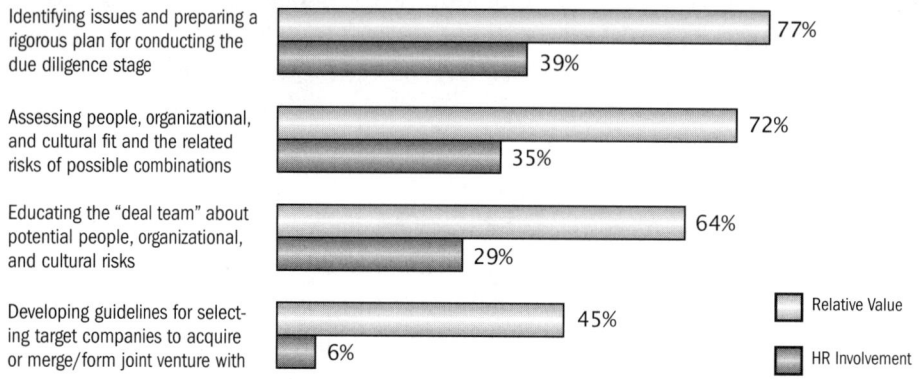

Note: Percentages indicate respondents that are highly involved and place a high level of value (4 or 5 on a 5-point scale) on the activity.

Source: Towers Perrin/SHRM Foundation Survey of over 440 HR executives worldwide.

Preparatory Activities for HR

As a first step in HR becoming a full partner in the M&A process, HR management must understand which of HR's resources have the relevant capabilities to support a merger or acquisition. HR can also lead in compiling a companywide resource directory for staffing M&A integration teams. An outline for an M&A resource directory is presented in the following box.

Functional Experts
- Finance
- Legal
- Market analysis
- Change management
- Corporate communications

People with M&A Experience
- M&A team members (e.g., people who conducted the due diligence stage for the company or for some other firm)
- Key managers from prior M&A (to help understand the other side's perspective)

Relevant Skills Needed
- Languages
- Geography
- Technology

If a company has an explicit acquisition strategy, the resource directory can be extended to include former employees of likely targets who are now working for the company or employees who have had significant interaction with the targets (for example, through joint ventures or professional associations). The directory can also include external resources such as law firms, accounting firms, actuaries, or consultants who have the experience and are qualified to participate in each stage of the M&A process cycle. The M&A resource directory does not have to be limited to people. It can include technical tools, previous evaluation criteria, data request and issue checklists, project management resources, sample reports, and so forth.

The experience level of an M&A team is related to the likelihood of success. HR should help identify potential members of their company's deal team, including representatives of the HR function itself, that have the right breadth and depth of experience. The HR members of the deal team, for example, should have a good understanding of significant trends pertaining to labor markets, productivity, and other people-related business performance issues. More specifically, HR should understand the following:

- Industry standard wages and benefits (as indicated, for instance, in industry-specific surveys)
- Typical turnover rates in the industry
- Employment practices and the structure of the rewards programs
- Overall wage levels, especially for likely acquisition or merger targets
- Overall level of employment at the most likely acquisition targets
- Recent people issues at likely targets (e.g., controversies or lawsuits)
- Union contracts at likely targets (if applicable)

This kind of information can be gathered from many sources. HR executives often have access to industry compensation surveys, for example, that can provide a good starting point. HR staff can also participate in professional groups that are a rich source of intelligence. Current employees who have held positions at the target companies or similar ones in the industry can provide other useful information on pay and benefits. Executive recruiters also keep track of compensation packages for senior management positions in many industries (though this information has to be validated).

Business publications and Internet searches can shed light on the job market in a specific industry or in some labor pools. Discussions with colleagues in these industries or markets can also provide input on market conditions. Much of this information can be gathered at little or no cost, although in all likelihood some gaps in the desired knowledge will exist at this early stage.

Companies with M&A experience should also compile their own knowledge and establish standards regarding best practices for future deals. Such knowledge is often gleaned at multiple levels. Observing how past deals fared may lead to many kinds of improvements, such as revising the HR due diligence checklists as new issues or better approaches are discovered. This, in turn, might have implications for how the HR function is best organized to respond quickly and effectively to future M&A inquiries.

Some companies use postmortems to formally review what happened and what went well or not so well. Usually, postmortems involve a gathering and debriefing of all key parties after the first 100 days following deal closure. While the internal postmortem can be extremely valuable, many participants may be reluctant to question or criticize their own efforts or those of their colleagues. An alternative is to have an independent team of outsiders review each major deal within a reasonable period of time following implementation. Generally, it takes from 18 to 24 months for the bulk of integration activities to be implemented and take effect.

The HR function can be a clearinghouse for this knowledge. At GE Capital, a very successful serial acquirer, corporate HR maintains files on M&A communication plans, 100-day plans, functional integration checklists, workshop agendas, consulting resources, and the like.

Proactive Role for HR in Pre-Deal Stage

To contribute fully to the pre-deal process, HR practitioners must demonstrate to the deal team that they have valuable experience and expertise that supplement the team's existing capabilities. Ideally, HR is a full member of the deal team. In fact, the Towers Perrin/SHRM Foundation research shows that when this is the case, capturing synergies and overcoming integration obstacles are more likely.

HR should educate the deal team about important people issues in M&A (e.g., how these issues contribute to the success or failure of deals and which issues are the most common obstacles to capturing synergies) and should be able to help address these issues. Having this kind of literacy and the supporting competencies is key to winning a seat at the management table during the pre-deal stage. The growing weight of intangible assets in stock market valuations adds greater importance to people issues and how people drive the valuation of the new company. Growth of cross-border M&As means that HR needs to develop skills appropriate for international M&As as well.

Once a list of potential targets is compiled, HR should be prepared to evaluate the people and organizational side of these targets. Seasoned HR professionals can often identify problems that would otherwise go undetected by other deal team members. For example, cultural incompatibilities and related issues are often significant obstacles to integration. In particular, HR can profile important cultural differences with the target companies, using tools and techniques matched appropriately to each situation—and within the time constraints of the pre-deal stage.

The skilled professional can make a qualitative assessment of the target from the public record (placement on "Best Places to Work" lists, etc.). A more in-depth examination requires interviewing people who have recent and direct knowledge of the target and gathering firsthand information (from plant visits, intranets, bulletin boards, employee meetings, etc.). This usually must wait until the due diligence or later stages of the M&A process.

In any event, HR should participate at this point in the selection of "best fit" targets. This is because a reasonably accurate cultural assessment might, for instance, have pre-

Exhibit 3.7 *Organizational and People Issues Gathered and Analyzed by HR in Pre-Deal*

Organizational Issues
- Backgrounds and management style of corporate officers
- Formal reporting structure (centralized, decentralized) and use of titles
- Shape and type of structure (matrix, functional, product/market, etc.)
- Ratio of line/staff or other measures of staff intensity
- Informal reporting structure and integrating mechanisms (use of teams, ad hoc arrangements, etc.)
- Details on design, resourcing, capabilities, and effectiveness of specific functions, such as sales and marketing organization

People Issues
- Demographics of the workforce, significant trends
- Skill base—education, amount of training, development activities
- Reward systems (philosophy, structure, etc.)
- Accountability system and links to other people management systems
- Performance measurement and other people processes
- Workforce engagement/commitment level
- Employee relations and union status
- Areas of current workforce tension
- Legal agreements (e.g., consent agreements)

Source: Towers Perrin analysis.

---

vented some of the less successful deals that have been discussed in the business press. The Quaker-Snapple deal, wherein old-line food company Quaker Oats tried unsuccessfully to incorporate a New Age beverage into its product mix, comes to mind. Of course, the valuation of Snapple's business and the difficulty experienced by Quaker in capturing expected distribution synergies were also major factors in this case example.

HR practitioners can also sensitize the pre-deal team to a wide range of important organizational and people issues and provide insights and information for diagnosing potential problems. *Exhibit 3.7* shows some of the information that HR can gather and analyze during the pre-deal stage.

Exhibit 3.8 shows data that have been collected using the techniques described in this chapter. The first example was created primarily from interviews with former employees of an acquisition target. It shows how different the compensation models of two competing companies are and helps anticipate likely integration issues.

Exhibit 3.9 (page 71) shows quantitative and qualitative information that one acquirer developed to help understand how a potential partner with offices around the world handles attrition. It also provides some valuable input on the culture and values of that potential partner.

HR is also qualified to assess the likely impact of a potential deal on current employees. This sort of assessment helps to identify potential integration difficulties, including negative reactions by various stakeholders, such as unions, or in terms of the skills required for the deal to be a success.

Exhibit 3.8 Comparison of Staffing Model and Cash Compensation

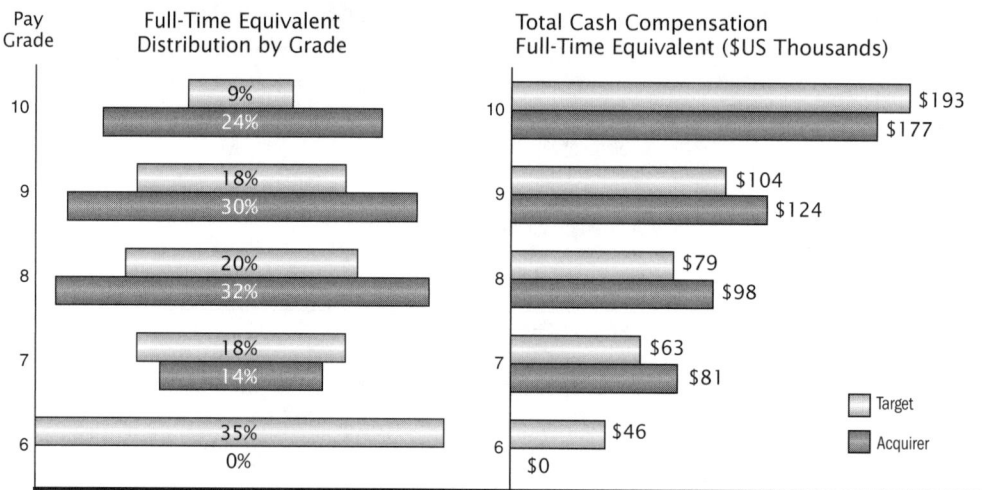

Source: Towers Perrin research and analysis.

Relatively few companies gather and analyze this type of information, even if it is accessible. However, given the high risk in M&As, this kind of analytical effort is strongly advised.

Preparing for Due Diligence

As part of its pre-deal role, HR needs to gear up for the next phase in the process. This means that HR must ensure that the right resources are available to support due diligence. Some policy issues also need to be discussed up front. In particular, the HR and Legal departments must coordinate their approach to communications so that the deal and its implications are communicated to the current staff in the most complete and appropriate manner.

Another important issue is change of control. A company should ideally place management in a position of neutrality before entering into a merger or acquisition; this is done through change-in-control protection (CIC), an agreement that specifies the financial compensation an executive will receive if he or she is required to leave the new company. An effective CIC program allows management to be totally objective and to keep shareholder interests paramount when considering any merger or acquisition opportunity. This is true for both acquirer and target. (See Chapter Five and Appendix D for more information on CIC agreements.)

Companies that wait until negotiations begin to make these arrangements are not as objective about change-in-control protection. Boards of directors are frequently asked to approve poorly designed, last-minute CIC plans that are in conflict with management interests. Some companies may elect to ignore CIC protection issues, leaving management vulnerable and unwilling to proceed on a potentially attractive deal.

Exhibit 3.9 Attrition and Retention Practices of Acquisition Target

Country	Attrition	Comment
U.S.	18–20%	■ Legal, financial, and operating structures differ ■ Manager level has highest attrition rate
Spain	20–30%	■ Technology group has highest attrition of any groups
U.K.	12%	■ Same attrition percentage at every level except for senior executive
Italy	20%	■ Highest attrition percentage at mid-level manager, followed by professional level ■ Highest attrition rate at professional level, followed by new manager level ■ Client Server Practice has highest attrition rate of any group
France	13%	■ Highest attrition rate at analyst level, followed by professional and manager levels
Japan	10%	■ Highest attrition percentage at professional level, followed by analyst level

Retention Strategies/Policies

No Counter-Offers	■ No counter-offers to employees who have already received offers from other firms ■ Exceptions may be made for "star" performers
Reduced Travel	■ Employees have the option of transferring to an assignment with much less travel ■ Initiated policy of "7 to 7" travel: Employee leaves for the client site no earlier than 7 AM Monday and returns home no later than 7 PM Friday
Salary Increases	■ Top performers receive considerably higher salary increases than average or below-average performers (Client Server Practice is the exception)
Paid Travel Home	■ In 1997, started paying for professionals to travel home every weekend, rather than every other weekend
Manager Initiative	■ Managers proactively seek information from their employees on what target can do better
Exit Interviews Committee Involvement	■ Attempts to understand employees' rationale for leaving ■ Provides opportunities for employees to work on various committees, with the intention of increasing their sense of ownership of the company
Community Service	■ Encourages employees to participate in outside activities for a worthwhile cause, with the intention of fostering a more balanced lifestyle ■ Partners frequently attend and sponsor these activities

Source: Towers Perrin analysis.

Exhibit 3.10 JDS Uniphase Recent M&A Activity (as of August 2000)

JDS Uniphase, a leader in the telecommunications hardware industry, was formed through the union of JDS Fitel and Uniphase Corp. in July 1999. Since then, the company has completed the following acquisitions:

- Epitaxx Inc.
- Optical Coating Laboratory Inc.
- Sifam
- Cronos Integrated Microsystems Inc.
- Casix Laser Inc.
- E-Tek Dynamics Inc. (US$15 billion all-stock purchase, pending U.S. Department of Justice approval)

JDS also announced a tentative merger with SDL Inc. (in which SDL is valued at US$41 billion). JDS sales for 1999 were about US$1 billion.

Source: Towers Perrin analysis.

HR should play a key role in implementing proper CIC protection at this early stage, an activity that will help position HR as a strategic partner throughout the balance of the M&A process.

Serial Acquirers and Pre-Deal

Most M&As are episodic events that companies manage with herculean efforts; few companies go through the process often enough to develop a pattern or a well-structured process. There are some exceptions: Companies such as GE Capital Services, Cisco, or JDS Uniphase have grown largely through multiple acquisitions. For these companies, it is important to learn how to manage M&As as a replicable process and not as a one-time-only event. *Exhibit 3.10* shows JDS Uniphase acquisitions from July 1999 and early 2000.

Some companies, such as GE Capital Services, have been working to make the post-acquisition integration process a core management capability and a source of competitive advantage. In doing so, these companies have developed models, processes, and best practices for pre-deal issues that can provide good benchmarks for less-experienced acquirers. These companies have also been able to identify weaknesses in the traditional approach to conducting M&As.

Many serial acquirers have a business development function that focuses on finding, analyzing, and negotiating acquisitions. This is often staffed with former consultants or investment bankers.

Traditionally, the business development function saw most deals through to closing. Afterward, line managers were expected to take over and begin the integration process. Serial acquirers have found this approach to be ineffective; specifically, it results in slow and costly integration. Through experience, they discovered that many integration issues can be anticipated and resolved before deals actually close if business development and line management work hand in hand from the beginning.

Summary

The pre-deal stage is a key element of the M&A life cycle process, as it sets the foundation for each potential transaction and its subsequent implementation. Poor analysis at this stage can lead to deals that will not be beneficial or to promises of synergies and other benefits that will not be attainable once a transaction is complete. What's more, a lack of preparation for the next stages during pre-deal will result in suboptimal results and possibly costly mistakes. Time is of the essence in capturing M&A benefits, and the pre-deal phase is a critical time for careful analysis and thorough planning.

Too often the focus of this stage is on the deal financials. Although financials are not to be neglected, pro formas are not a reliable indicator of long-term success. Issues related to culture, management style, organizational capabilities, and the ability to implement change while maintaining business continuity are among the most common pitfalls of M&A transactions. As such, they need to be addressed as early as possible.

Recent transactions highlight the growing importance of intangible assets, which are largely the talents of people, in the valuation of potential deals. Retaining and leveraging human capital is thus becoming more critical for successful M&As than it was in the past. As the number of cross-border transactions increases, the merging of cultures and HR systems is also getting more complex.

Unfortunately, the pre-deal stage is the one in which HR is least involved, yet the HR function is uniquely suited to tackle some of the previously indicated issues—provided it has built the required skills and capabilities and is given the opportunity to play the role of a strategic partner during the pre-deal work. ■

CHAPTER FOUR

The Due Diligence Stage

Andrew F. Giffin

"Due diligence is extremely important, and HR must be at the deal table from the beginning."

Senior Vice President, Human Resources
Energy Company

It is wise to learn as much as possible about a potential mate before marriage, and the same can be said about a possible partner in a merger or acquisition. In fact, the due diligence process is intended to uncover potential deal wreckers before closing. During the due diligence stage, there's still time to call off the deal or to significantly change its terms. Once the deal has been signed, regrets may abound, but it is too late to do anything about them.

The planned extent of integration strongly influences the substance and process of due diligence. (See Chapter Two for a discussion of the different integration philosophies.) For instance, in a limited integration, having managers across the two organizations get to know one another or work together may not be crucial. In these instances, due diligence is generally focused on the target's ability to maintain its performance after the deal is closed and to produce the incremental results needed to offset the acquisition premium, as its results will be consolidated with those of the new parent company.

On the other hand, a complete transformation of two companies into a new organization requires a deep understanding of their comparative resources and organizational capabilities, as well as an accurate assessment of the new entity's ability to achieve the expected transformation while maintaining its business momentum.

The intensity of due diligence also depends directly on a company's exposure. If the combination is a limited partnership with only partial ownership by a company contributing business or assets to that combination, the risk is less than if all liabilities are assumed, as in an acquisition.

Tailoring the due diligence process to the type of mergers and acquisitions (M&As) transaction and intended integration philosophy is a critical first step, especially since the time available for completing this process is often limited and the resources required can be extensive.

The most important information to uncover during this process is whether the target company or potential merger partner has the organizational capabilities and resources to deliver the anticipated synergies and benefits of a deal. For instance:

- Does the target have the marketplace position and/or competitive capabilities to meet strategic expectations?
- Will the target's profitability justify its price?
- Do qualified managers and other critical talent understand the deal's business rationale and specific performance goals and enthusiastically support them?
- Does the target have significant liabilities and exposures that could reduce its future value?
- Are critical organizational capabilities operating at competitive levels?
- Will the key people stay and work well together?
- Does the target's information technology (IT) system meet industry standards and fit with the acquirer's technology?
- Are there any potential issues or problems with the target's foreign or domestic subsidiaries?

These are just a few of the multitude of issues that must be examined during the due diligence stage. The process is intended to pinpoint issues that could give rise to major problems later. Still, no matter how exhaustive the due diligence process, experience demonstrates that deal breakers can surface later in any area—even in areas that seemed only marginally important at first glance.

Take the case of the British life insurance company that acquired a similar firm in Italy. The acquirer made the deal so that it could expand geographically. Due diligence concentrated on the target's life insurance activities, but a careful examination of a non-life insurance subsidiary *after* the acquisition was completed revealed that its liabilities greatly exceeded its assets, wiping out much of the value of the deal. As a result, the acquired company was later sold at a loss.

The human resources (HR) professional's role in due diligence is not limited to consideration of pay, benefits, and other HR policies and costs. Rather, HR should be a full-time member of the due diligence team and contribute professional expertise to the whole process.

The Towers Perrin/SHRM Foundation survey showed that HR involvement in due diligence varied significantly between successful mergers and unsuccessful ones. As shown in *Exhibit 4.1*, companies that indicated their mergers were successful had more HR involvement in key aspects of due diligence than did those companies that called their acquisitions unsuccessful.

In this chapter, we highlight both the obvious and not so obvious areas that must be addressed during the due diligence stage.

Scope of Due Diligence—Common Areas of Investigation

The primary goal of due diligence is to validate the deal. Nonetheless, the information uncovered during this process should also be used to plan for implementation.

Exhibit 4.1 HR Involvement in Due Diligence Activities

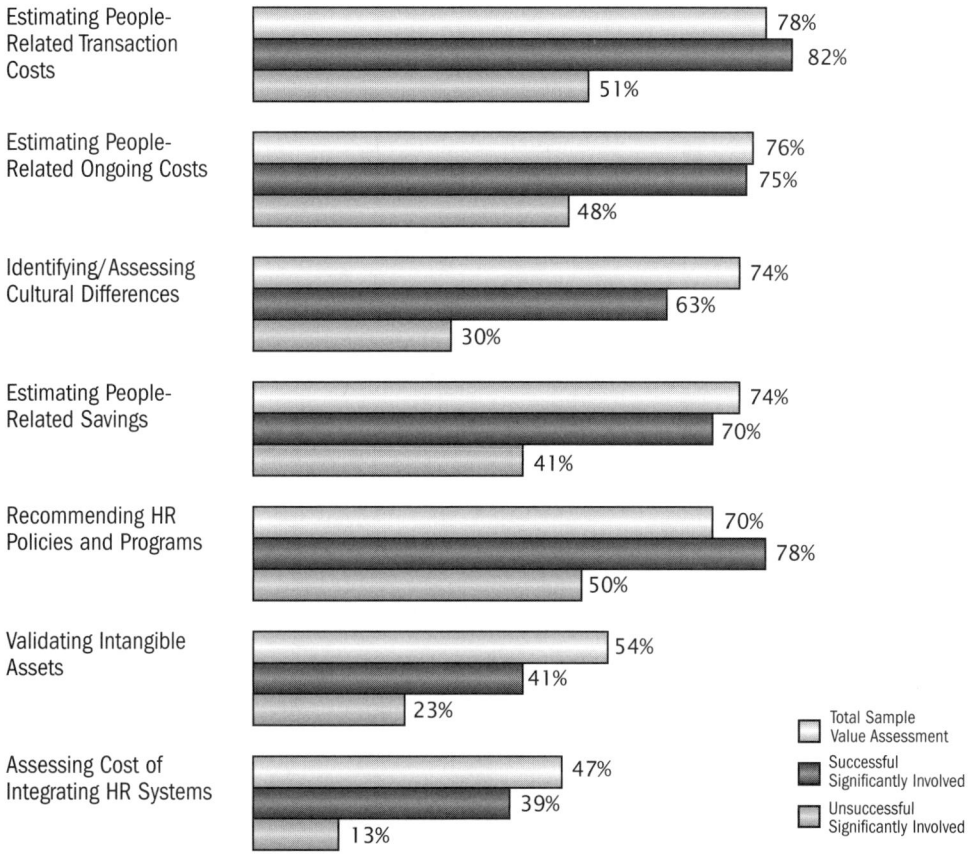

Notes: a) Successful companies are those that attained intended synergies in their mergers, while unsuccessful companies did not.
b) Percentages indicate respondents that are highly involved and place a high level of value (4 or 5 on a 5-point scale) on the activity.

Source: Towers Perrin/SHRM Foundation Survey of over 440 HR executives worldwide.

Due diligence has the following multiple purposes:
- Verify strategic expectations
- Validate the price
- Confirm leadership commitment
- Discover significant liabilities and exposures
- Confirm legal ability to combine
- Verify expected organizational capabilities
- Analyze people issues such as retention, cost, and cultural fit
- Evaluate IT position
- Understand variations among company units and jurisdictions

Here's an in-depth look at each step of the due diligence process, with emphasis on the critical roles that HR should play.

Verify Strategic Expectations
Some questions often asked during this step of the due diligence process follow. While all of the questions are applicable for deals employing the "mutual best-of-both" and "transformation" integration philosophies, many also apply to situations where "limited" and "dominant" philosophies are followed.

- Are the target company's de facto strategies consistent with stated directions?
- Do senior managers from both companies involved in the deal have consistent views of these strategies?
- Are the two companies' strategies historically similar, or are they in conflict?
- Do managers understand and accept the business rationale for the deal?
- Do managers share the same vision, values, and strategic objectives (e.g., growth, profit, and community responsibility) for the new company?
- Do managers appreciate the scope and implications for the integration of businesses, organizations, and management teams?

Although these questions may appear straightforward, many deals are struck with only vague notions about future strategic direction. Exploring such questions may challenge deal architects to fully develop and support their assumptions about potential synergies. For instance, will eliminating projected staff redundancies leave sufficient talent and motivation to achieve these synergies?

The recent acquisition of a consumer services company by a peer competitor is a textbook case of what can happen when strategic expectations and their implications are not understood. Although the acquirer intended to leverage the target's distribution capability, due diligence failed to evaluate its distribution system's effectiveness and how that system would perform under an integrated structure. The due diligence team reviewed production records and organizational charts but failed to uncover that the target's sales representatives were so dissatisfied with working conditions that they were planning to leave the company en masse. As a result, after the deal closed and many salespeople quit the new company, the value of the combined distribution synergy was drastically reduced. This is what can happen when the due diligence process fails to see and verify the crucial link between employee commitment and successful implementation of business strategy.

Another key goal of due diligence is to confirm the fit between the new company's intended strategy and its competitive environment and market requirements. Essentially, due diligence should verify that the new company's intended strategy is supported by objective and thorough competitive analysis, especially the competitors' likely responses to the deal.

The new company's prospects for future marketplace success can also be evaluated by examining established and potential customer relationships of the legacy companies. For instance, how strong is the target's relationship with its customers? How are customers of both companies likely to respond to the new combination and its strategy? Similarly, how are key distributors and suppliers and joint venture or alliance partners likely to respond?

Cost savings and operating synergies are part of the rationale for most M&As. Due diligence should objectively explore the basis for these kinds of cost and synergy expectations. For example, is there hard evidence of redundant activities, organizations, and jobs that could be eliminated? Equally important, would a smaller workforce be able to handle a larger—and more complex—combined operation?

Insider views may be biased by wishful thinking, so external analysts (e.g., regulatory agencies, rating agencies, business consultants, and investment analysts) can enhance the quality of the due diligence process. Their observations can also influence how a merger or acquisition is perceived and valued (e.g., customer acceptance, share price) by each company's stakeholders. They can also have a major impact on perceptions of management credibility. For example, analyst reaction was initially cool when Vivendi, a French conglomerate with worldwide interests in utilities, transportation, telecommunications, construction, and commercial real estate, announced its intent to purchase The Seagram Company, Ltd., the Canadian company that owns Universal Music and Universal Pictures and theme parks, in addition to its traditional alcoholic beverage businesses. The negative response was due in part, according to Geraldine Fabrikant's July 31, 2000, *New York Times* "Market Place" column, to investor perceptions that management had made insufficient disclosure and provided little explanation about the merger's rationale. The result was depressed stock prices for both companies.

For their part, HR professionals should also understand the acquirer's strategic intent to ensure that the right kinds of people issues are pursued during due diligence. HR must alert the due diligence team to the ways people and related organizational or cultural issues can affect the deal's key strategic assumptions. As one senior HR professional put it, "HR needs to have more room at the deal table in due diligence, starting with the negotiation process. People at the table currently can only take it one layer deep. You need someone with implementation experience because there may be different (human resource-related) agreements at the table, and implementation planning will be more realistic if you have people who know it better."

Cultural due diligence, while crucial, is often overlooked, in part because HR professionals often lack the required assessment competencies. Nonetheless, such assessments are closely linked with strategic expectations. For example, a regional bank considered a merger with an insurance company whose geographic market coverage overlapped its own. Strategic and cultural differences killed the deal, however, and the companies' respective annual reports showed how deep their differences ran. The bank's report highlighted its financial performance in detail while the insurance company filled its report with examples of its employee contributions to community service, with only summary financial results. These obvious differences, along with the unproven benefits of combining retail banking and insurance, made it clear to both parties that integration would be very difficult.

Validate the Price

The price of a deal is typically expressed as a dollar-per-share value or a multiple of earnings, revenue, or assets. But when one company buys another, as discussed in Chapter One, value is ultimately determined by the target company's ability to generate sufficient incremental earnings when combined with the buyer. For the buyer to gain *added* economic value, the target must be able to contribute earnings greater than the level implicit in the sale price.

In due diligence, financial statements are reviewed to identify financial and operating assets, liabilities, and historic and projected financial results. Of course, during due diligence, financial statements are not taken at face value. Asset values must be verified (e.g., securities valuations and building appraisals). Liabilities reported on the balance sheet must be investigated. People costs (salaries, benefits, programs, etc.) and potential cost reductions must also be validated. Equally important, the full impact of transaction costs must be anticipated, both costs involved in completing the purchase or merger and in implementing it afterward.

Financial controls, accounting methods, and internal reports are examined for reliability. Critical items, such as tax treatment, must be investigated to determine what could change as a result of the combination (e.g., how the transfer of ownership is treated for tax purposes).

The financial models used to determine the deal offer price are also validated during due diligence. Because acquisitions assume future profits, these models are used to forecast profitability on the basis of assumptions about expected merger synergies and cost reductions. In the pre-deal stage, covered in Chapter Three, these future profitability assumptions are typically made with little or no internal information about the target company. In hostile takeover situations, for instance, the prospective acquirer does not have access to internal information needed to validate price assumptions, which are often based on a multiple of earnings. During due diligence, however, such assumptions can be substantiated with actual data.

The life insurance business is one of the more complex environments for due diligence, especially due to the difficulty of projecting future profits. The reason is that such profits come from insurance policies that are in force for a number of years. Profit on each policy is estimated on the basis of revenue and expense trends. Actual profitability, however, will be affected by future policy retention, premium payments, claims experience, expense levels, and other factors. Cash-flow models must be used to account for the many variables that will affect profit potential.

Similar issues can arise in any business with long-term contractual obligations. But whether the dynamics are long- or short-term, the results of due diligence need to confirm that the assumptions used in the price-setting models can be achieved in future operations. This is particularly relevant to those deals where synergies are expected to strengthen competitiveness and reduce costs.

Confirm Leadership Commitment

The future roles of senior executives of the acquired company (or junior partner in a merger) are often a major stumbling block, both in closing the deal and in implementing it. Commitment from these executives often depends on their satisfaction with the roles and compensation they will have in the new company. If many of the incumbent executives are going to be replaced, the impact on the business and the rest of the organization must also be considered. That applies to any special treatment that the acquired company's founders or senior management receives, as it might affect the attitudes and motivation of the acquirer's current management.

Commitment is especially important when the target company's value depends to a large degree on retaining its key executives and other talent. For example, the value of high-tech companies is often highly dependent on whether their founder(s) remain with an acquirer. In an M&A, these entrepreneurs can be the first ones to jump to another venture or simply to cash out. That's why it is essential for due diligence to attempt to assess key people's commitment to staying with the acquiring company longer than the term of their employment contracts. Their commitment, always difficult to evaluate, will be influenced by the acquirer's actions, culture, and other tangible and intangible factors.

Aside from commitment issues, selection decisions can affect the attitudes of key employees. For example, in a merger of two large financial institutions, the new company's senior management faced the challenge of integrating two very different cultures. One culture emphasized professional staff autonomy and rapid decision-making. The other valued staff control. The new company's employees carefully watched the behaviors of executives to see whether they were biased by the attitudes of their former companies. They assumed that their new bosses would exemplify the management style of their former organizations. Significant defections were threatened when key employees found out they would be managed by someone from the other company because they believed their work environment would deteriorate. In this case, although due diligence identified the potential for major defections, senior management did not fully evaluate key employee reactions or anticipate solutions that might help to reconcile the cultural differences. Management did not reassure key employees about the new company's work environment or even recognize this was an important issue that needed to be resolved quickly in the integration process. As a result, key talent, believing that their concerns would not be addressed, began considering job offers from competitors, and many defected before the new company's leadership could react.

Discover Significant Liabilities and Exposures

Exposure to significant liabilities can influence the target's purchase price or even cause an acquirer to lose interest in closing the deal. Among the warning signs seen during due diligence are the following:

- Unresolved but contested tax liabilities from previous years
- Potentially expensive contracts (e.g., commitments to acquire major equipment, long-term supplier agreements) that depend on highly uncertain future events

- Active litigation that carries the risk of significant adverse judgments (e.g., punitive damages)
- Significant environmental risks that could expose the target to huge liabilities well into the future
- Change-of-control provisions in employment contracts that require special benefits (e.g., additional severance pay) to protect senior managers and other employees if they lose their jobs
- Aggressive response by competitors to neutralize or even frustrate the potential synergies underpinning a deal
- Uncertain union reaction (e.g., concerns about potential job losses or reduced benefits can spark union demands for new negotiations and contract changes)

Due diligence lists developed during earlier deals provide an initial screening device. Past due diligence experience also helps a company to develop a "nose" or instinct for potential problems. Particular attention should be paid to hidden costs and to factors that influence the "needed to win" organizational capabilities the new company must have to succeed.

For example, in a recent acquisition, the buyer discovered a special severance arrangement that had been made with former employees of the target company as part of an early retirement offer. This grandfathered arrangement was not uncovered until after the deal closed, when angry retirees called to complain and provided written documentation of the promises made to them by the target company. This arrangement required extensive time and effort to resolve and resulted in unanticipated payouts to cover the special obligations triggered by the acquisition.

The above example underscores another important point. For reported liabilities, as well as those that come to the surface during due diligence, acquirers must either assume the obligation or secure a warranty or guarantee to shift the associated obligation back to the seller if the target company is a subsidiary of another company. Even so, when these liabilities are significant, the acquirer must be confident that the target company's parent will be in a position to honor its commitment to the acquirer. If there is no continuing entity that can be relied on to accept responsibility, the acquirer must assume the risk and make any needed adjustment to the price.

Confirm Legal Ability to Combine

Corporate charters, bylaws, board of director minutes, and other documentation need to be reviewed to confirm the legal status of the entity being acquired and to verify the legal right of the owners to sell the business. Complex ownership structures (e.g., family trusts) can require extraordinary measures to ensure that all interests confirm the transfer.

For some targets, this review process may include external authorities. Companies regulated by governments (e.g., banks, insurance companies, and securities firms) are subject to regulatory requirements for changes of control. The new owners' right to continue operations may also be subject to similar regulatory scrutiny and approval.

Particularly when foreign operations are involved, special conditions may be placed on the approval of the combination. For example, the mega-merger between America Online and Time Warner had to comply with stringent antitrust requirements in the United States and also faced an additional set of restrictions to satisfy the European Union's competition authorities. It was also required to pass muster with U.S. communications regulators. Anticipation of these and similar issues and an assessment of their impact is a necessary step in due diligence.

Furthermore, local officials commonly require the acquiring company to retain existing locations and personnel, a condition that may or may not fit with the new company's strategic plans.

Confirm Expected Organizational Capabilities

Even if the target company's leadership seems fully committed to the proposed deal, the due diligence process must examine whether the target can generate the expected earnings improvement needed to justify closing the deal. Due diligence should identify the competitive requirements needed for the success of the new company and compare the organizational capabilities of the target with these requirements. In particular, due diligence should analyze the risks of losing the people whose skills or competencies are critical to the long-term success of the merger or acquisition.

The type of integration philosophy contemplated (see Chapter Two) determines the specific tests needed to assess organizational capabilities and retention of key talent. When little change in the scope and manner of operations is anticipated, due diligence can focus on reconfirming that the right capabilities are in place to achieve economic and competitive success. When the target company is to be absorbed by the acquirer or dominant partner in a merger, or when the new company is expected to establish an entirely new mode of operation, the new business model must be verified. If new strategies will be adapted, the analysis must test whether the combined organization will be able to adapt to the new competitive positioning.

A common example involves the merger of two businesses that are in the same industry but have very different operating styles. One is conservative, closely following industry trends and adopting well-defined rules for the roles of units and individuals. The other is an industry trendsetter with high levels of autonomy enjoyed by managers and employees. Both have been competitively successful. Unless the need to reconcile these style differences is identified in due diligence, the integration process may be both difficult and prolonged, leading to lower-than-expected cost savings and, in certain situations, even failure of the combination.

Corporate attitudes and management style differences are illuminated by people programs and policies, in both the target and the acquirer. During due diligence, the acquirer needs to investigate the target's approach to these important people matters and the ways in which services are delivered to employees. For example, do pay policies help attract and retain the types of employees that are demanded by the new company's stated strategy? Do incentive structures fit with the new company's performance expectations? Also, how does the HR staff interact with HR representatives in the operating units and with line managers and employees? How are policies affecting people management communicated? What employee feedback systems are used? How are needed adjustments to people programs and policies implemented? And how do these people management policies and approaches compare with those of the acquirer?

Analyze People Issues

HR professionals should be familiar with the full range of issues addressed in due diligence. This is fundamental for playing the broadest and most effective role in the due diligence process. Nevertheless, HR participants will naturally be most interested in those issues related to people management, organizational effectiveness, and cultural compatibility.

A total rewards model can be a useful guide to key areas of due diligence inquiry related to such topics. Total rewards includes every investment a company makes in its people, including the quantifiable ones such as pay and benefits as well as the less tangible ones such as flexible work schedules and on-the-job development. (See Appendix C for more detail.)

The ability to retain key employees and to recruit new ones depends on having the right reward elements in the integrated (total rewards) program. However, in a merger or acquisition, this may create a dilemma if the new company believes it cannot achieve stated cost reductions if it continues expensive reward programs that employees find valuable. Nor can an acquirer expect to change employee behavior to meet the needs of the newly combined operations if those programs do not encourage employees to modify their behaviors.

Company documentation can provide much of the background needed to investigate existing reward elements. Personal interviews may also prove invaluable for understanding employees' desires and expectations, including their views on existing programs and the need for changes to those programs for achieving desired new behaviors. A related benefit of employee interviews is that they help identify who should fill key roles in the new company and who should receive special retention bonuses.

Evaluate Information Technology Position

Computers, telecommunications, and the Internet have become central features of business strategy and essential ingredients in building competitive advantage. For instance, M&As in many industries are motivated in part by the need to upgrade technology, so due diligence should carefully investigate the target's technology strategy and infrastructure. How do they compare with those of competitors? Will they meet the future competitive challenges from e-businesses and other applications? How do their applications fit with those of the acquirer or merger partner?

Although most M&As assume synergies and cost savings will come from moving to a common technology platform, more often than not, this is not easily achieved. To challenge a prospective deal's assumptions about technology, due diligence must examine the following:

- Strengths and weaknesses of current information architecture, systems, and databases
- Differences in existing platforms that may make transition difficult
- The ability to move applications systems from one platform to another
- The costs and benefits of changing applications to facilitate a single platform (e.g., the volume of activity may not justify a conversion)
- The availability of personnel to support the new company's combined information infrastructure and related operations
- User (internal staff and suppliers, distributors, and customers) requirements needed to adapt to changes in the information infrastructure
- The current and future use of outsourcing capabilities in information and related functions
- The impact on service accuracy, speed, and quality during the integration process

The technology considerations of a merger or acquisition are examined later in Chapter Nine.

Understand Variations Among Company Units and Jurisdictions

The foregoing elements of due diligence apply to all of the business units and jurisdictions of the target. Targets with multiple business units, particularly when they are located in different countries, may have a wide range of characteristics and special issues to consider. It cannot be merely assumed that one method of operation applies or one culture dominates them all. As noted earlier, it can be a flaw in an inconsequential subsidiary that eventually makes the merger or acquisition fail.

Some Specific People Issues

A number of people issues in the due diligence process warrant particular attention. Although we have treated these issues separately here, they span the breadth of the due diligence process, and that fact reinforces the importance of a strong HR capability on the due diligence team.

Identify Key Talent

Acquirers often assume naively that they will keep the target's key managers and other talent in sales, research and development (R&D), finance, HR, and operations. This assumption is wrong more often than not. A major reason is that competitors take advantage of the transition from legacy companies to a new company to poach key talent. For example, when a telecommunications company purchased a cable networking business for a hefty price in the late 1990s, the strategic rationale for the deal was that the acquirer (an old "bricks-and-mortar" company) could simply "morph" itself into a cable-based New Economy competitor. Although the acquirer did an excellent job of anticipating cultural integration needs and total rewards for the new combined workforce, much of the deal's potential was lost when many of the target's key talent left the company during the transition stage. Because these people constituted the target's human capital, they took much of the acquirer's prospects for future success with them. Due diligence could have stemmed this loss of talent by identifying early who the key players were and planning concrete actions that would help retain them.

By contrast, when a large engineering conglomerate acquired a smaller innovative company to pioneer robotics technology, first- and second-line managers, as well as a significant part of the R&D team, were interviewed and assessed to determine their individual competencies, roles, and potential for advancement. In addition, from the day the deal was made public, a constant stream of tailored (i.e., personal) messages, one-on-one meetings, e-mail, publications, and a voice response help line kept these people informed about what was going on and allayed their concerns. As a result, turnover was minimal, and the acquirer achieved its goal of harnessing the full potential of the acquired company's human capital.

As noted earlier, once a pending merger or acquisition is made public, employees—particularly those with the most valuable skills—are often the target of aggressive recruiting by competitors or executive search firms. That is why it is so critical to know who these people are, how they perceive the deal for themselves and their careers, and how they can be persuaded to stay. In addition to identifying the key players and clearly communicating with them every step of the way, special efforts can also help retain the best people when strategic objectives, incentives, and performance measurement systems are aligned in a logical way. When all three are in sync, employees understand the results they're expected to achieve *and* the rewards they will receive for their performance contributions. For that reason, successful integrators have learned that reviewing alignment during due diligence can help define the specific changes needed during the transition period and beyond to enable the new company's strategic direction.

Evaluate Prospects for Cultural Integration

As previously discussed, managing cultural differences between companies during the integration process is often the single highest barrier to success. Failure to account for cultural differences and their consequences is often attributed to the disproportionate attention typically given to strategic and financial issues, both in the pre-deal and due diligence stages. In truth, these stages of the M&A process are typically managed by strategic planners and financial managers (e.g., treasurer, general counsel, chief financial officer) who may have limited knowledge of some of the critical people, organization, and—perhaps most significantly—cultural issues. They may not be sensitive to signs that such issues are present in any given deal and may not fully appreciate the attendant risks.

As part of a recent pharmaceutical and chemical company merger that embraced the "best-of-both" integration, two operating divisions were combined—one with an entrepreneurial, sales-driven culture and the other with a long-standing bureaucratic, slower-moving work environment. Tensions derived from the underlying cultural origins of the team members became apparent during meetings between the joint integration teams. As tempers flared, several key people who had participated in the earlier deal making and integration planning left the new company—out of sheer frustration. Although the senior management continued to declare the merger a success, this talent drain continued long after the transition period.

To avoid this kind of situation, the due diligence investigation needs to identify the potential for "culture clash," providing the integration teams with the facts necessary for them to design a transition process that includes understanding and reconciliation. This is critical in a case such as that discussed above in which the best-of-both or transformation philosophy is intended to govern the integration. By the same token, if understanding and reconciliation are not considered feasible, the rationale for the combination should be questioned very seriously.

As with culture, organizational issues can influence how people contribute to the combined entity formed through a merger or acquisition. At issue is whether it is feasible to meld the two companies' organizations and workforces and still remain competitive. If so, what steps will be required during integration to achieve this end?

Due diligence activities directed toward assessing integration needs include the following:

- Deciding on the approach to and timing of integrating specific businesses units and support functions
- Understanding the risks of unplanned turnover from integrating business units and functions
- Profiling cultural differences and examining whether they are likely to disrupt or compromise the integration process
- Estimating the effort and time required to communicate the new company's strategy and integration philosophy and to build broad-based employee support for the merger or acquisition, especially its stated benefits
- Evaluating the tasks required to address the key cultural issues and the ability of the new company to complete the tasks successfully
- Assessing the ability of management to execute the integration plan

These activities help facilitate successful integration by anticipating potential obstacles. Even more important, the analysis will also help determine the feasibility of the deal in the first place by identifying potential delays and associated costs.

Status of Employee Relations

The target's current work environment is another critical area for due diligence. Among the important questions that must be answered are the following:

- What is the target's philosophy regarding people management?
- How is this philosophy exemplified through HR policies and practices?
- What is the labor climate in the target or merger partner?

- Are there frequent labor disputes? If so, why? How successful have past contract negotiations been?
- Are discrimination or other complaints common? If so, why?
- What is the target's safety record? For instance, is the number of workers compensation claims unusually high? What does this imply?

Prior Experience with Combinations

Consolidation of business has been on the rise. But organizations have a wide range of experience with the integration process. Some of these are good experiences and some are not. Therefore, during due diligence, companies should ask: Have both organizations demonstrated the ability to integrate? Has a bad experience made them resistant or wary? Are they fed up with the integration process? Such people-related considerations are critically important to the success of any combination and demand that HR and the entire deal team work in a collaborative fashion to reach the right answers.

Business Locations and Employee Relocation

Resolving the headquarters location of the combined entity and its major subunits should be considered during the due diligence stage. This decision involves evaluating the alternatives, determining stakeholder attitudes to each, and anticipating numbers of employees to be relocated and the relocation process and terms once final selections are made.

Case in point: Two large corporations created a joint venture operating in a specialty chemical market. The joint venture was intended to combine the strengths of both companies' research facilities, which were in different locations. Although the two research staffs understood the joint venture's purpose, the location of this new venture had not been determined. Subsequently, the uncertainty about the choice of location and relocation terms led to unrest in both research groups. And once the location decision was finally made, considerable time and expense was required to encourage one of the research groups to move—with limited success.

As the example suggests, whenever consolidation plans call for relocating people, considerable resistance is likely. Many relocations result in substantial loss of talent. In addition to replacement costs, the potential loss of crucial knowledge, experience, and continuity must be built into contingency plans.

HR Policies, Plans, and Programs

Each company's HR policies, plans, and programs should be compared and contrasted to assess their compatibility and determine how the new company's key people are likely to react to significant changes. The scope of the assessment should encompass current benefits programs and ongoing costs for all active employees (including full-time, part-time, expatriate, temporary contract, and union employees), inactive employees (disabled, eligible for post-termination benefits, those on leaves of absence), and retirees. These obligations are frequently underestimated and potential cost savings

Exhibit 4.2 Due Diligence: HR Programs Examined

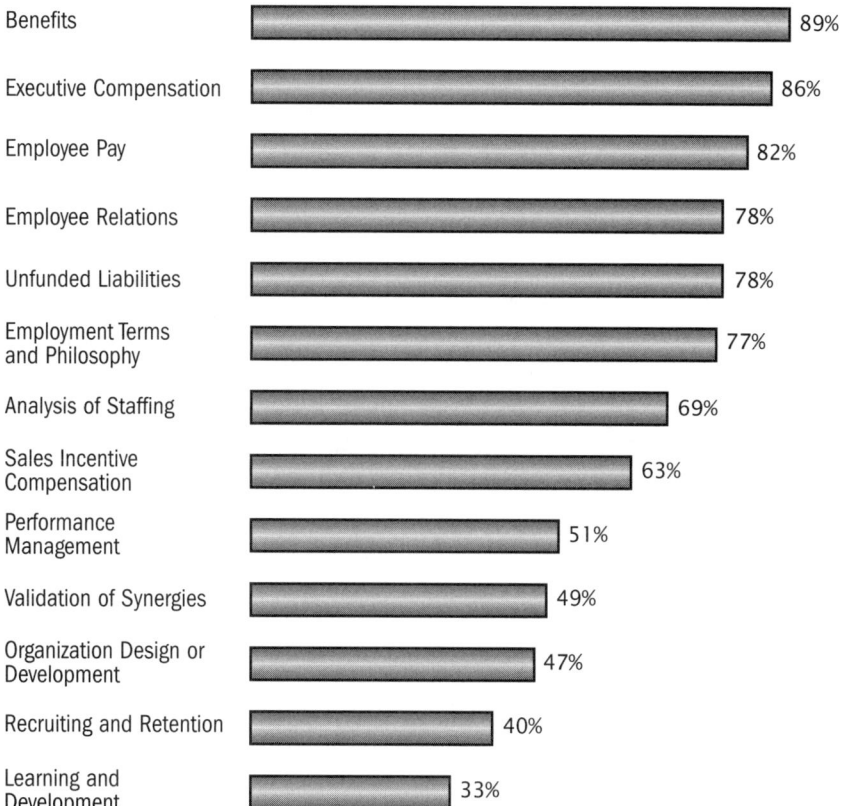

Note: Percentages indicate those stating that the area was examined in their most recent M&A activity.

Source: Towers Perrin/SHRM Foundation Survey of over 440 HR executives worldwide.

from combinations overestimated. Assessment of these obligations is key to identifying any large, unanticipated liability that could affect the deal's value or viability and is an important source of information for analyzing the impact of changes in the programs.

Exhibit 4.2 shows which HR programs were examined during the due diligence process by respondents in the Towers Perrin/SHRM Foundation survey. Not surprisingly, those programs with obvious potential for financial or legal impact on the new company were most likely to be examined.

Pay Strategies and Liabilities

The M&A head of a large manufacturing company recently said, "If I were allowed to look at only one thing in due diligence, I would choose the target's pay programs. They tell me more about what an organization values and how it works than anything else."

This executive is right: Pay programs flow directly from a company's values and are deserving of special attention during due diligence.

Among the areas of due diligence inquiry into base pay and incentives, change of control, and other pay-related issues are the following:

- Compatibility of pay levels across companies and with competitive benchmarks
- Role of variable pay in cash compensation
- Links between pay and performance goals
- Consistency of current practices with expected incentive plans for the new company and an assessment of changes in behavior that the new plans should motivate
- Potential costs of golden parachutes, accelerated pay provisions, and stock option triggers
- Impact of incentives and financial obligations on retention of key talent
- Cost impact of expected severance and turnover; commitments to future pay increases, relocation, and compliance costs; and transitional program costs (e.g., retention bonuses)

In addition to pay, understanding the related benefits program costs, liabilities, and risks is another vital aspect of due diligence.

Retiree/Disabled Employee Liabilities

For retirees and disabled employees, due diligence issues typically focus on life insurance, defined benefit pension, and health plans. Careful investigation of liabilities and future costs is particularly important when the target company has acquired other companies in the past. A recent merger of two financial services companies provides an example of what can happen when these potentially large costs are overlooked. In this case, the acquired company had made several previous acquisitions without fully integrating their benefit programs and related administration, and it did not have a complete account of its plan participants. As a result, the new company had no prior knowledge that the company it acquired had been providing benefits to about 200 retirees—that is, not until it terminated its relationship with the plan administrator. At that point, the company was forced to buy costly bridge coverage until a suitable replacement could be found for the plan administrator.

A key decision for a new company is whether to terminate, freeze, or integrate the acquired company's retirement plans. Although restrictions may limit the choice by requiring continuation of particular coverage under union contracts or by law in some jurisdictions, this decision usually swings on comparative costs. Indeed, retirement plan costs (and liabilities) are influenced by several factors that require careful scrutiny during due diligence.

- Employee/Retired Member Population: Will the liability for former employees be transferred to the acquirer's plan? Have the acquired company's costs been determined by using average costs for a larger plan or do they reflect only the employee population being acquired? Are there special arrangements for particular groups of employees/retirees?

- Plan Benefits: Are additional change-in-control benefits triggered by the acquisition? What is the potential one-time cost of special termination benefits for employees who are departing due to the acquisition?
- Actuarial Assumptions: What assumptions have been used to date by the acquired company in determining its liabilities and the costs of these benefits? How do these assumptions compare with those used by the acquiring company?
- Accounting Treatment: Is a specific accounting treatment mandated for the merger or acquisition? For example, in the United States, M&As are accounted for under "pooling of interests" or "purchase" methods. Although companies often prefer the pooling of interests method for tax and other reasons, in some instances they may be required to report costs using the purchase method.

To illustrate the interplay (or combined impact) of these factors, consider the software company whose strategy was to acquire other software firms with applications related to its own software portfolio. In one transaction, it was assured in preliminary discussions that the target's pension plan was "fully funded." This conclusion was based on a calculation using current salaries of the target's employees. When future salary escalation, transaction-triggered benefits (e.g., change-in-control, early retirement), and acquiring company changes in actuarial assumptions were factored in, the acquiring company was left with a $50 million deficit. Given the size of the acquirer, this could have been a deal breaker or worse had the problem not been uncovered during due diligence.

The transfer of retirement plan assets is another due diligence issue. If the acquired company has been participating in a master trust made up of a large group of companies, the acquirer must decide how the transfer of assets should be made—in cash or in kind (i.e., in the form of securities). This may become an important negotiating point. Moreover, if securities are being transferred, which ones and how their value is determined must also be clarified, particularly if market price data are not available.

Master trust or parent company plan participation also raises questions about appropriate cost assumptions. For example, are historic plan average costs relevant for the acquired employees as a stand-alone group?

Future retirement plan costs for all acquired employees should also be considered. As plan benefits are integrated, these costs may change considerably. For example, most U.S. companies tend to have distinct practices with respect to post-retirement life insurance and health coverage. That's why the acquirer must decide before closing whether responsibility for this coverage will shift from the parent (i.e., the target's parent) to the acquiring company.

Unidentified arrangements for retirees and disabled employees can open a Pandora's box of unanticipated costs. Take the case of a large telecommunications company that purchased a division of another telecommunications company. Before the acquisition, the parent company of the acquired division provided health and welfare benefits for approximately 6,000 active employees and 2,000 retirees. However, due diligence failed to identify liabilities for disabled employees. After the acquisition, all of the liabilities for active, retired, and disabled employees were transferred to the acquiring company. However, since the acquiring company did not offer the same benefit programs and vendor-provided services as the parent of the acquired company, it was forced to obtain benefit coverage for the disabled employees. Further, because a complete list of disabled employees was not provided to the acquiring company before closing, the life insurance carrier denied death claims for disabled employees of the acquired company on the grounds that no coverage had been negotiated for them. This oversight left the acquiring company with the choice of negotiating coverage after the fact or covering the death claims directly.

To avoid similar issues, details of the target's retirement plans and employee obligations should undergo painstaking scrutiny in due diligence. The inquiry should include the following:

- Have all plans and benefits, including transaction-triggered benefits and unfunded plans, been disclosed?
- Are the acquired company's actuarial reports current and complete?
- What benefits have and have not been included in the valuation reports?
- What actuarial assumptions and methods were used in the valuations, and were any costs or liabilities estimated?
- Have any plan improvements recently been negotiated or added but not included in the valuation reports?
- Are there union requirements to maintain certain plan benefits?
- Are there compliance or reporting problems with the applicable regulatory authorities (e.g., in the Employee Retirement Income Security Act [ERISA] or Pension Benefit Guaranty Corporation [PBGC] filings or premiums)?

Although defined benefit plans are the most complicated to review, defined contribution plans can also raise problems that must be explored during due diligence. For instance, employees of the new company resulting from a merger or acquisition can face difficulties with benefit eligibility rules (e.g., are employees "terminated" when they move from one unit to another, changing their "tenure" position?).

Retirement liabilities can pose a particular challenge when foreign subsidiaries are involved. For example, a U.S. conglomerate was recently interested in purchasing a German-based company with more than 26,000 employees in 27 countries. Due diligence showed that retirement liabilities were reported with overly aggressive financial assumptions and that methodologies used were out of line with U.S. requirements. Moreover, in some countries, liabilities were unfunded. Practices that were permitted in local countries failed to meet U.S. requirements. The overall balance sheet impact of these issues (liabilities) was more than 10 percent of the original purchase price. Fortunately for the acquirer in this case, the liabilities were discovered before the deal was closed, so the negotiating team was able to adjust the purchase price accordingly.

In addition to assessing the obligations under existing plans, it's important for due diligence to anticipate consolidations or plan changes. For example, there is a strong trend today to move from defined benefit to defined contribution plans. Where such a transition is being considered, it's important for due diligence to identify restrictions or special obligations that may influence either the choice of plans or the terms applied to different classes of employees.

Health Plan Liabilities

The growing importance and cost of health benefits makes them a subject for due diligence. As with retirement benefits, obligations to active employees must be identified. Key areas of inquiry include the following:

- Current costs of active employee programs for the acquired population
- Commitments for future cost increases (e.g., cost-sharing agreements)
- Exposure to cost escalation from medical inflation, utilization trends, and medical technology development
- Plan offerings and vendor positions
- Compliance of plans with regulatory requirements

Estimating Benefit Plan Cost Savings

To justify acquisition premiums and to demonstrate the economic synergies in M&A, companies are usually eager to estimate cost savings from benefit plan consolidation. In the final reckoning, these savings often fail to materialize or even to reach expectations. For example, when two large telecommunication companies merged, each company used the same national health care vendors within the same geographic area. The acquirer anticipated a 20 to 25 percent savings, or about $750 million, from combining their health programs. But after the companies were combined, the acquirer discovered that instead of providing economies of scale, the large size of the combined workforce actually increased program costs by roughly $350 million. Bottom line: Due diligence failed to validate a very large synergy projection.

To avoid inaccurate cost-saving projections, due diligence should include an investigation of the contractual arrangements and internal processes required for health programs. For instance, are the anticipated economies of scale realistic? Are there groups of active, retired, or disabled employees who require special benefits or accounting treatment? Will the costs of consolidation still allow the expected cost savings? What steps will be required for a successful consolidation during the integration stage?

Termination Benefits

In the United States, Canada, and the United Kingdom, retirement and health benefits tend to pose the most significant employee-related liabilities. In many other countries (including some Latin American and European countries), state-mandated termination benefits (some funded, some not) may carry potentially large liabilities. This is because termination benefits are significant and are not covered by funded arrangements. Due diligence should therefore include a review of local laws on employee and termination benefits to ensure that a full and accurate picture of exposures is developed before closing.

Exhibit 4.3 Due Diligence Time Frames

Time Frame	Respondents
Less than 3 Months	62.9%
3–6 Months	29.7%
7–12 Months	6.9%
More than 12 Months	0.5%

Source: Towers Perrin/SHRM Foundation Survey of over 440 HR executives worldwide.

Navigating the Due Diligence Process

No magic formula exists to guarantee successful due diligence. Nonetheless, navigating the due diligence process can be facilitated by keeping in mind the time constraints and other limitations that will be faced and by following some of the proven approaches summarized in the following paragraphs.

Outside Expertise

If due diligence is not a routine activity for a company—that is, M&As are not frequent enough to justify building a world-class management competency in due diligence—it is important to include outside advisors—attorneys, consultants, and engineers—who have that experience.

Time Constraints and Priorities

The deal-making process often leaves insufficient time for complete due diligence. In many instances, an initial agreement (e.g., a letter of intent) is structured to provide a mandate for due diligence. The time frame for this process can be limited to a few days or extend for several months. According to the Towers Perrin/SHRM Foundation survey, about 60 percent of respondents experienced due diligence time frames of less than three months, and some 90 percent had less than six months. These tight time constraints require careful prioritization and planning. *Exhibit 4.3* shows the time frames respondents and their companies used for the due diligence process.

Because of time (and also cost) constraints, due diligence requires careful prioritization of issues and of the work to be done in resolving them. Although the hope is always that no information will be uncovered that would unravel the deal, focusing on the most significant issues helps identify potential deal breakers early so that they can be fully examined. *Exhibit 4.4* shows the HR due diligence activities that the Towers Perrin/SHRM Foundation survey respondents ranked as most valuable and their degree of involvement in those activities. Not surprisingly, issues that carry the greatest financial risk ranked highest.

Exhibit 4.4 Due Diligence: Most Valuable Activities and HR Involvement

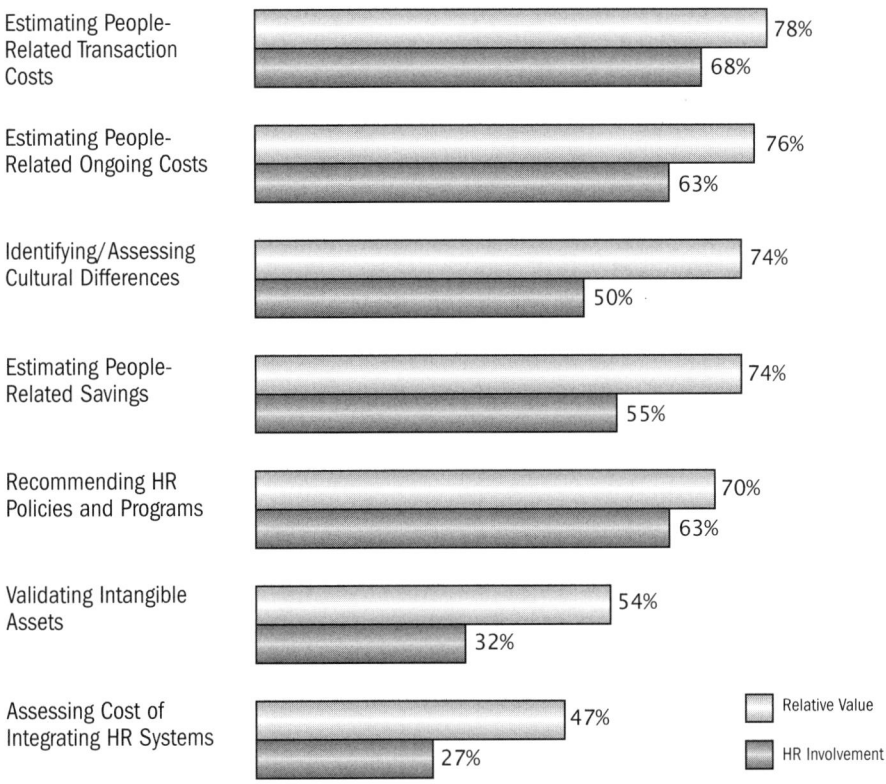

Note: Percentages indicate respondents that are highly involved and place a high level of value (4 or 5 on a 5-point scale) on the activity.

Source: Towers Perrin/SHRM Foundation Survey of over 440 HR executives worldwide.

Data Availability Limitations

For competitive reasons, target companies sometimes limit severely access to their data, either directly or by imposing unrealistic time constraints on due diligence. As mentioned earlier, in hostile takeover situations, information may be limited to public sources. Acquirers must decide whether the risks permit them to proceed or to hold out for additional time and/or data access. The acquiree may be able to condition an initial agreement on the successful completion of particular due diligence steps.

Target companies may also fail to disclose known problems. Or, because available documentation may not provide a complete picture of the current situation, the acquirer may need to interview the target company to develop the right perspective. If the target's management is open to such inquiries, the acquirer can be more confident that relevant facts have been discovered and that the decision to proceed is sound.

It is also common for a target company to make pertinent files available to a potential acquirer via a data room, particularly when there are multiple bidders. Review of these materials may be limited, however, to the data room itself, and even then may be subject to strict time limits. To make the best use of this opportunity, it is essential to carefully plan data room activity in advance—for example, by assigning different data room tasks to specific members of the due diligence team. Bringing outside experts with extensive data room due diligence experience can also make the process more efficient.

Time and access limitations, along with the dynamic nature of the due diligence process itself, require the team to prepare a well-conceived plan before getting immersed in details. The emerging results of due diligence analysis must be promptly translated into reports, and identified problems and recommendations must be immediately communicated to the full team. Resources can then be reallocated as needed to the highest priority due diligence activities.

Get to the Decision Point

As preliminary conclusions are formulated and circulated for reaction and comment, the key questions for the due diligence team to ask are the following:
- Have any potential deal breakers surfaced?
- What is the risk of a deal breaker surfacing in the future?
- What additional follow-up is required?
- Is the due diligence team overlooking anything significant?

Some conclusions, such as incompatible distribution systems, will clearly be deal breakers, while others, such as unanticipated weakness in a particular division's competitiveness, will warrant only advisory notes for future consideration. Still others, such as the target's guarantee against loss from a potential liability, are appropriate issues for renegotiation.

Many companies with little experience in due diligence find this open-ended form of analysis particularly difficult. Often, they are forced to close the process—or a phase of it—prematurely with incomplete information. At this point, the due diligence team must ask itself, "Given what we know now, do we proceed, withdraw, or request a change?" Answering this question requires accepting the ambiguity created by not having a complete picture of the target's strengths and weaknesses.

Integration Planning and Implementation

Due diligence sets up the subsequent integration planning and implementation stages by disclosing issues that will need to be addressed as the M&A process evolves further. For example, the target's human resource policies and programs may vary from those of the acquirer. The due diligence process should develop the necessary facts for a comparison of the approaches used by each company, confirm the potential for reconciliation, and anticipate a path to a new formula.

Understanding the Downside Risks

Inadequate due diligence has contributed to major failures in M&As. These failures may be couched in terms of abrupt resignations of discontented executives, irreconcilable culture clashes, unresolved tax liabilities, huge costs incurred in a breakup, disclosure of adverse market conditions that changed company values, and in many other ways. Due diligence will not anticipate all deal breakers or mitigate all of the risks that may be present. (In fact, the legal requirement—that is, the duty to protect shareholder interests—is to exercise reasonable prudence.) That said, completing the due diligence process by drawing on best-practice experience and being attentive to potentially critical issues is critical to improving the odds of a successful outcome. Although acquirers cannot uncover every issue, successful integrators know that when potential problems are ignored or buried, they usually surface when it's too late and too costly to correct them.

Summary

The search for deal breakers in due diligence needs to be thorough and efficient, accommodating the distinct needs of the deal in question. At the same time, it must lay some of the groundwork for the subsequent integration planning and implementation stages.

It is important for HR professionals to be involved throughout the due diligence stage. HR should help negotiators and business leaders understand the potential impact of people, organizational, and cultural issues and thereby enhance the deal's chances for success. This role is not limited to consideration of personnel activities or concerns; it includes the broader impact of people issues on the full range of business issues. However, to allow an appropriate level of HR participation, practitioners must have specific M&A competencies.

Due diligence is a discovery process. All members of the due diligence team, including HR professionals, must apply their areas of expertise to the whole of the due diligence scope and process to complete an analysis that meets the often difficult combination of uncertain priorities and limited time frames. ■

CHAPTER FIVE

Integration Planning Stage

Brent L. Rice

"The deal is in the details."
The Industry Standard

Imagine that you're a chief executive officer who has worked hard to identify a merger or acquisition target, evaluate the merits of the deal, and sign the agreement. Your next challenge is to figure out how to integrate the two organizations without losing business momentum. This should be relatively easy, shouldn't it? Your own company is very successful, you picked the target because it was the best business fit, and many talented people in the organization have mergers and acquisitions (M&A) experience. Maybe you had to pay a large premium to acquire the target, but this will easily be recovered once the companies are combined and those promised synergies begin to materialize.

Flash forward 12 months. You've picked some of the low-hanging fruit, mostly expense reductions (though the employee terminations were painful), but several major problems remain. Your competitors took a hard run at your best customers—and you are stunned at how successful they were. They were also able to lure away many of your top sales people and national accounts managers. Worst of all, anticipated revenues and earnings are well below expectations, and the stock price is trending downward with no bottom in sight. The chairman is calling with increasing frequency, and stock analysts are not convinced that the business will rebound any time soon. Where are those synergies? Maybe the next move is to cut jobs even more.

Unfortunately, this scenario plays out all too often. Companies enter the integration process with great expectations but become frustrated when projected synergies fail to develop. As discussed in Chapter One, research shows that whether the intention was to enhance brand reputation, succeed in new markets, grow market share, or cut costs, more than half of the companies undertaking a merger or acquisition have been disappointed with the results.

Fortunately, careful design and efficient implementation of the integration plan leads to a very different, positive outcome. And human resources (HR) must provide leadership and expertise in planning the integration of business and functional organizations, people, and cultures to overcome these obstacles.

Past M&A practices, which confined HR involvement to integrating compensation, benefits, and other HR programs, are insufficient in view of the strategic importance of people to M&A success. This is a crucial point: HR must lead the planning for many key aspects of the integration process.

As *Exhibit 5.1* shows, a significant gap exists between survey respondents who participated in successful M&As and those who were not successful in terms of their involvement in integration planning activities.

As one seasoned veteran of M&As put it, "HR needs to be as involved in integration planning as the finance and information technology departments. HR needs to know the organization's business so well that the CEO can trust HR to find and value the talent that must be maintained."

If HR leaders have not been actively involved in the pre-deal and due diligence stages, what can they do to position themselves for a key role in integration planning? First, they must demonstrate knowledge of the people, organizational, and cultural challenges of integration and be able to effectively communicate these challenges to senior management and the deal team. This may require a significant investment of time and effort to build M&A competencies through research, workshops, and best-practice visits to successful acquiring companies. Next, HR must acquire the tools and methodologies to support key aspects of integration planning, such as culture assessment, organization design, and project management. Finally, HR must be able to gain the attention of the M&A process owners who may have a blind spot to these challenges.

Given the importance of managing the people, organizational, and cultural aspects of any merger or acquisition, HR can help to ensure integration success through three major roles.

Support for Overall Integration

As part of senior management, HR should play a leadership role in the following activities:

- Determining what skills and competencies are required to build or maintain those organizational capabilities necessary for supporting the new company's business strategy
- Identifying critical people integration issues and designing programs for dealing with them, including transition programs for retention, severance, relocation, and staffing for the new organization
- Profiling and assessing significant cultural differences and identifying the changes required to bridge the gaps
- Identifying future leadership requirements in conjunction with an assessment of current leadership capabilities
- Advising and counseling line managers throughout the integration process

Exhibit 5.1 HR Involvement in Integration Planning Activities: Successful vs. Unsuccessful

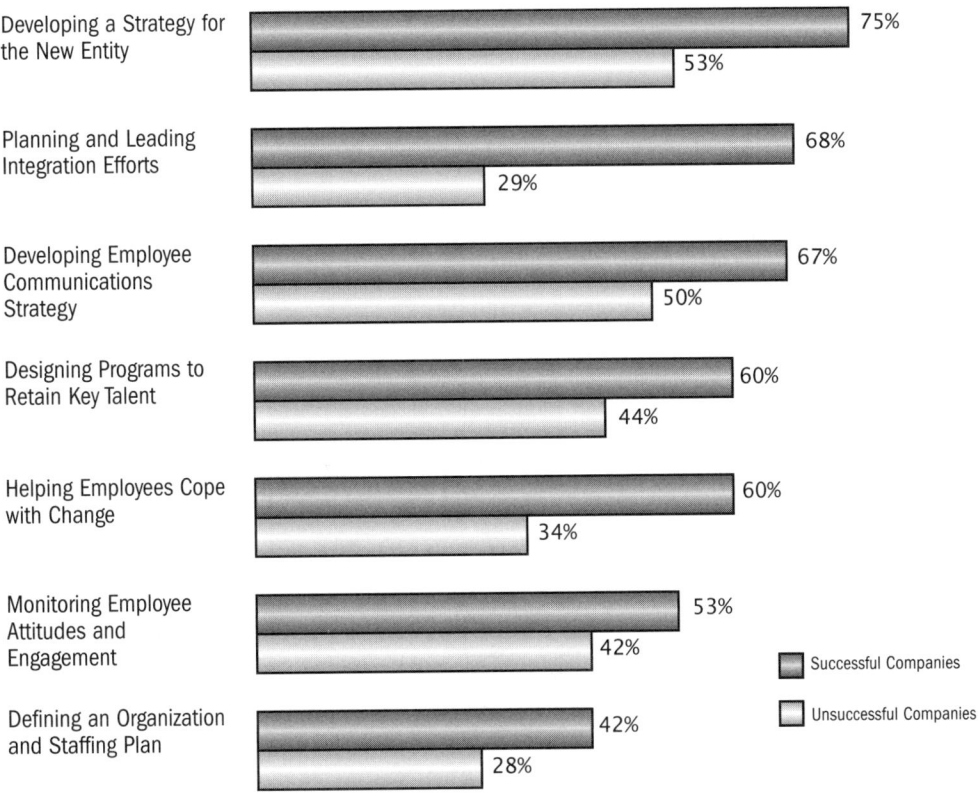

Notes: a) Successful companies are those that attained intended synergies in their mergers, while unsuccessful companies did not.
b) Percentages indicate respondents that are highly involved and place a high level of value (4 or 5 on a 5-point scale) on the activity.

Source: Analysis of Towers Perrin/SHRM Foundation Survey data.

Policies and Reward Program Design

HR must develop the policies and programs to help maximize the new company's investment in human capital. This role includes the following:

- Developing a total rewards strategy for the new company (Chapter Eight provides details on the concepts and approaches), including the guiding principles and design parameters for total rewards programs
- Developing a timeline for unifying or transforming HR services and practices

Reinvention of the HR Function

This requires a thorough assessment to determine the most effective and efficient way of organizing HR to support the newly combined organization and its employees. (Chapter Seven contains a detailed treatment of this topic.)

Exhibit 5.2   Stakeholders' Perceptions of M&A Success

Customers	Investors	Employees	Suppliers and Distributors	Communities
■ Products and services are the same or better after the merger (prices, availability, and quality) ■ Innovation is a strong feature of the new company (R&D, technical support, and service, etc.) ■ Synergies are shared with customers where appropriate (marketing, sales, and distribution) ■ Customer service and support does not erode during transition	■ Merger synergies are quickly realized, as promised by management ■ Market value of the newly formed company's shares rises faster than the general trend for the industry ■ The financial performance of the new company is consistent with the expectations set forth before closing	■ Though jobs may be lost, those that remain are challenging and rewarding ■ Where practical, displaced employees are offered other positions in the new company ■ New opportunities are created to promote on merit and eliminate underperformers ■ The positive aspects of the current employment contract (explicit and implicit) are unaffected or improved	■ Key relationships and networks are preserved and strengthened ■ Synergies are shared with suppliers and distributors where appropriate (value chain) ■ The new company's commitment to its current strategic partnerships and alliances is resolved quickly	■ The new company uses its financial and people resources to serve the community ■ Civic and charitable initiatives are not compromised by job losses, relocation of company headquarters, or spending cuts ■ The new company maintains its social responsibilities to the communities in which it does business

Source: Towers Perrin analysis.

Planning for Success

In some M&As, extended regulatory approvals leave a lot of time for thinking about integration plans. But regardless of the situation, as one senior vice president of HR said, "It's very important to have a cast-iron plan for integrating programs. What's more, that planning should start as early as possible." Integration planning should begin before the final stages of due diligence (or even earlier, if possible); starting to seriously plan for integration only after the announcement of the deal is too late. At the announcement, stakeholders expect management to have answers about the way the integration process will unfold. Management's credibility hinges to large extent on its ability to provide clear, unambiguous direction about the stakeholder needs and concerns about the integration process.

So how do the company's key stakeholders—customers, investors, employees, suppliers, distributors, and the communities in which the new company will do business—measure success? Success should be measured in terms of the value created for each of the key stakeholders (see *Exhibit 5.2*).

As discussed in Chapter Two, integration success requires a multi-stakeholder point of view and proceeds from a master plan with the following elements:
- Strategic framework or context for the deal
- Performance expectations and the actions required to realize them
- Project organization, including team structures, composition, and mobilization
- Master schedule and key milestones
- Approach to decision-making and project coordination
- Integration plans for organization and workforces, people systems, culture, work processes, and technology
- Communications and change plan

Let's look at each of these elements in more detail, with an emphasis on what HR needs to know to lead and support integration planning.

Strategic Framework

The strategic framework provides the context for integration planning. Its development is the responsibility of senior management, generally with support from the finance and strategic planning functions. The framework outlines the vision and strategy for the merged organization and the rationale for the deal (why it was undertaken and what benefits will accrue). These prospective benefits must be stated in understandable terms that resonate with the key stakeholders.

Articulation of Financial Expectations

As the deal is being formulated, the architects and negotiators (the deal team) determine the cost savings and revenue enhancements and other synergies (value drivers) that must be achieved to justify the costs of doing the transaction and to ensure its success. Most important, the deal team must also show how these value drivers will be expressed (e.g., X percent reduction in staff, Y percent increase in customer base) and what their contribution will be to the transaction's success.

The next step is to translate these value drivers into meaningful objectives for the integration teams, which will then develop detailed plans for integrating the businesses and organizations of the integration partners. (More detail on the role of integration teams is provided in the next section.) For example, when overall cost and workforce reductions are expected, synergy targets should be provided to each functional and operating integration team.

Project Organization

Project organization arrangements depend in large measure on the intended integration philosophy and on the deal's specific value drivers. If the targets for the value drivers are aggressive and implementation speed is an issue, the integration project must have an extensive infrastructure and more internal and external resources than would be needed for a less aggressive plan.

Exhibit 5.3 Typical Integration Project Organization

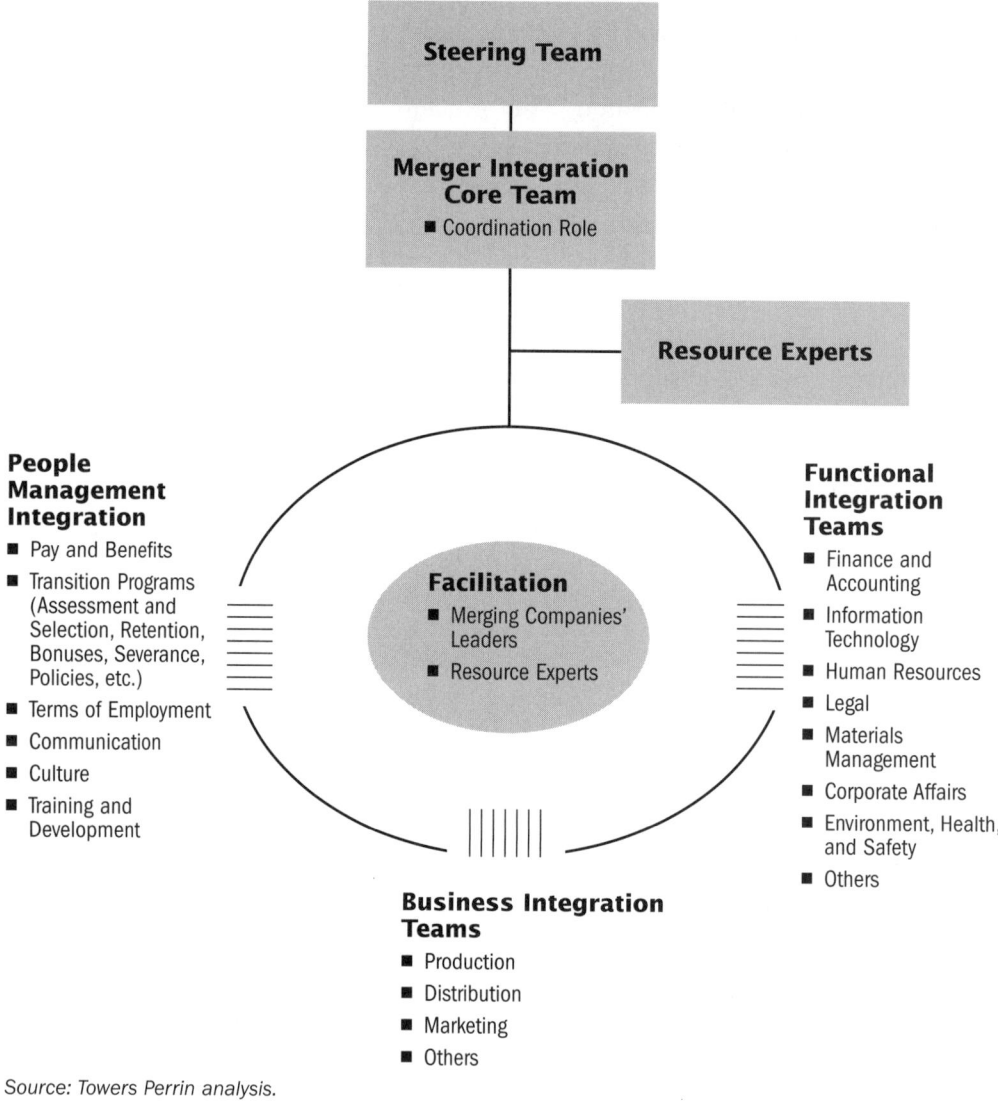

Source: Towers Perrin analysis.

Following are several examples of how a specific type of integration can influence the project organization:

- Limited integration may face little more than overlapping functions and activities in the two corporate staff and support organizations. A single integration project team often can address these overlaps.
- Dominant integration requires a modest project infrastructure; it is often used in industry consolidation by serial acquirers and when the target's value depends on physical assets (e.g., a natural resources company). These companies often have an established, well-documented process and dedicated resources for inte-

gration planning and implementation project management. Dedicated integration teams have the expertise to plan and manage the myriad activities that make up the integration process. Serial acquirers may also retain external resources, such as legal or accounting advisors and consulting firms, to provide the specialized expertise needed to support peak integration activity—for example, when the number of deals in the pipeline are more than their internal resources or capabilities can handle.
- Best-of-both and transformation approaches typically require a more elaborate integration plan and project infrastructure and more time to implement than do the other approaches. In both, it is important to involve enough operating and support function representatives from both organizations to leverage their expert knowledge of the legacy companies' respective application systems, management processes, and work practices.

The best-of-both and transformation approaches use a project management organization similar in form to the example presented in *Exhibit 5.3*.

The key elements of this project organization are described in the following paragraphs.

A steering team—made up of senior executives from each organization, including HR, who define the integration philosophy and vision for the combined entity—reviews and approves integration recommendations, assigns implementation responsibilities, and monitors progress. Members are usually responsible for leading key portions of due diligence. Accordingly, the makeup of the steering team is generally communicated shortly after the deal is announced.

A core team is also assembled after the announcement. This team, which should include HR, identifies and addresses the tactical integration issues that arise between the announcement and the launch of integration teams. The core team is typically led by an integration project manager (or co-managers), who may also serve on the steering team. The project manager is responsible for establishing and managing the integration process until the new company is established and its management is in place, and for building an integration project office to direct and support the day-to-day integration activities.

The integration project office should continue to operate as an integrating force for the new company until managers are selected and have assumed all responsibility for ongoing business and remaining integration activities. A typical integration project office consists of four to seven people selected from the two integration partners (and sometimes from an outside firm). The project office is primarily responsible for supporting project management and logistics, including the following:
- Development, maintenance, and communications of the master schedule
- Ongoing administration of integration and support team work plans to ensure proper coordination with the master schedule
- Creation and dissemination of status reports, actions, and decision requirements and of interim and final presentations

Exhibit 5.4 Typical HR Integration Team Structure

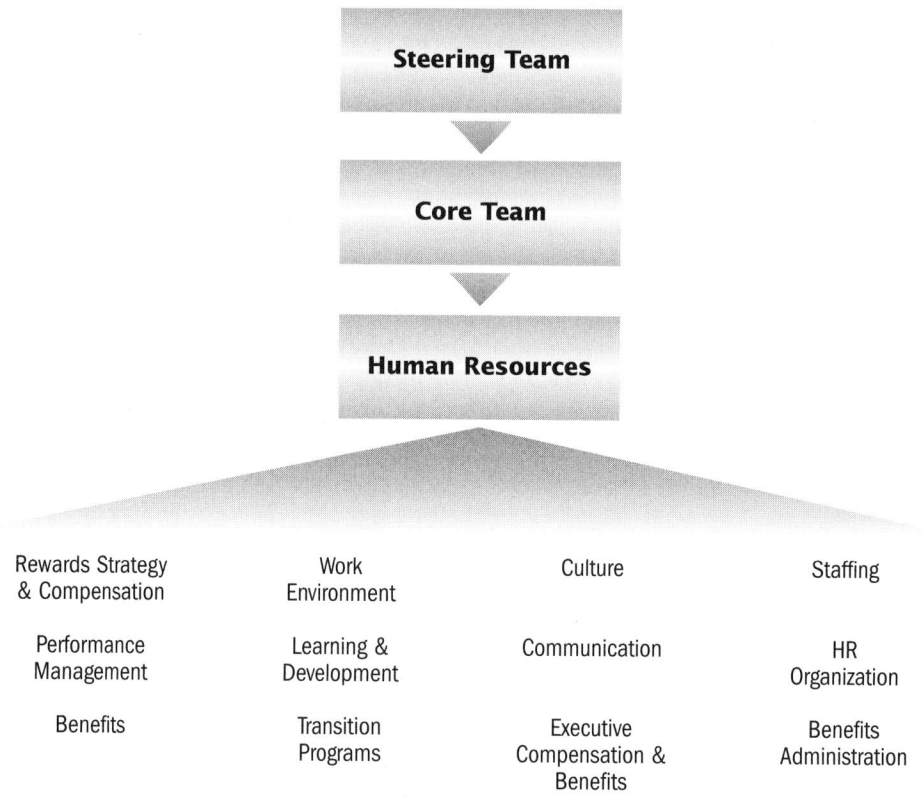

Source: Towers Perrin analysis.

- Planning, facilitation, and supporting core, integration, and support team meetings
- Development and maintenance of financial and cost information and models for existing ("as is") organizations and combined ("to be") organizations by function, business unit, and so on
- Training on organization design tools and templates to be used by the integration teams

Integration teams encompass general operations (e.g., manufacturing, logistics) and business unit integration teams, as well as functional integration teams for staff support and service units (e.g., finance and accounting, information technology [IT], human resources, and purchasing). Depending on the priorities and sequencing of the major activities along the integration timeline, these teams may be launched at different points during the integration process. For example, functional support teams for communications, HR support, and IT are often launched soon after the deal is announced. Members

Exhibit 5.5   Models for Resourcing the M&A Process

Type of Approach	Companies Using
Dedicated Team	■ Allied Signal ■ Honeywell
Project Managers plus Subject Matter Experts	■ Bank of America ■ Citigroup
Core Team plus External Resources	■ Ford Motor Company ■ American Express
SWAT Team (for each deal)	■ Astra Zeneca ■ Air Products
Global Network	■ Deutsche Bank ■ BP Amoco
Center of Excellence	■ McDonald's

Source: Towers Perrin analysis.

of teams participate in team-building and orientation sessions, and receive extensive training through the integration project office on the integration tools, approaches, processes, and the deliverables expected from them. As appropriate, team members analyze current function or business unit practices, costs, and structures in view of the benefits and synergies to be captured, and identify and evaluate actions that need to be taken. They recommend organization designs that are reviewed and challenged, usually by the core team, before steering team approval. Integration teams also develop implementation plans for their recommendations once approved.

An HR or people management team should be formed immediately after the deal is announced to provide crucial support on people, organizational, and cultural transition issues. The team's leader should also serve on the core team to ensure that these issues have all due visibility and emphasis. The most effective integration model involves multiple subteams, which can be phased in as necessary (see *Exhibit 5.4*). During integration planning, HR has multiple strategic, design, and business support roles that place intense resource demands on the function.

Resourcing the Integration Team

Once the structure for managing the integration project has been determined, management must focus on providing resources to the various teams and subteams that make up the structure. Three issues in particular must be considered when making project resourcing decisions: the integration philosophy, the availability of internal resources to support the integration process (while maintaining continuity of the current businesses), and the integration time frame.

That said, most integration efforts employ one of several resourcing models, as shown in *Exhibit 5.5*.

- Dedicated Team: In this model, full- or part-time resources are dedicated to M&A activities. The dedicated team usually represents most or all staff functions, and sometimes members rotate. Its members report to both their corporate functions (through a direct line) and a business development office (by a dotted line). The dedicated team is the focal point for all staff work (including outsourced tasks) and is responsible for coordination within each function. Given the sensitive nature of this team's work, it is often populated by high-potential managers. This model is widespread and well adapted to pre-deal activities. *Exhibit 5.6* shows a typical dedicated team project organization model.
- Project Managers plus Subject Matter Experts (SMEs): In this model, dedicated (professional) project managers are tasked with process oversight for deals. SMEs supply technical advice and expertise, as required. This model is commonplace in the "merge, acquire, divest" environment (i.e., for companies with an active portfolio management approach). Project managers move from acquisition to acquisition; this requires well-trained and relatively senior project managers with the judgment and experience to coordinate potentially complex projects. The issue of long-term integration remains a limitation on this model, assuming integration is a desirable end. (Turnaround situations are not always concerned with this issue.)
- Core Team plus External Resources: In this model, a dedicated team works with strategic partners for ad hoc and ongoing support associated with M&As. This model often relies on a standard approach for determining roles, responsibilities, and timelines. It is a typical model for companies with decentralized management and a multiple-deal portfolio. The strategic partners might dedicate resources and teams to work with a particular acquirer and are often on a retainer agreement. Such a model is best suited to companies that pursue M&As infrequently. That's because the approach allows them, when needed, to tap into expertise that would be too costly to develop and maintain internally.
- SWAT Team (for each deal): In this model, a unique team is assembled to investigate each possible deal or family of deals. This model is common among highly diversified and serial acquirers. Often, the team includes dedicated specialists from the business development office who can help ensure due process is followed and that previously acquired experience is used. Because team members can stay involved with the acquired company for a relatively long period of time, the SWAT team is also well suited to deals for which synergies are specific and/or earn-outs are relatively far off.

Exhibit 5.6 Resourcing Model Example: Dedicated M&A Team

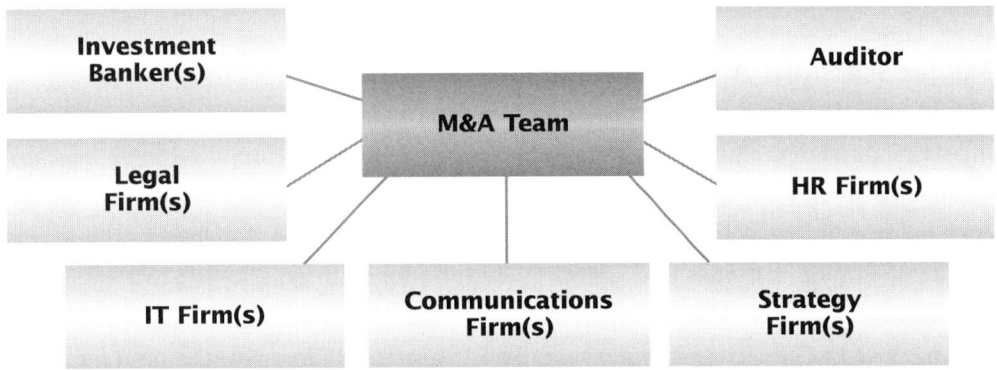

- Predetermined understanding of "who does what, when, how, etc."
- Prominent in companies with a decentralized M&A activity and multiple deal portfolio
- Suppliers regularly on-site for "huddle" meetings
- Suppliers often dedicate resources/teams within their firm
- Interdependencies typically managed by M&A team
- Suppliers often on retainer-like agreement

Source: *Towers Perrin analysis.*

- Global Network: This model is commonly used for acquisitions with global operations. Because it relies on regional teams, it allows for a speedy and effective analysis of large international deals. For such a model to work smoothly, however, a sophisticated project management structure has to be in place to coordinate the work of multiple integration teams, including regional, functional, and operating teams. Increasingly, this model requires external partners because of the size and complexity of M&As, particularly cross-border combinations.
- Center of Excellence: Popular with some serial acquirers, this model is also adaptable for holding companies. The Center of Excellence focuses on rapid assimilation of multiple, often very similar, acquisitions. While not recommended for mergers or joint ventures, this model fits well for some industry consolidators. For instance, taken together, the U.S. holdings of the four largest consolidators in the funeral industry exceed 3,000 funeral homes and 1,000 cemeteries, and new deals are always in the works. Given the similarities among the many individual deals that these companies undertake, the Center of Excellence approach is well suited to them.

Despite efforts by many companies to routinize their transactions, the structure of most deals remains unique. Each acquisition target has its own distinctive personality, culture, and potential, and its own integration issues. No matter how many insights and models previous transactions generate, the next deal is almost always different in very important ways. Drawing lessons from its own experience allows a company to be better at managing M&A transactions, but that said, M&A is still more an art than a science.

Master Schedule: A Focus on the First 100 Days

The master schedule is a high-level view of the major tasks, key deliverables, regulatory milestones, and due dates for the integration process. It is the primary vehicle for establishing the integration plan and timelines and coordinating the multiple concurrent streams of activities comprising the integration process. It should clearly outline the major integration activities and identify key milestones to ensure that the impact of schedule changes is understood and addressed. The master schedule is influenced and informed by the new company's vision, the integration philosophy, the time frame to closing date, and the nature and scope of planned changes. Several commercially available software programs are useful in developing the integration plan and tracking progress.

It is important to note that the integration planning period itself must be accounted for in the master plan. This planning period may vary widely, depending on industry, size of the companies involved, and other circumstances. For instance, the period from announcement to closing date is typically short in the technologies sector (two to four months) but often much longer (18 to 24 months) in the utility industry because of the need for lengthy regulatory review and approvals.

Many factors affect the implementation timeline. Nonetheless, to enhance the likelihood of success, 75 to 80 percent of integration activities should be completed in the first 100 days after closing the transaction. This time frame is critical because most organizations have limited tolerance for disruption to their ongoing businesses and for large amounts of added work. Change must occur quickly to avoid apathy or allow "business as usual" attitudes to set in.

Development of the master schedule is typically one of the first responsibilities of the integration project manager and core team. If the integration project organization has not been set up, either the deal team or a group of senior managers must draft the initial master schedule. Ongoing maintenance and communication of master schedule revisions to important stakeholders (e.g., integration teams, employees, customers) are the responsibility of the project office.

What does integration planning and the first 100 days of implementation look like for HR? HR must determine which key steps must be taken in the first 100 days after the deal closes and which implementation activities will be deferred. Since HR is often involved in several teams and subteams, senior HR executives need a consolidated work plan to view so that they can manage the multiple work streams. *Exhibit 5.7* shows an example of a high-level consolidated work plan for HR integration planning and implementation.

Exhibit 5.7 Sample of Consolidated HR Integration Plan

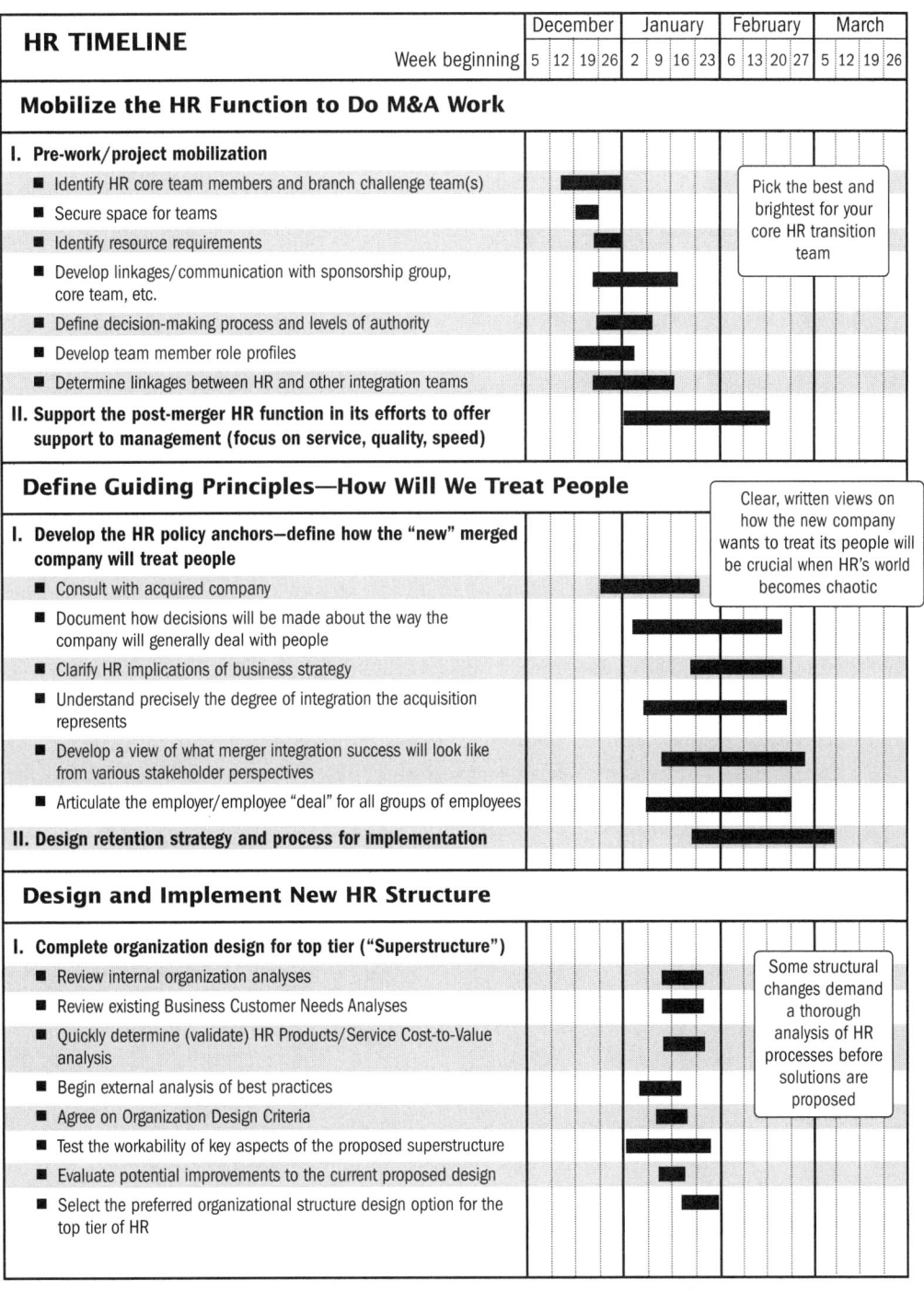

Source: Towers Perrin analysis.

Approach to Project Coordination

The integration project manager and the integration project office have primary responsibility for developing protocols and methods for project coordination, including the following:

- Establishing project infrastructure and managing logistics, including arrangements for meeting and workspace, security access, parking, travel arrangements, computers and network access, printers and copiers, telephones and voicemail, facsimile machines, and so on
- Developing charters, including roles and responsibilities, for integration teams
- Defining milestones for progress measurement
- Providing ongoing monitoring of the integration process
- Tracking and validating master schedule updates and coordinating required revisions to integration team work plans
- Identifying "hands-off" and tracking crossover issues between integration teams
- Assessing team performance and providing periodic feedback
- Developing project communication vehicles and regularly disseminating information to integration teams

Detailed Integration Plans

The detailed work plans developed by the integration teams must address all of the major elements for building the new combined company, including the following:

- Structure: Decisions must be made about the architecture of the new organization (e.g., whether it will be largely centralized or decentralized; whether it will be organized around products, markets, or geographies), plus the structures for all component units—both the business units and the functional support units (such as Finance, Human Resources, and Legal/Regulatory).
- Processes: Typically, there is not enough time at the outset of integration to make major changes to administrative and operating processes. "Re-engineering" is better left for later, when there is less risk of major disruption within the new organization. However, key management processes, such as the manner in which major business and investment decisions will be made in the new company, must be clarified.
- People: Assessment and selection of staff for the new company; integration or new design of HR systems; and ongoing attraction, retention, and development of staff are among the most important people-related issues for integration planning. In addition, the immediate integration concerns for HR plans are pay, including base pay, short- and long-term incentives, and executive compensation; and benefits, including retirement, stock, savings, and health and welfare plans. Training, performance management, work/life programs, and other elements of the new company's HR offering can usually follow near-term integration activities.

Having said that, transition programs are needed for employees who stay and those who leave involuntarily. For remaining employees, these plans typically include special retention arrangements to keep key staff at least through the initial period when the bulk of integration tasks must be accomplished and when the risk of lost business is the greatest. Special arrangements may also be required in the event of staff relocation or retraining. For departing employees, special arrangements will also be needed to ease their transition out of the new (combined) company. These arrangements might include severance payments or special retirement benefits, immediate vesting of retirement benefits, and outplacement services.

- Culture: This permeates everything in the new company: the way people work with each other, the way people are rewarded and promoted, the work behaviors that are valued by the company, and the manner in which communication flows across the organization. Integration planners must be sensitive to and understand significant cultural differences, decide what culture will be most successful going forward, and establish plans for making any related changes.
- Technology: Major decisions will have to be made regarding applications software and systems architecture. Technology changes require the longest time to implement, and they carry the largest implementation costs. Delays in designing and implementing technology integration plans can, moreover, seriously affect customer service, the speed and accuracy of information available to management and employees, and the realization of anticipated cost savings.

Development of the high-level organization architecture, or superstructure, and the associated staffing and selection processes are two factors that require priority attention during integration planning. These activities are typically the responsibility of either the core team or the steering team, with assistance from the HR or people management team. Because of the importance of these activities to the successful launch of the integration process, a detailed treatment, provided in the following paragraphs, is required to ensure that HR is prepared.

Organization Design

At the integration planning stage, only high-level organization architecture needs to be developed for the new company. In most cases, integration teams will develop detailed organization structure for the subordinate business units and support functions later, during the implementation stage.

The high-level architecture includes design of the top management organization, the recommended functional support and services delivery approach, high-level specification of organization charters and reporting relationships, guidelines for span of control and for organization levels, and governance design.

An objective, efficient, fact-based approach for top management organization design is crucial because it can be a source of subsequent conflict for the new management team. In any case, the approach should facilitate alignment of the organization's

Exhibit 5.8 Case Example—Organization Architecture

> An objective, fact-driven design process helps minimize potential disagreements among the new company's management groups by promoting discussion and consensus-building.

A. Plan the project
- Agree on overall process
- Schedule meetings
- Agree on assumptions

B. Conduct information-gathering survey
- Select interviews
- Benchmarking

C. Determine management philosophy elements

D. Identify structure elements

E. Refine structure drivers

F. Identify design criteria
- Minimum levels
- Speed of decision-making
- Small corporate center

G. Develop criteria weightings

H. Prepare viable alternative structures and validate

I. Discuss and select top 3 options

J. Identify roles and responsibilities associated with each option

K. Evaluate top 3 options against criteria

L. Make recommendations

Source: Towers Perrin analysis.

---

structure with its business strategy, capitalize on benchmarking data and best-practices information, and provide an audit trail for decisions. *Exhibit 5.8* shows a sample approach for a high-level organization structure design.

Staffing

The staffing process used by the new company not only heralds the birth of the new organization but significantly influences the effectiveness and perceived fairness of the overall integration process. Indeed, the Towers Perrin/SHRM Foundation research demonstrates that "loss of key talent" (listed by 53 percent of the respondents) and "selecting the wrong people for key jobs" (listed by 51 percent) are two major obstacles to successful integration.

The staffing process, or its outcomes, serves as an early indication of the true values and cultural biases of the new company. Consider, for example, a new company formed through a merger that seeks to create a work environment characterized by candor, involvement, and open-door management. If the staffing process is entirely top-down, with little employee input, employees will question senior management's real commitment to nurturing these values in the new company.

Exhibit 5.9 High-Level Staffing Approaches

	Description	Advantages	Disadvantages
Cascade Approach	▪ Staffing process takes place in waves, with each successive level of management staffing the next level down	▪ Involves a large percentage of employees in the staffing process (which tends to improve perceptions of fairness and reduce resistance) ▪ Increases the likelihood that individuals making staffing decisions are familiar with the performance of employees being staffed ▪ Provides greater flexibility in placing employees in jobs (e.g., if they are not selected for their first choice, other opportunities may become available)	▪ More time-consuming and resource-intensive than back-room approach ▪ May not be an option for companies that need to move swiftly
Back-Room Approach	▪ Staffing decisions are made all at once by a select group of individuals	▪ Faster and less resource-intensive than cascade approach ▪ Reduces period of uncertainty about staffing outcomes	▪ May be perceived as less fair than cascade approach ▪ Those making staffing decisions may not be familiar with job performance of the individuals they are staffing
Hybrid Approach	▪ Combination of cascade and back-room approaches used in different parts or levels of the organization	▪ Provides flexibility to move quickly in parts of the organization where this is necessary (e.g., top leadership, sales force)	▪ May generate perceptions of inequity because groups are handled differently

Source: Towers Perrin analysis.

In our experience, companies will typically choose from among the three staffing approaches outlined in *Exhibit 5.9*.

Many successful integrators employ the cascade approach, which has several major advantages.

- It allows leaders at each organization level to actively shape the new management team and the workforce.
- It eases the pressure on maintaining business momentum because selection decisions are sequenced rather than being made all at once.
- It allows employees who are denied their first job choice an opportunity to find alternative placement in the new organization.

What constitutes effective design of a cascading staffing process? A few things stand out. First, the staffing process should involve representatives from both organizations, including line management as well as HR advisors. Standardization across different parts of the organization also lends consistency, structure, fairness, and credibility to the selection process. And for certain operating units or support functions, the process can be tailored to fit unique circumstances (e.g., vary the timing or use different selection criteria for specialized technical skills in short supply).

Selection counts. Despite the premium on speed of integration, companies should not lose sight of the basic requirements for making sound people selection decisions. Choosing the best candidate for the job should take precedence. For the selection process to be fair and legally defensible, the new company must define its specific job requirements by answering the following key questions:

- What are each job's key responsibilities?
- What knowledge, skills, and experience are needed to perform the job effectively?
- What career path(s) does this job offer?

After building a solid understanding of the knowledge, skills, and experience required to perform a given job effectively, management must agree on the specific criteria for evaluating potential candidates. A pharmaceutical company that had merged with another developed selection criteria based on

- alignment with company values;
- skills, including education;
- demonstrated competencies; and
- individual performance documented in annual performance appraisals.

While not as effective as other tools for predicting long-run job success, face-to-face interviews are often used for staff selection decisions in an M&A. Not surprisingly, managers are uncomfortable selecting from among otherwise qualified candidates without the benefit of a face-to-face interview. These interviews incorporate questions derived from the selection criteria and rating scales for assessing each candidate's strengths relative to those criteria. Structured interviews, in particular, are seen as equitable because all candidates for a given job are asked to respond to the same questions and are rated on the same scale, generally by the same people.

Staffing selection criteria should encompass the distinct skills needed to perform a job effectively. Some skills can be assessed in an interview; others, however, are best assessed using other methods. A work sample test can be extremely effective. A candidate for a sales position, for example, could be asked to give a sales pitch to a potential customer, played by the assessor. The customer/assessor can gauge candidates' persuasiveness and how well they think on their feet. Similarly, candidates for IT jobs could be given a test that describes various computing, programming, or networking problems for which the candidate makes diagnoses. Tests of this type are better predictors of job performance than is an interview alone. For that reason, interviews are best used in combination with other selection techniques.

Staffing opportunities. Mergers and acquisitions provide a unique opportunity for revolutionary change in the way staffing decisions are made. For instance, companies may choose to

- introduce competencies into their selection criteria, including desired behaviors;
- apply creative selection techniques such as the practical tests mentioned above;
- identify the job skills required for success in the future, not just the present; and
- fill key positions by hiring externally if internal candidates lack the right mix of knowledge, skills, and experience.

Using a rigorously designed staffing and assessment process that starts with the selection of senior managers can have a very positive impact on the retention and engagement of the broader workforce. In fact, such a process can be used to help reshape the organization's culture.

Communications and Change Plan

Communication and change activities lay the foundation for and help create the new company's integrated culture. Although some chief executives and M&A experts downplay the importance of culture, the Towers Perrin/SHRM Foundation research demonstrates clearly that integrating cultures is essential to making M&As work.

> "Study after study of past merger waves has shown that two of every three deals have not worked. ... Look behind any disastrous deal and the same word keeps popping up—culture. Culture permeates a company and differences can poison any collaboration." (*The Economist*, "After the Deal," January 1999)

A Bureau of Business Research study at the American International College (*CFO Magazine*, April 1996) of chief financial officers and other top financial executives of 45 Forbes 500 companies found that organizational and cultural problems are "more likely ... than financial factors to sink a merger." Incompatible cultures prevent people from contributing all they can to integration efforts. People become territorial, and disputes about details become overblown. Too much time is spent feuding over roles, longing for the past, and fighting decisions. These internal conflicts prevent people from focusing on what is important: customers, products, markets, and operational efficiencies.

Cultural integration addresses these issues essentially by establishing a new corporate identity with which key stakeholders, including employees of the new company, can identify. The integration process encourages senior-level discussions that illustrate the differences and mutual aspirations of the original companies and help develop a shared vision for the future. It also provides a foundation upon which strategic and organizational systems can be built.

An Integrated Approach

The integration master plan, described earlier, provides the "what" of integration; change management and communications provide the "how." The "how" drives

employee perception of what work life will be like in the new company. Every merger or acquisition should have change management and communication plans that use these change drivers:
- Leadership (what leaders say and do)
- Communication (what signals the organization, employees, and the outside world send and receive)
- Involvement (how employees and external audiences participate in and lead work activities related to the integration)
- Measurement (how teams track progress and stay focused)
- Support (how employees are supported through the transition process)

Incorporating these change drivers in the plans increases the likelihood that the new company's employees will adopt new behaviors and embrace a new culture. Based on our experience, we strongly recommend that companies create communication and change teams when planning for integration of M&As.

An integrated approach to communications and change minimizes conflicts, bolsters leadership's credibility, and improves the company's ability to retain and motivate employees. For example, a utility company announced to its employees that its merger with another utility would combine the "best of both." However, its senior leadership sent a completely different message when one company dominated staffing decisions. As a result, employees became cynical and discounted many of the new company leadership's other messages.

Building on Critical Success Factors

One of the most important factors in any successful merger or acquisition is building on the experiences of other companies—and of your own company. During integration planning, teams have the opportunity to use what they have learned. In this regard, our experience has identified eight factors for communications and change success.

Success Factors for Effective M&A Communications and Change
- Adopt an employee perspective
- Stay fast and flexible
- Help drive the integration plans
- Work at corporate, functional, and department levels
- Balance high-touch and high-tech media
- Don't overwhelm the audience with data
- Align all sources of information and data
- Provide anchors and road maps

The implementation chapter discusses these success factors in detail. However, a few of these factors are extremely important for communications and change planning and warrant some discussion at this point.

Exhibit 5.10 Employee Responses to Change

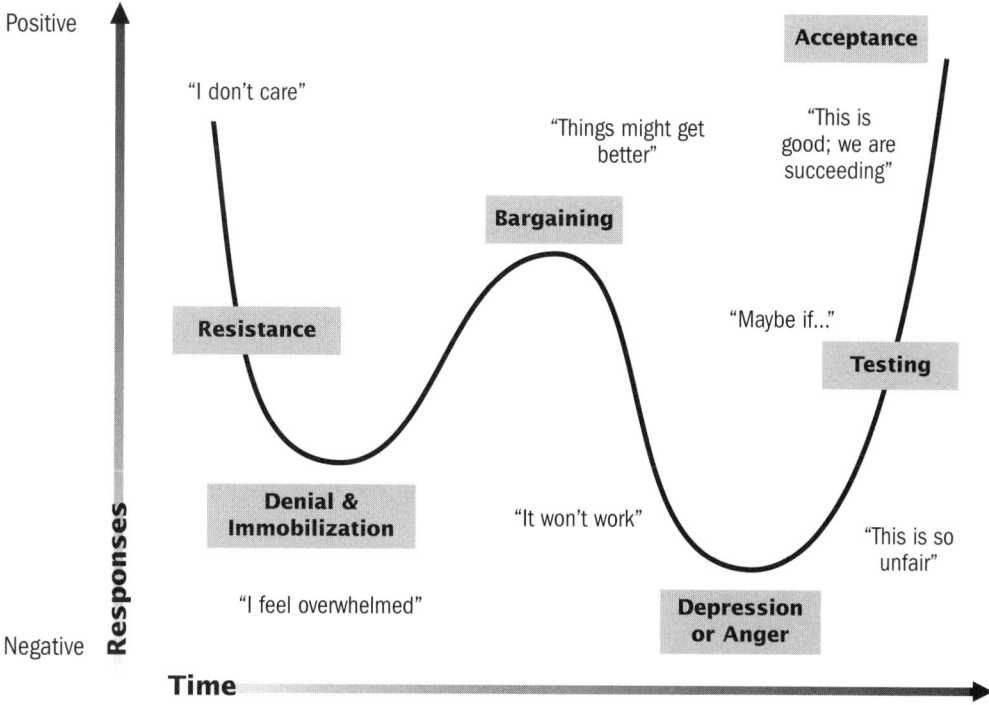

Source: Towers Perrin analysis.

Adopt an employee perspective. Senior leadership and integration teams often have difficulty understanding the employee perspective because these groups frequently are further along in the change process than the rest of the organization. Most people in the combining organizations don't have the same involvement or information and don't feel as confident about the future as senior leadership does. *Exhibit 5.10* illustrates the cycle of change and how employee perceptions evolve over time.

Stay fast and flexible. In M&As, the pace of change is almost always fast and furious. Decisions are made (and may be changed) from one day to the next, and even when the decision is final, the plans for implementing it undergo constant revision. The new company's leaders must have a core set of messages and responses to crisis situations.

Work at corporate, division, and local levels. Too often, integration planning occurs only at the corporate level. To be effective, communication and the change process must be tailored to all major levels of the new company's organizations: corporate, division, and local.

Balance high-tech and high-touch media. The communication and change plan needs to include the technological options available today to most companies: intranet, Internet, voicemail, e-mail, and videoconferencing. These tools provide new ways to reach and involve people throughout the integration process. However, they are not enough. The new company's leaders are still the people to whom employees go to for personal information, reassurance, and help dealing with the stress that occurs during integration. The communications and change plan equips leaders with needed tools and support so that they can act as the new company's primary communicators and change managers.

Provide anchors and road maps. When designing the communication and change plan, the new company's leaders need to identify anchors (things that won't change or that employees can hold on to) and develop road maps that tell employees where the company is going. Anchors and road maps help employees feel more secure in a time of rapid change and high ambiguity. For example, letting employees know that their benefits programs won't change for a year or two after implementation provides a very tangible anchor. Letting people know which functions won't be consolidated is an even more powerful message (although you must also be well prepared to deal with the areas that will be affected).

Planning Communication and Change

Successful M&As follow a disciplined process for change and communication that is planned early, linked to business and integration plans, and focused on the perspectives of employees and other stakeholders. The initial steps in the process are creating the communication and change (C&C) team, assessing culture, setting direction, and developing a plan.

Creating the team. The C&C team is responsible for equipping the new company's leaders and employees to make the transition to the new company. It should also develop or review external communications to ensure consistency with internal messages. Finally, during integration planning, the C&C team works closely with other integration teams in highlighting the implications of their decisions and in developing tailored communication and change plans to support the work of those teams.

Given its role, the C&C team must draw on the resources of many functions across the combining organizations: corporate communications (including investor/external relations), organizational effectiveness/development, human resources, public affairs, legal, and line management.

The C&C team leader needs to be a visible and respected member of senior leadership. This sends a strong signal to the legacy organizations that the new company is committed to "doing communication and change right." In addition, the C&C team must have subject matter experts who can start implementing the communication and change plan during integration planning. Many companies employ external resources

Exhibit 5.11 Communication and Change Team Composition

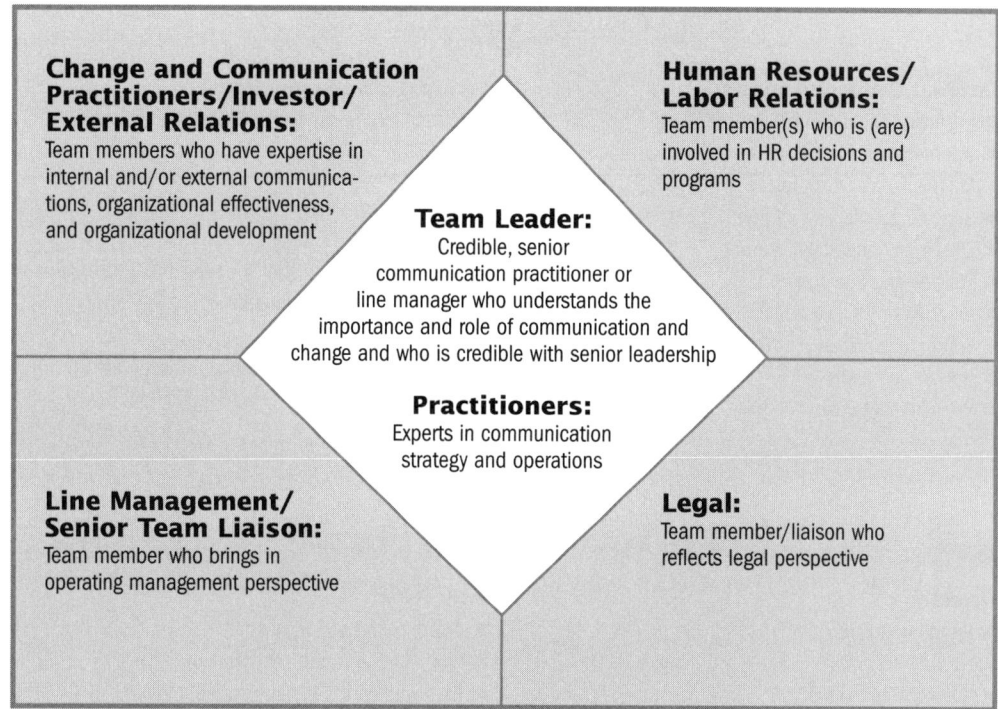

Source: Towers Perrin analysis.

to support the C&C team and help build the skills that the new company's leaders need for managing change in the combined organization. *Exhibit 5.11* shows a representative C&C team.

The C&C team also has to stay connected to other integration teams and their broad change initiatives. Sometimes, however, legal constraints dictate that two separate teams develop communication and change plans for the combining organizations. Obviously, in such cases, a process for information sharing and coordination is paramount to ensuring that the separate communications send consistent messages and timely information to all employees.

Assessing the cultures. Understanding the cultures of the two companies—ideally before the formal change in control takes effect—is the starting point for people integration. Culture can be profiled in various ways, depending on the situation and time constraints. (See *Exhibit 5.12*.)

Profiling culture using the sources presented in *Exhibit 5.12* requires skill, experience, and judgment. That said, with these profiles as a foundation, the new company's leaders can prepare to integrate organizations, processes, and workforces in a way that promotes the desired culture for the combined organization.

Integration Planning Stage ■ 121

Exhibit 5.12 Methods for Profiling a Company's Culture

What the Company Says About Its Culture

Internal Communications
- M&A team-supplied information
- Top management output
- Memos, newsletters, releases
- Specific people/culture publications
- Employee handbooks, manuals
- Policies and procedures
- Program and process literature
- Performance reviews
- Succession plans
- Replacement charts

External Communications
- Annual report, especially CEO's letter to shareholders
- Press releases
- Marketing materials
- Investor relations data
- Financial data, especially management discussions
- Speeches, presentations by senior executives

Note: Various mediums of communication are assumed: voice, paper, video, electronic, etc.

What Employees Say the Culture Is

Directly
- Random interviews
- Select interviews
- Segment interviews
- Focus groups
- Culture surveys
- Climate surveys
- Special surveys
- Multi-rater surveys (360s)
- Chat rooms

Note: The items above may come from prior M&A activity or may be used as primary HR tools in the due diligence stage.

Indirectly
- Ability to attract top talent
- Promotion and transfer practices
- Participation in learning/development
- Attrition/turnover data and analysis
- Retention activities
- Complaints, grievances, cases
- Legal, regulatory compliance
- Union peace/avoidance
- Safety and health program records
- Total rewards programs
- Choices, flexibility offered employees
- Reward, recognition clubs/programs
- Quality of work/life programs

Source: HIGH Performance Strategies, *Don Howard, SPHR.*

Profiling cultures during integration planning offers many benefits, including the following:

- In M&A situations, anecdotal accounts of the respective cultures are rife. A proper assessment provides an objective understanding—a kind of "cultural due diligence."
- It provides a springboard for integration planning and allows key activities to be launched early from a solid foundation of understanding.
- The assessments can provide benchmarks for determining how well the new company is achieving its integration objectives.

- It tangibly demonstrates the new company's appreciation of the good in both legacy organizations.

Employee research during integration planning is helpful in focusing communication and for receiving valuable feedback from the workforce. Although extensive research is usually hard to compile at this stage, HR can help the new company's senior leaders identify the best research opportunities. Leadership must be committed to following through on the results of the research it authorizes—by acting on employee concerns and suggestions or by letting employees know why things are not changing as they had envisioned.

Although the C&C team and senior leadership need to know about employee concerns and reactions to the merger or acquisition, the integration teams may need more specific information on topics such as benefits, organizational, and cultural differences between the two companies. This research can take many forms: employee meetings, interviews, surveys, focus groups. The C&C team should coordinate these efforts to avoid duplication and research "fatigue." In one merger, for example, four different teams were conducting interviews but were not communicating with each other. When the third team's request for interviews arrived, many executives became annoyed and refused to participate further.

Setting a direction. An important element of integration planning is to build in ways of conveying the organization climate that will characterize the new company. At a minimum, senior leaders should define the integration philosophy and any related principles early in their integration planning. Once the new leadership team has been named, it should move quickly to define the vision and values for the new company. This helps people in both companies stay focused on the current businesses while facilitating the work of the integration planning teams. (For more information on this process, see Chapter Six.)

Developing the change plan. The C&C team participates in the processes for developing the new company's overall strategy and for planning how to combine the organizations, workforces, and cultures. In addition, the C&C team should develop a supporting change plan. This plan addresses the management of the integration's impact on employees, the gaps between where people seem to be now and where they need to be in the future, and the actions necessary to close those gaps. The change plan must be developed from an employee perspective by laying out required behavior changes and explaining what employees stand to gain by conforming to them.

The change plan should be coordinated with the integration project office because it often encompasses business performance and integration milestones that the steering team and integration teams can use to gauge progress. The milestones should account for the major elements that affect the stability of the new organization (e.g., work processes, business events, people programs, leadership actions, and external events).

For example, the change plan for one global merger explicitly identified the dates on which the senior management and other leaders were slated to meet together. These meetings served as a forum for the integration progress and helped prepare the new company's leaders for upcoming milestones.

Although content will vary with the specific circumstances of a merger or acquisition, the general outline of the change plan includes the following:

- Communication and change objectives (linked to business objectives)
- Statement of communication and change principles
- Pertinent research and assessments (internal and external)
- Description of the new company's values and associated behaviors
- Core messages and themes (and implied actions)
- Information sources, feedback mechanisms, and media for communications
- Processes and responsibilities for carrying out a communications plan and change interventions
- Measures of communication and change effectiveness and their fit within the overall performance measurement system for the merger or acquisition
- Contingency planning and crisis management processes
- Schedule outlining key milestones and their timing

Equipping Leaders

The new company's leaders must be equipped to deal with the changes they and their employees will experience during the integration process. Those leaders who are members of the integration teams may need coaching to help them understand the impact of their decisions and behaviors on employees. All leaders benefit from orientations and reference materials that provide a complete picture of the integration process, specifics about their roles in that process, and tools for communicating with employees and for sensing their reactions as the integration process unfolds. Helping leaders understand the role and importance of communication and change management, and equipping them to play their roles effectively, is a key job for the C&C team.

Summary

Integration planning is a crucial stage of the M&A process. Companies that do it well have a good chance of overcoming obstacles to success. Most activities in this stage revolve around the development of the integration master plan and schedule. The nature of integration planning (e.g., deciding on the integration philosophy) is such that it must begin long before a deal is actually announced.

The best integration plans encompass the needs and perspectives of all stakeholders in a merger or acquisition. They address not only the details of the integration process and activities but also include communication and change management.

During the integration planning stage, HR should support the new company's senior management and participate in or even lead the core team. HR should help to ensure that important people, organizational, and cultural issues are found, evaluated, and resolved in a timely and expert manner. The most important activities for HR in the integration planning process include the following:

- Helping employees at all levels of the existing organizations cope with change
- Defining the organization architecture and staffing plan for the new company
- Designing and administering the selection and placement processes
- Outlining people management goals and guiding principles
- Developing employee communications and change plans
- Designing new total rewards strategies and aligning policies, practices, and programs accordingly (discussed in detail in Chapter Six)

According to the Towers Perrin/SHRM Foundation survey, respondents believe that HR must increase its involvement in most of these activities. For that to happen, HR must close capability and skills gaps in a number of areas. The focus should be on developing in-depth M&A literacy and integration know-how as well as a strong ability to plan and lead complex integration projects, particularly in areas such as culture assessment and organization design.

This new role may be a stretch for many HR practitioners. But those who have been successful at developing and using these competencies say their roles in M&A have been the most rewarding experiences of their careers. ■

CHAPTER SIX

Implementation Stage

Mary Cianni

*"Planning without action is a daydream;
action without planning is a nightmare."*

Old Chinese saying

Implementation is the final stage of the mergers and acquisition (M&A) life cycle. In this stage, all the planning comes to fruition, and the two companies begin to become one. It is a challenging time because the two companies are trying to merge cultures and processes quickly (the bulk of implementation takes place during the first 100 days of the deal's closing) and at the same time continue to successfully run the day-to-day business. All this must be accomplished under the scrutiny of customers, employees, competitors, regulators, and securities analysts.

It is also a challenging time for human resources (HR). Many of the new company's most delicate implementation tasks are HR's responsibility, and after months of working with management and functional units to plan for implementation, HR employees must now help put those plans into action.

Implementation is about action. After the strategies are set, the goals defined, and the plans approved, HR must ensure that people-related implementation is proactive, seamless, and fast-paced. *Exhibit 6.1* shows the eight most important factors to ensure a successful implementation.

The integration plan sets the direction for implementation. As the new company enters this stage, several questions should already have been answered, including the following:

- What are the near-term implementation priorities? Who is responsible for achieving them?
- How will decisions regarding implementation issues be reached? Who will have input?
- What are the key implementation milestones, deliverables, and timelines? Which activities depend on the completion of other activities?
- What charters have teams been given?

Exhibit 6.1   Eight Factors for Successful M&A Implementation

- Clearly articulated overall business strategy that connects with all stakeholders
- Detailed road map and sufficient project management infrastructure to ensure adherence to implementation priorities, general timelines, deliverables, and milestone dates
- Involvement by employees of both companies in developing and implementing organization, workforce, and process changes
- Clearly communicated roles and responsibilities for all integration teams and their members
- Visible and forceful executive sponsorship for managing the implementation and resolving issues or conflicts
- An unwavering focus on the customer and on the stated growth and cost-savings goals
- Multiple communications channels for enabling a continuous dialogue between the new company's leaders and employees
- Tangible, objective performance measures to evaluate progress, celebrate successes, and make adjustments and modifications where necessary

Source: Towers Perrin analysis.

- How will communications be managed and delivered?
- How will implementation success be measured?

Although much of the implementation activity occurs immediately after closing, the full implementation stage can last anywhere from six months to three or four years. For the first several months, the focus is on sustaining business momentum, generating near-term growth, achieving promised cost savings, and designing and staffing the new organization. In fact, high-level appointments within each major organization in the new company are almost always determined, staffed, and announced before the closing—often within 60 to 90 days of the deal's initial announcement. (A long regulatory review process could make this impossible until after approval, however.)

During implementation, the integrated total rewards programs for the new company are put into place. (See Chapter Eight for a complete discussion of total rewards.) Several key programs may be ready fairly quickly, but some—for instance, a new pension plan—may take two years or more to fully implement. Once staffing of the new organization is completed and its combined operations have been launched, the arduous task of integrating the two companies' business and management processes and technology systems can begin. At this point, the real work of creating a truly new company begins.

Managing the implementation process requires a coherent and understandable road map that is developed during integration planning (see *Exhibit 6.2*). The road map is important not only to guide the integration teams, but also to provide employees with a fuller sense of the journey that the new company is taking. Knowing what the end state will look like helps the teams to focus on the right issues at the right time.

Maintaining business momentum is a major challenge during the implementation stage. To do so, executives leading the new company must mobilize the integration

Exhibit 6.2 Implementation Road Map

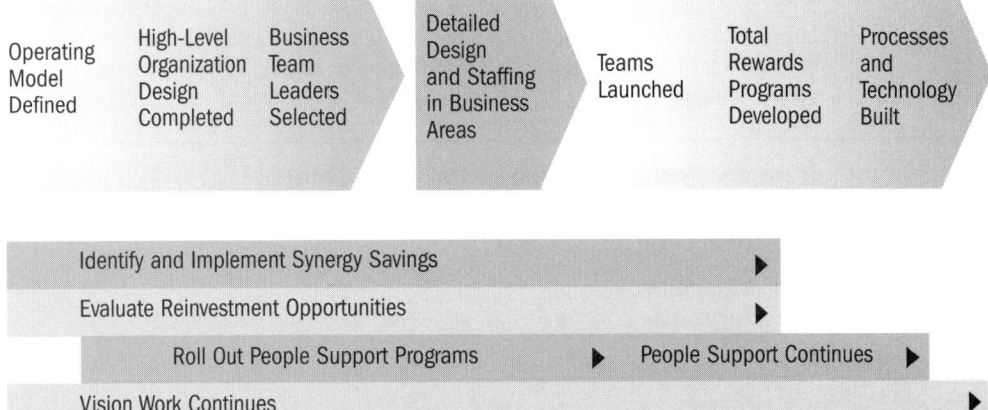

Getting Together
- Begin using "NewCo" name/logo in market
- Communicate New Company vision
- Define operating model based on outputs of visioning work
- Identify synergy goals by business area
- Develop organization design for each business area
- Appoint managers and employees within business areas
- Roll out people integration programs (severance, out placement, relocation, etc.)
- Integration task forces under way

Moving Forward
- Launch new teams
- Engage people in further definition of vision, culture, and "business as usual" goals
- Build processes and technology for new organization
- Develop and roll out new total reward programs
- Drive out synergy goals
- Wind down integration task forces

Sustaining Performance
- Monitor established performance metrics
- Reward individuals and teams that exemplify desired cultural norms

Source: Towers Perrin analysis.

teams in a timely fashion and empower them to act. A large pharmaceutical company, for example, had its integration teams follow what was referred to as the "80/100 rule," meaning that they would move quickly 100 percent of the time, even if a given decision was only 80 percent right. The message: Don't wait until you have all the answers because you never will.

If they don't understand that moving quickly is important at this stage, integration teams may fall into the trap of "analysis paralysis" and everyone will become frustrated by the lack of progress. Tight time frames coupled with measurable action also help the

Exhibit 6.3   Day One Sets the Tone for Implementation

Many organizations mark the beginning of implementation with a celebration of Day One of the new company. Any of several milestones can be used to mark Day One: shareholder approval, regulatory approval, launch of the new brand. On Day One or shortly after, the integration teams must be ready for action. This marks the beginning of the honeymoon period for the new company, and as such, it provides the window of opportunity for change. Wise companies take advantage of it to build employee support and excitement.

Here are some examples of Day One events:
- A global telecast involving all senior leaders of the new company held at local convention centers around the world throughout the day
- A welcome bag for all employees containing consumer products and marketing collateral from both companies
- Unveiling of a new company intranet, with stories about the new organization

Source: Towers Perrin analysis.

---

new company keep its focus on its customers and its current business during the implementation of the merger or acquisition.

Demonstrating visible progress in the early stages of implementation also helps to build employee commitment to the new company. Every action sends a signal about how the new company will be managed and operated. As implementation begins, many employees are conflicted—stuck somewhere between the vision and culture of their old organization and the as-yet-undefined new organization. Senior leadership, with strong support from HR, needs to help employees move toward the future by acting quickly and in a manner consistent with the defined vision and values for the new company. See *Exhibit 6.3* for examples of some activities HR can sponsor for all employees on Day One to set the tone for a successful merger.

The Role of HR During Implementation

HR must emphasize the importance of change and help manage it at the organizational and individual level. More specifically, HR's role is to provide senior executives and line managers with the requisite skills and the support to handle change across the organization.

The HR function's role during implementation can be intense, encompassing six primary areas of responsibility, as shown on *Exhibit 6.4*.

As discussed in Chapter Five, there are several ways to organize integration teams, but finding enough of the right resources can be a challenge. Many organizations rely, therefore, on outside resources for help and expertise. However, to meet the demands of the implementation process, HR might also have to curtail some of its discretionary services during the first 6 to 12 months of implementation.

This frees HR resources to help business units facilitate change-management sessions for employees and conduct integration team start-up sessions. Of course, any

Exhibit 6.4 HR's Multiple Roles During Implementation

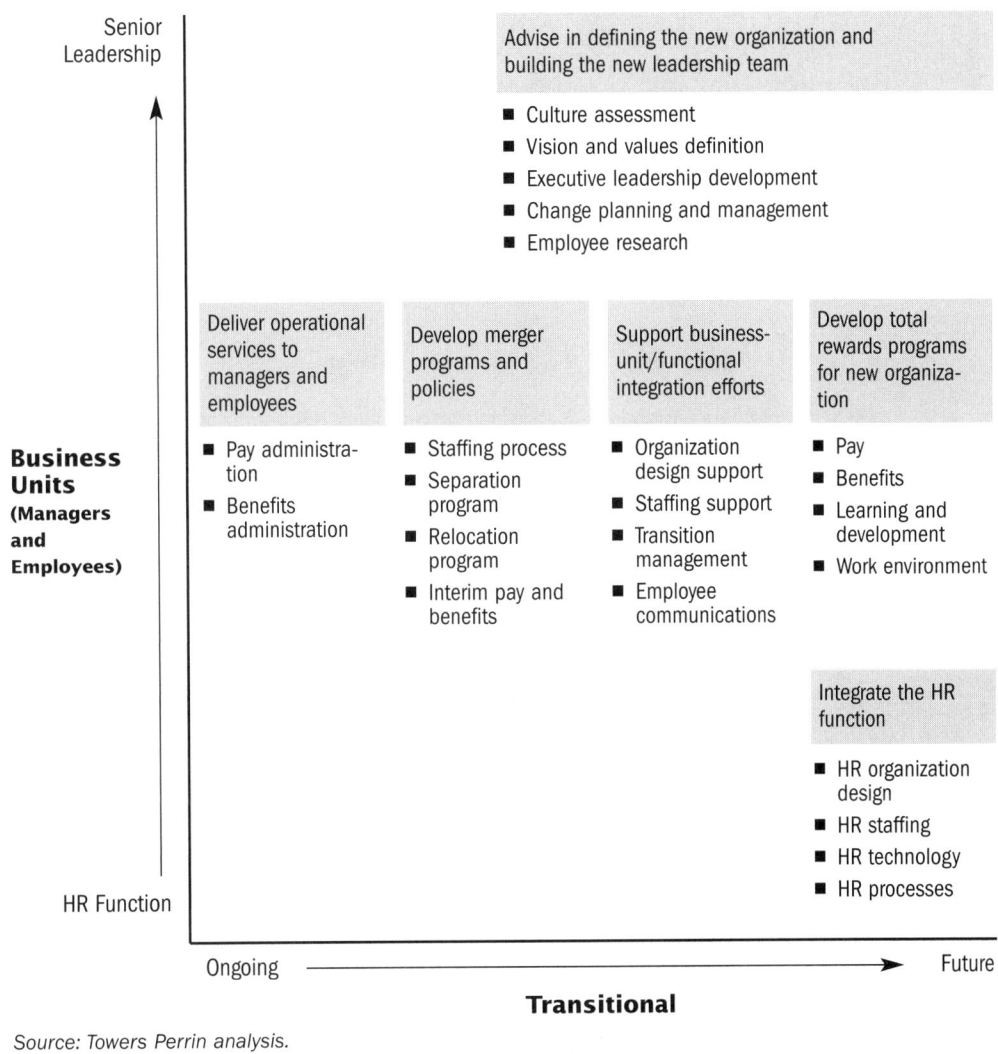

Source: Towers Perrin analysis.

changes in HR service levels may be disruptive for the employees of the legacy companies, so these changes should be endorsed by the senior leadership team of the new company. *Exhibit 6.5* outlines the effective use of external resources.

Building and Staffing the New Organization

HR has two primary areas for implementation support:

- Organization-wide people integration—leading the change process by helping the combined entity establish, design, and deliver organization-wide people and policy programs
- Business unit/functional integration—helping each new business unit or function, including the HR function itself, align itself with the new company's over-

Exhibit 6.5 Effective Use of External Support During Implementation

Understand your needs first

Always assess needs by balancing the work effort (especially priorities and required expertise) against internal capacity. During integration planning, HR develops work plans that describe implementation activities. Now is the time to take a fresh look at these activities and determine how to supplement internal resources. Very rarely will HR find that it has all of the resources necessary to support implementation, provide ongoing services, and begin to build the new HR function. The key is to understand where the biggest resource gaps lie and then supplement appropriately.

Pick the right firm for the situation

Whatever the decision about sourcing external support, finding the right partner is crucial. Few, if any, firms can provide the breadth of services generally required, and many firms have poor reputations for partnering with rivals in multisourcing relationships.

Use external resources wisely

It is important that HR own the outcomes of the organizational, people, and cultural aspects of implementation. Consultants and other external support should not run the show.

Source: Towers Perrin analysis.

---

all business strategy, identify and shape its required organizational capabilities, redesign processes and structures, define roles and responsibilities, and staff new positions

Organization-wide People Integration

Understanding and addressing cultural issues and helping to ensure effective, frequent communication among members of the new management team account for much of the organization-wide integration. Consistency is important here for two reasons: First, it keeps the focus on the stated goals of the merger or acquisition; second, it improves the chances that the desired synergies, such as lower costs or higher productivity, will be achieved.

Implementing the new company's total rewards program is absolutely crucial for HR at this stage. Rewards are of major interest to employees, and by quickly implementing—and communicating the benefits of—a new rewards program, HR helps promote fair and objective management decision-making, make certain that the right people are in the right jobs, and ensure that key talent is retained. What's more, communicating these programs and processes to employees helps calm their anxiety and keeps them focused on maintaining their own performance.

Business Unit and Function Integration

In approaching organization design and implementation at the business unit and functional levels, best practice entails taking the following steps:

- Step 1: Align business unit and functional strategies with the overall business strategy for the new company
- Step 2: Identify and evaluate current and needed organizational capabilities for implementing the strategy
- Step 3: Compare process and workforce requirements with existing and needed organizational capabilities and develop a plan to address gaps
- Step 4: Create a strategic staffing model (policy framework, documentation, tools, etc.) for the new company
- Step 5: Develop a detailed organizational structure, beginning with the governance and top-management tiers and continuing through the operating and staff support tiers
- Step 6: Finalize organization design recommendations, secure management approval, and implement the plans

In the first step, the new company's leadership provides each business unit and function with a clear and concise definition of the new company's business strategy and an explanation of the major design implications. Using this as a foundation, business unit and function leadership teams clarify and articulate their own supporting strategy and ensure alignment with the business strategy for the new company as a whole. The business unit or function strategy must, of course, be validated by the new company's executive leadership before the unit proceeds to the next step. In cases where HR has credible organization development expertise, practitioners may be assigned to facilitate the working meetings of the leadership teams.

In Step 2, HR may consult with the business unit or function leadership teams to identify and benchmark the specific organizational capabilities required to deliver their post-integration strategies. For example, if creating double-digit revenue growth in Europe is the objective of a global business unit's strategy, then evaluating and negotiating business alliances with European firms may be a required organization capability. Each capability's importance to implementing the strategy should be measured (say, on a scale of 1 to 5), and the business unit or function's existing capability should also be measured. Capabilities with a high importance and low current performance rating must be addressed immediately via an explicit action plan. The reasons for poor current performance tend to reflect several common problems, such as the following:

- People (e.g., shortage of critical skills, weak performance commitment)
- Culture (e.g., reactive versus proactive, fragmented versus collaborative)
- Process (e.g., lack of processes to ensure efficient and effective performance)
- Structure (e.g., overmanaged or cumbersome structure that slows decision-making or weakens accountability)
- Technology (e.g., inefficient, out-of-date, or disconnected systems)

If, for example, the organizational capabilities analysis suggests that poor performance is due to a talent shortage, then HR can begin to address the gap through a new resourcing strategy, as noted in Step 4. In Steps 3 and 4, HR works with business unit or function leaders to determine the best processes and people resources for building the needed capabilities. In Step 5, HR and management may look at alternative organizational structures that better address the new company's capability requirements.

In the last step (Step 6), each business unit and function leader presents final recommendations to the new company's executive management to ensure proper alignment with the overall strategy and goals of the new company. Modifications are made as required, and implementation begins.

After the new company's required capabilities are understood and the gaps and surpluses in the current organization are identified, an action plan with a logical business rationale as its foundation can be developed to drive implementation in the right direction. Our experience and the research done for this book demonstrate unequivocally that managing lasting change requires a logical foundation that can be communicated to and readily understood by employees at all levels. Too often, changes are introduced without first preparing the affected people and other stakeholders. When that happens, either resistance or indifference is the inevitable result.

The workforce of the new company is shaped through selection and deployment, learning and development, rewards and recognition, and performance management programs. These programs should align with and support organization-wide integration. Once the programs are ready, HR helps each business unit and function implement them by managing the related communications and, when needed, by troubleshooting.

Organization Design

Integration of business units and staff support functions in a merger or acquisition provides an opportunity for creating a new, leading-edge organization. Because of the limited time available for launching the new company after the deal is closed, organization design and implementation are frequently managed in discrete steps. Most companies create a transitional organization for the first year and a plan to reach an end-state or ideal organization in later years. This allows the two companies to continue their previous businesses during the immediate post-merger period. Near-term stabilization of these businesses is critical to long-term success. Moreover, stakeholders usually expect the "bugs" to be worked out during the first year of transition.

HR's involvement in the development of the new company's organization is critical for several reasons. First, HR can provide business unit and functional management with the necessary design and implementation expertise. Second, HR's perspective is usually broader than that of the business unit or function, which can help ensure that the proposed organization design suits the company as a whole. Third, HR can promote a fair and defensible process that is in compliance with all legal and regulatory requirements and helps promote achievement of synergies.

Staffing the new organization goes hand in hand with the design process. HR can alert management to any adverse implications that may result from the new design (for example, if the elimination of certain types of positions would result in a disproportionate number of members of a protected class being displaced).

Staffing Implementation

The selection process used to staff the newly built organization must be legally defensible and transparent to and perceived as fair by all employees. It should address the types of employee concerns that surface during the implementation process, such as the following:

- Will I lose my job?
- Will I have to work for a new boss?
- Will I lose the status I've gained in my current organization?
- Will I be demoted?
- Will my job responsibilities change?
- Will I lose my co-workers?

As noted in Chapter Five, selecting the right people for important positions is a key aspect of successful integration. In the first 100 days, the following staffing initiatives should be completed:

- Communicate guiding principles for the screening and selection of staff and present an anticipated timeline
- Select people for the top levels of the organization and, once appointed, involve them in the selection of people for the remaining positions

Communicating and adhering to the timeline can be challenging. In any merger or acquisition, tension exists between making staff selection decisions quickly and having a well-conceived staffing and rollout plan. On one hand, there is an impetus to get it done so that some semblance of normalcy can be re-established as quickly as possible. On the other, there is pressure to be strategic and careful about staffing decisions. This means taking the necessary time to assess the skills and behaviors needed for each position. Here, the 80/100 rule could apply as long as the selection process is fair, transparent, and legally defensible.

Still, a balance can be difficult to achieve. For example, one company was determined to move through the staffing process quickly and did not allow enough time for making sound selection decisions. Unrealistic artificial deadlines meant that hiring managers often did not interview all of the qualified candidates and instead focused on candidates they already believed to be qualified.

This practice had a number of unpleasant consequences. First, qualified candidates who were not interviewed because of time constraints felt justifiably frustrated and angry. This led to low morale, which decreased productivity and increased the potential for litigation. Second, a disproportionate number of the people selected for jobs in the new company came from the same operating division, function, or department as the hiring manager, which created inevitable friction and unrest. Finally, the staffing process did not achieve its primary objective, which was to fill each job in the new organization with the best candidate.

Another example illustrates the other end of the spectrum. In this case, management was so concerned about the fairness and precision of the staffing process that it took too long to prepare for each wave of staffing, particularly for the top and middle levels of the organization. Despite this company's good intentions, employees grew increasingly restless as months passed with little evidence of progress. Morale and productivity suffered, and many employees began searching for other jobs. Subsequent focus groups and exit interviews showed that employees were simply tired of being in limbo, with no end in sight. The new company's leadership responded by adopting a more aggressive staffing timeline and managed to curtail its turnover somewhat. This example demonstrates not only the importance of moving the staffing process along, but also the value of employee research in understanding issues and making necessary adjustments in the process.

Guiding Principles

Making staffing decisions is never an easy or popular task. Nonetheless, a few principles should guide implementation of the staffing process. Adherence to these principles helps minimize workplace disruption, making it easier for employees to focus on their core job responsibilities. The six guiding principles for staffing that have worked for many successful companies are discussed in the following paragraphs.

Make the selection process creditable. Before beginning the selection process, establish and communicate a framework that is fair, clear to everyone, and legally defensible.

Communicate, communicate, communicate. Because staffing decisions hit home for everyone, the importance of staffing-related communication cannot be overemphasized. Even if there isn't anything concrete to report at the outset, telling employees that information will be available at a specific time in the future can make a huge difference in containing rumors and speculation.

Involve people. A broad cross section of people from both companies should be involved in the design and administration of the staffing process. Ideally, all employees should have a voice in the process. Employee involvement can take various forms, including the following:

- Hold focus groups or working sessions during the design and implementation phases of the staffing process to gather employees' input and provide a format for hearing their concerns
- Provide a practical means for employees to communicate their accomplishments and job qualifications. Even something as simple as providing everyone with a standard resume form or offering interviews can have a positive effect on employee attitudes toward the staffing process

- Establish an appeal or grievances process for employees who believe they have been treated unfairly in the staffing process
- Reassure those who are displaced that they will be treated fairly and made eligible for other positions if possible

For example, one company sponsored biweekly open-forum breakfasts at which employees were invited to share their thoughts about the integration process with members of the new management team. Management said these sessions were invaluable in understanding employee concerns about the integration process and their attitudes toward the new company.

Support managers. The support and commitment of managers, both in the incumbent organizations and those selected for the new company, are critical to the success of the integration process. Managers must orchestrate the integration process, help other employees cope with change during the transition and keep them focused on their current jobs, and deal with the uncertainties surrounding their own careers.

The new company should support its managers' active participation in the implementation process, as this increases the likelihood that integration will take place in a coordinated, concerted way. The following types of support can be given to managers during the staffing process:

- Training seminars on topics such as coping with change, developing interviewing skills, providing feedback (both positive and developmental), communicating staffing decisions, and handling disappointed employees
- Online bulletin boards with interviewing tools, major talking points for communicating staffing decisions, answers to frequently asked questions, and contact information for querying HR and other resources
- Networking and support opportunities such as online or actual discussion groups, "brown bag" lunches, and panel discussions with leadership of the new company
- Work/life balance initiatives for managers who contribute above and beyond the call of duty, such as extra vacation days or gift certificates for a dinner or a visit to a spa

Train those involved in the staffing process. Hold training for anyone making assessments of employees even if they have had related experience beforehand. This includes detailed training for individuals who conduct interviews or make other assessments and for individuals who administer the staffing process. It also includes information exchanges for explaining to employees how the staffing process works and what their role will be (e.g., filling out standard resume forms).

Provide outplacement support. Invest generously in outplacement and be creative about the types of support offered to displaced employees. Relatively inexpensive initiatives can make a great difference to employees, for example, offering workshops on resume writing or preparing for interviews, offering seminars on Internet-based job search techniques, and providing office space (complete with fax machines, telephone lines, and Internet access) for employees to use in their job search, even after their termination dates.

By embracing these principles, management can help employees maintain the sense that, even with the uncertainty surrounding the integration, they still are in control of their futures. When they know what is happening, what their options are, and what services will be available to them, employees have less anxiety about the prospect of losing their jobs. The result is less distraction, greater productivity, and a smoother integration process. That's a "win-win" situation for the new company.

Managing the Change Process: Building a New Culture

Managing change during a merger or acquisition is fundamentally about ensuring that stakeholders receive value promised. This is an extraordinary challenge because, as discussed in Chapter Two, mergers and acquisitions must recoup the value each company would have achieved without the deal, plus the premium payment and integration costs. This means that previous levels of performance are no longer good enough—no matter how well each company was doing. Today's mergers and acquisitions continue to ratchet up performance expectations to ever greater heights. As a result, implementation must be guided by a change management strategy that unlocks discretionary effort in the combined workforce, engages employees in the vision and aspirations of the new company, and rewards them well for superior performance.

At this juncture, HR's role is to help manage the transition employees have to make from their old to the new company, while ensuring they continue to focus on the day-to-day business of satisfying customers. This can be a challenge because each employee is riding an emotional roller coaster, and that fact, combined with the confusion and uncertainty that often characterize the implementation stage, can paralyze an organization that is unprepared.

For a successful implementation to occur, commitment, culture, and connections all must be taken into account.

Commitment

The extent to which people are dedicated to the new company and are willing to expend their full energy on making it a success is the measure of their commitment. Companies can no longer expect employees to commit their loyalty to whatever new venture their executives think is best for the company. If employees don't buy into the deal, believing that it can enhance their careers, their teams, their business units, or the company as a whole, they will resist change. High performers, who have other employment options, may leave if they become too frustrated or anxious about the new company's prospects. Accordingly, companies that hope to succeed with a merger and acquisition must use the implementation stage as an opportunity to involve, inspire, and inform employees.

Culture

In earlier chapters, the importance of addressing culture issues early and explicitly was discussed in detail. Creating a new culture or assimilating people into the established culture of the acquiring company is a major activity during implementation. Inspirational leadership, common values, clear measures, challenging work, and worthwhile rewards provide the impetus and energy needed to fuel the change process and facilitate a true melding of cultures.

How the integration plan is implemented speaks volumes to employees about what the work environment of the new company will be like. When the new company leaders publicly state one set of values for the company, while exhibiting an opposite set of values during implementation, they put themselves in a deep hole right from the start. Employees will become suspicious and cynical about the new company's leaders, impeding a fast and smooth transition from the culture they know to the new one.

Culture change does not occur separately from other changes taking place in the newly combined organization. Whether explicitly or implicitly, culture touches every action, every word, and every decision. While cultural messages may be communicated and reinforced through web sites, newsletters, and e-mails, culture is embedded most firmly within the company through the actions of its leaders. Stated more bluntly, culture failures in mergers and acquisitions are failures of leadership.

Connections

The faster people feel connected to their new company and their work unit, the faster they are likely to fully embrace the goals of integration. One way connections are established is by keeping employees informed about integration and business-related decisions. The communication media used must give people information when and where they want it. Combining high-tech and high-touch media (e.g., intranet, video, and face-to-face meetings) can help to ensure connections remain interactive and collaborative and have a human touch.

Effective communication is only part of the connection equation. During implementation, the most powerful connections are formed when communities of people begin working toward common goals of the larger organization. This is why successful integrators pay careful attention to the formation, nurturing, and management of teams. These teams need clear mandates, explicit goals, empathic leadership, and opportunities to achieve recognizable success early. These early wins will help to solidify the connections and foster the energy and confidence needed for future successes.

Successful integrators also have an adventurous spirit. In some ways, this quality is akin to the discipline of soldiers in combat, the stamina of marathon runners, and the empathy and patience of saints. These are the behaviors everyone must exhibit to some extent during any change process. The employees of companies involved in M&As must understand that change is inevitable and that it demands openness to new ideas and willingness to surrender old ways of doing things. Managers, while coping with their own mixed feelings about the merger or acquisition, must empathize with the concerns of their employees while keeping them focused on existing work and future possibilities. Both employees and managers must become comfortable with some degree of ambiguity because answers to many important questions may not come as quickly or completely as everyone would like.

A successful transition from separate companies to a new integrated company must be led by executives who can define clearly where the respective team, unit, or company is headed; seek ways to influence and collaborate with others, regardless of which company they came from; and remain flexible while implementing the integration plan. America Online's Mayo Stuntz, who is managing the details of the integration for the AOL-Time Warner merger, fits this profile. As described by Walter Isaacson, a former editor of *Time* magazine, "Mayo has the ability to get a bunch of people in a room, figure out ways they can work together, and then make them feel happy to do so."

Critical Success Factors

Implementing M&A demands a thorough understanding of the art and science of change management. We have identified four factors that drive effective change implementation: leadership, communication, involvement, and measurement.

Leadership

Leadership is probably the single most powerful and misunderstood variable in the success of a merger or acquisition. It is powerful in that it determines whether implementation is launched with the speed and force necessary to overcome the apprehensions and inertia in both organizations. It is misunderstood in that it arouses strong passions and opinions from just about everyone in the affected organizations—particularly the organization undergoing the most significant change (usually the acquired company or the junior partner in a merger).

Who do we mean when we talk about the leaders of an organization? Our focus is on the senior leadership team, including the senior officer responsible for the HR functions, all of whom play vital roles in guiding and directing integration activities before, during, and after implementation.

During implementation, senior executives of the new company can become so consumed by details that they forget the single most important role they have—that is, to engage, inform, and motivate workers. When leaders have different priorities, the new company's people (managers and nonmanagers alike) may feel anxious about their own status and ambivalent about the prospects for the new organization. Worse still, disengagement can spread quickly through the workplace and run so deep that it may take a very long time to undo the damage that could have been avoided with competent leadership in the first place.

A central challenge for the senior executive of the HR function for the new company is to convince the CEO and other members of the senior leadership team that they should be concerned about how the combined organization perceives the quality of their leadership—both individually and collectively.

The implementation stage is a window of "leadership opportunity." Particularly at the outset of this stage, everyone in the combining organizations pays very close attention to the actions, words, and behaviors of leaders, and people may be more open to being led now than at later points in the integration process. People who are in the throes of change they did not create must be given a clear sense of direction and purpose. Only the most capable organizational leaders can provide this, and they must do so before the new company's concrete starts to set.

The most successful M&As are led by teams whose members have the courage and take the time to be leaders. Their leadership style can take many forms, but in most cases, it involves simply getting out into the new organization, fielding hard questions, admitting what is known and what isn't, and providing a sense that someone is in charge who cares deeply about the new company's employees, customers, and other stakeholders.

Mandate for HR Leadership

Members of the new company's senior leadership team must get to know one another, establish norms, clarify roles, assign accountabilities, determine how decisions will be made, deal with conflict, and perhaps most important, determine exactly how they intend to guide the development of the new organization. The senior HR executive on the leadership team must push these issues to the top of the new company's agenda. By convincing the senior leadership team to invest real time and energy in developing its own strengths, HR can demonstrate its ability to add value when and where it is needed most.

Our empirical research, presented throughout this book, underscores that how credible and effective the HR senior executives are as leaders has much to do with M&A success. HR leaders must recognize this opportunity to make a positive impact on the entire M&A process, become energized by it, and invest significant time and attention in preparing themselves for the challenges ahead. They must embrace their natural role as experts on people, organizational, and culture issues and demand a powerful voice and due influence within the senior leadership team. An HR leader who misses this opportunity is not likely to be a serious force for change or an equal partner on the senior leadership team.

One of the most valuable contributions HR can make is to provide candid and insightful observations regarding how the new company's senior leaders are viewed by the rest of the organization. More than anyone, the senior HR executive should have firsthand, up-to-date information regarding the mood of employees throughout the new organization and whether or not the integration process is gaining positive momentum.

It takes a fact-based perspective and self-confidence to stand up in a senior leadership team meeting and convince one's colleagues that their leadership is falling short. The best way to do this effectively is by

- backing up opinions with facts and data (e.g., research from "pulse" surveys);
- expressing empathy for the stress each individual is feeling;

- offering practical, tangible actions that can be easily implemented; and
- providing personal assistance and other resources as needed.

Communication During the Implementation Stage

During implementation, people in the organizations to be combined will experience firsthand the changes they have been worrying about since the deal was first announced. Providing them with the information they need to understand and cope with these changes is the primary purpose of M&A communication and another key role for HR practitioners.

Until this point in the process, employees have been hearing about the many changes that will take place during implementation. Now these changes will become a reality, and a well-conceived and -executed communication strategy is an effective means for helping employees make sense of their changing work environment. Some specific communication challenges typically faced during implementation include the following:

- Employee reactions to losing a position, getting a new position (promotion, demotion, transfer), or seeing colleagues leave or change positions
- The realization among managers and employees that change is now a constant, not a short-term event
- An overload of messages and priorities from current managers and those appointed to management positions in the new company
- Burnout as people continue to carry out the heavy burden of their current responsibilities while supporting implementation of the new programs and structures
- Stress as people from the combining organizations begin working with each other more closely and differences in style and approach become visible and often aggravating

During this stage, the communication and change (C&C) team should also establish connections with the business units and other operating entities of the new company to ensure that information is developed and disseminated in ways that have a beneficial impact on performance. Often, communication begins and ends at the corporate level; however, most effective change occurs when communication responsibility resides at the work unit or department level.

The primary goals of communication during implementation are to prepare employees for their new roles, help them accept specific changes and the reasons for them, and enable them to see how the many different change initiatives fit together during the implementation stage. In fact, communication often pertains to specific implementation initiatives. Examples of such communication include the following:

- Meetings to explain the staffing process and for presentations by each business unit function or department leaders
- Articles in the new company's newsletter (with sections on regular business and merger-related news) that explain the change programs

- Specific communication vehicles for managers such as a type of e-mail used only when managers need to act on the information, a web site that provides background and detailed information, or urgent voicemails for breaking news
- A hotline that responds to anonymous inquiries about rumors circulating within the workforce
- An electronic bulletin board that keeps HR professionals up to date on emerging issues, provides consistent answers to common questions, and so on
- Scripts for call center employees who answer employee questions about benefits and other issues
- Background information and supporting reference materials for people with direct customer contact (Q&As, template letters for customers, scripts)
- Open houses to explain new processes, relocation issues, new programs (e.g., benefits), and new business issues (e.g., products)
- Fact sheets on the new company and its products

HR should be a champion and catalyst for communication in the implementation stage. Some key roles for HR are the following:

- Answer questions about specific human resource programs (e.g., relocation, new benefits and retirement programs, new compensation programs)
- Help to equip line and staff leaders throughout the new organization to identify communication issues early and share information quickly and accurately
- Develop communication messages and materials regarding the various changes being introduced; work with vendors or internal resources to produce and deliver these materials
- Model the new communication style and environment for the rest of the organization—both in the HR function and in employee-related communications
- Help gather and deliver messages regarding ongoing employee research to senior management and to the new organization as a whole
- Evaluate communications frequently during implementation to assess alignment with integration objectives

Chapter Five emphasized that communication must be an integral part of the change management plan, not treated as a tactical device simply to inform employees of change. This approach helps to ensure consistent messages, programs, and leadership actions. Several communication best practices are described in *Exhibit 6.6*.

Involvement

Involving employees in implementation increases their commitment to the new organization and to the integration plan, builds a foundation for developing a high-performance work environment, and connects employees to the business and with each other. Several principles can be used to guide employee involvement in the integration process and improve employee performance and motivation while enhancing the new company's bottom-line results.

Specifically, employee involvement during an M&A can

Exhibit 6.6 Communication Best Practices

1. Provide anchors and road maps

Provide anchors (things that won't change) and road maps (pictures of where the new organization is headed) to help employees and their managers focus on their work, rather than on uncertainties.

2. Bundle information

Bundle information, particularly about what matters most to employees and managers. For example, communications related to job postings, tuition reimbursement, and training and development programs can be packaged as "Helping People Develop." Bundling information enables people to see more easily how changes that are part of implementation fit together.

3. Facilitate multiple communication flows

Electronic channels for providing feedback need to be accessible and implemented by other channels (e.g., manager meetings).

4. Balance high tech and high touch

Using the web to communicate fast-breaking news, daily updates, and detailed information can be very effective. However, managers should be an integral part of the communication strategy. In general, managers should communicate information that personally affects employees, answer the hard questions, weave core messages into day-to-day work, and act in ways that reinforce the new company's desired culture.

Source: Towers Perrin analysis.

- increase employee awareness and understanding about why change is necessary;
- unlock previously untapped organizational knowledge that can lead to better-informed and -evaluated decisions;
- motivate employees by demonstrating that their ideas and opinions are important and valued;
- challenge employees in ways that can enhance their job satisfaction;
- help to retain high performers and employees with "hot skills";
- increase employee buy-in and build a critical mass of support throughout the workforce;
- improve the quality of decision-making by incorporating diverse viewpoints;
- teach decision-making, team-process, and business-literacy skills; and
- liberate managers from the notion that they must have all the answers.

Most important, involvement is used to change employee behavior. During the integration process, people need to let go of the old, embrace the new, and navigate through change, while raising their individual performance levels. This is a tall order for many employees at a time when they find themselves overwhelmed by anxiety, stress, and confusion. The temptation to check out emotionally and disengage from the integration process is high. On the other hand, when employees are engaged, they energize the change process and help build momentum to carry the organization to a higher level of performance.

Three levels of involvement are typically used during a merger or acquisition: input, participation, and decision-making. As employees move from one level of involvement to the next, they are more likely to become advocates and agents of the change process rather than its detractors.

Input from employees is the most common form of involvement used during a merger or acquisition, and it can provide critical—and sometimes surprising—information about employee perceptions, feelings, and attitudes. Employee input is often collected through activities that take relatively little time and effort. Some common examples are surveys, focus groups, Q&A sessions during all-employee meetings, e-mail suggestion boxes, and employee breakfasts or lunches with senior leaders.

HR executives and practitioners who seek employee input during a merger or acquisition should understand that soliciting feedback from employees can backfire if not done properly. To avoid such problems, HR executives and practitioners should

- make certain that decision-makers value the input and use it in their deliberations,
- set clear ground rules for focus groups to prevent them from degenerating into gripe sessions or problem-solving exercises disconnected from the new company's decision-making process,
- set employee expectations by clearly communicating the purpose of seeking input and the process for how it will be used by decision-makers, and
- tell employees how their input was used or how it affected the decision-making process.

Participation, the next level of involvement, allows employees to identify and solve problems, envision a future state, brainstorm ideas, and build action plans. This takes employee time and effort but, if done right, can increase the pace and quality of the change efforts.

Common forms of participation used in a merger or acquisition include employee advisory boards, rapid-response teams, process-design teams, customer-response teams, and change teams.

When asking people to invest their time and energy in helping implement the integration plan, the new company must ensure that they have an opportunity to make a difference in approach and outcome. For instance, in one merger, employees were asked to join an employee task force to advise senior managers about the new company's marketing function. The managers had excellent intentions; each selected people for the task force and sought help from HR and outside consultants in establishing, facilitating, and managing the task force. However, managers soon became so involved with the issues related to designing and staffing the function that they had little time to focus on the task force's activities. After a few months, the leaders forgot about the task force, participation levels fell, and HR disbanded the work group. Employees were left frustrated and deeply suspicious of the sincerity of their leaders' commitment to employee involvement and, for that matter, to employee contributions in general. Some lessons that can be taken from this experience are listed below.

- Employees don't want to be substantively involved in the integration process just for the sake of involvement. They want to make a positive contribution to the decisions and policies that shape this process.
- Senior leadership endorsement of employee involvement is not enough. The active and continuous participation of those leaders is critical for successful participation efforts. If, in the case above, leaders had committed to facilitating the working sessions and had spent time with the task force rather than outsourcing these tasks to HR and consultants, the outcome might have been very different.
- Employee work teams need clear, mutually agreed-upon, and realistic mandates. Expecting a deliverable like a proposal, template, or action plan can help make the mandate tangible. An objective like "providing advice" is not specific enough for work teams to successfully contribute to the integration process. By contrast, appropriate mandates include the following: developing a proposal to decrease turnover to a benchmark or target level in a particular function, creating a guide for how a physically dispersed team can work together, or identifying specific skills and behaviors that employees need to succeed in the new company.

Decision-making engages employees at the highest level of involvement. Good opportunities for manager and employee joint decision-making include redesigning work processes and determining the best ways to communicate news and information across all parts of the new company's organization. Engaging employees in decision-making processes gives them some influence over those decisions that affect them.

Measurement in M&A

In implementing a merger or acquisition, measurement processes or techniques should be used to gauge employee attitudes and opinions about important aspects of the integration process. Because measurement takes time and can produce as many questions as it does answers, it often faces stiff resistance from some people in management.

Nonetheless, the implementation stage is exactly the right time to measure stakeholder attitudes and opinions and to look carefully at the impact of the messages that underlie the integration philosophy and process. Why?

Because employee perception is reality. Investment analysts tend to look at financial data, not employee perceptions, in rating company potential. And yet, employee perceptions figure prominently in creating a "new" company. These perceptions are important at the implementation stage for one compelling reason: There's nothing else to go on! The new company does not yet have a track record, a shared history, a mutual brand, or even a joint product. So positive employee perceptions—driven, of course, by effective organizational communication—of the rationale for the deal and the potential for success are fundamental drivers for building commitment and are strong retention devices. Looking again at our own research data, developing a strategy for communicating with employees of both companies is the highest-rated value for the integration planning stage.

Because there's no progress without a baseline. Much like the often-quoted mantra of the movie *Jerry Maguire*—"Show me the money"—employees (and analysts) will demand to see early progress against stated goals. Financial measures are only half the picture. Favorable employee perceptions about the organization's ability to respond to market needs, provide real learning and development opportunities, reward competitively, and so on become "proof" that the new organization is succeeding. And this perception is something that employees will share with customers, distributors, alliance partners, and others through their commitment and positive outlook about the future.

Because stakes are high. This final point remains true today, when M&As often involve multibillion-dollar transactions of publicly held companies. More to the point, companies that are growing aggressively through mergers and acquisitions often pay a significant premium for the privilege. (As we discussed earlier, sustaining financial performance is the top-rated obstacle in capturing intended synergies.) Given this premium, who can afford to misunderstand what makes an acquired company or a merger partner attractive in the first place? Measurement helps to prevent possible failure from becoming a reality.

How Measurement Adds Value

While there are a host of "products" that can result from the capture and analysis of organizational intelligence—from value and mission statements to workforce engagement indices to turnover drivers—the following points demonstrate the fundamental value of measurement in the M&A environment.

Naming the "hippo in the room." As the expression suggests, organizations (much like individuals) are remarkably adept at ignoring what may in fact be rather glaringly obvious facts—especially when the facts suggest some degree of failure or imperfection. Data collected through employee research can be both representative and confidential and can provide a forum for identifying and addressing issues that are otherwise often difficult even to name. The most obvious example—and one that is quite common in M&A situations, especially during the first 100 days—is the concern that the new company does not have a clearly defined, coherent business strategy. Employees do not generally have channels through which to express this anxiety. Managers with access to the senior leadership, on the other hand, may not feel comfortable discussing this issue, fearing that perhaps they simply don't understand the strategy. Even among the new company's senior leadership, there may be concerns that are difficult to air in the hectic

Exhibit 6.7   Health Care Industry Example: Turnover Drivers

> A large health care employer uncovered a relatively high level of potential turnover ("intention to leave in the next year") at its senior manager level. Analysis of the data showed that opinion on this item was most influenced by the degree to which these individuals felt they were being *included* in shaping the market strategy. In essence, this was a relatively simple process issue that, if left unresolved, could have led to the significant loss of management talent.

Source: Towers Perrin analysis.

---

pace of the integration process. However, with survey or focus group data, the message can be delivered clearly (and without personal risk) to the senior leadership. If the strategy is clear, communication can be improved. If the strategy is not settled, then employees can be reassured about the process in place for completing and communicating the strategy. Employee research is a simple tool that can have a big impact on employee confidence and commitment.

Addressing "drivers," not symptoms. Employee research helps management understand the interrelationships among discrete issues. For example, retention is generally a concern when two organizations come together. Although some turnover is to be expected, significant loss of talent can disrupt ongoing operations and degrade the inherent value of the deal. Without real measurement, turnover issues are likely to be addressed in fairly traditional ways (short-term stay bonus, long-term incentives, etc.). With research data, it becomes possible to document the true relationship between turnover and operational performance. As the example in *Exhibit 6.7* suggests, what shapes opinion is not always obvious, nor is it always difficult to resolve. However, the data allow for precise identification and appropriate channeling of follow-up activities and resources.

Measuring means communicating. At the implementation stage, managing ongoing changes and employee communication processes had the top value rating from our survey participants. Surveys are frequently overlooked vehicles for supporting this process. The act of gathering data—whether through individual leadership interviews or an all-employee survey—sends an important message. At the most basic level, the fact that questions are being asked demonstrates an interest in employee viewpoints and input. More important, *what* is being asked communicates what is "on the agenda"—either from the senior leadership or human resources point of view—and allows employees to contribute to the new organization's development. Ironically, this is exactly why some management teams object to conducting research in the first place—a fear that these questions imply that issues are entirely open for debate. While this is certainly a valid concern, a sound research process will produce instruments (dis-

Exhibit 6.8 Matching Context and Approach in Employee Research

Context	Suggested Approach
Hostile takeover; position overlap ■ Low sponsorship ■ Extreme concern about making "a bad situation worse"	■ Low visibility ■ Selected interviews with senior leadership of acquired company ■ Small number of employee focus groups at both companies ■ Focus on integration process
True merger of equals; no position overlap; complementary service offerings ■ High sponsorship ■ Leadership of both organizations eager to develop synergies	■ High visibility ■ Create profile of each culture (focus groups and culture survey); compare and contrast differences ■ Communicate results as platform for defining new (ideal) work environment
Friendly acquisition; minimal position overlap ■ Mixed sponsorship ■ Long-term strategy not yet clearly defined ■ Concern about raising expectations	■ Low visibility ■ Employee focus groups within both organizations to determine current perceptions about business model and desired culture ■ Results fed into strategy clarification process; high-level communication to all employees

Source: Towers Perrin analysis.

cussion guides, questionnaires, etc.) that yield usable data, not unrealistic expectations. Finally, the process of reporting research findings provides a natural platform for senior leadership to build credibility, share a vision for the future, and reassure employees that their concerns are taken seriously.

The Research Approach

One reason that measurement is perceived as discretionary—especially in merger situations—is that many companies do a poor job of matching their research methods with their research needs. The result is that their research yields information and data that are not especially useful in helping the new company achieve its goals. Even worse, the research process, when not well suited to the organizational climate, can be a destructive force, raising unrealistic expectations or consuming employee good will with no visible outcome or impact.

How, then, do we ensure the right match? The following three factors, when assessed properly, help the new organization design an effective approach.

Exhibit 6.9 Real-World Example: Research Disaster of a Defense Contractor

A heavily unionized defense contractor commissioned research to understand its employees' perceptions about existing benefit programs. Employees completed a survey with the expectation that their input would help in some way to improve these programs. While the survey results indicated high satisfaction with various program elements, a companion cost analysis and other factors led to significant benefit cutbacks. Not surprisingly, employees were unhappy and felt they had been betrayed. And, not surprisingly, the company is now extremely skittish about any further employee research. In this case, employees should never have been engaged in a process intended to provide ideas for cutting their benefits. Any future research will need to acknowledge this past experience, clarify the reasons for the research, and describe the specific uses of the results.

Source: Towers Perrin analysis.

Visibility and sponsorship. Should employees be aware of the measurement activity or should data collection be accomplished in a quiet manner? The answer depends on several factors, including the level of sponsorship by senior leadership. With strong management support, research becomes a vehicle for involving employees in the process of creating a new company. On the other hand, even if senior leadership is unwilling to involve most employees in the process, focused research should still be conducted, albeit in a low-key manner, with results shared only with management.

Whether an organization uses a quiet or direct approach depends on what is appropriate to its specific circumstances. The company may not be ready to involve most of its employees in what is essentially a dialogue with senior leaders about the shape of the new organization's functioning and culture. *Exhibit 6.8* offers some guidelines but is certainly not intended to be prescriptive.

Organizational "will" and resources. The research process can (and often should) be largely outsourced to ensure objectivity and confidentiality. Nonetheless, employees and management must invest their time if the research is to deliver credible results. During the first 100 days of implementation, it is very difficult for employees to spend their time away from day-to-day operations. Accordingly, an effective research program must support and energize (rather than distract or frustrate) the integration process.

Research history. Few things are more frustrating to employees than to be asked for the same input more than once. That is why the research program design should be informed by previous employee surveys or other research efforts. Even when the results of prior research are not relevant to the questions at hand, the research process employed may be instructive. An effective research program (one that produces information of value for the investment required) should pick up where the available research information ends. By building on available data, the new company's senior leadership can send a message that past research in both organizations is important to shaping what will happen. During the implementation stage, collecting and using the results of past employee research is a worthwhile task for all of the integration teams. However, care should be taken when conducting employee research. As *Exhibit 6.9* shows, the research process can be misused.

Summary

Implementation is the time when the rubber meets the road. All of the integration planning must be made real, and the promise of the combined organization must be kept. More than any other factor, employees will influence the success of this stage, and HR's actions will in turn influence employee attitudes and behavior. The importance of listening to employees and communicating with them throughout implementation cannot be overemphasized. Much of the responsibility for that communication falls on the new company's leaders, with the support of the HR function. Continuous measurement of the effectiveness of the implementation process can help the new company correct its course if necessary and can provide important information for future mergers and acquisitions. Successful integration requires commitment, dedication, enthusiasm, decisiveness, and a very clear focus on the goals of the new company. ■

SECTION III

The New HR Emerges

CHAPTER SEVEN

Transforming the HR Organization

Mary Cianni

"Human resource people must speak the language of the business and their activities must reflect the priorities of the business."
Clifford J. Erlich
Senior Vice President, HR, Marriott Corporation

In implementing a merger or acquisition, the human resources (HR) function must help address myriad people issues, communicate resolution of these issues across the combined organization, and troubleshoot as the need arises. In a complex merger, for example, using a mutual best-of-both or transformation approach, the HR function itself is caught in the same currents of change as the entire organization. HR managers must support the new company's formation and at the same time transform the HR function itself. That's not an easy thing to do: The HR function must become both an agent of change and a changed agent.

Within the first 100 days of launching the new company, HR participates in the organization design process. Within the first year, its focus shifts to building the integrated HR function so that it can both deliver day-to-day human resource services and help complete the alignment of human resource policies and programs with the business goals of the new company.

Because HR must juggle these dual roles, correct prioritization of its activities becomes paramount. As a first priority, HR must apply the management processes, change programs, and policies of the new company to itself. It must also ensure that sufficient resources are available to support the ongoing integration activities of other functions and business units.

At this point in the process, HR is operating with the same uncertainties that everyone else in the combined organization faces. These individuals are supporting the new company's operating units and staff functions and also dealing with issues such as reductions in force, relocation, retention, and restructuring. They may see some of their colleagues displaced as a result of outsourcing or restructuring. They may wonder whether they will have good jobs in the new combined HR organization and, if so, how their roles and career prospects may change. Furthermore, HR staff assigned to integration task forces must work productively with new colleagues while maintaining their "day jobs" during the transition—managing compensation plans, filling vacancies, drafting communications for clients, answering benefit questions, and so forth.

Notwithstanding these challenges, mergers and acquisitions (M&A) also create new opportunities. For example, the integration process can provide the impetus for significant change in HR by

- demonstrating HR's project management expertise regarding business transformation and organizational change, thus setting the stage for a strengthened role in the new company;
- shifting resources within the HR function from transactional and personnel administrative work to more strategic and consultative roles;
- leveraging information technology—to enable employee and manager self-service applications and processes, for example; and
- redesigning HR programs in ways that can help achieve business purposes such as attracting and retaining talent for the new company.

All this must be accomplished with extraordinary speed and skill. This means that HR has to get its own house in order quickly after a deal is closed so that it can be prepared to support implementation once it begins. One way to accomplish this is to use third parties to handle administrative activities related to integration. For example, a vendor could establish and operate a temporary call center to answer employee questions.

HR can also ensure that its services are used to best advantage during integration by assigning HR staff to business unit integration teams; this allows HR to both stay close to business issues and build relationships with the new business unit management.

The sections that follow discuss the important decisions HR must make in the first 100 days of implementation. These decisions will define the image of the HR function in the new company and influence the impressions that operating and functional executives have about HR's senior leaders. During the implementation stage, HR has the opportunity to demonstrate its expert knowledge and skills and to make a significant contribution to the future success of the combined organization. Conversely, HR can lose credibility if it fails to display the necessary leadership for raising the HR function's profile within the combined organization. With this in mind, three roles are fundamental to successful positioning of HR within the first 100 days.

Set the people-related strategy. HR helps build the capabilities the new company needs to execute its business strategies by advising the new leaders on which people strategies best support both their integration goals and the needs of their ongoing business activities. This entails initiating discussions on synergy targets, retention plans, resources, and capability requirements. For example, if improving retention is a goal of the new company, HR will focus on professional growth opportunities and learning and development strategies. In this way, the HR function can demonstrate from the very inception of the new company how it can help business leaders meet business needs.

Build and develop the senior leadership team. Senior leadership of the new company must clarify roles, assign accountabilities, agree on decision-making processes and norms, deal with conflict, and, perhaps most important, determine how they will work together in guiding and directing the company. HR should push these leadership issues to the top of the new company's agenda. By convincing the senior leadership team to invest sufficient time and energy to perfect its own functioning, HR demonstrates in a highly visible way its ability to add value early in the implementation stage. This kind of support is particularly important because senior leadership teams sometimes do not resolve very basic issues related to their early days of implementation. The HR managers and practitioners should serve as role models for the team behaviors that the new company should embrace.

Establish HR's credibility with senior executives. How the HR function is used and its degree of clout often vary between the companies involved in M&As. In one company, for example, HR might concentrate largely on administrative work and transaction processing. Its focus may be on such issues as whether people are paid accurately, health claims are handled in a cost-effective manner, and managers are able to hire (or fire) people without a lot of red tape. Meanwhile, the other partner in the merger may take a more strategic approach to the role of HR. For example, management may regard HR as an expert on the design and implementation of innovative solutions to people-related business performance issues. Building consensus on and communicating the future role of HR in the new company, and having a concrete plan for achieving it, provide a clear mandate for transforming the HR function.

Our view, for the many compelling reasons covered in this book, is that smart companies elevate the HR function and leverage its expertise in ways that are important to achieving business performance.

Designing the New HR Organization

As a first step toward creating a world-class HR organization, the HR functional integration team must propose a people strategy for the new company. For example, in one global merger, the new company's leaders said the organization's strategic intent was to "win through innovation." HR then translated this intent into specific design guidelines incorporating the elements listed in *Exhibit 7.1*.

After clarifying the people strategy, HR should design the organization structure for the new company's integrated HR function. Beyond the organizational architecture itself, the integration team should specify related components of the new company's management system, including the following:

- People: Identify the HR function's job structure, competencies to match the structure, and candidates for the jobs to be filled.

Exhibit 7.1 Designing the New Organization **EXAMPLE**

BROAD STRATEGIC INITIATIVES

| Research aggressively | Know our customers | Win through innovation | Contain costs | Maximize people contribution |

Process for translating a broad initiative into a specific HR initiative

| **Operational requirement:** Effective link between R&D and manufacturing to enhance speed to market for new products | ▶ | **Organizational implication:** Move people with the product as it proceeds through the development cycle (i.e., core product development team) | ▶ | **Impact on people:** People need systems and incentives to align their work with the product development stages | ▶ | **HR implication:** Create work environment in which people view their jobs as rotating through successive product development teams (incentives/motivation to rotate positions) | ▶ | **HR program "Rotation for Innovation":**
■ Defined roles/jobs
■ Structure
■ Requirements/eligibility
■ Incentives
■ Links to succession planning and learning and development |

Source: Towers Perrin analysis.

- Culture: Describe the desired work environment for HR, a change management strategy for achieving it, and metrics for measuring progress.
- Process: Define roles and responsibilities for major activities in the core processes in which HR is to be involved.
- Technology: Develop a technology strategy for supporting administration of the core HR processes and for delivering HR services to managers and employees (see Chapter Nine).

With the people-related strategy clarified and the new organizational arrangements defined, HR should next devise a scorecard for the HR functional community as a whole and for its components.

- Linking HR to the business: Measures HR contribution to the new company's financial performance
- HR process delivery: Measures efficiency and effectiveness of HR processes and service delivery
- Customer satisfaction: Measures the degree to which support and service expectations of the new company's managers and employees are met
- Workforce capability: Measures progress toward enhancing the skills and competencies of the new company's workforce

When to Transform HR

How changes to the HR function are sequenced within the master integration plan depends on many factors, including the deal's size, whether it crosses national borders, and the state of HR information systems.

HR Goes First

HR leaders should begin thinking about how to integrate and transform the HR functions of the combined companies as early as possible. For example, a 100-day integration plan and initial designs for the new company's HR unit should begin once a deal is disclosed—but before the head of the new company's HR function has been named. The planning and design work should be done during the integration planning stage. That way, the new leader can move into action immediately.

The advantage to HR of going first and moving fast is clear: It gives stability to HR and allows it to focus on helping leaders and other staff units through the integration process. However, because HR will adopt an organization model for itself before the company as a whole does, that model may need to be revisited later, especially in a best-of-both or transformation approach to integration. In an M&A with a dominant partner, the new company's organization design usually resembles that of the dominant company; so, too, the design of the combined HR function usually ends up mirroring the dominant company's, generally with only slight modifications.

If HR goes first, the new company's HR leadership may have difficulty arguing for an elevated role if such a role breaks with past practices of one or both legacy companies. For this reason alone, HR might consider the following alternatives.

Concurrent HR Design

In most cases, HR is integrated concurrently with the other functional units. Accordingly, there are large resource demands on HR as it manages its multiple roles during the integration process. For this reason, companies often fast-track the design and staffing of the integrated HR function. Fast-tracking stabilizes HR because managers and practitioners alike understand their individual status and that of the future HR organization early in the implementation stage. They can then devote their energies to supporting the integration activities of other functions.

HR Goes Last

The advantage of going last is that the HR team is able to focus all of its resources and energies on building and integrating the new company. Then, with the new company's structure and strategy in place, HR can design itself to fit. However, going last requires HR to live with uncertainty about its future, which may cause some key talent in HR to leave. It may also make integrating the two HR teams more difficult, because people who are unsure about their future may view colleagues not as collaborators but as competitors for jobs in the new company.

Regardless of the timing, the HR functional integration process should be guided by the following principles:

Build an HR function based on what is best for the new company. Cherry-picking best practices from the two HR organizations too often ends up in horse trading, compromises, and, in the end, disappointment. It tends to create an HR function that lacks coherence, consistent form, and clear messages about management philosophy and the best work environment. A better approach is to align HR policies, programs, and practices with the new company's business requirements, then design the HR function to meet these requirements effectively and efficiently.

Be bold and consider all reasonable options. Outsourcing or centralizing HR functions in a service center can offer superior value and give HR the opportunity to move from being a largely administrative function to being a fundamental and strategic part of the business. By answering the myriad questions that employees have about changes to benefits, relocation, and severance packages during the integration process, temporary service centers relieve HR of a huge burden and allow it to focus on higher value-added consultative and expert support activities. Once service centers are in place, they can also serve as a foundation for an entirely new approach to handling HR's transactional work and for leveraging web-based technology to deliver services in the future.

Leveraging integration tools such as web-based communications can jump-start a high-tech approach to HR transactional work, thereby freeing HR to focus more of its talent and energy on strategic roles. In addition, using technology to break the mold for delivering HR services signals a fresh start for the new company's integrated HR function. In fact, in one large cross-border combination, HR modeled a new way of doing business within the integrated company by pioneering web-enabled services delivery to managers and employees globally.

Engage the HR staff in the design process. Bringing people together in ways that build a solid foundation for a new HR team is another important principle for successful HR integration. Representatives from both of the combining organizations should serve on the HR functional design teams, sharing information and creating a vision of the future. To expedite the design process, team members gather and assess information on the "as is" HR organizations, sharing best practices from their prior experience and creating new concepts and a design that will better suit the new organization. Once the new organization model is developed, the design team, with advice and support from a communication and change (C&C) team, can identify involvement opportunities for the HR staff as a whole, such as formulating a new vision and values statement, creating new role profiles, and developing new performance metrics. This plan gives all HR staff members a chance to shape their future in partnership with the design team while building a new sense of community within the combined HR function.

Exhibit 7.2 Context for HR Transformation of a Large Manufacturing Company

Strategic Objectives:
- Become the low-cost provider in its industry by reducing waste and complexity as the two companies are integrated
- Grow market share by providing the best products and customer service in the industry

HR Function Objectives:
- Improve HR's cost-effectiveness by increasing the efficiency of HR service delivery
- Eliminate or streamline HR routine administrative activities
- Build strategic HR capabilities needed to improve the company's overall performance (e.g., attracting and retaining people, managing performance, improving labor relations)
- Strengthen the partnership between HR and line managers (mutual respect and trust) to become accepted within the new company as a strategic partner

People Management Objectives:
- Build a workforce with highly competent people in all operations and support functions and at all levels of the organization
- Help to foster a corporate culture of shared commitment to the new company's vision, values, and strategies that energizes and unites the new workforce
- Make sure people embrace common values that will help everyone achieve results consistent with the new company's business objectives and aspirations

HR Mission:
- Serve and consult with business management on strategic people issues
- Work tirelessly to champion and lead the change process within the new company
- Provide functional expertise on people management at all organization levels

Source: Towers Perrin analysis.

Develop a change plan as early as practical. For HR, applying its own expertise in communication, involvement, measurement, and leadership to its new HR organization is key to successful transformation. In addition, more and more HR organizations are designing and implementing intranets to facilitate change management within the HR community during the busy and chaotic time after the deal is closed.

Steps of HR Organization Design

The organization design process for HR is the same as for any business unit or support function within the integrating organizations, and it comprises five steps.

Step One: Determine the HR Philosophy and People Strategy

HR transformation should focus the combined HR function on value-added activities that strengthen the new company's competitiveness and build its associated organizational capabilities. These activities cover everything from building workforce competencies to shaping a new culture to attracting and retaining top talent. How the new company's strategic objectives influence HR transformation is illustrated by the example in *Exhibit 7.2*.

Exhibit 7.3 Activity Analysis for Top-Level HR Processes

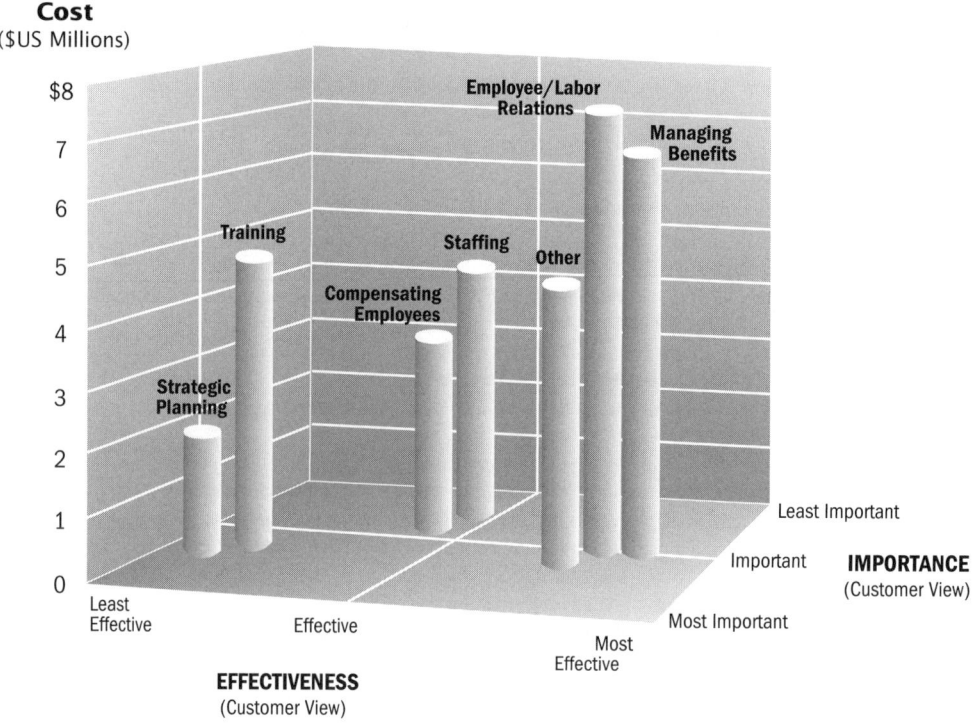

Source: Towers Perrin analysis.

Step Two: Prioritize Data Collection Early in the Process

An authoritative source must be established to provide critical HR data and eliminate the possibility of conflicting information being fed into the design process. These data will help HR create a picture of the current state of the two HR organizations so that differences and design requirements can be uncovered and action plans prepared. It is important to establish in advance the purpose of the research and how the data will be used so that adequate time can be set aside for data collection. The research should answer questions such as the following:

- What combination of HR programs and services has the greatest perceived value among employees of the new company?
- Is the current service delivery model of each company meeting or exceeding promised levels of quality, cost, and service?

Some tools that can be used for data collection include activity analysis, process mapping, technology assessment, and outsourcing analysis.

HR activity analysis measures what HR does in terms of full-time employee equivalents and associated costs for activities such as designing compensation plans, delivering learning and development programs, and recruiting new hires. Combining the activity analysis results with the results of employee satisfaction and program cost measurements provides an excellent analytical tool for identifying opportunities to redesign HR programs, processes, and major organization building blocks (e.g., work units, job structures). For example, the technique described in *Exhibit 7.3* can be used to pinpoint HR processes that are high cost relative to their importance to customers.

Assessing effectiveness, importance, and cost helps identify opportunities for HR to refocus its resources to provide more effective service.

Process mapping describes the "as is" situation regarding HR workflow, allowing analysis of the effectiveness and efficiency of HR's work. This "as is" process mapping can provide the basis for designing HR processes.

Technology assessment evaluates the scope for increasing the cost-effectiveness of HR processes and service delivery through the use of advanced technologies (see Chapter Nine).

Shared services and outsourcing analysis helps to assess the risks, costs, and benefits of centralized HR activities and outsourced activities.

Step Three: Engage Managers in the HR Design Process

The M&A integration process is an excellent vehicle for holding discussions with managers of the combining organizations about the value of current HR programs and practices and about what is needed for the future. One useful approach for such discussions is to assess the new HR function's required "organization capabilities"—those things that the organization must be especially good at (e.g., attracting, retaining, and developing the right people) to accomplish its strategic business objectives.

Integration planners should identify the new set of required organization capabilities and the current performance level (relative to competition or other standards) of each of the participating companies. Results of this analysis can help determine which features of each company should be retained and which external best practices should be adopted.

The gaps that surface from this analysis can show HR how its resources should be allocated in the new company. The assessment can also help clarify the strengths and weaknesses of the combined HR function as root causes for the gaps are uncovered. For example, the combined HR function may capitalize on complementary strengths such as the administrative and technical expertise of one legacy HR unit (for delivering HR transactional services) and the organization development strength of its new partner. An HR change management plan can then be developed to address the need for competencies that neither legacy function has (see *Exhibit 7.4*).

Once a preliminary HR design is formulated, each legacy function can test the design against its own requirements, with particular attention to the design's impact on service delivery and work processes.

Exhibit 7.4 Evaluating Capabilities in the HR Design Process

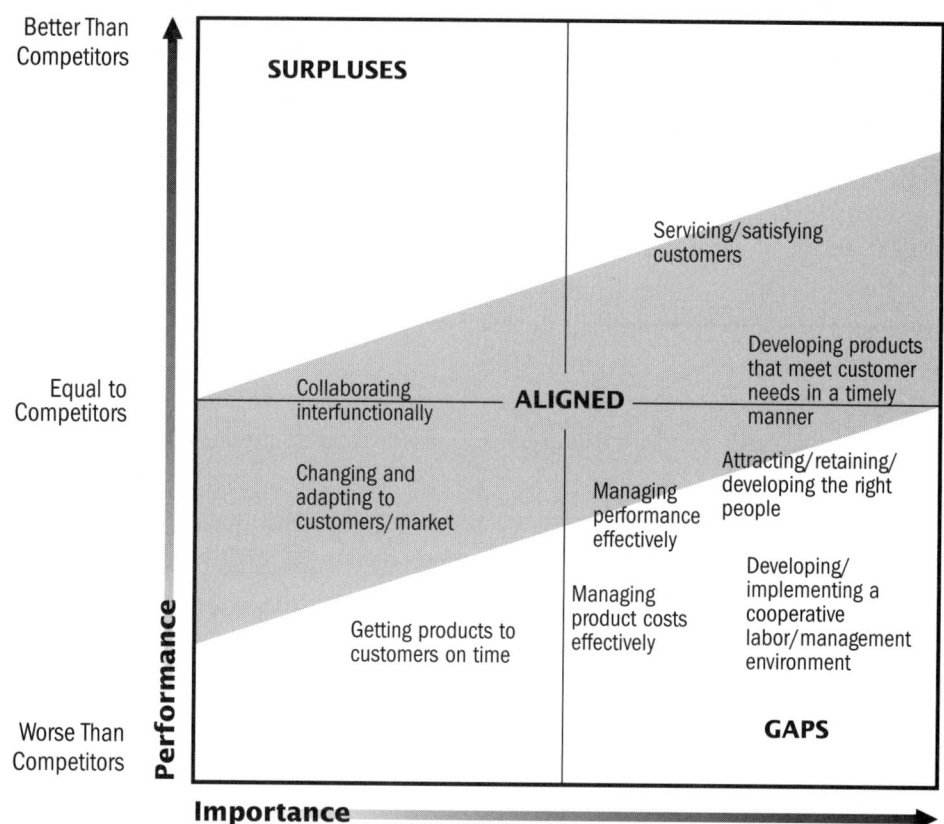

a) **Needed to Play:** Capabilities that are required for the successful execution of the strategy, but that do not, in and of themselves, provide a source of sustained competitive advantage.

b) **Needed to Win:** Capabilities that not only are required for the successful execution of the strategy, but that also provide a source of sustained competitive advantage in the business.

Causes of Gap
- **People** (e.g., lack HR skills in developing strategic staffing models)
- **Culture** (e.g., react to current needs rather than plan for future)
- **Process** (e.g., no process to conduct effective workforce planning)
- **Structure** (e.g., no assignment of responsibility for strategic staffing)
- **Technology** (e.g., no systems to enable efficient workforce planning)

Source: Towers Perrin analysis.

Step Four: Use HR Building Blocks When Designing the Function in Detail

In M&A situations, the design team should focus on three types of HR activities—transactional, consultative, and strategic. These activities should be distributed across the major HR organization building blocks: corporate role, center of excellence, administrative shared services, and support for line operations. Each building block is summarized as follows:

Corporate role. In large organizations, corporate HR staff members often lead the development of organization-wide people strategies and policies to help ensure consistency across the organization. Corporate HR roles also include oversight of the HR function, particularly in such areas as budgeting and setting performance goals and in the following types of activities:
- Helping to set strategic priorities for people management
- Providing leadership and professional standards for the entire HR functional community
- Leading initiatives in HR program research, assessment, and integration
- Managing HR professional resource allocation and performance management systems

Center of excellence. For some HR functions, deep technical expertise is required. As an example, executive compensation requires an in-depth knowledge of executive pay, incentive plans, and stock options. Concentrating expertise in centers of excellence makes knowledge capital and best practices available to all operational units in a cost-effective manner. HR staff assigned to centers of excellence provide high-value expertise to line managers and to their HR partners in the field. It used to be that HR centers of excellence were typically located in corporate headquarters; however, enabled by technology, virtual centers of excellence are also becoming common.

Administrative shared services. Increasingly, HR services delivered directly to managers and employees are being deployed through shared service functions responsible for entire operating divisions or regional operations. Centralizing administrative services, such as updating employee information, processing terminations, and administering benefits, is a cost-effective way to run HR. Many leading-edge companies are moving these services to web-enabled, self-service systems that allow employees to change their own personal information and that give managers electronic access to all the necessary forms for processing new hires and promotions, enrolling employees in training, and conducting other HR transactions.

Support for line managers. HR staff work hand in hand with line managers to develop and implement people strategies. Specifically, they help line managers determine the capabilities required to support the business and then translate these needs into people programs such as attraction and retention of talent, development of future leaders, and creation of work environments that fully leverage the new company's human capabilities. In this HR/line management collaborative model, HR staff members are often called on to provide value-added expertise, coaching, advice, and execution support. They also serve as liaisons with their colleagues in HR centers of

Exhibit 7.5 Case Example: Support for Line Operators

Employee Service Center	Management Service Center
Key Responsibilities ■ Deliver low-cost, highly automated employee transaction and information processing ■ Deliver quick, responsive answers to employees' questions ■ Refer issues as needed to the most appropriate source for resolution	**Key Responsibilities** ■ Deliver quick, responsive answers to questions about people management issues from line management and field HR ■ Use diagnostic tools to help customers identify people management issues ■ Provide services to address critical people management issues ■ Refer issues as needed to the most appropriate source for resolution
IMPACT	**IMPACT**
■ Significant efficiency gains ■ Elimination of administrative work from field HR ■ Improved consistency ■ More focused customer service ■ Self-sufficiency for employees	■ Leveraging best practices ■ Enabling field HR to provide better support for key business issues ■ Significant efficiency gains ■ Self-sufficiency for line management

Source: Towers Perrin analysis.

excellence to design HR programs that meet local business needs (e.g., a sales incentive program for a business unit).

For example, *Exhibit 7.5* describes how a hospitality company addressed its need to reduce costs, keep key employees, and hire new talent by creating employee and management service centers.

Step Five: Build an Integrated HR Technology Solution

Today, technology drives HR service delivery. With enterprise-wide software and widely available intranet and Internet tools, HR can deliver customized services that support the distinct needs of a company's businesses. This step involves customizing HR services to meet the needs of each business segment in the company and motivating employees to go online to "buy" HR services directly. It is necessary to have a technology platform in common in order to create a web-based self-service offering that will be of value to employees and managers.

For employees. Personalized rewards information, matched to demographic profiles and analyzed to determine optimal investment profiles, provides employees with a useful financial planning service. Online job posting systems, combined with sophisticated competency assessment tools and online catalogs of internal and external training opportunities, provide a career planning service unique to each employee.

For managers. Online workforce demographics, internal climate survey data, and staffing information support a strategic staffing plan and help managers improve the organization's productivity. Online forms and applications speed manager-initiated HR transactions.

Global HR Transformation

Transforming the HR function is most difficult when companies are joining forces to create a new global enterprise. Even among companies that label themselves as "global," the HR function often is a collection of stand-alone HR functions serving the needs of individual countries and national employee groups. This country-specific focus does not work if employee databases cannot connect with one another or if a disparate set of HR practices fails to send clear and consistent messages to employees. More important, this decentralized approach to managing the HR function may lead to policies that meet local country needs but that are not aligned with the overall corporate strategy. By contrast, in a truly global company, people within the organization can go anywhere in the world and feel at home in the corporate culture.

Although many companies develop HR policies and programs that are ostensibly global in nature, they often are deployed through a disjointed regional and line-of-business operating model. Truly global organizations see no distinction between domestic and international people. This does not imply a lack of recognition of national differences but suggests that HR leadership in a global organization must possess a functional expertise that can be applied in situations requiring knowledge of international cultures and issues.

When redesigning the HR function in a global company, the process follows the same principles and approaches as for nonglobal companies.

Global HR Structure

Client/server technology, the Internet, and telecommunications create new possibilities for sharing information across borders. A truly global HR function can manage and analyze data for the entire workforce. For example, employees can access job opportunities in any part of their global employer's operations.

Although technology is used to create global HR functions—service centers, web-based self-service applications for managers and employees, and a single HR information system—certain types of HR work are best performed locally. Certainly, HR services in a global company must take into account national laws that may prohibit certain practices.

When redesigning HR to be a global function, two principles should guide the final design. First, corporate HR should focus on the entire organization. Second, regional and local HR should be responsible for services that touch individual employees. These principles are discussed in detail below.

The specific duties of corporate HR in a global model concern policies and practices that benefit the organization in its entirety, including the following:

- Support of key corporate business initiatives to ensure an approach that reinforces the unified culture of the new company
- Stewardship of an overall mission, vision, and set of values to drive consistent application of all core HR practices, regardless of location
- Delivery of executive services—including compensation, succession planning, and development—that focus on attracting and retaining senior talent
- Development and oversight of the implementation of a global mobility strategy, along with the administration of supporting programs that build a truly global workforce
- Stewardship of leadership development, including the design, implementation, and administration of programs for high-potential individuals; development of corporate recruiting initiatives for filling leadership positions worldwide
- Development and administration of policies and frameworks that foster a common approach to employee communications; development of messages that reinforce the desired corporate culture and work environment
- Design of the technology infrastructure and HR web strategy to help unify and enhance delivery of HR services
- Participation in and coordination of centers of excellence to provide high-quality expertise and consultation to line managers and to local HR practitioners in the field

Geographic (regional or local) deployment of HR expertise is best suited to the design and delivery of HR services that need to be "close to the employee." Generally speaking, those activities can be done most efficiently from a regional service center. A few examples include the following:

- Employee pay and benefit design and administration
- Management development programs
- Employee learning and development programs
- Performance management systems
- Processing functions (e.g., payroll)
- Sourcing functions (e.g., recruitment, advertising, vendor management)
- Compliance and legal functions

Some HR functions may need to be pushed down further into the organization—to the plant or office level—for example, functions that usually require face-to-face interaction with the employee or the manager such as employee relations support, interviewing support, labor relations and works council management, and data entry and other forms of technology support.

Implementing the New HR Organization

Implementation of the new company's HR organization focuses on the functions of HR units and the ways in which the work will be done. The implementation plan should result in the following documentation:

- A description of HR's relationships to other units, such as finance, legal, and line management, and the processes and services it will provide
- Profiles of the roles and responsibilities of each position in the HR unit
- Competency models for each HR position and a plan for developing competencies throughout the HR unit
- A list of ways to enable members of the integrated HR unit to work together effectively, including development of an understanding of cultural differences (meeting styles, communication processes, and decision-making accountabilities) that may influence behaviors
- Measurement tools for assessing progress throughout the implementation stage
- A communication plan that makes use of both written and face-to-face initiatives such as employee meetings, newsletters, web sites, and skip-level meetings (meetings with non-direct reports)
- A supporting HR technology plan that covers HR applications integration, enhancement, or replacement as well as the steps and time frames for building an optimal technology architecture and infrastructure

This implementation plan needs to address how employees will be informed about HR programs and services and how they can access them (e.g., toll-free number, web site, direct call). The plan should include ways for people to provide feedback on an ongoing basis (e.g., quick pulse surveys via the web, interviews, response cards).

Summary

Although building new HR programs and systems in the midst of the chaos and turmoil of the integration process is a herculean task, the payoff is the opportunity to create a new, improved, more effective HR function. Leveraging this opportunity—whether to enhance technology, upgrade the HR competencies and skill levels, position people strategy in a new light, or redefine the role of HR leaders—can lead to a re-energized and upgraded HR function. In many merged or combined companies, the resultant HR function assumes a new role as a business partner. A merger or acquisition gives HR an exceptional opportunity to think about what it needs to do to become a world-class HR organization. Fresh perspectives gained from the merger partner or acquired company can instill a more innovative approach to business issues. Letting go of the past and forging a new future will not only provide managers and employees with better HR services but also give the HR staff different challenges and career opportunities that will contribute to the success of the new company. ■

CHAPTER EIGHT

Planning the Integration of Rewards

Kenneth T. Ransby and John M. Burns

"The most important factor in a merger isn't numbers, it's people."

Herb Marchand
Vice President and CFO, Toshiba International Corp.

In the Towers Perrin/SHRM Foundation research, HR executives reported that two of the three efforts considered most critical to integration planning were designing programs to retain key talent and developing a total rewards strategy for the new entity. The respondents also noted that those activities required the highest level of HR involvement.

Sound planning for the integration of rewards programs can set the stage for a revitalized, successful enterprise; inadequate planning can produce cultural friction, increase costs, and impede productivity and growth. This chapter presents best practices for the integration of rewards programs that help avoid these pitfalls and thereby contribute to the success of a merger or acquisition.

A Total Rewards Perspective

In recent years, the human resource community has begun to take a broader perspective on rewards—a perspective that includes not only pay and benefits but also learning and development and the work environment (see *Exhibit 8.1*). In fact, learning and development and the work environment are now major elements in the effort to attract and retain the "right" talent.

Consequently, rewards planning in M&As should span the "four quadrants" of total rewards, as shown in *Exhibit 8.1*.

Establishing the Integration Strategy

If the limited integration model is used, the approach to total rewards is simple: retain the separate rewards arrangements, perhaps with a few minor exceptions. Under the dominant model, the acquirer's rewards programs are usually applied to the acquired company, although the time frame for implementation will vary. Under the best-of-both

Exhibit 8.1 Total Rewards Quadrant Chart

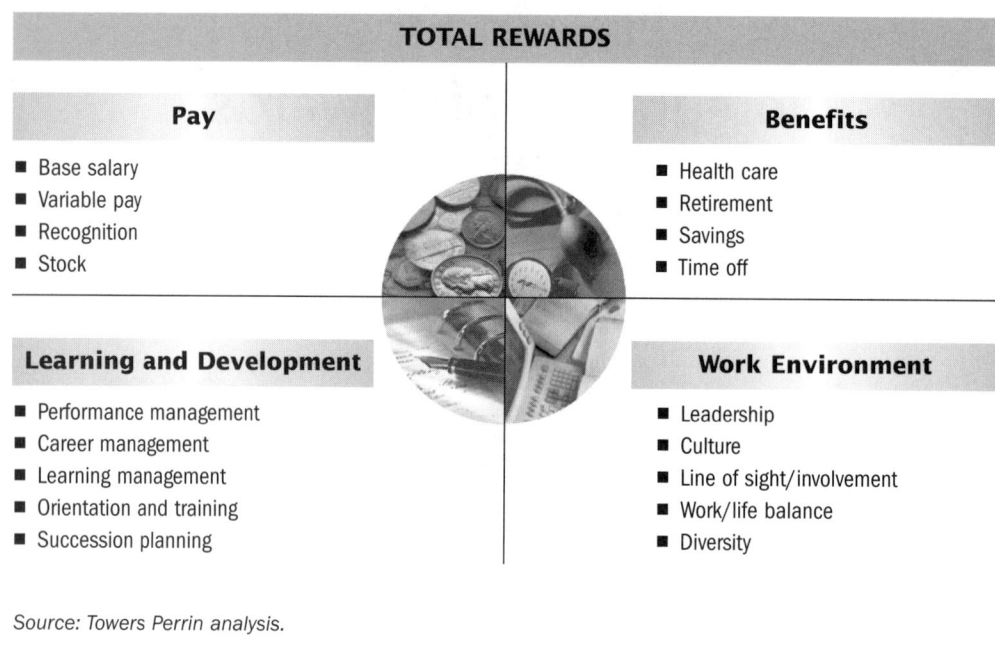

Source: Towers Perrin analysis.

and transformation models, a more strategic approach is required. In such cases, rewards programs must reflect the new company's business and people strategies. That means rethinking the total rewards strategy.

Total Rewards Framework

The total rewards framework incorporates the company perspective, the employee perspective, competitive factors, and internal realities, all of which are used in assessing important trade-offs. Applying this framework in M&A situations helps ensure the adoption of best practices, not simply the most expensive ones.

Exhibit 8.2 illustrates how the rewards strategy can balance the perspectives of the company and its employees by focusing on the "deal" or implicit employment contract. This is a key concept—that is, a deal must be mutually beneficial if employees are expected to act and behave in ways that consistently support desired business results.

- The company perspective flows from the strategic framework for the merger or acquisition as discussed in Section II. The new company's management needs to identify what it expects from employees and what it can afford to offer through total rewards.
- Depending on the time available, the employee perspective can be gleaned from focus groups, brief pulse surveys (or more comprehensive employee surveys, if possible), and interviews drawn from major demographic segments of the merging organizations. The resulting information can provide important insights into

Exhibit 8.2 A Balanced View—Integrated Framework

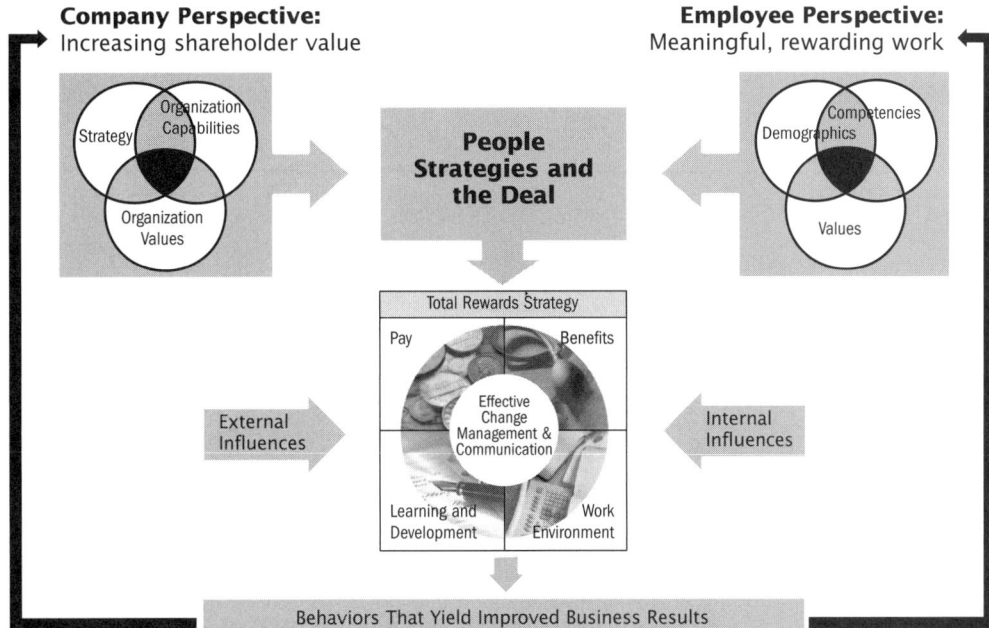

Source: Towers Perrin analysis.

employees' expectations about what they will be asked to contribute to the new company and what they will receive in return.

Employees as Assets—or Investors?

> "Employees are our greatest assets."
> —Anonymous CEO in annual report

You have probably read or heard this statement many times from senior executives. In his book *Human Capital: What It Is and Why People Invest It* (San Francisco: Jossey-Bass, 1999), Thomas O. Davenport argued that the worker-as-asset notion is passé. Employees no longer just want to make good wages. They know that they could work elsewhere, so they behave more like free-agent owners of investable capital.

Davenport wrote in his book that assets "are passive—bought, sold, and replaced at the whim of their owners. ... It is time to ... think of workers not as human capital but rather as human capital owners and investors." In short, modern high-skilled employees want to be well-rewarded for the time and energy that they could productively invest elsewhere. And the rewards for their investment extend well beyond cash and benefits to intangible elements that usually carry more weight than financial rewards in individual career decisions.

The "stickiest" work settings (the ones that people want to join and that they leave less frequently and more reluctantly) have an abundance of opportunity and empowerment. In her book *Evolve! Succeeding in the Digital Culture of Tomorrow* (Boston: Harvard Business School Press, 2001), Rosabeth Moss Kanter wrote, "Knowledge workers want to build their human capital—their individual package of skills and accomplishments—as much as their financial capital."

Exhibit 8.3 Case Example: Global Total Pay Strategy

Business Strategy	Total Pay Strategy	Supporting Plans
Customer Focus	Variety of pay vehicles designed to encourage employees to anticipate and respond to customer needs	Competency development tied to performance management, training and development, and base pay raises Focused short-term incentives and recognition program
Performance Achieved through: ■ Revenue growth ■ Market share ■ Product innovation ■ Cost control ■ Quality ■ Leadership	Pay linked to company's financial success—base pay at 50th percentile, total direct compensation at 66th percentile and higher for exceptional performance Bonus goals and measures tied to the six key corporate performance areas	Competency-based salaries, performance management, and training and development. Base pay levels and benefits tied to market. Incentives tied directly to results Different market comparison groups used for ■ Management ■ Exempt employees ■ Non-exempt employees ■ Technology workers
Building Engaged Workforce	Choices in benefits; ownership opportunities; all supported by extensive communications	Flexible benefits, including lifestyle benefits; profit sharing; financial planning education; stock purchase and stock option plans

Source: Towers Perrin analysis.

Total rewards strategy balances the needs and interests of the new company with those of its employees. There is an even more practical argument for total rewards in M&A. Just when the company is embarking on the integration planning exercise, competitors are very likely to be targeting its key employees. The new company's management must make the design and implementation of a strategic total rewards program a priority and must inform the employees of the two combining workforces about the program.

- External influences are both competitive and financial in nature: the new company's employment costs relative to those of competing companies and the competitiveness of rewards programs for key employee groups. Addressing such influences may be quite complicated, especially if one of the partners has a sig-

nificantly more generous total rewards program—what are the cost/benefit trade-offs associated with moving to a uniform approach?
- Internal influences are largely associated with the demographic characteristics of the combined employee population and the administrative capabilities of the new company. Both may be significantly affected if staff reductions are planned, and they will undoubtedly shift in the future as the new company grows.

Linkage with Business Strategy

The total rewards strategy should provide broad program design guidance that is consistent with the combined organization's key business strategies. A high-technology manufacturing company summarized its post-merger global "total pay" strategy as shown in *Exhibit 8.3*.

Fundamental to this strategy was the decision to make specific market comparisons with groups of peer companies relevant to major employee categories, including employees with special skills (e.g., technology workers). The global total rewards strategy was then used as a guide for developing country-by-country rewards programs consistent with local competitive practice, tax considerations, and legal/regulatory environments.

"Show Me the Money"

If an acquirer has assured the investment community that the deal it proposes will result in substantial reductions in the combined company's fixed costs of doing business, significantly revising the rewards programs may be necessary to achieve the promised synergies. In this instance, a holistic approach to a total rewards design can prevent the new company's management from investing in programs that won't really create value for the business. In addition, this approach may satisfy any contractual commitments that were made to protect compensation and benefit levels for employees of the target company without duplicating specific components of the target company's total rewards program.

Change Opportunity

A merger or acquisition provides an excellent opportunity for making fundamental changes in total rewards strategy and for sweeping away tired or expensive programs and practices. Moreover, most employees expect change during M&As, and the new company's management can use their receptivity to reinvigorate the employer-employee relationship via total rewards.

Nonetheless, time limitations may mean that at least during the first several months after the closing date, the company will change only what absolutely needs to be fixed, postponing detailed analysis of broader, more fundamental changes until later. But to take advantage of the readiness for change within the workforce, decisions on broader actions should not be deferred beyond a year or two. By then, the new company will have gone through one or two performance and pay reviews. The employees will have

Exhibit 8.4 Total Rewards Development Process

Phase I	Phase II	Phase III	Phase IV
Set Objectives	**Assess Rewards Programs**	**Develop Rewards Blueprint**	**Implement and Measure**
Establish clear, complete, and shared statement of strategic objectives	Evaluate performance of current rewards programs	Confirm current rewards programs or develop new rewards programs	Develop implementation programs and processes; measure results
■ Leadership research ■ Strategy clarification ■ Capability assessment ■ Change management strategy ■ Communication strategy ■ Reward objectives ■ Outcome measures	■ Change readiness assessment ■ Employee research ■ Competitive analysis ■ Gap analysis for component programs ■ Allocation assessment ■ Communication audit	■ High-level design ■ Cost and funding assessments ■ Change management and communication requirements ■ Initial implementation strategy	■ Detailed design ■ Detailed implementation plans ■ Continuous improvement and measurement ■ Administration

Source: Towers Perrin analysis.

become comfortable with the new status quo, and the window of opportunity for fundamental changes may close. Therefore, beginning with the integration planning stage, the new company's management should emphasize to employees that it will continue making adjustments to total rewards in order to align the component programs with the new company's business strategy.

The Total Rewards Development Process

A systematic process should be followed in designing and implementing total rewards programs. The recommended process for M&A comprises four distinct phases (see *Exhibit 8.4*).

This process is useful not only in the M&A context but also for ongoing program refinement. In fact, periodic reassessment of total rewards alignment is necessary whenever material changes are made to the new company's business strategy, its workforce management, or the environment in which it operates.

In many ways, the total rewards process resembles the M&A life cycle discussed in Chapter One. Phase I is similar to pre-deal target selection, Phase II to due diligence, Phase III to integration planning, and Phase IV to implementation.

Satisfying the Consumers

The new company's employees can be viewed as the "consumers" of its total rewards program. The new company's senior executives and other employees alike are keen to

Exhibit 8.5 Case Example: A Merger of Two Regional Energy Companies

In this 1999 merger, a thorough review of total rewards programs was undertaken during integration planning. Towers Perrin interviewed all members of the two senior management teams. These interviews provided excellent input for designing the new company's total rewards program, including the following:

- Clarity on the requirements for success of the new company, including the key organization capabilities needed in each major business segment
- The key elements of rewards that would foster a high-performance culture in the new company (e.g., *every* executive pointed to learning and development and the work environment)

The total rewards design team used this input, as well as employee opinions expressed during focus groups, in its design work. When the design for the new company's total rewards program was later submitted to the Compensation Committee for approval, the program objectives and its design were tied back to the input from employees and senior management gathered previously.

Source: Towers Perrin analysis.

---

learn how the rewards program will affect them as individuals. The attitudes of employees about the existing rewards structure and the likely impact of potential changes must, therefore, be understood and factored into the total rewards design process (see *Exhibit 8.5*).

Allocation of Reward Dollars

When two companies combine, their respective rewards programs need to be examined in relation to each other (and in relation to the key objectives of the new company). In what areas are they similar? Where—and to what extent—do they differ? One tool to help with this analysis is a total rewards allocation diagnostic (see example in *Exhibit 8.6*).

The allocations to base pay and the work environment are roughly the same for both companies in *Exhibit 8.6*. However, there are appreciable differences in pensions, variable pay, and learning. Company A allocates a significantly higher percentage of its total program to deferred rewards, which might be a negative factor in the recruitment and retention of younger workers. Such differences must be recognized when the rewards programs are redesigned for the combined organization.

It is also useful to make direct comparisons between total rewards for the combining organizations to the extent that the component elements of rewards programs can be readily quantified. *Exhibit 8.7* illustrates two examples of benchmarks that may be used.

Exhibit 8.6 Example: Analysis of Total Rewards Allocation

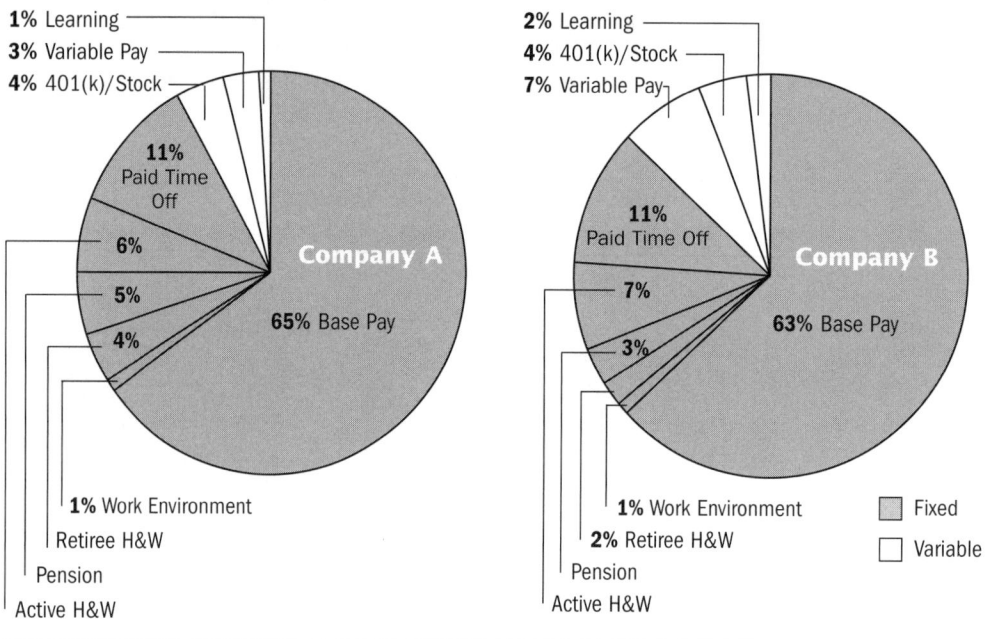

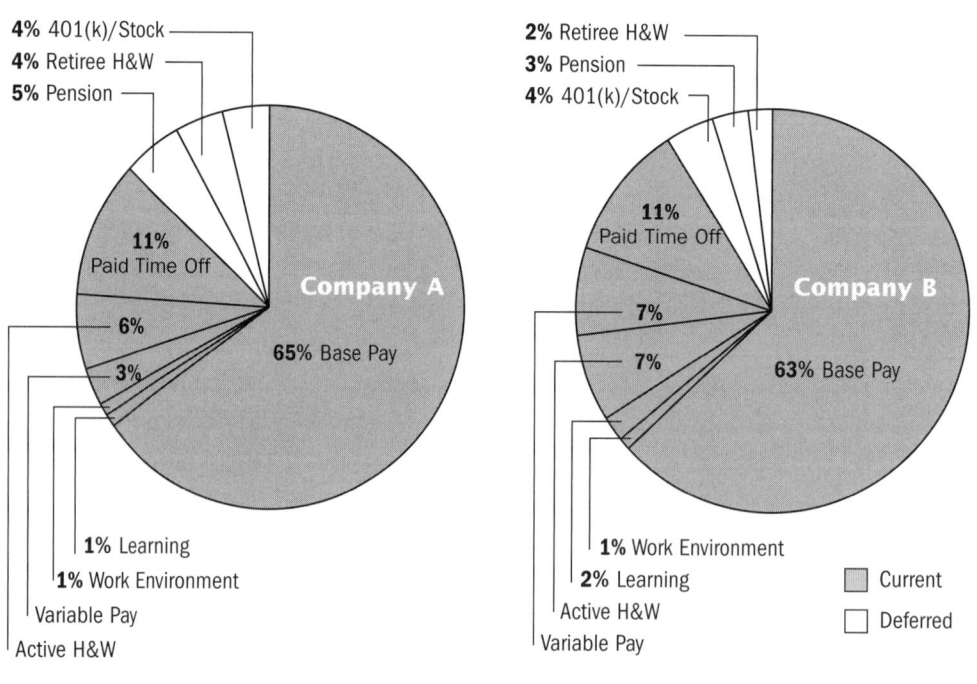

Source: Towers Perrin analysis.

Exhibit 8.7 Example: Use of Benchmark Comparisons for Total Rewards

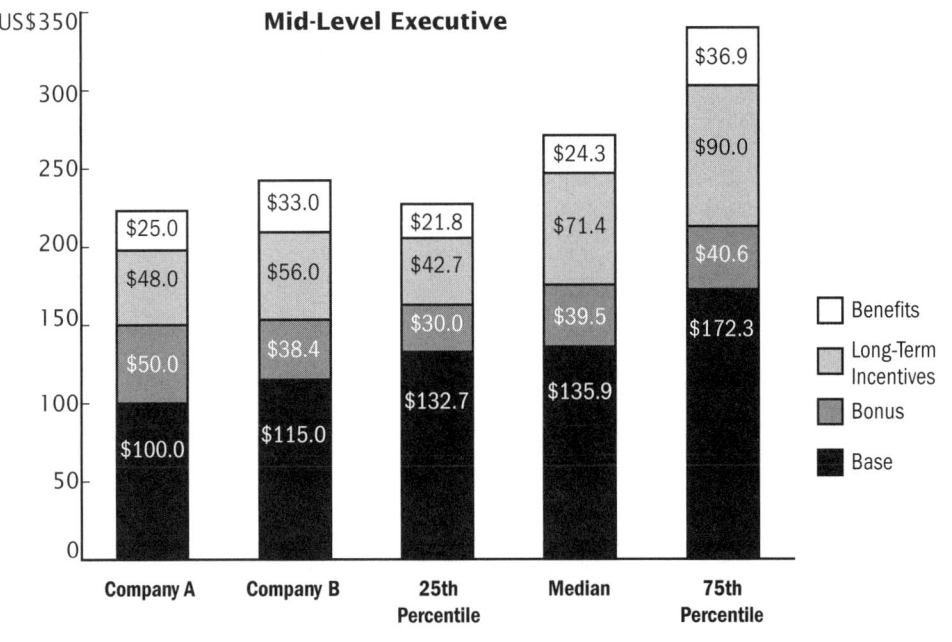
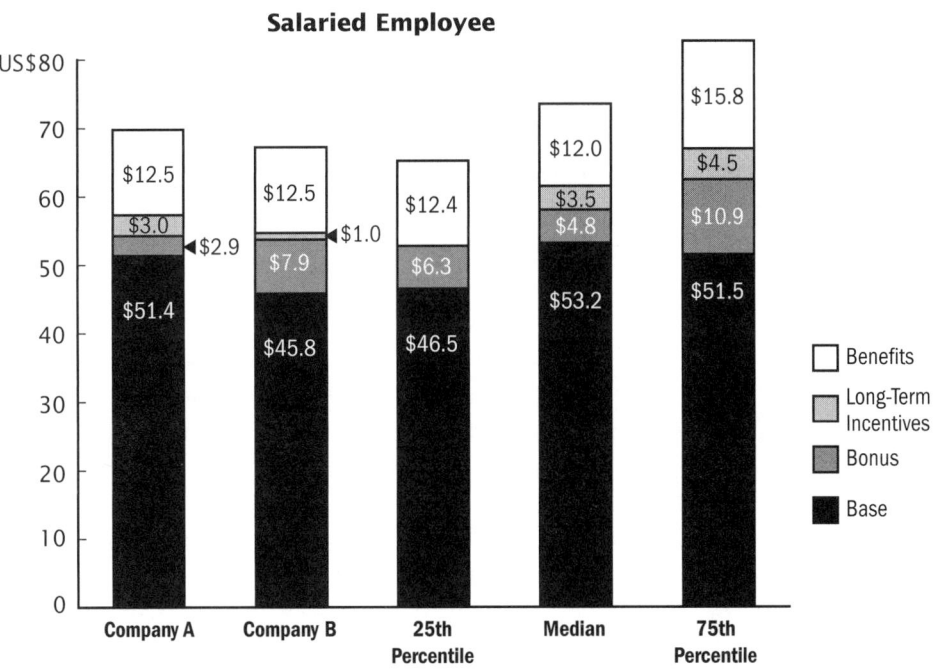

Note: All dollar figures in thousands.

Source: Towers Perrin analysis.

Planning the Integration of Rewards ■ 179

Exhibit 8.8 Case Example: Using a "Workout" to Plan the Integration Quickly

After a major merger within the hospitality industry, management had to move quickly to integrate the rewards programs of three large companies in a matter of weeks. More than 100,000 employees were involved, not only across the United States but also in many other countries around the world.

The total rewards strategy and the fundamental design of the main programs were developed in the course of a one-week, off-site "workout" session. Members of the workout team included the heads of human resources, directors of compensation and benefits, and Towers Perrin consultants having specialties in both rewards and change management.

The workout approach was successful for several reasons:
- In advance of the workout, leaders of the design team interviewed the CEO and other senior executives of the new organization. This provided a clear reading on the business strategy, financial objectives, and other requirements for future success.
- The design team had done its homework in advance of the workout, assembling side-by-side program comparisons, cost information, and employee data summaries.
- The workout agenda was structured in a manner to produce a thorough but expeditious review of the program.
- Above all, the team was committed to completing a large volume of work under a tight deadline.

Source: Towers Perrin analysis.

The Importance of Timing

The implementation timetable dictates how much total rewards analysis can be practically accomplished at this stage. To move quickly, some companies rely on existing analyses (if they are reasonably current) or use a streamlined analytical approach. For instance, the results of a recent employee survey may serve as a useful basis for analysis of worker needs and perceptions. A "serial acquirer" may also depend on a fast but insightful review of the target's rewards strategy; moving to the acquirer's programs is only a question of priorities and timing. In any event, it is always wise to establish the new company's total rewards strategy and high-level integration plan early so that subsequent detailed design and implementation can proceed as soon as practical (see *Exhibit 8.8*).

Program Issues: Pay

The integration of pay programs is a critical M&A step because these arrangements are fundamental to focusing employees on the business goals of the new organization. The integration process must also address internal equity issues to ensure that individuals with comparable roles receive comparable compensation.

Integration planners must determine whether the new company will move forward with the existing programs of one or both predecessor organizations or will need to develop new programs. Before deciding, the new company's management needs the right information (see *Exhibit 8.9*).

Exhibit 8.9 Inventory of Existing Pay Programs

As a first step, the new company's management must inventory the programs and policies of the combining organizations. This inventory should cover the following:

- Up-to-date job descriptions
- Types of jobs in each organization, including the matching of comparable jobs
- Methodologies used to slot employees into salary ranges, including the use of formal job evaluation processes
- Compensation philosophies and objectives (i.e., where each of the combining organizations seeks to position its compensation package vis-à-vis the competition)
- Salary structures, including the number of salary ranges used, and salary range minimums, maximums, and midpoints
- Salary administration guidelines, including the criteria used to move employees through a salary range
- Timing of salary increases and incentive award payments
- Types of incentive plans used, including target award levels, eligibility criteria, and frequency of payments
- Use of other cash compensation programs, such as retention bonuses, hot skills bonuses, premium pay, and ad hoc bonuses
- Policies regarding matters such as overtime pay eligibility and payment schedules
- Performance management systems used, including approaches for setting performance objectives, evaluating results, and linking pay and performance

Source: Towers Perrin analysis.

An analysis of existing pay programs should address the following two fundamental questions:

- How do the programs of the merging organizations compare with one another?
- How well do these programs align with the strategic direction and business needs of the new company? (Neither of the current pay programs may be well aligned with the new business strategy.)

Integration planning becomes particularly complex when there are significant differences in the ways the combining organizations have traditionally managed their pay programs. This complexity can increase even more if one company provides appreciably higher pay levels for comparable positions than the other or includes a wider range of positions in its incentive programs.

If pay differences are acute, the new company needs to proceed with caution: Simply adopting the "richest" programs could unnecessarily drive up future costs of doing business. Conversely, adopting a "leaner" approach to compensation could put the new company at risk of losing key talent or facing litigation from employees who believe their implicit employment contract has been breached.

To have an appropriate framework for managing pay, the new company should establish written objectives that articulate where it intends to position the various elements of pay (e.g., base pay, target bonus percentages, total cash) as opposed to its competitors. These objectives also define the types of performance, results, or behaviors that the elements of pay should reward.

Exhibit 8.10 Case Example: Joint Venture of Manufacturing Companies

A manufacturing company entered into a joint venture with another company to expand its production capabilities. As part of the joint venture, the manufacturer integrated a division of the second company with its own operations.

During the integration planning process, the manufacturer reviewed the existing pay programs. This review included the following:

- Competitive market analyses to assess the competitiveness of the existing base pay structure, incentive plans, and benefit programs
- Internal research, including leadership interviews, focus groups, and an employee total rewards survey to obtain opinions about the existing programs and needs for the future
- Auditing the current pay program designs to assess strengths and weaknesses, considering both the joint venture's business strategy and "best practices"

By using the research findings, the joint venture's leaders designed a pay program that addressed its emerging business needs. As compared with current practice, it adopted a streamlined base pay structure that had fewer, broader pay grades, and a new bonus plan that incorporated business performance measures aligned with the goals of the joint venture.

Source: Towers Perrin analysis.

Once pay objectives are established, the new company can begin to outline a specific plan design. HR professionals must address the methodology for assigning employees to salary ranges, the new base pay structure, the new incentive plan design, and the other types of cash programs. The analysis should also identify which employees gain or lose ground relative to their current pay under different design scenarios.

Integration planning should also address communication issues associated with introduction of the new programs, as well as a transition strategy for dealing with individuals who are put at a disadvantage by the changes. From a communication perspective, employees must understand what is expected of them in the new company and how their contributions will be evaluated and rewarded in the future (see *Exhibit 8.10*).

Program Issues: Health and Welfare

Benefit Design

In the United States, employer-provided health and welfare benefits typically include the following: health care benefits (e.g., medical, dental, vision, and employee assistance programs), income protection plans (e.g., life insurance, accidental death and dismemberment insurance, and short- and long-term disability), and paid time-off plans (e.g., vacation, holiday, personal time). Integration planning should address these and other programs such as adoption assistance, tuition reimbursement, spending accounts, and a growing array of employee-paid voluntary benefits.

Exhibit 8.11 Typical Benefits Objectives: High-Performance Companies

- Benefits are necessary, but not distinguishing, elements of total rewards in the attraction and retention of talent. Other rewards should create competitive advantage.
- Benefit programs should appeal to the preferences of employees who are critical to the company's success.
- Benefit programs may vary across operating companies only where such differences are proven to be necessary to attract and retain key employee groups, or where the corporate program should be cut back for cost competitiveness within a particular industry.
- Overall benefit program values should be at or below competitive medians. Other rewards should be above median to differentiate the company in the marketplace.
- Benefits should be financially equitable for employees in similar jobs.
- Benefit programs should reinforce shared responsibility between the company and its employees.
- Benefit programs should support workforce diversity and help employees meet their work/life needs.
- Benefit program design and communication should foster understanding of the programs and how they support business and personal objectives.

Source: Towers Perrin analysis.

As with other M&A issues, the underlying philosophy of the merger or acquisition should drive the approach to benefit integration. For example, in a dominant model, the usual strategy is to absorb the acquired employee population into the acquirer's plans. For other models, the merger or acquisition presents an ideal opportunity to revisit the overall benefit strategy to ensure that the new company's program will meet both employer and employee needs and will be structured as cost-effectively as possible.

The benefit objectives should be driven by the total rewards strategy and provide clear criteria for plan design. Some of the objectives often found in high-performance companies are shown in *Exhibit 8.11*.

Manager and employee input is essential for improving program effectiveness or perceived value. With this input, HR may decide to conduct a thorough evaluation of all current programs—including designs, costs, liabilities, vendors, administrative arrangements, and communication effectiveness. In addition, HR should benchmark the current programs against competitive norms or best practices.

There can be great disparity between health and welfare plans, particularly among companies in the United States. Similar companies often place different emphasis on the various components of these plans, thereby affecting both the relative value and the cost of the programs. *Exhibit 8.12* illustrates a cost comparison of the health and welfare plans of four organizations in related industries that merged. It underscores the importance of analyzing the value of the plans in total rather than on an individual component basis.

In the best-of-both or transformation models, selecting the best elements in each plan is tempting because it ensures that no employee ends up at a disadvantage. However, the total benefit package must be kept in mind to ensure that coverage and

Exhibit 8.12 Example: Analysis of Health and Welfare Benefit Costs

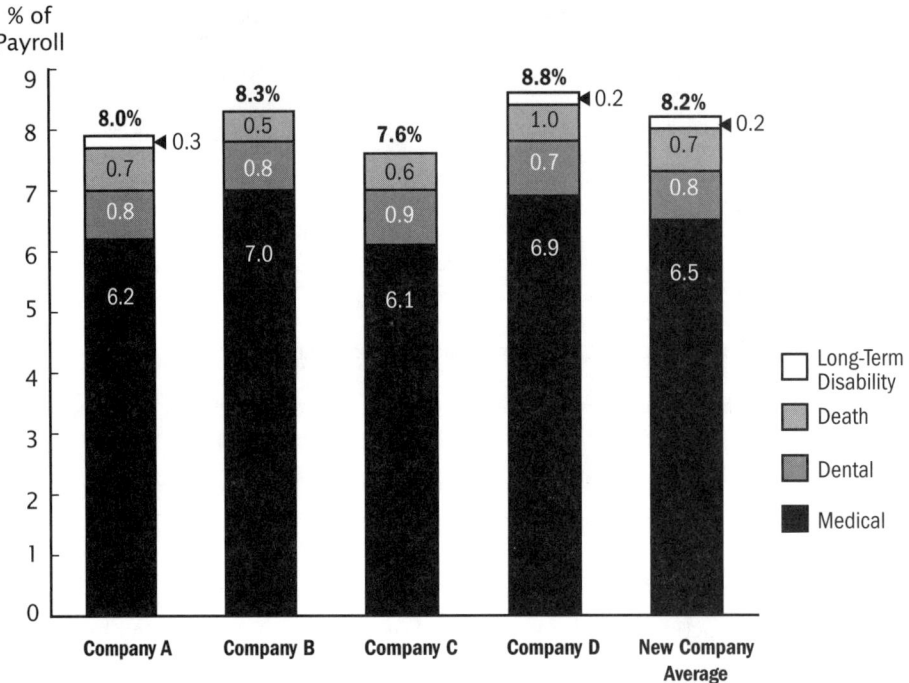

Source: Towers Perrin analysis.

costs are in line with the total rewards strategy, the specific health and welfare plan objectives, and the terms of the sale/purchase arrangement.

Some types of coverage are provided under different parts of a benefit program in different countries (e.g., disability is often provided under retirement plans in Europe). Consequently, the benefits integration strategy for a global M&A should reflect desired cost-sharing arrangements and tax efficiencies that are appropriate for each country.

A merger or acquisition provides an excellent opportunity to address contemporary health care issues and update the design and delivery of the new company's rewards programs. Some of the major health care issues employers are now examining include

- the role of technology in educating health care consumers, facilitating employee decision-making, and improving benefit administration;
- health care cost-management initiatives that address the characteristics of the specific employee population;
- integrated disability and absence management programs to control costs and enhance productivity;
- enhanced employee choice to respond to the diverse needs of today's workforce; and
- revamped communications to emphasize the total rewards philosophy.

Funding Considerations

The financial advantages of consolidating the two companies' plans are compelling unless the acquired company is very large, is in a different business, or has a very different cost structure. Cost savings can be captured even if the new company retains previous benefit or employee contribution levels.

The manner in which the new company funds its welfare plans—including the use of self-funding, stop-loss insurance, and fully insured arrangements—is key to the integration planning process. Given the larger employee base of the combined organization, it is often advisable for the organization to assume a greater degree of risk, thereby lowering insurance costs. Opportunities for cost reduction may also be possible with certain benefit programs through the use of multinational financial pooling techniques. These techniques can not only generate savings on the order of 20 percent of premiums paid for offshore coverage but also increase underwriting flexibility on a global basis.

If the acquired company participates in the plan of a larger parent, it is important to determine the impact of the purchase on the acquiring company. The actual health and welfare costs for the acquired company may be significantly more, or less, than the average costs previously assessed by the acquired company's former parent.

Administration

It is never too early in the integration planning stage to develop a strategy for benefit administration. To that end, the new company should do the following:

1. Assess the current administration and technological environment of both organizations. This step, which is critical in determining a strategic direction for the new organization, allows management to highlight differences between organizations, benchmark the current environment against common and best practice models, and identify areas for improvement.
2. Evaluate interim versus long-term solutions. There may be significant opportunities for making benefit administration more efficient and cost-effective. The integration process may be the perfect opportunity to assess various alternatives, such as outsourcing some or all administrative functions, improving the value of existing systems, or implementing customized HR intranets and web portals. In evaluating alternatives, potential efficiencies and cost savings need to be weighed against the time and expense associated with undertaking the analysis and the related conversion. Given time constraints, the organization may need to identify interim solutions such as maintaining separate systems or converting all populations to an existing system.
3. Consider using a specialty call center during the transition period. Given the amount of change and the uncertainties involved in integration, HR can expect to be inundated with questions from current employees and retirees. Call centers (either internal or external) can be very helpful in answering many straightforward questions such as, "How do I enroll in my benefits?" or "What physicians are in the managed care network?"

4. Identify employee populations that will lose access to administrative services. For example, a company with a decentralized approach to benefit administration may purchase a division of a company with a centralized approach, thereby eliminating access to HR administration for the employees of the acquired division. Bringing these issues to the surface as soon as possible gives the new company time to establish the appropriate HR administrative solutions for these populations.
5. Keep in mind the administrative needs of other populations in rolling out new programs. Because active employees are typically the largest and most influential group affected by a merger or acquisition, employers tend to focus on the enrollment of the active population before dealing with inactive populations. The effort necessary for enrolling and administering benefit programs for the inactive population, including retirees, disabled employees, and COBRA (Consolidated Omnibus Budget Reconciliation Act) beneficiaries, is often underestimated. It is prudent to anticipate the needs and heightened level of support that are often required by the inactive population and plan accordingly.

Communication Strategy

Communication of the new company's benefit program is often the first visible indication of the merger's impact on employees. By their nature, benefits represent security and protection. During a merger or acquisition, employees lose that sense of security, and, as a result, communication about the benefit package speaks volumes about the kind of employee-employer relationship that can be expected from the new company. The following are tips for effective communication about benefits during a merger or acquisition:

- Announce a high-level benefit overview as soon as possible. Communicating information about the program early in the process will provide less opportunity for employees to speculate about changes.
- Focus on employee education, providing as much detail as possible about program components, design, vendors, and costs. Employees need to have access to accurate, detailed information that will help them evaluate and select the plan options that best meet their personal needs. In addition to employer communication materials, vendor capabilities—such as web sites, brochures, and customer service representatives—can provide useful information to employees.
- Address the distinct information needs of different constituencies or audiences. For example, a disabled population may not have the same benefit options or access to information as the active population and may need to have the content and delivery of communication materials altered to fit its needs.
- Emphasize the total rewards package. Because there may be many new or modified features in individual plan components, the communication strategy should call attention to the value of the total package.

Exhibit 8.13 Case Example: Communication Plays Key Role in Bank Merger

> The merger of two major banks demanded the design and communication of a benefit plan that was aligned with the new total rewards philosophy. The communication of the new plan to 100,000 employees was a critical event because it marked the first major internal communication since the merger was announced. Messages about benefit changes, the necessity for new-plan enrollment, and the specifics of how to access provider information were needed for the large and diverse employee population.
>
> A one-day "workout" session was used to develop the communication plan. During this meeting of senior human resource leaders of the two banks, the "merger of equals" philosophy was discussed, as were other objectives such as the need to aggressively manage the total costs of the benefit programs. There were many cultural differences between the two organizations, and their respective benefit programs were also dramatically different.
>
> During the workout session, the senior team identified key audiences, the managers who would need to be involved in the communication process, the media that would be most effective in reaching this diverse population, and the theme for the campaign.
>
> The detailed communication plan identified the need for special messages to explain the rationale for the changes, the health care cost environment, and what the bank would do to assist employees through the transition. Media for the campaign included posters, post cards, articles posted on the intranet, an enrollment book, a newsletter for managers, new-hire and recruitment materials, benefit comparison charts, an interactive voice-response system, and call centers for answering questions and sending provider information.
>
> The result? Over a two-week period, 100,000 employees were successfully re-enrolled in the new plan.

Source: Towers Perrin analysis.

- Allow sufficient time and budget. In establishing a strategy that addresses the language and cultural challenges across global operations, it is easy to underestimate the effort and expense required to communicate effectively (see *Exhibit 8.13*).

Program Issues: Retirement

By their very nature, retirement plans involve long-term rewards for employees and obligations for employers. Accordingly, dealing with retirement plan issues requires special insight and planning by the integration team.

Benefit Design

Under the dominant model, the integration strategy is usually straightforward: consolidate the benefits under the acquirer's plan. However, some acquirers adopt the acquired company's plan if it is more in line with the acquirer's emerging total rewards strategy. In the best-of-both and transformation models, the total rewards strategy process should again be the reference for guiding plan modifications in terms of

- retirement plan goals (e.g., continue a reasonable level of employment income in retirement, encourage savings for retirement, promote ownership in the company) and
- design criteria (e.g., retirement benefit objectives, market competitiveness, company cost objectives, employee cost sharing, integration with government and statutory plans, and communication objectives).

In recent years, many high-tech and dot-com companies (and some large employers such as Citicorp) have shifted to equity-based rewards for retirement. These companies may have only modest retirement programs—or none at all—because they provide significant wealth accumulation opportunities via broad-based stock option plans. Differences between these and traditional retirement programs—either defined benefit (DB) or defined contribution (DC)—go to the heart of the employment "deal," and they must be resolved in terms of the total rewards strategy and retirement plan objectives for the new company.

As a starting point, the design team should examine projected retirement benefits for benchmark employee profiles, for both companies and for a comparable competitor group. *Exhibit 8.14* illustrates comparisons of retirement benefit replacement ratios for two benchmark profiles.

After examining a few of these benchmark profiles, the design team will start to see who will be the winners and the losers in any benefit redesign. It is important, however, to move beyond a simple analysis of retirement programs by income group: Impact at different ages must be studied, particularly if a change from a DB plan to a DC (or cash balance) plan is being considered. *Exhibit 8.15* (page 190) illustrates the different patterns of accrual of value for a DB plan versus an equivalent cash balance plan.

This graph underscores the different accruals by age under the two plans. Note also the sharp increase in value for the DB plan at age 50. This is because the DB plan illustrated has a large early-retirement subsidy that commences at that age. These types of comparisons help to clarify whether transition guarantees (or "grandfather" allowances) should be made and how to communicate plan changes.

Another issue concerns the handling of past service credits. If two DB pension plans are being merged, the formulas for past service are typically left unaltered (for cost reasons), unless the formulas are so similar that any additional cost incurred in moving to the more expensive plan is more than offset by corresponding administration or communication cost savings. If the move is from a DB plan to a DC plan, the following issues will need to be addressed:

- Leaving accrued benefits in place instead of converting them to present values that are transferred to the DC plan
- Determining the interest rate for calculating the present values of accrued benefits
- Choosing the method of valuing special early-retirement subsidies

Exhibit 8.14 Example: Petroleum Industry Comparison of "Replacement Ratios" for Retirement Benefits

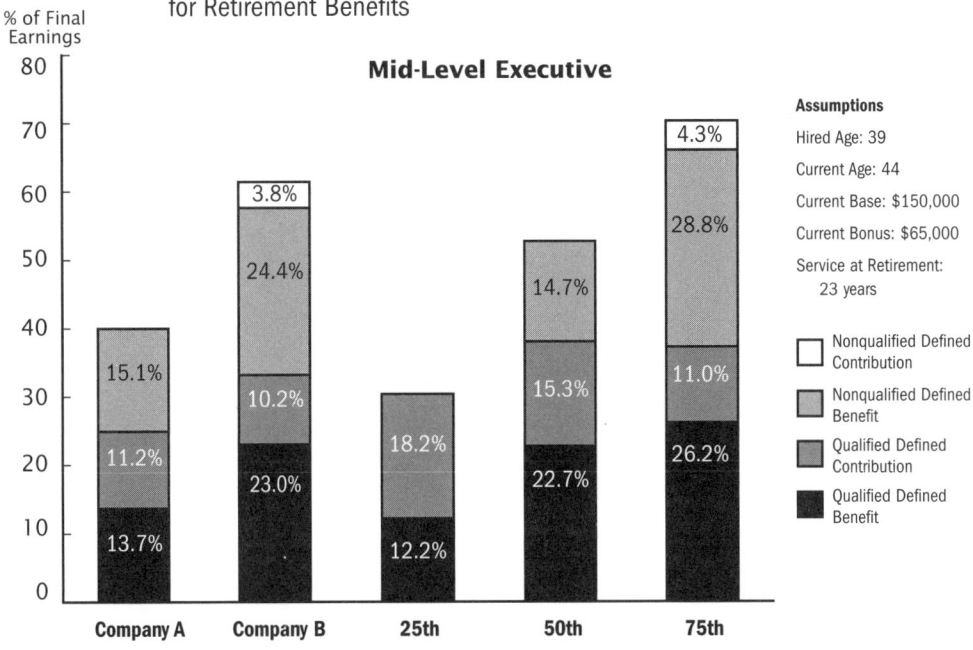

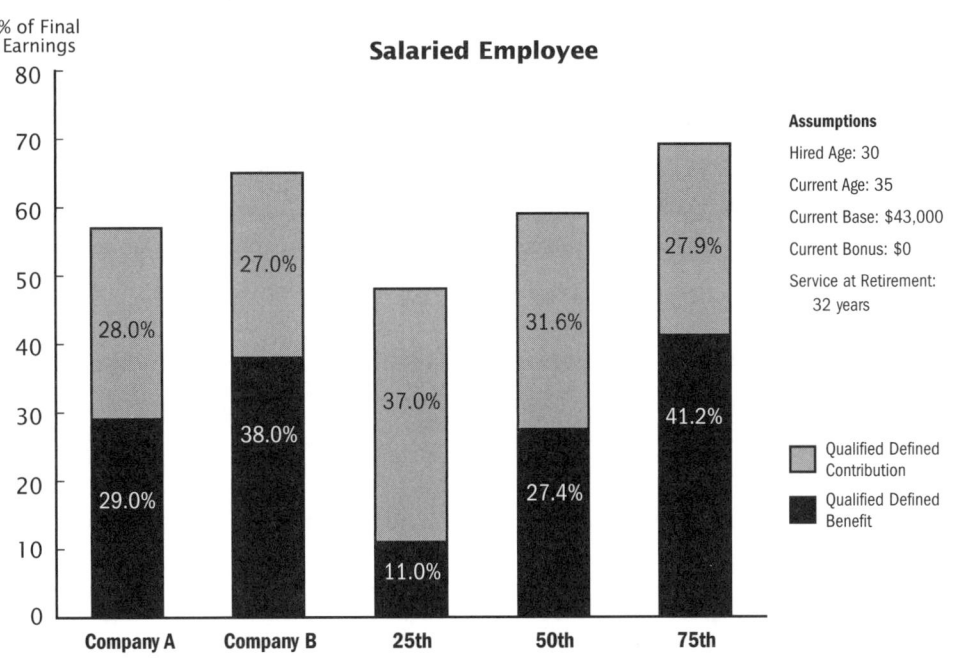

Source: Towers Perrin analysis.

Exhibit 8.15 Example: Defined Benefit Versus Cash Balance Retirement Plan

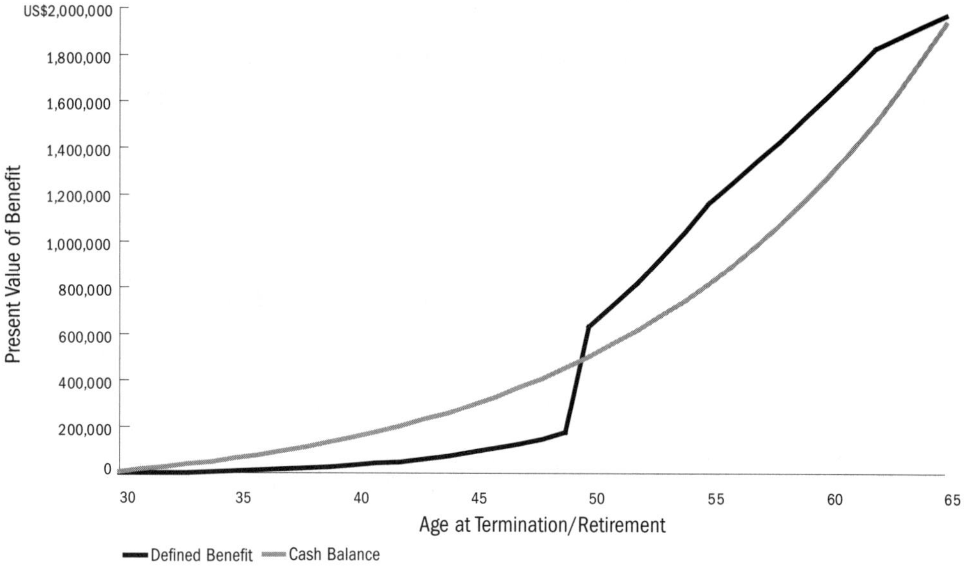

Source: Towers Perrin analysis.

Any of these issues can have a major impact on employee attitudes and on the plan's cost to the new company.

Although thorough planning is essential, it is also important to identify "quick hits" that may be possible as a result of the merger or acquisition. For example, depending on applicable pension law, it may be possible to achieve significant gains by merging an overfunded DB plan with an underfunded one. Typically, this can be done immediately after the closing date of the merger or acquisition. It does not require a change in the benefit plan design, and it reduces the overall cash-flow requirements for the new company.

In DC plans, the structure of employee-employer cost-sharing arrangements is critical. Defined contribution plans can be expensive, but they are also an opportunity to strengthen the link between employee performance, the performance of the business, and employee rewards. Decisions about the matching contributions by the employer and how to link these contributions to the success of the combined business should be based on a well-defined total rewards strategy.

In retiree life and medical plans, deciding what to offer employees depends on whether the new company will continue to provide an existing plan. If not, the existing plan generally is restricted to those who are currently retired or are eligible to retire. Other active employees are transferred to the new company's plan, which may be more modest or offered in the form of a service-related lump sum on retirement.

Funding and Investment Considerations

In combining either DB or DC plans, companies often renegotiate service provider contracts to achieve significant cost savings. This may also be an opportune time to assess the level of service and recalibrate investment performance measures for the new company's retirement plan.

There may be significant philosophical differences between the two companies regarding the investment of funds in DC plans. For example, one may be directing employer (and even employee) contributions to purchase company stock, whereas the other may be using external market funds exclusively. Such differences are fundamental and should be resolved in terms of the total rewards strategy and retirement plan objectives for the combined company.

Administration

In a large merger or acquisition, either company may have superior administrative processes that could generate significant cost savings or performance improvement if applied to the other company. Nevertheless, the administrative requirements for the new company's plans should be explored, along with the extent to which present facilities and systems can fulfill these requirements. If a gap surfaces between these requirements and the new company's administrative capabilities, outsourcing to a third-party administrator may be appropriate.

Communication Strategy

If significant amendments are made to employee retirement plans, management must develop a strategy to inform participants about the planned changes and their potential impact. Because of the long-term nature of retirement plans, employees may wish to adjust their other savings and capital accumulation arrangements to compensate for the impact of retirement plan changes. In addition, employees may be asked to direct their investments to new vehicles and make new levels of contributions to plans. In many mergers over the past decade, defined benefit plans have been replaced with defined contribution plans. From the employee's perspective, such a change prompts numerous questions that require sophisticated communications, including the following:

- What happens to my accrued pension?
- What impact will this change have on my retirement security?
- What should I contribute to the new program, and what are my investment options?

Program Issues: Performance Management

Reviewing the performance management (PM) system in a merger or acquisition provides an outstanding opportunity to reinvigorate the organization. PM systems should promote the best talent and communicate what the new company will expect from its employees. A well-designed PM system can align employee actions and behaviors with the vision and strategy of the new company and significantly increase operating and financial performance.

Performance Management Goals

Before a PM system is developed, the leaders of the new company need to establish the design framework for the system. For example, how do they want the system to drive the achievement of strategic goals? What is the employment "deal" and how is this reflected in the system? How should the new company's external and internal brand image align with the new PM system? And most important, how aggressively should the new company pursue the building of a high-performance culture? The PM system can reinforce a new culture by clearly articulating which employee contributions and behaviors will be valued.

Asking the following questions can help test the urgency for and organizational receptivity to performance management:

- Is the new company willing to terminate weak performers? (For example, will the new company implement an A, B, C employee-rating process, where "C players" are put on probation and then dismissed if they do not become "B players"?)
- Does the new company want to reshape its image as a higher-performance workplace?
- How closely will performance be linked to pay and promotion?

Also, consider the impact of the new company's PM system on culture. In some cases, the PM system will be a radical change. Management should anticipate and be prepared to address employees' anxiety about the new system.

Defining Performance in the New Organization

Traditionally, companies have evaluated individual performance against broad performance factors such as quality of work or productivity. In today's more sophisticated organizations, performance is measured both by what employees accomplish (i.e., results) and by how they accomplish it (i.e., competencies).

When measurement is tied to performance outcomes (the "what"), integration planners should determine how the outcomes will be measured. Key issues to be addressed include the following:

- Will the kinds of results differ by job category or role (e.g., exempt versus nonexempt employees)?
- Will the results measured be team-based or individual-based?
- Will individual performance goals be linked to the business strategy?

Companies that clearly define individual competencies (knowledge, skills, behaviors, and attributes—the "how") that are needed to deliver on organization capabilities and to integrate them into the PM system are taking a key step in communicating and building a new corporate culture. Important issues that will have to be addressed include the following:

- Does each of the merging companies have a competency model? If yes, should they be integrated or should a new model be developed?
- In what other ways are the new company's values being communicated to employees? Are the messages consistent?

If the new company's PM system is to influence pay decisions, this fact must be communicated to employees. Even more important, the company's managers must follow through on that policy. Any variation (such as use of manager discretion to determine pay) also must be clearly communicated.

Program Issues: Learning and Career Management

A thoughtful approach to the design of ongoing learning and career management programs can have an important impact on successful integration.

First, communicating the new company's strong commitment to learning and people development is a powerful retention factor during the integration planning period and beyond. Second, the opportunities created by web technology may help reduce costs and improve the access to and functionality of learning programs (see Chapter Nine). Finally, a performance-based culture is reinforced if managers and employees are engaged in all aspects of learning and development to ensure the success of implementation. Such a culture may include offering training for new skills, behaviors, and knowledge; communicating career opportunities in the new company; clarifying performance expectations; and encouraging behavior that is aligned with the new company's intended culture.

Learning and development questions to consider during the integration planning stage include the following:

- What are the current best practices of each organization? For example, one acquirer selected the acquired company's rotational assignment approach for developing sales managers because it was clearly superior to its own program.
- What is the new company's vision for how learning occurs? For example, many companies are reducing high travel costs associated with traditional classroom-based training by moving to web-based and videoconferencing platforms.
- What messages does the new company's management want to convey about the role of learning and development—now and in the future? Some of the possible messages are that it (1) builds strong, versatile leaders, (2) builds organization capabilities, (3) improves organizational performance, or (4) improves retention of key and "hot skill" employees.

The HR function can positively influence employee attitudes about learning and development in the new company as it designs and delivers training that supports the integration teams. In doing so, the HR function is also seen as an instrument of change in the organization—a critical role for HR to play if it is going to be a true partner to the business units.

HR integration planners should consider the following questions when determining how to use learning and development to stimulate higher levels of performance:

- What learning and development programs will build and reinforce the employee competencies that are required for the new company to succeed?
- How should these programs be designed to deliver the best results at the lowest practical cost?
- What roles will HR, senior business leaders, business unit and functional managers, and employees play in executing the learning and development strategy?
- How should other HR systems (e.g., salary structures) be modified to dovetail with the new approach to learning and development?

As the new organization brings together two companies with unique structures and career paths, it also needs to plan how career opportunities will change in the future. Communicating new opportunities can be very effective in retaining employees who are looking for a new challenge.

Program Issues: Work/Life

Employee research consistently shows that work/life programs are highly valued components in the total rewards package. A wide range of corporate initiatives fall under the work/life umbrella, including flexible work arrangements, flexible work hours, and numerous programs designed to help employees manage their time, address family responsibilities, and cope effectively with stress.

Work/life programs contribute measurably to business performance and support the achievement of business goals by helping employees maintain a better balance between their work accountabilities and their personal obligations—thus enabling them to be more focused and productive on the job.

To determine which types of programs can best contribute to business performance, the new company's integration planners should address the following types of questions:

- What are the demographics of the combined employee population, and what does each employee segment value in a work/life program?
- What kinds of programs did the organizations offer before the merger and how did employees receive them?
- What challenges will employees face in working at the new company (e.g., long hours during the integration process)? What types of work/life programs will help employees cope with these challenges?
- What challenges will the new company face in recruiting and retaining talent? To what extent can work/life programs help management position the new company as an employer of choice for both prospective and current employees?

Selecting the most appropriate work/life programs is a complex task. Research that provides an objective understanding of employee needs helps planners develop work/life programs that are meaningful to the greatest number of employees. For example, is support for child care a priority issue? What about elder care? Do employees want more flexible work hours or would they prefer to work from home a few days per week? Would employees value a concierge service to assist with extra chores? Would an on-site massage therapist be a plus?

Work/life programs are especially beneficial for employees with family-related responsibilities or for employees engaged in high-stress jobs. Programs that can help employees better manage their time and well-being can go a long way toward building a work environment that fosters both high performance and employee commitment to the new company's vision and values, strategies, and goals.

Program Issues: Executive Compensation

Executive compensation plans are important to the success of the business, and this is particularly evident during the integration process. Because such plans—see Appendix D for a detailed discussion of change-in-control (CIC) and incentive compensation arrangements—influence management behaviors, they must be designed with great care to avoid unintended adverse consequences. Moreover, because of the importance of CIC contracts, retention plans, and other key executive compensation issues, both integration planning and implementation tasks for these executive compensation arrangements should take place soon after the deal is struck, if not before.

The following executive compensation issues can have a profound influence on M&A success and must be addressed early in the integration planning stage:

- How will the new company retain the senior and mid-level executives it needs to prosper in the long run? Today, most public companies (and a growing number of privately held companies) use CIC agreements to protect key management during a merger or acquisition. If properly designed and executed, a CIC plan gives management the economic security to objectively evaluate a potential M&A transaction with the best interests of shareholders in mind. Most large public companies adopt comprehensive CIC plans well in advance of initiating M&A activity, although some wait until M&A discussions are under way or nearing closure. Regardless of the timing, CIC arrangements can be designed to offer management a reasonable degree of security and help the acquirer retain key executives to manage the new company.
- What are the costs of top management terminations, and how can the company cut redundant management positions? As early as the due diligence stage, acquiring companies analyze the costs associated with the possible termination of executives during the integration process. The costs of such terminations, in the form of CIC and severance compensation, are often 2 to 3 percent of the price paid to complete a deal. If they are factored into the economic calculus of the costs for transition early, they should not be a cause for concern later.
- How should stock options be settled, and can they be converted into the stock options of the new company? In most stock option plans, options are immediately vested upon a change in control of the company. If such a provision is not included in the supporting plan document, then such protection is often provided in CIC agreements for individual executives.

In certain instances, depending on the type and nature of the transaction, unexercised stock options may be exchanged for new options in the combined or

Exhibit 8.16 Integration Principles for Executive Compensation

1. *The executive compensation program must be aligned with the new company's overall business strategy.* This means having annual and long-term incentives that support the new company's business plans, whether they are to integrate sales and marketing activities, capture additional market share, increase product development activities, or achieve other goals.
2. *Incentive compensation plans should be based on a thorough analysis of the relevant industry and performance metrics that reflect shareholder value creation.* Financial models should be applied to show the impact of proposed incentive plans under various business scenarios.
3. *Executive incentive plans should target the synergies and other outcomes that are important to successful integration.* Business analysts and investors will look carefully at the ability of the new company to capture synergies during the first 6 to 12 months of integrated operations. Management should be rewarded for early achievement of planned synergies.

Source: Towers Perrin analysis.

---

surviving company. The key is to ensure that the company does not incur an accounting charge for the new option by providing the executive with a current gain greater than the amount implicit in the exchanged option. This can be accomplished by adjusting the share price and the number of shares associated with the new option to match the underlying gain and number of option shares implied in the existing grant.

- What should the executive compensation program be for the new company? When combining two companies, the easy path is to take existing compensation and benefit plans and retrofit them for the new company. In the case of executive compensation, there is a great temptation to take the best of each company's plans and create the most generous program possible. This tactic can lead to a very expensive executive compensation plan that fits neither the new business strategy nor the industry's competitive environment. *Exhibit 8.16* provides several integration principles.

Special Retention Incentives for Other Staff

Most senior executives have appropriate CIC agreements during the M&A process, thereby negating the need for additional retention vehicles. However, the value of an acquired organization can be significantly undercut if the acquirer fails to retain other talent (e.g., key middle managers and professionals) needed to make the new venture a success. These employees, who may be in information technology, legal, accounting, or human resource functions, must be retained for at least the first 12 to 18 months to implement a successful merger or acquisition.

To develop an effective retention strategy, the new company's integration planners must address the following issues:

- How will the new company define the talent it must retain to secure its near- and long-term success? Which specific individuals or groups meet this definition?
- How long will these individuals be critical to the success of the merger or acquisition? Are they required only for the transition period, or are they needed for the longer term?
- What can the new company afford to do to retain these individuals?

Typically, special compensation programs are developed to support the retention of this talent pool. These often take the form of cash retention bonuses that are paid only if the individual stays with the organization for a specified period of time. The retention bonuses are sometimes paid out in accordance with a specified schedule, with a portion paid up front and other payments made at specific times (e.g., after the first year of the new company's operation) or to correspond with the achievement of project milestones.

A Total Rewards Case Study

Following is a case study in which a merger provided the opportunity to create an entirely new total rewards program.

Background

In recent years, deregulation has brought profound changes to the energy industry. To an ever-increasing extent, gas and electric companies are no longer considered utilities with monopolies in specific markets and concomitant regulation by state and federal authorities. These former monopolies now function competitively, as companies in most other industries do. The associated economic pressures have in turn led to mergers among many gas and electric energy service providers.

In the late 1990s, a Midwest holding company acquired various energy service companies both in the United States and abroad with the goal of establishing a highly competitive, broadly based energy services organization. In addition to retaining its local regulated utility, the newly configured organization was preparing to compete in the deregulated power generation market.

The New Culture

The old utility company culture was clearly unsuited to the needs of the merged organization to be a forceful competitor. Substantial changes were necessary. The first step management took was to develop a change agenda and process, with a particular focus on the design and implementation of a new rewards framework that would reinforce the changes to be made.

This multifaceted change process began with a vision for the new organization, which influenced the design of an integrated set of people and rewards programs to build and sustain a high-performance work environment. Equally important, to better reflect the new organization's business strategies and the needs of its employees, there had to be a significant reallocation of investments in rewards.

The New Total Rewards Strategy

The new total rewards program reflected the structure of the merged organization, which was divided into separate business units, some subject to regulation and some not. This separation resulted in the following distinctive strategies for each of the four quadrants of total rewards:

Pay. Pay would be on a par with competitors, with the specific competition defined by each strategic business unit. Pay would be performance-driven, with significant rewards for top performers. The performance of each business unit would fund the incentive programs.

Benefits. The overall package would be competitive within each sector of the energy industry, and a cost-containment strategy would be implemented. Programs would be designed and administered at the corporate level, with each business unit able to select plan elements and benefit levels. There would also be meaningful employee choice.

Learning and development. These programs would be competency-based. The corporate programs group would focus on broad organizational change while each business unit would offer skills development programs tailored to its specific needs. The most talented employees (100 to 250 corporate-wide) would be identified, and special attention would be devoted to their development needs.

Work environment. Core policies—such as flexible work arrangements and dress codes—would be developed at the corporate level, but business units would be encouraged to develop critically important local policies.

The Results

With its new culture firmly in place and the new rewards program implemented, the organization has emerged as a highly competitive force in both the power generation and distribution sectors of the energy industry. It is also making serious inroads into the energy marketing sector.

Employees have expressed satisfaction with the new total rewards program. This reaction is particularly notable because the corporation reduced the fixed-cost elements of total rewards and emphasized performance-oriented programs.

As this case study shows, the success of a merger or acquisition relies on achieving a close alignment between the total rewards strategy and the new company's business strategies and goals. ■

CHAPTER NINE

HR Technology Integration Strategy

Alfred J. Walker

> *"HR professionals can address the IT challenge in novel and innovative ways."*
>
> Homa Bahrami, UCLA, and
> Stuart Evans, University of Cambridge

The merger of two companies raises some immediate and crucial issues about human resources (HR) technology that can keep both the chief information officer and head of HR up at night: What should our HR technology integration strategy be? How will we deliver on fundamental services like payroll, benefits, and compliance reporting? Should our longer-term strategy be to use the HR technologies that reside in the dominant company? What if the acquired company has better systems? What about adopting an entirely new strategy, perhaps using a new HR technology platform, even one exclusively web-based? Or should we have a hybrid solution, with some elements from both companies—some web-based, some call center-based, and some using voice response?

The answers to the myriad technology questions begin with another, broader question: What will the new company's long-term HR services delivery strategy be? While HR answers this question, it must also meet the immediate needs of the employees, dependents, and retirees of both companies. In integration planning, these short-term obligations must take precedence over long-range planning, at least until they are satisfied. Senior management, as well as the HR and information technology (IT) staffs in both companies, may wish to expand the use of service centers, use more external vendors, and move more applications to the web. However, these steps may have to wait until management has ensured that no vital services will be disrupted. Clearly, a well-grounded integration plan is called for—one that can meet both short- and long-term needs.

Integration Purposes

Let's look at why an HR technology integration plan is necessary, and what its purpose is. Is it another bureaucratic document that demands a great deal of work to put

---

Adapted from Chapter 12, *Web Based Human Resources*, by Alfred Walker. Copyright © 2001 The McGraw-Hill Companies, Inc. Reproduced by permission of The McGraw-Hill Companies, Inc. For more information on this topic, please see *Web Based Human Resources*, by Alfred Walker, available at bookstores.

together but in reality is never acted on? Or is it a highly useful instrument that helps guide the HR technology investment for the new company?

The primary purpose of HR technology integration in a merger or acquisition is twofold: to build a realistic framework specifying the technology and supporting infrastructure that HR will need to meet the business requirements of the new company, and to develop a workable plan for getting there, considering both near-term and longer-term needs. The integration plan should aim to increase the effectiveness of the new company's HR programs, processes, and service delivery mechanisms by speeding up cycle times, raising service levels, reducing costs, and adding new service capability. The mechanisms for delivering HR services should address the distinct needs of employees, managers, retirees, and, perhaps, candidates for employment of the newly created entity.

Scope of Integration Planning

The HR technology integration planning should cover the following areas:

- Base HR record-keeping systems (e.g., SAP™, PeopleSoft®, Oracle®, GEAC™)
- HR service center technologies such as case management systems, knowledge bases, and call tracking
- Web-based solutions ranging from an HR portal to manager/employee self-service
- Single-purpose applications such as succession planning and recruiting
- External vendors (e.g., benefit firms that handle 401(k) plans, payroll suppliers)

Management of the new company may decide in due course that some of these areas should not be integrated, but all should be on the table at the start of the planning process.

HR Technology Integration

Companies involved with mergers and acquisitions (M&As) frequently underestimate the difficulty of integrating technology solutions while at the same time overestimating the expected technology capabilities, performance, and usefulness to the end user. Integration planners tend to be optimists at heart, and when they base their expectations on inaccurate beliefs and assumptions, they set goals that cannot easily be met. The user community for HR systems, too, often underestimates the work required to change systems and the underlying HR programs and processes.

Influences

Several factors influence HR technology integration. Planning integration is not as simple as adopting one company's systems and programs, even if that company is the dominant one in the merger or acquisition. HR technology integration deals with a wide range of complex issues, such as those listed in *Exhibit 9.1*.

Exhibit 9.1 HR Technology Integration Issues

- Understanding the overall business objectives, initiatives, and needs of the new company
- Developing the major strategies, goals, and objectives for the people aspects of the integration process
- Developing realistic IT strategies, given the pace of technology development (advances are made every day, and new technology can render an existing strategy obsolete in a matter of months); ensuring the ability to support legacy systems in both companies
- Developing HR function integration and transformation goals; re-focusing HR on activities that bring greater value to the business; redesigning HR processes to meet the needs of the new work environment
- Recognizing that there is usually a limited budget for technology integration, which requires a constant re-prioritization of systems projects
- Deploying overworked HR and IT staffs with uneven skill sets
- Providing technology maintenance for the business changes (such as new HR program releases and reorganizations) taking place during integration
- Understanding that HR technology integration and implementation are by their nature slow and expensive, and during implementation of a new HR system, user needs are often difficult to meet satisfactorily
- Choosing among several software products that offer solutions to an HR service administration or delivery problem
- Meeting hundreds of federal, state, and local regulatory and compliance requirements for the legacy companies for some time after the new HR technology decision is made
- Meeting the backlog of unmet user needs and demands for new applications (e.g., modifications or enhancements to HR, benefits, and payroll plans and programs, ranging from staffing systems to pension calculators, almost all of which need to be delivered with a technology solution)
- Coping with the complexity of balancing services and support to different customers and constituencies (e.g., employees, managers, applicants for employment, retirees)

Source: Towers Perrin analysis.

HR Technology Integration Issues

These issues present many conflicting demands, so a well-conceived HR technology integration plan becomes a necessity for successful implementation of M&As.

HR Technology Decision Framework

Development of a technology integration plan must take into consideration the following questions:

- What HR programs and services will be delivered in the new company? Each functional area within HR has distinctive programs and plans, along with underlying processes and attendant transactions.
- What audiences are covered by each of the HR programs and plans? Are programs and plans different for employees of each legacy company? What other differences are seen in the plans—for example, differences for hourly and salaried employees? Will each plant or division have the same plans? What about senior management, applicants, retirees, expatriates?
- How will the new company's programs and benefit plans be delivered? Will the primary delivery vehicle for HR services be the web? A service center? Or will

delivery be via an outsourced provider or application service provider (ASP)? Aside from the primary delivery vehicle, some types of HR transactions are best handled on a face-to-face basis. How will these be dealt with?

- When are HR programs and plans to be delivered? What timing is associated with each HR program, plan, transaction, or process? What are the controlling dates in the implementation plan? When do decisions about technology need to be made, considering the urgency of meeting the immediate needs?
- Who manages the content for HR services delivered through integrated technology? Who is the plan or process owner for each service and for each served population?
- Who is responsible for HR service delivery and support: the HR technology support group? HR service center? IT function?
- What is the cost of HR service support and delivery? How will the service be charged: by unit costing methods, by transaction, or on a per employee basis?
- How will the company maintain quality in the delivery channels (i.e., what measures should be used in which processes to ensure timely and accurate service delivery)?

HR Technology Integration Plan

The integration plan, while different in each situation, should contain at least the following components:

- A short-term plan for continuing vital services through the transition period
- A vision of how HR services will be delivered in the new company—at least for the next several years
- A framework or outline for HR technology integration and migration—including investments for software, people, hardware upgrades, and so on—and application priorities over the next several fiscal years
- New enterprise-wide information and technology platforms for HR
- The objectives and charter of the HR technology group or groups
- Specific recommendations for technology solutions (e.g., which company's systems to use, when to use the web, when to use the call center)
- Introduction of technology upgrades and new releases for the new entity, with an emphasis on ensuring that all systems work when the merged company opens its doors for business
- Outline for the launch and management of HR technology projects in the future
- Suggested organizational structure and roles for the HR, benefits, payroll, and IT staffs
- Data accuracy and measurement standards for key HR information and processes
- Global jurisdictional and reporting requirements
- Confidentiality, security, and privacy policies

Exhibit 9.2 Example: Aligning HR Services with Business Needs

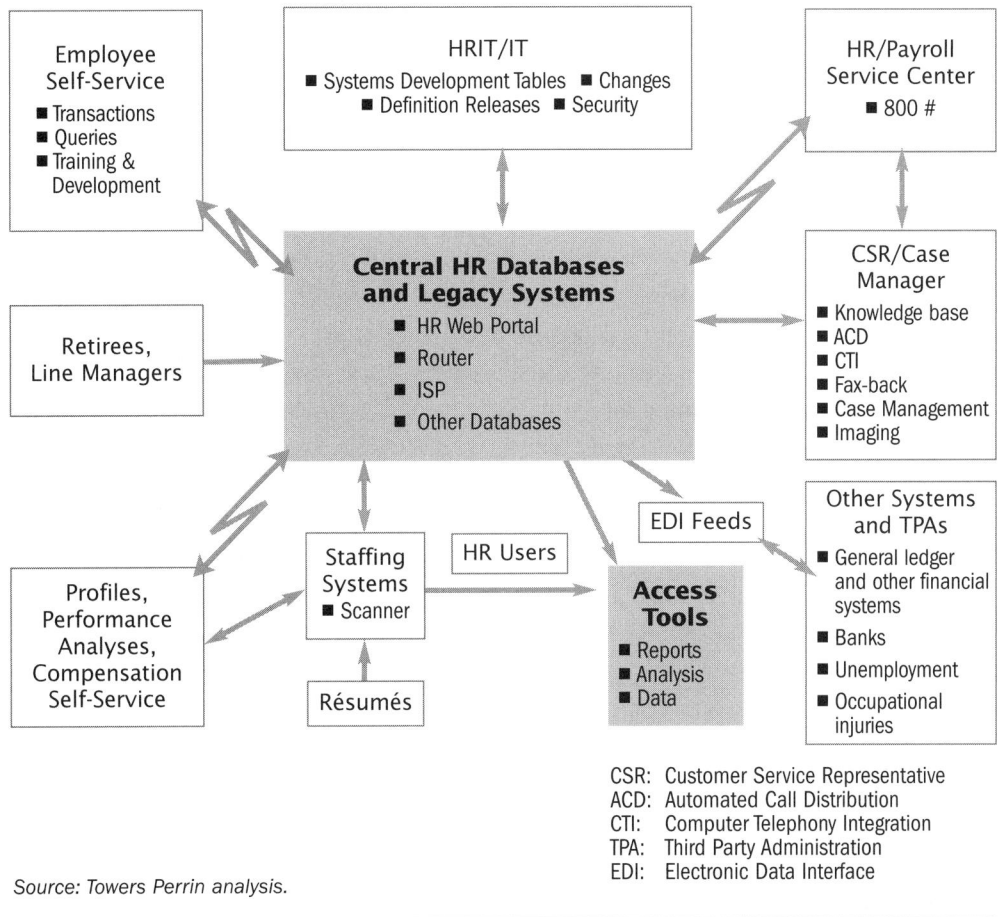

Source: Towers Perrin analysis.

Stages in HR Technology Integration Planning

Stage 1. Create a Vision of the Future Delivery Model
After management has ensured continuity of services in the short run, the new company should develop consensus among senior management in the HR and IT functions—with concurrence from the primary business managers—of how HR services will be delivered and through what specific technologies. In essence, this consensus is a description of the future state of the HR function.

A highly successful method for gaining consensus is to develop a preliminary picture of that future state and then have employees and management react to it through focus groups or interviews. The following is an example of such a delivery model.

Model for HR service delivery—high tech as well as high touch. *Exhibit 9.2* shows how transactional and information services could be delivered through HR technology to the various users in the integrated company. It presents a future picture of both HR technology and HR service delivery. The model makes a distinction between the HR work delivered to the new company's various businesses through HR generalists and HR staff assigned to those businesses and work delivered with HR technology. Face-to-face advice and counsel is preserved and enhanced in this model. Transferring transaction processing and administrative work from HR generalists to the web or a service center gives the new company's HR staff more time for the role of business partner and consultant.

Stage 2. Select HR Technology Components

HR technology solutions hinge on several technological and service-related concepts. Collectively, these concepts frame the final design of the new company's HR service delivery model. They include the following:

- Choice of the HR plans as the driver of the technical solution. When management decides which employees are in which HR plans, then the technical delivery choices can be made.
- Seamless transition. Employees and managers should have as few service interruptions as possible during the implementation process.
- 24 × 7 × 365. The technology solution must give all managers and employees access to HR systems and their own personal information, along with HR applications, any time and anywhere during and after the implementation.
- Support for key business applications. Key applications such as learning must be supported to facilitate knowledge and skills building.
- Automated workflow. The system should eliminate routine, redundant, manual, and paper transaction processing.
- Streamlined processes. The system should eliminate non-value-adding handling of paper and reduce or eliminate excessive numbers of approval signatures and redundant process steps.
- Solutions that increase manager and employee self-sufficiency. These include interactive voice response, intranet/web applications, fax-back, and Lotus Notes databases, among others.
- Capture and build the organization's intellectual capital. The system should be easily accessible, reducing or eliminating lost "business knowledge" during and after a merger or acquisition.
- Help reduce unwanted turnover. This is a priority both during and after the closing of a merger or acquisition.

Preferred service delivery methods. Each HR process, transaction, or event needs to be analyzed and the preferred method of delivery chosen. Such methods include technology, in-person delivery, paper systems, and outside vendors and application service providers (ASPs). Many companies use a merger or acquisition as the catalyst for fundamental change. For example, one company may use an interactive voice response

Exhibit 9.3 HR Service Delivery Model

Source: Towers Perrin analysis.

solution for employees to access account balances in their 401(k) plans because it is easy to do by telephone, perhaps even easier than using the web. But the web would be a better means for delivering the full range of total reward information. So choices have to be made about what the HR services or processes will use as their primary delivery vehicle—that is, Company A, Company B, or neither. Further, these choices have to accommodate different audiences. For example, retirees most likely do not have access to the company local area network (LAN), but they do have access to the web, so their access might be more limited than that of current employees but still be acceptable.

Application priorities and rollout. With limited resources—time and budget—applications must be prioritized using an appropriate methodology. The best way to prioritize is for management to align applications with business needs or objectives: Those with the greatest impact may deserve favorable treatment in the plan. Selection of which applications to deliver, and when, is a pivotal component of the HR technology integration plan, as *Exhibit 9.3* illustrates.

One vendor, two vendors, or best of breed? The selection of the base system from one company or the decision to leave both systems in place will determine the extent of integration necessary for HR programs, plans, and technology systems. The proliferation of systems solutions in most companies normally requires a plan that covers numerous technologies, not just the base HR system that is selected. Web-based technologies will most probably be used to deliver HR services. Major vendors in this market, such as PeopleSoft, Oracle, Lawson, and SAP, offer such products. But the ideal HR technology solution will likely need more applications, including multimedia solutions; resume reading and handling methodologies; and optical scanning, imaging, and voice recognition systems. So neither one technology nor one vendor will be able to meet all of the new company's needs.

For the HR service center, the same applies. Technology may well encompass unified networks with case management systems, voice networks, knowledge bases, and call-pathing capabilities, among others. And in the future, more expert-based applications and multimedia software products will be available.

The ideal model for HR technology provides access to key business data—primarily employee and organizational information—anywhere, any time. In addition, embedded workflow capability by authorized personnel permits work to be delivered more efficiently and from a distance. Manager and employee self-service is also a necessary component, and the model has to support the information relationships contained in the HR business model. Finally, the model's success depends on its acceptance by all stakeholders.

Before you decide, list assumptions. Because of the complexities of the merged business and a newly merged workforce, it is impossible to fully understand and have access to all user needs, requirements, and environmental impacts when developing strategy and project plans. In our rapidly changing, highly competitive environment, a company's business strategies and processes can change within 6 to 18 months, and there is always the chance of further mergers and acquisitions. Much effort, cost, and time are generally necessary to collect all relevant information in one location. For this reason, the future HR business model, and the technologies and IT (HR applications) organization to support it, must have input from HR, IT, and line management.

Possible Assumptions. A future-looking HR technology integration plan must build on assumptions regarding the new company's business in the future. Will it be sufficiently profitable to implement the plan? Can it be assumed that there will be no further mergers or acquisitions? What about continued management and user support? The following is a list of possible assumptions:
- Current systems and vendor-supplied services in both companies will continue to operate until the longer-term plan is implemented.
- Major processes will be redesigned for speed and simplification where possible, taking the best of the processes from each of the merged companies.
- Not all HR processes or programs will require that information on employees, plans and programs, and organizations be maintained in a central HR informa-

tion system (HRIS), web site, or data mart (e.g., medical data can be stored separately).
- HR technology implementation priorities will have to be altered in a year or two, and the HR objectives and long-term HR technology strategies will have to be reassessed.
- Experienced HR staff will be committed to the technology integration project during the implementation stage.
- Qualified HR technology professionals will be assigned to each major process and application and will interface with users and manage the integration work (testing, training, etc.).
- Suppliers of data that feed HR applications will need to properly update their respective data elements and ensure that their data are available to support a smooth transition from old to new applications.
- IT staff as well as management at all levels will support the technology integration priorities and plans.
- An HR service center will handle most HR transactions and data requests flowing from the integration process. The center will serve as a single point of contact with employees for web-based support and will handle queries regarding HR plans and programs during and after the merger implementation stage.
- Sufficient funds will be available to carry out at least the major near-term priorities of the merger or acquisition in an acceptable manner.
- Reporting relationship data will be maintained in the new company's database.

Stage 3. Select HR Technology and Service Delivery Approach

Step 1. Establish guiding principles for technology integration and selection. Guiding principles (agreed to by all parties) set the context for the new service delivery architecture and for the associated roles and responsibilities. These principles might include the following:
- Technology integration will adhere to the new company's standards and methodology for project management.
- Certain technologies and platforms can cover both companies, thus reducing costs and facilitating support and maintenance.
- Scale economies will be exploited to take full advantage of valuable IT competencies and skills, to leverage technology investments, and to better manage the processes they support.
- Data elements will be mapped to a standard lexicon.
- Uniform and consistent methods will be used for presenting key HR data (which provide "intelligence") in order to improve and expedite decision-making and enhance understanding of the data captured and maintained in HR systems.

- Responsibility for data entry will move to the source (i.e., employees, managers, applicants) in order to improve data accuracy, integrity, consistency, and timeliness.
- The new company will collect and provide access to detailed data that allow system users to define their own data requirements rather than just get back summary statistics.
- The data collected and maintained in the new company's HRIS, legacy systems, and data mart will have sufficient integrity and accuracy to gain the trust of management in the new company.
- Data that supply the web site (HRIS or data mart) will be maintained and updated on a timely basis to the desired level of accuracy.
- The new company will maintain the proper privacy, security, and access levels to the data. (This principle takes on special significance in a cross-border merger, where data protection issues can arise.)

Step 2. Creating the architectural framework. The HR service delivery architecture should be robust, scalable, flexible, and secure. In addition, it should allow for access by managers and employees from any point on the globe at any time. Integration of legacy databases demands a complex network of applications, processes, databases, and servers, comprising internally maintained systems as well as those from external vendors and hosts.

A three-tiered model, as illustrated in *Exhibit 9.4*, should be considered for the core of the HR technology architecture. The first tier represents the technology that would be evident to the employee, manager, or HR program/plan (the client or client-side) and that is maintained on a desktop, computer, or kiosk. Here, the customer interface technology would contain the presentation graphics, or graphical user interface (GUI) components, along with a browser to access the web, and would present a common look and feel to the user. This tier also permits the user to activate a channel to an external web site or go directly into the corporate (intranet) site. In addition, the desktop should contain standard office applications such as a word processor, spreadsheet, and access to the LAN.

The middle tier (server-side) contains the Internet servers, application servers, and all the presentation and business logic, HR processes, system calculations, and core HR systems such as SAP or PeopleSoft, as well as supporting logic and content carriers such as knowledge bases. In addition, active server pages handle the HTML formatting tags. Component objects (or COM objects) are housed there as well. COM objects execute transactions and move data from databases to the user within the established editing and workflow rules. This middle tier also handles queries dealing with multimedia components and IVR, and provides access to or from a call center.

The third tier (enterprise information) houses the data on a database server and can access certain native HR systems or store data in a data mart or data warehouse for access, reporting, and analysis.

Exhibit 9.4 Three-Tier Model for Future Architecture

Three-Tier Architecture		What Gets Done
User Interface Tier	Access Devices • Telephones • Computer Terminals • Palm-Size PCs (PPCs)	• Source of user request for information/transaction
tpConnect™ Presentation Layer		• Understands access device characteristics • Formats data for user by device
XML (SOAP)		
Business Logic and Integration Tier	Enterprise Application Integration (EAI) • Directory Services • Work Flow • Personalization • Search • Report Engine • Usage Metrics • Content Management	• Defines how and what work gets done via rules and work flow • Validates/authenticates user • Identifies required information and sends requests to XML connectors
XML Connectors		
Data Access and Applications Tier	• ERP • HRMS • Legacy Data • Knowledge Base • Applications (e.g., Kadiri) • ASPs	• Generates request for information from applications and databases • Applications and databases provide information requested from single or multiple sources

Source: Towers Perrin analysis.

Step 3. Choosing technology and service delivery platforms. The methodology for selecting a specific HRIS, web hardware and software platforms, ASPs, and service center technologies should be covered in the integration plan. The specific choices should be made jointly by the HR and IT functions within the context of the current IT standards. The plan should consider functionality, ability to meet future requirements, adapt-

Exhibit 9.5 Process for HR Systems Integration **Example**

Get Your Act Together
- Establish integration HR tech team
- Develop HR service delivery model
- Understand users' needs
- Develop evaluation criteria

Systems Evaluation
- Screen against new HR plans
- Screen against future needs
- Screen for IT platform issues

Detailed Evaluations
- Examine codes and database designs
- Assess cost and supportability
- Make final selection

Source: Towers Perrin analysis.

ability and acceptability of server hardware (e.g., Microsoft's NT server, LINUX servers), compatibility with standard e-mail systems such as Lotus Notes, network architecture, desktops, and interaction with any Internet and telecommunications protocols.

Software platforms must also be within the IT standards and should also cover the enterprise resource planning (ERP) standards, use of HTML Access and Java Applets, security firewalls, sign-on levels and authentication, Active X, Java or VB Script, workflow technologies, call center technologies, and development tool kits. Security interfaces with the directory server should use the Lightweight Directory Access Protocol (LDAP) to authenticate end users and manage their system access privileges.

Costs, capabilities, security, and appropriateness all are important in the choice of platforms. But just as important is the new company's strategic direction and conformity to the overall HR integration principles. The combined effect of process redesign, new technology deployment, shared services, and outsourcing will increase the speed of service delivery and the level of employee satisfaction. The platforms and architecture that promote these goals should be given the highest priority.

Step 4. Selecting specific technologies. After Steps 1 through 3 are completed, the technology integration work teams can choose the HR delivery vehicles. This is a multipart process that can differ from company to company, but it is best done within a framework similar to that shown in *Exhibit 9.5*.

Criteria used in the assessment should include the following:
- Strategic alignment with HR, IT, and business needs (ERP tie-in)
- HR functionality and specific applications
- Technical robustness and web compatibility
- Database structure and content
- Scalability and flexibility to meet future needs
- Ease of user access and user satisfaction
- Costs and supportability

Specific delivery vehicles can be chosen after the technology integration team considers these criteria.

Other considerations. In addition to conducting its basic assessment, the technology integration team should consider any contracts that must be honored with technology vendors and consultants, as well as support and enhancement capabilities of these vendors that will be involved in the integration process. There may be some applications that must remain with particular vendors for a period of time after the merger, whether or not the new company desires it.

Selecting the web deployment strategy. The web delivery environment for HR services will be even more complex in the future than it is today, when there are commonly 40 or more web-based applications to maintain. A key decision will be whether the web-based applications will be delivered by in-house staff or moved to an external service provider.

Developing a web site map. To help overcome differences of opinion about where content should reside, a site map should be drawn to plan out the potential use of the web and show the design and flow for users. The mapping should be driven by usage and event processes, not necessarily by organizational responsibility. For example, a web page that has a name change feature could also handle beneficiary changes, despite the fact that an employee name change may be handled by the HR records function, while the change of a beneficiary may be handled by the benefits function. The best practice is to gear the natural process flow to the user, who should drive the design. The general rule for usability remains: The fewer clicks needed to reach the desired page, the better.

Stage 4. Organizational Roles and Responsibilities for the Integration Plan

Management and user input and communication. In the past, technologists (i.e., programmers) developed most of the HR technology integration plans. User involvement was minimal, and the planning documents never came close to matching what actually happened. As a result, the HR technology that was delivered, the sequence in which the related software applications were delivered, and the priorities of the developers may not have matched management's expectations. It is essential to manage these expectations because unforeseen business needs, regulatory requirements, and workforce demands crop up constantly and quickly. Involving users throughout the entire integration process is key to a good outcome.

User involvement in technology implementation. It is critical to involve users in conversion and testing when implementing new HR systems. Whether an application is internally developed, a purchased HRIS/payroll software package such as PeopleSoft, or a call center, the focus should be on delivering technology solutions that meet the HR programs/plans, policies, and employee needs.

Users should ensure that before system implementation or process redesign, a service delivery sequence is mapped out for every major HR event. For example, in the case of annual performance appraisals, does an employee go first to the web, HR staff, service center, or another path, such as voice response? And which system or pieces of systems are to be installed?

Subject matter experts (SMEs) should be involved in these decisions during conversion, testing, running in parallel, and cut-over. Some users (HR, payroll, line managers, and others) may find this interaction time-consuming and confusing, but it is vital to the success of the integration effort. While systems are being evaluated and converted, HR, payroll, and the other parts of the organization must continue to deliver services while dedicating a significant amount of their time to the implementation project. If not enough good SMEs are available, the applications may not meet the new company's requirements, and the success of the HR technology implementation project could be jeopardized.

Integration Plan Impact on HR

For some HR staff, the introduction of the new technology will have relatively little impact on their jobs, particularly if they deal with sensitive, high-touch issues such as performance management or pay issues. Most HR staff, however, will find their work altered in some fashion; for example, many transactional parts of their work may be shifted to the HR service center. Even if the work they do remains the same, many of the processes that they had been involved with in the past may now be done in new ways.

In all likelihood, the new HR service delivery model resulting from a merger or acquisition will use more technology than before. Most high-volume processes will be web-enabled, with workflow and self-service introduced. For example, employees will now handle some routine matters themselves through the web site and will be able to connect with an HR system directly or with an operational data store (ODS) or data mart fed by the HR database. Another innovation may enable local HR staff to pull up a computer screen, click on the appropriate icon, and review those transactions that are passed on to them for approval, rather than handling paper-based administrative transactions. In this case, their work is automatically forwarded to the appropriate line manager or HR unit, depending on the particular workflow desired by the process owner.

Other changes to the HR work environment will take place as well. With the growth of hosting and outsourcing and the introduction of shared services units, it becomes necessary to reexamine supplier activities that could be managed centrally—a function perhaps now handled by a number of HR specialists.

Joint IT/HR Technology Integration

Because of the complexities and workloads involved, systems integration and support of the new HR technologies and systems become shared responsibilities. The HR technology and IT functions must partner on assignments and determine where the lines of responsibility will be drawn for each application. Normally, HR technology supports the applications (user needs, definitions, changes, cost benefits, user testing, training), and IT supports the infrastructure on which the enterprise applications depend (networks, workstation configuration, intranet, enterprise system security, firewalls, etc.). However, the merger or acquisition may change this approach, depending on staff expertise and resource constraints. In any event, HR technology and IT depend on each other for support and for balancing requirements and solutions.

Change Management Role

It is critical that HR and IT staff communicate with the various constituencies regarding the objectives of the integration effort and chosen systems applications. The evaluation process, the reasons for the selection, and information about costs, benefits, output, and so forth must be shared with all affected parties. New technology solutions can be extremely helpful, but they also involve change—change that perhaps was not invited and that for some users will involve learning new tasks and competencies. In addition, with the new HR service delivery model, there is an expectation that certain technology solutions (e.g., the HR web site) will be used by employees in every business unit, making communications extremely important for the success of the solution.

Managing the introduction of new technology applications during a merger or acquisition is one of the more difficult aspects of integration because it involves all HR staff, managers, and employees; the integration plan should address this point. Gaining buy-in requires expertise in change management and communications, competencies not always in great abundance in IT or HR technology organizations. The higher the expectations, the higher the risk to successful implementation if they are not met; the lower the expectations, the more difficult it may be to obtain support and to make a compelling business case for change. Balance must be sought, and a proper level of communications regarding each new implementation must be carefully planned.

Summary

The HR technology integration plan is aimed at achieving the service delivery level that management desires in the new company. It is a mixture of short-term and longer-term considerations, technical and organizational plans and initiatives, that ties the two companies, their vendors, and the employees of the new company together in an integrated fashion. ∎

SECTION IV

The Next M&A Wave

CHAPTER TEN

M&A in the New Millennium

Thomas O. Davenport

"You can never plan the future by the past."
Edmund Burke
British Statesman, 1791

The previous chapters have brought into focus the current role of the human resources (HR) function in helping companies to merge or acquire effectively. We have seen how merger and acquisition (M&A) activity tends to take place in waves, driven by market opportunity, inspired by the perceived value of conglomeration, and fueled by stock market valuations. Now let's exchange the clear lens that has magnified our analysis for a cloudy crystal ball. We will look ahead into an uncertain future to discern what we can about how changes unfolding now will affect the ways that organizations approach future M&A opportunities and how the role of the HR function might evolve. The future of business raises a number of critical M&A questions, such as the following:

- What motives and goals will compel companies to merge or acquire in the future? In other words, what will the next M&A wave look like?
- Will organizations look for combinations within national boundaries, or will cross-border combinations increase?
- What sources of shareholder value will companies pursue when they undertake a merger or acquisition?
- Will organizations do a better job of integration and value creation than their predecessors have done?
- What must HR do to ensure that future mergers and acquisitions yield the highest possible value for all stakeholders?

Forces That Will Affect the Future of Business

At least four forces will change how companies do business in the future—globalization, technology development, the rising importance of knowledge assets, and workforce evolution. Each force has implications, in turn, for how companies will approach mergers and acquisitions and for the expected role of HR in the M&A life cycle.

Globalization

Global trade (the transfer of goods and services across borders) has grown sixfold since the end of World War II. In fact, world trade is growing faster than world production (the rate at which companies produce goods). Foreign direct investment (FDI), or investment in physical plant, equipment, and organizations by companies from another country, exhibits faster growth than does world trade. Whether the trade is in crayons, computers, or cars, the boundaries that formerly separated countries as economic units have become increasingly permeable.

Today, the world's 500 largest multinational enterprises (MNEs) based in the United States, the European Union (EU), and Japan account for more than 80 percent of the world's total FDI and about half of all world trade. Of all the automobiles produced in North America, 90 percent come from factories owned by Japanese or European MNEs or the large U.S. automakers; no other part of the world has a significant role in producing cars for U.S. consumers. In Europe and Japan, the story is the same. In specialty chemicals, more than 90 percent of all paint comes from MNEs in these three regions and is used within those regions. In steel, electrical equipment, and much of the rest of the manufacturing sector, production and trade stay largely within the triad. When it comes to commerce, global has come to mean trade within this triad rather than across worldwide regions. Only consumer electronics (with Korean manufacturers having a role) and high value-added goods with low transport costs constitute truly global markets.

Look for things to change, however, as we move farther into the twenty-first century. Most of the future opportunities for U.S. companies will come from countries that today are hardly an economic blip on most global radar screens. Consider, for example, the way population growth patterns will influence the size of future consumer markets. In the EU, prominent countries like Germany, France, and the United Kingdom will experience population decreases over the next 50 years. In 2000, these three countries had a combined population of about 202 million. By 2050, according to the U.S. Census Bureau's International Data Base, their population will fall to approximately 197 million, a drop of 2.5 percent. Over that same period, the Census Bureau projects, Japan's population will fall from 126 million to 101 million, a plunge of some 20 percent. U.S. population is projected to increase a robust 46 percent over the first 50 years of this new century, from 276 million to 404 million.

In contrast to Japan and the EU, dramatic population growth will take place in countries like India, China, Indonesia, Nigeria, Pakistan, Ethiopia, and the Congo. *Exhibit 10.1* shows expected population increases in each of these countries.

China and India will continue as the world's largest consumer markets, with India taking over the title of world's most populous country (India will *add* more people in the first half of the century than the United States will have as its *total population* in 2050). Much of the rest of the world's population growth will occur in developing countries near the equator. Brazil will emerge as the seventh most populous country on the planet; Mexico will occupy the twelfth position. U.S. and European countries looking for new markets and for potential new merger or alliance partners will pay close atten-

Exhibit 10.1 Expected Population Increases

Country	2000 Population*	Projected 2050 Population*	Change*	Percent Change
China	1,262	1,470	208	16.5%
India	1,014	1,620	606	59.8%
Indonesia	225	338	113	50.2%
Pakistan	142	268	126	88.7%
Nigeria	123	304	181	147.2%
Ethiopia	64	188	124	193.8%
Congo	49	182	133	271.4%

Note: * In millions

Source: U.S. Census Bureau, International Data Base.

tion to these shifting demographic patterns. Later in the chapter we will consider the cross-cultural implications (and the resulting HR challenges) of doing business in attractive but unfamiliar regions of the globe.

Technology Development

Technology developments will press the accelerator pedal of global trade. Improvements in computer efficiency and telecommunications reach have already lowered the costs of production abroad for U.S. MNEs. U.S. investments by foreign multinationals have similarly benefited from new technology. National Semiconductor Corporation, for example, uses the global reach of the Internet to expand its network of distributors and connect with customers. National Semiconductor publishes data on some 30,000 products on its web site. Customers worldwide can order product samples without charge, which not only avoids many tax and customs issues but also simplifies accounting conundrums (such as where and when revenue should be recognized). The Internet also saves the company money. A call-center inquiry costs about $5 per call, whereas an Internet contact currently costs 12 cents.

There are two verities associated with technological change: It's fast and it's unpredictable. To those two we can add a third: It's bound to affect how companies conceive of and undertake M&A activity in the future. As the computer chip has become ubiquitous—in your computer, your TV remote, your child's electronic toy—virtually everything has become smarter. But software, not hardware, is king; it has replaced plastic boxes and glowing screens as the key element of information technology. Software, more than hardware, has driven the development of networking. In the future, we can expect that the Internet, the ultimate network, will dramatically influence how business gets done and how companies define the prospective advantages (and challenges) of corporate marriages.

Business-to-business (B2B) e-commerce will continue to reconfigure how information, products, and service are created, promoted, and delivered by American companies. Total e-commerce traffic in the United States (B2B and business-to-consumer) could exceed $1.5 trillion by 2004. Driving the nearly 100 percent per year growth is an age-old business imperative: keeping costs down. One recent research report cited in *Electronic Buyers' News* indicates that supply-chain automation software could slash procurement costs by more than 70 percent.

North America continues to account for the major share of B2B e-commerce revenue. Europe, however, shows the fastest growth in the B2B market, with 1999 e-commerce revenue of US$31.8 billion, headed toward a projected US$2.34 trillion by 2004. Aggressive forays into B2B by companies like BMW, Phillips, KLM, and British Telecom will fuel this growth. Asia, which is currently well behind the United States and Europe in e-commerce, will start to catch up over the next several years. In 1999, B2B volume in Asia amounted to just US$9.2 billion. Research by the Gartner Group suggests, however, that the region will generate close to US$1 trillion in revenue by 2004, an annual growth rate of 155 percent.

Like any industry in its infancy, e-commerce has experienced a flood of market entrants. Expect to see rationalization among the many e-commerce providers as companies look for a competitive edge. Gartner Group estimates, for example, that as many as 85 percent of Internet pure plays in the Asia Pacific region will fail or be acquired by 2003. With technology companies worldwide coming and going, merging and failing, HR will need to play a critical role in vetting the value of prospective acquirees and ensuring that that value carries over into the combined organization.

Even the fundamental definition of value continues to evolve rapidly in the e-commerce market. This changing value calculus has implications for companies seeking to increase prosperity through future mergers and acquisitions. For example, recent academic research suggests that the way securities markets value Internet competitors changed significantly over the first few months of 2000, when Internet equity values dropped like a rock.

The implication? Managers hoping to derive value from an e-commerce merger or acquisition must have their fingers on the pulse of the investor community. Cash burn became important overnight in 2000; other factors may take on (or lose) significance just as quickly. Yesterday's assumptions are stale already, and the conventional wisdom (going all the way back to last quarter) is already passé.

Rising Importance of Knowledge Assets

In the February 1999 issue of *CFO* Magazine, in an article entitled "Seeing Is Believing: A Better Approach to Estimating Knowledge Capital," author S. L. Mintz summarized the growing importance of intangible assets: "The industrial revolution has given way to an age of computers, information, and global competition. Decisions are made more quickly, and superior knowledge of products, markets, methods, and cultures often determines who prevails. The desire for mobility favors assets that can move over those

Exhibit 10.2 Knowledge Capital Management

Averages[a]	R&D as Percent of Sales	Advertising as Percent of Sales	Capital Spending as Percent of Property, Plant, and Equipment	1998 Total Shareholder Return
High	7.2%	3.1%	31.3%	54.8%
Medium	4.4%	2.2%	24.0%	29.3%
Low	3.8%	1.4%	23.3%	5.6%

Notes: a) Grouped by change in the ratio of knowledge earnings to book value. Knowledge earnings are net revenue derived from all sources other than financial and tangible assets.

Source: CFO *Magazine*, February 1999.

assets rooted to the ground. This spurs additional investment in assets that may affect the balance sheet, but are not recorded there." When Mintz refers to mobile assets, he means knowledge-based assets: customer relationships, innovative products and services (especially those under patent), and structural capital such as operationally excellent processes.

And just how important are knowledge assets to a company's financial success? Assume that an organization manifests its ability to use knowledge assets in three indicators: ratios of research and development expenditures to sales, advertising to sales, and capital spending as a percentage of property, plant, and equipment. Organizations that manage knowledge capital more effectively will not only have higher ratios in these indicators, but will also show a relationship between these indicators and the holy grail of a market-driven economy, total shareholder return. *Exhibit 10.2* shows how these elements of knowledge capital management relate to such returns.

The point is not simply that more (as in more research and development investment or more advertising spending) is better. Rather, more and better (as in more creative and fruitful research and development investment and more effective advertising) is better. And this phenomenon will only hold truer over the next decade, across a range of industries.

The increasing importance of knowledge in creating shareholder value assets reinforces the idea that acquiring and retaining talented people will continue as a make-or-break capability for twenty-first century companies. HR will play a central role in helping managers deal with their sources of knowledge capital, especially with mergers or acquisitions intended to build knowledge assets.

Workforce Evolution

Despite the recent economic correction, when economists peer into the murky future, what they see warms the hearts of workers and sends chills down the spines of managers: continued economic expansion over the next eight years, with unemployment roughly reminiscent of 1998 levels. At the end of 1999, economists from the U.S. Bureau of Labor Statistics (BLS) projected that growth in the gross domestic product would average about 2.4 percent per year approaching 2008, compared with 2.6 percent per year from 1988 through 1998. With accelerating exports and imports dominating the U.S. economy (globalization again!), employment should grow steadily. Even if the economy softens more than these projections suggest, labor markets should remain tight, especially for technically skilled workers.

And where will the most dramatic growth in employment take place? According to the BLS, two sectors dominate—technology and health care. Of the twenty occupations expected to grow fastest, eight are health-related and eight are computer-related. Computer systems analyst positions will grow the most, with an increase of 577,000 jobs (a 94 percent increase). Not far behind are computer support specialists (projected to add 439,000 jobs, a 102 percent increase) and computer engineers (323,000 new jobs, a 108 percent increase). The increasing emphasis on technical skills will manifest itself in growing educational requirements. Occupations that usually require at least a bachelor's degree will account for 6.6 million new jobs during the 1998–2008 decade, or about a third of all job growth, according to the U.S. Department of Labor. Put another way, occupations requiring a college education will grow almost twice as fast as the average for all occupations.

The challenge for companies looking to hire technical talent centers on the mismatch between growth in available jobs and growth in the population of workers eligible to take them. The BLS projects that between 1998 and 2008, the U.S. economy will add about 20 million positions. Over the same period, the labor force will increase by 17 million. Coming out ahead in what looks increasingly like a zero-sum game will call for astute workforce planning, aggressive recruiting, and insightful retention strategies. Accomplishing all this while combining two companies will pose a daunting task for HR management.

Implications for M&A and for HR's Role

As if each of these forces weren't dramatic enough on its own, the relationships among them add to their power and their ability to confound. Advancing technology hastens pan-global interconnections. Technology also drives up the value of knowledge capital, which in turn makes a tight labor market all the more troublesome. Forces this powerful and this intertwined can't help but change the ways companies view the benefits, challenges, and implementation requirements of M&As in the future.

So, what will impel the next wave of mergers and acquisitions? The swell of that wave may be building already. Over the next decade, the need for new capabilities and resources that build innovation power will drive M&As. Indeed, companies that have the human capital and organizational capabilities to generate great ideas, turn them into compelling products and services, and deliver them faster than the competition have been able to create competitive advantage since before Adam Smith wrote *The Wealth of Nations* in 1776. The difference between then and now, however, is urgency. Innovation is no longer a way to get ahead—it's a requirement for staying even. Only the truly inventive, the extremely radical, and the dwellers at the edge of reality can use innovation to get a sustainable competitive edge. That's where the power comes in. Truly good ideas are worth a pound of gold, but the ability to systematize innovation and commercialize ideas is priceless. Organizations that can sustain continuous innovation, survive the twists and turns of an unmapped competitive landscape, absorb failures, and move on (and do all this without burning through stores of cash) are the companies that will boast stratospheric returns on investment in the next decade.

Building that kind of strength organically is a worthy goal, but who has the time? The next wave of mergers and acquisitions will be led by companies that realize they can achieve innovation power better and faster through M&A than through any other means. They will merge or acquire to maximize scarce talent, harness knowledge capital, exploit technology, and reach global audiences.

As innovation power drives new mergers and acquisitions, what will happen to the future role of HR? We can expect that the contribution of HR will—indeed, must—evolve as well. The following sections consider the new forms that evolution might produce in the coming world of M&A.

Globalization—A New (and Old) Definition of Culture

According to John Sullivan, business professor at San Francisco State University and former chief talent officer at Agilent Technologies, increasing global competition will put the quest for top-line revenue growth at the top of managers' M&A wish lists. Cost-reduction synergies that made past mergers and acquisitions attractive will decline as a rationale, Sullivan says. Recent stock market performance has suggested that equity value goes up as revenue goes up; companies will look to combine when they believe they can add to the top line of the income statement, rather than merely reduce the operating cost lines in the middle.

One way to grow revenue is to gain access to new markets. Consequently, mergers and acquisitions involving U.S. and European companies will continue as organizations on both sides of the Atlantic look for hospitable markets for their products and services. What BP and Amoco, Deutsche Bank and Bankers Trust, GlaxoWellcome and SmithKline Beecham, and even Unilever and Ben & Jerry's have done reinforces a precedent for others to follow. Future deals like these will dwarf the deals of the late 1990s.

In some instances, organizations may prove willing to pay substantial premiums for a presence in a new market. Witness the July 2000 bid by Deutsche Telekom (DT) for American wireless company VoiceStream. The German telecommunications giant made an initial bid that amounted to $20,000 for each VoiceStream subscriber; previous deals in the sector had valued subscribers at about $6,000 each. Why did DT value VoiceStream so highly? It boils down to two words: global player. By acquiring its way into the U.S. market, DT leapfrogged over its two main European competitors, the UK's Vodafone Airtouch and France Telekom's Orange group. Deutsche Telekom hoped its American acquisition would yield better growth than it could find in its European backyard. Acquisition premiums based more on market access than on company fundamentals may become commonplace over the next decade.

Perceptions of cultural compatibility will add momentum to cross-border M&A activity between North American and European companies. In one study, for example, managers were asked to choose the country of origin for their most preferred merger partner. Managers from British, Dutch, and Swedish companies said they most preferred a partnership with a U.S. company. The survey respondents said that they perceived American managers to have a positive attitude and professional approach to business. American managers, in turn, said they most preferred to merge with a British company, again citing professional approach as the reason. In contrast, managers in the UK, France, Germany, and the United States said that they least favored a merger with a Japanese company. The managers pointed to language barriers and lack of cultural understanding as the reasons. We can expect, given these kinds of perceptions, that business-specific cultural affinity will increase M&A activity between U.S. and Northern European companies.

That said, the global population trends discussed earlier will compel managers to split their hitherto undivided attention on Europe, North America, and Japan. The most dramatic future market growth will occur elsewhere. Therefore, we expect companies to acquire or pursue other forms of alliance to get access to emerging markets such as those in India, Indonesia, Pakistan, Mexico, and Brazil. Indeed, incompatible laws governing corporate structure, ownership requirements, and taxation may preclude formal mergers of U.S.-domiciled companies with counterparts in developing nations. Early news of the Deutsche Telekom purchase of VoiceStream produced regulatory grumblings in the United States, for example. A U.S. senator quickly introduced legislation that would prohibit the Federal Communications Commission from permitting the transfer of American wireless licenses to any German firm for at least a year. The stated fear focused on national security, a potential issue given that the German government owned 57 percent of DT at the time of the acquisition offer (and would hold 45 percent of the combined entity).

Regulatory barriers to merging or acquiring will not discourage companies from seeking to increase market reach, however. Companies will simply look for other kinds of partnerships. One way or another, desire for access to markets and to resources (increasingly, knowledge-intensive resources) will increase cross-border activity in areas unfamiliar to many U.S. companies.

The prospect of increased cross-border mergers, acquisitions, and alliances means that HR will need to move beyond the current definition of corporate culture to consider the broader questions of how country and regional cultures affect business practices. Indeed, assessment of cultural fit must increasingly take into account the broader, country-specific notion of culture, as well as the narrower, company-centric definition. HR will need to become the source of knowledge and insight for managers who contemplate forging alliances with their counterparts in countries having unfamiliar cultural conventions.

To play their role in broad-scale analysis of cultural fit, HR leaders will need to have a framework for assessing cultural elements and determining the implications for management action. In performing cultural analysis, they must consider the influence on company culture of such dimensions as the following:

- Individualism/collectivism: Expectations differ as to whether business success depends more on individual initiative and contributions or on team contributions and group loyalty. Some management teams in some countries show strong individualist tendencies, whereas collectivist tendencies emerge more strongly in other countries.
- Power/distance: This refers to the amount of power wielded by managers at different organizational levels, relative to each other and to their employees. Some companies display less power/distance; in others, the boss has much more power than subordinates. Employees in low power/distance cultures have more individual autonomy and feel freer to challenge authority and status.
- Assertiveness/consensus-seeking: Cultures in which managers act with great autonomy tend to value ambition, decisiveness, and the desire to achieve recognition through good work and increasing earnings. Consensus-seeking cultures, in contrast, place higher value on interpersonal relationships and group harmony.
- Risk-seeking/avoidance: Companies in cultures where risk, ambiguity, and uncertainty are avoided tend to evidence control mechanisms such as authoritarianism and dogmatism. In contrast, companies from cultures in which uncertainty is more readily tolerated show fewer rigid control mechanisms.

Given the rate at which companies merge, forge partnerships, acquire, and exchange ideas across borders, it is risky to assume that historical cultural stereotypes apply to all companies in a country. Rather, the above dimensions can serve as guidelines for HR, which should ensure that the smoothest path is followed to cultural integration.

These cultural dimensions can profoundly influence the ways managers conduct negotiations, establish social contracts with employees, set expectations for production quantity and quality, and formulate plans for the future. The DT deal with VoiceStream points up some of the cultural challenges cross-border merger partners will face. Unlike DaimlerBenz, a German company that had decades of experience in the United States before its purchase of Chrysler, DT has no North American operating experience. Instead, the acquisition places a company accustomed to operating as an effective monopolist in its home market in a new and unfamiliar competitive position. More precisely, deregulation has steadily reshaped the American telecommunications landscape since 1984, creating a highly competitive marketplace. Also, about one-third of DT's employees are government employees (in U.S. parlance, "bureaucrats"); they cannot be fired no matter how strong the cost-cutting rationale. Imagine how they will cope with the freewheeling U.S. telecommunications market. Cognizant of these challenges, DT placed an American executive on the company's management board in 1999. Will that kind of move become commonplace in the future as organizations struggle to adapt to the new business cultures that international mergers and acquisitions bring? And will it be enough to inculcate new ways of doing business? Only time and experience will tell.

HR can be a source of insight, expertise, and training on how to anticipate and deal with the cultural challenges that, left unanticipated, can scuttle even the most sensible deal. Further, HR must be prepared to constantly update its knowledge base on the cultures of the companies to be combined. At the pace of business today, keeping up with culture means hitting a moving target. The best HR functions will keep up with the change, helping managers deal with shifting cultural reality in ways that facilitate, rather than hinder, cross-border alliances.

Technology—Walking the Talk

The earlier discussion suggested that we have entered a world where technology rules. Indeed, exploiting technology must be a fundamental goal for accelerating innovation. If that is true, we can expect more companies to merge or acquire for two specific reasons:

- To obtain new products, services, and distribution channels, which are the outputs of applying technology
- To build the organization capability required to create future technological innovation

Despite its recent problems, Cisco Systems stands out as a current model of a successful technology-focused acquirer. Cisco's acquisition strategy focuses squarely on strengthening its product line for customers who want integrated data, voice, and video services. By combining these communication modes, Cisco (like such competitors as Lucent Technologies, Nortel Network, and 3Com) hopes to give businesses and consumers new Internet-based communication services. The company could rely on research and development and new product creation to fuel its expansion. Instead, it bet that acquisition would get it the critical mass it needs more quickly. Interestingly, Cisco has not limited itself to North American (or even European) acquisitions. As of mid-2000, Cisco had made four acquisitions in Israel; the new globalization is alive and well! In one recent deal, Cisco acquired a company that manufactures computer-access equipment critical to the network it is building. The acquisition strengthened Cisco's product line for integrated communication networks.

Over the long run, acquisitions focused on the second technology-centric goal—building not just the current technology product line, but also the underlying capability to continue innovating—may create greater value for M&A partners. Companies good at innovation have the people, organization, processes, culture, and assets necessary to consistently deliver new, advanced products and services to market. Smart acquirers get access to innovative products; really smart ones strengthen their capability to innovate. Here, too, Cisco excels. It consistently holds on to the talented employees of acquired companies, employees whose knowledge, skills, and energies are critical to continued innovation.

Adding to innovation capability is a dramatic way for HR to become a true partner with line managers. HR professionals should be able to contribute alongside strategic planners, manufacturing executives, marketers, scientists, and financial managers and assess the fit with a target company's market offering and capabilities. HR should also help define the strengths and weaknesses of the acquirer's own innovation capability and assess whether a given target company would help address deficiencies. These are business issues, not classic HR concerns; a fully contributing HR function will have a firm place on the team that addresses them.

The HR function of the future must also guide management in how best to achieve organizational integration. Consider, for example, the organizational issues that might surround an acquisition designed to bolster a company's e-commerce capability. HR could lead in helping a management team answer a set of thorny organizational questions such as the following:

- Should we integrate the e-commerce unit into the company or spin it off (fully or partially)?
- Who should own e-commerce: marketing, line operations, information technology, an independent business unit?
- How should we structure the unit (layers of management, functional groupings, reporting relationships)?
- How should we educate the rest of the company about our intended e-commerce strategy?
- Who, if anyone, from the existing organization should transfer to the new e-commerce unit?

For HR to have the credibility required to take a place at the technology-planning table, the function must demonstrate technological sophistication in its own right. This means pushing its ability to innovate by developing new technology well beyond the transactional systems that often dominate HRIS today. HR technology must increase individual and manager productivity (for example, by helping managers connect business planning systems with workforce planning systems to project postmerger staffing needs). Beyond that, HR must work toward creating smart systems that learn and improve as they are used (for instance, expert systems that compile information and then develop algorithms to predict turnover). In some cases, these systems will play a critical role in the merger integration effort. In all cases, they offer proof that HR has the innovation capability and technological sophistication to contribute to a technology-driven acquisition effort.

The engine that powers innovation capability and generates technology-based products has become, for twenty-first century companies, the fundamental value source: knowledge capital. In no other area of merger and acquisition management is the role of HR more critical.

Knowledge Capital—Preserving Value

Embedded knowledge has become the key to innovation capability; the investment markets have increasingly awakened to this reality. Baruch Lev, Philip Bardes professor of accounting and finance at New York University, notes that growth in the ratio of market capitalization to net book value for companies on the S&P 500 comes largely from what he calls knowledge assets, the intangibles that drive company prosperity in an information-intensive, technology-focused world. Even if we chalk up some of this difference between market and book values to stock market exuberance, Lev says, "We haven't seen anything yet." He points out, "We're close to the limits of efficiency for physical capital. There is no doubt in my mind that the knowledge assets will continue to climb, however."

Companies that acquire customer and supplier relationships in new markets, products that complement current offerings, or patents on specialized manufacturing techniques have acquired knowledge assets. Prospective acquirers of such assets face a twofold challenge:

- Holding on to the sources of knowledge assets (that is, the smart people who created them)
- Ensuring that, even if the organization retains those sources, future productivity justifies the purchase price

HR has a role to play in helping companies address both challenges. In the pre-deal stage of the M&A process, HR should help the company identify acquisition candidates that have the capabilities and the people to bolster knowledge capital (intangible assets). Conversely, HR should avoid mergers or acquisitions (or help negotiate better prices) where the added value from intangible assets is insufficient.

In the due diligence stage, HR should deeply probe the critical capabilities of the candidate organization. The goal is to determine the extent to which key capabilities (e.g., innovation, product development, brand creation) depend on finely honed processes, efficient organization structures, well-adapted culture, state-of-the-art assets, or highly qualified people. Capabilities most often depend, of course, on a combination of all of these factors. Nevertheless, all components of a capability will not contribute equally; one or two elements will usually rise above the others in importance. HR can work side by side with line management to perform the capability assessment. Often, the human capital (knowledge, skills, talent, and behaviors) of key people will emerge as the preeminent reason for successful creation of knowledge assets. It is in the preservation and enhancement of people-centered value where HR can—indeed, must—earn its stripes.

HR should have the capability to zero in on the most critical individual contributors and marshal the resources required to ensure their commitment to the new company and their continued engagement in their jobs. The complexities of engendering commitment and engagement are well documented but are by no means simple. Building commitment and fostering engagement rely on a comprehensive "deal" between individual and organization, a deal that involves an entire portfolio of rewards, both financial and nonfinancial. The point is that HR must turn its attention chiefly to the few key people whose contributions are vital to preserving the most important acquired capabilities. This means addressing two imperatives:

- Building bonds of commitment to the organization so that key contributors don't walk out the door before they deliver their full potential contribution
- Providing jobs and a work environment that keep them engaged and producing in ways that will fulfill the promise of the merger or acquisition

Whereas HR has often focused its attention on achieving general alignment and equity between the reward programs of two combining entities, the future calls for greater focus. In a business environment where knowledge assets produce economic value, HR must concentrate on identifying key contributors and forging powerful bonds with them. Program alignment may be worthwhile for the organization at large, but having deals in place that can help bind the most productive individual asset-generators to the company is crucial.

Of course, it's not easy to identify the top talent accurately—especially in large global organizations. If their identity does not become obvious from the analysis of organization capabilities, HR needs to call in outside experts. One source of expertise is headhunters. They know who has the skills, experience, and talent to be interesting to other companies. Ask the headhunters for their appraisal; then make sure that the people they identify feel so much commitment and such high levels of engagement that they ignore the headhunter when he or she calls later with an offer from another company.

Keeping an acquired company's key people requires more than great individual deals, however. Cultural compatibility between the organizations comes into play again. HR should have in its toolkit a methodology for describing corporate cultures and comparing the cultural elements of the two companies. To the extent that culture may be a phenomenon of business units (rather than whole companies or even regions of the world), multiple analyses may be called for. Tools exist for culture profiling and assessment. The simplest approach (and possibly the best) for culture assessment (pre-closing) is to determine what an organization chooses to measure, reward, and punish. That intelligence says much about whether two companies are likely to encourage common approaches for achieving and recognizing success.

At present, most companies have poor (or nonexistent) ways of measuring the value of knowledge assets and monitoring how that value changes as a consequence of a merger or acquisition. Interestingly, Baruch Lev, Joshua Livnat, and Benjamin Segal, in their working paper entitled "Identifying and Valuing Individual Intangibles," found that the reported value placed on human capital in 10 acquisitions involving technology companies ranged from 3 to 12 percent of the purchase price, with an average of 5 percent.

Here again, HR should step into this breach to create (and advocate) a set of tools for valuing knowledge assets of both acquirer and acquiree, or merger partners. Like all good measurements, these tools should be simple to apply, focused on what really counts, understandable to everyone who needs them, and indicative of any corrective action required.

The recent merger between Pfizer and Warner-Lambert demonstrates how a company can estimate a deal's impact on knowledge capital. There is knowledge capital in every business, but seldom to the degree found in pharmaceuticals, where research and development, brand reputation, patents, and product development capture most of an organization's stock market value. Pfizer Chief Financial Officer David Shedlarz referred specifically to these resources when he described the goal of the merger as creation of "a new competitive standard in developing a breadth and depth of research capability."

Wall Street expected the combination of the two companies to be a financial winner. Instead of two separate organizations, each expected to increase earnings at 20 percent annually, the new company carried the expectation of a 24 percent annual growth rate. Pfizer had premerger knowledge capital of $82.5 billion; Warner-Lambert was worth $50.0 billion in knowledge capital, for a total of $132.5 billion. Postmerger, Wall Street expected the figure to grow to $166.9 billion. Thus, the merger appeared to add $34.4 billion in knowledge capital. Subtract the $28 billion premium over Warner Lambert's market price paid by Pfizer (knowledge capital doesn't come cheap), and you get a net knowledge capital gain of $6.4 billion, according to an article by S. L. Mintz in the April 2000 issue of *CFO* Magazine. By developing this kind of information, HR can advance the cause of financially rigorous, value-oriented metrics. Such metrics are central elements of a modern management information system, whether in a merger and acquisition context or in an ongoing business.

Unfortunately, valuation is a major literacy gap, according to the research done for this book. Nearly 80 percent of the survey participants felt valuing human capital is an extremely important area of HR knowledge; however, fewer than one-third believe they possess this knowledge today.

Workforce Evolution—Planning Beyond the Merger

HR functions across North America are already struggling with workforce evolution. Undertaking mergers and acquisitions that depend on obtaining and preserving access to scarce talent makes the challenge all the more difficult. In the narrowest sense, preserving the people-related value of two organizations requires a personal touch with key people. From a broader perspective, keeping the people who create knowledge capital means astute analysis and integration of company cultures. At a higher level, HR must help managers understand the realities of workforce evolution in their planning for implementation while continuing to meet the existing competitive challenges.

In a tight labor market demanding ever-higher technological know-how, skilled contributors will have substantial control over their work lives. The well-documented phenomenon of worker free agency will gain further momentum in the evolved workforce of the future. Moreover, the desire for freedom is not limited to veteran technomasters with impressive resumes. In June 2000, the National Association of Colleges and Employers reported that 62 percent of the visitors to its JobWeb site (geared toward graduating college students) said they expect to stay at their first job three years or fewer. Workforce flexibility, it seems, starts young.

Given worker mobility, even a thoughtful retention strategy will face pressure from the tightening labor market in a merger or acquisition. External forces militate in favor of increasing use of nontraditional social contracts between people and companies. Indeed, an organization that can, through merger or acquisition, develop the capability for defining and managing such relationships will gain a potentially large competitive advantage. Expect to see more M&A activity driven by one company's desire to capitalize on another's capability to devise and manage a diverse set of worker/company relationships.

In many ways, a merger or acquisition simply adds urgency to crafting a forward-looking people strategy and workforce planning effort. In the integration planning stages, HR must lead the new company in identifying the human capital required to succeed, both immediately and over the long term, and in formulating the strategies for filling the gaps it identifies. Understanding the new company's business and current human capital within the combining organizations, and having deep insights into future labor market conditions, will empower HR to take initiative to ensure that the new company has people

- with the right skills, knowledge, talents, and behaviors;
- in the right number and combinations;
- in the right places;
- at the right times and for the right duration; and
- at the right costs.

Given the technology and innovation imperatives discussed earlier, HR faces a specific challenge (and a commensurate opportunity) in using a merger or acquisition to increase available talent in a few key areas. Recent research conducted jointly by Towers Perrin and the Economist Intelligence Unit pinpointed two such areas: innovation and e-literacy. The research indicated that executives of major North American and European companies believe that these are the two most important employee skills in terms of contribution to future strategic success. And here's the challenge—the same executives said that the greatest gaps between present employee skills and future requirements are in those two skill areas. The HR function that helps an organization come through the integration process with enhanced employee competency in these areas will have made a dramatic contribution to the performance of the combined entity.

HR must understand the myriad trade-offs inherent in workforce planning: choosing experienced people or recruiting new college graduates, investing in training or hiring workers with the necessary background, substituting technology for people or changing business practices, keeping veteran employees or bringing in fresh blood.

HR will need creativity to deal with these trade-offs. As one expert puts it, "Competition for strategic talent will drive the implementation of new team-centered practices that include drafting, trading, and free agency concepts similar to those found in professional athletics. The workforce staffing function will be responsible for the proactive scouting of talent—again similar to athletic scouting activities."

Once the integration planning teams have a good handle on the new company's human capital needs, the contracting process begins. In a world where stock market value comes largely from human capital (i.e., people) and where the right people are harder and harder to find, imaginative employment contracts, in the words of one observer, become a needed-to-win organization capability. This capability not only strengthens competitiveness, it also has the potential for providing the HR function with a strong identity and a new set of service performance benchmarks to achieve, say Mary Mallon and Joanne Duberley in an article in *Human Resource Management Journal*, "Managers and Professionals in the Contingent Workforce" (first quarter 2000).

Contracting requires HR to deal with a host of ambiguous issues. As more and more workers approach their careers as free agents, the simple dichotomy of "employee" or "not an employee" disappears. For example, with whom should you create a traditional employee relationship ("core" employees, for example), and who should have a transaction-type contract? After all, the best contributors usually have the greatest freedom, so what's the point in trying to tie them down with a contract? Should you provide training to contract workers, or should learning and development be limited to regular employees? How much involvement should free agents have in helping to devise and implement strategy? How much flexibility should employees have to negotiate customized deals?

Findings from the Towers Perrin study with the Economist Intelligence Unit indicate that, at present, only about 10 percent of employees in large North American and European companies have any real opportunity to customize their reward packages. But the executives in these companies believe that by 2003, the percentage of employees with at least some control over their reward packages will swell to 56 percent. HR departments that can accommodate this growing flexibility while still getting the most out of reward investments and minimizing administrative costs will be heroes to managers and shareholders alike.

Notwithstanding the difficulty of these questions, as Mallon and Duberley note, "The growth of contingent work provides the field of HRM (HR management) with an opportunity to shift its focus from employment to managing the work done for the organization, opening up substantial opportunities to contribute to the bottom line of the business."

Indeed, sophisticated workforce planning and creative contracting are important HR capabilities regardless of whether an organization engages in M&A activity. In a merger or acquisition, the challenges of unifying separate workforces provide an opportunity (indeed, an imperative) to raise workforce planning and contracting to an entirely new level.

Changing Gears (and Everything Else)

We began this chapter with a set of questions that established a context for discussing HR's future role in M&A. The chapter has provided answers—however speculative—to those questions. As for management's motives in pursuing mergers and acquisitions, revenue growth (from new markets, products, and innovation capabilities) emerged as a top priority. Cross-border M&A activity is likely to continue, although targets in developing countries will play an increasingly important role in future alliance plans. Intangible assets will continue their ascendancy as the principal sources of value in future mergers and acquisitions.

One question remains unanswered: Will organizations do a better job of integration and value creation than their predecessors have done? We can expect that the securities markets will become ever savvier about granting high multiples to management teams who do the best job of effectively executing well-conceived mergers and acquisitions. Conversely, the financial markets will punish management teams that don't have the wherewithal to bring companies together. Companies in which the HR function contributes in all stages of the M&A life cycle will, one hopes, find themselves in the former group.

HR roles in future M&As are clearly challenging. But, like all things challenging, mergers and acquisitions are both a threat and an opportunity. The threat is clear: Fail to deliver the needed capabilities, and the merger or acquisition fails. Failure damages HR's credibility and may label the function a bureaucracy incapable of meeting critical business needs. Succeed, and the merger or acquisition has a good chance of yielding value. Success can only increase the credibility (and influence) of the HR function.

What more can HR do to ensure its place on the core team that plans for and implements future mergers and acquisitions? Following are a few ideas.

- **Expand points of reference.** HR should not set its sights on being the best HR function it can be. Instead, HR should strive to be as good as the best functions in the new company at the things that matter most. HR should be able to measure implementation progress and business performance as well as finance; make deals that are as creative as any the legal department could devise; be as technologically sophisticated as people in MIS, at least in implementing the applications that count most for people management; and provide service as good as that available in the company's best customer service unit.
- **Focus on what matters.** HR must pay attention to people, organizational and cultural integration, opportunities, measurement, and benchmarks that make a difference.
- **Change—and manage change—at electronic speed.** HR must do what needs to be done "just in time." By anticipating and preparing for change and improving its use of technology, HR can accelerate its conventional pace.
- **Build manager competencies.** HR must work to shift direct responsibility for ownership of people issues—before and after a merger or acquisition—to line managers.
- **Become the organization's conscience—and its source of information and insight—on the value of knowledge capital.** HR must suggest ways to monitor changes in this critical intangible asset as a foundation for analyzing how it might change through a merger.

An HR function that hopes to contribute directly to successful mergers and acquisitions must comprise managers, professionals, and administrative staff who have, in addition to the traditional skills, a distinct set of competencies not common among HR practitioners today, including the following:

- Tolerance for constant change: Responding to, and thriving in, a state of continuous flux; making sure HR moves and adapts fast enough to keep up with the M&A integration process.
- Business insight: Understanding how the new company will need to compete and to prosper, and being able to translate that understanding into a direct contribution to the integration process; beyond business acumen, this means knowing the new company's business well enough to advise and counsel line managers on how to build human capital and how to deploy it for the greatest effect.
- Technology expertise: Possessing an advanced understanding of web-based and other technologies that can ratchet up the performance of HR.
- Comfort with criticism: Having a propensity to seek regular feedback from internal customers and to act on that feedback responsively and quickly.
- Presence and self-confidence: Being secure in the knowledge of belonging in the M&A integration planning and implementation activities with the most senior, seasoned managers in the new company.

Despite the current hype about HR as a "business partner," the evolution of the function as a strategic contributor is still more hope than reality. According to a 1999 survey summarized in the June 2000 *Human Resource Department Management Report*, "Is It Wishful Thinking or Has HR's Role Really Changed?" HR still spends almost two-thirds of its time maintaining records, auditing procedural compliance, and administering programs and practices.

Skill at these kinds of activities will not enable HR to contribute to successful mergers and acquisitions. Instead, HR practitioners must help find ways to grow revenue, anticipate and adapt to workforce changes, and help line managers widen their understanding of how to build human capital. An HR function that can do these things will be a real player at every stage of the M&A process. ■

Appendices

APPENDIX A
The Global Transaction

Jeffrey A. Schmidt

Cross-border mergers and acquisitions follow the same life cycle and face the same types of issues as domestic transactions, with the added complications of language barriers, differences in management styles, organization and pay philosophies, and cultural and regulatory hurdles. Nonetheless, despite the additional risks, global mergers and acquisitions are accelerating.

Let's briefly examine some of the distinctive aspects in the life cycle of a cross-border merger.

Due diligence. Due diligence is a crucial step in any proposed deal, but the process is both more complex and more crucial when the potential partner or acquiree is located in a foreign country or countries. A target company may have operations in many nations on as many as six continents, and it is neither efficient nor logical to conduct equal due diligence in each country. Instead, the acquirer should focus on those four or five places that matter most—those with the highest revenue, the greatest number of employees, the strongest potential for growth or cost savings, and the greatest level of risk. While HR should be involved in every stage of a cross-border deal—from target selection through implementation—HR involvement in due diligence is especially critical because of the complex and sensitive organizational and cultural risks involved, including pay and benefits issues.

The process begins with the development of country-specific due diligence criteria, which must be based on the underlying business and economic rationale for the deal. Specific people-related issues to be considered will vary by country, but they usually include the following:

- Severance costs
- Acquired rights

- Union and other labor agreements
- Employment contracts, especially for executives
- Laws governing employee terminations
- Pension and benefit plans
- Unrecognized liabilities

Much of this research is collected at data centers established by the acquiree in each country. The due diligence team should include people who speak the local language and understand local laws, regulations, customs, and business practices. If these skills are unavailable within the acquirer, they must be hired from the outside.

It is not unusual for due diligence to reveal hidden liabilities in the funding of a target company's pension program. Sometimes, such liabilities can be large enough to kill the deal or significantly reduce the price the acquirer is willing to pay. This problem can crop up in any deal, either domestic or foreign, but there is less chance of discovering it when there are operations in several countries, each of which has its own regulations for the governance of such plans.

HR comprises only one component of a companywide due diligence team and must maintain regular communication with other disciplines. In one instance, careful due diligence uncovered a pension plan that was underfunded by $60 million. The target company had evaluated the liability at $20 million and was as surprised as the acquirer to discover the $40 million discrepancy. The result: a $40 million reduction in the purchase price.

Total rewards. In the area of total rewards, underfunded pensions are not the only cross-border problems that can arise. Others—such as employee pay—may be less dramatic, but they too can be significant. For example, the acquirer may already operate a subsidiary in a foreign country where it is considering an acquisition. Pay levels at the current subsidiary may be significantly higher than those at the target company, presenting the acquirer with a difficult choice. Failure to raise wages appropriately may have a deleterious effect on morale, but doing so may not be financially feasible.

Executive compensation also presents challenges—especially when U.S.-based companies are involved—with the key issue being stock options, not salary. Such options have been an integral component of total rewards in the United States for many years but are used less often elsewhere.

Cultural integration. While cultural issues can be a major factor in domestic mergers, the challenge is compounded when the cultures of different countries are considered. Employees in different countries may be motivated by different factors, and certain aspects of one culture may be difficult for another to accept. This could become an issue for an acquiring company and requires that the appropriate integration philosophy be selected and that implementation proceed with an eye toward flexibility and sensitivity to national employee attitudes, perspectives, and feelings.

Communication. All HR professionals understand that communication can play a key role in successful integration, particularly during the regulatory review period after the deal is announced. In a cross-border deal, it is obviously necessary to communicate in the language of the acquired company, but this cannot be accomplished merely by translating documents from headquarters. The tone, manner, style, and wording of a printed or e-mail message must be reviewed by those who truly understand both the language and culture of the target company. To do otherwise is to risk offending and perhaps even permanently antagonizing employees. And in some countries, one-to-one communication is the only acceptable means of delivering important messages to employees.

Cross-pollination. For global companies, integration is an ongoing process. There are cultural and operational advantages to fostering regular contact among employees at every location and at virtually every level. Long-term, the most effective way to bring the corporation together is by managing a unified, globally diverse workforce, with employees from subsidiaries spending time at corporate headquarters, and with similar corporate-to-subsidiary and subsidiary-to-subsidiary programs.

The formula for cross-border success. There are no easy answers, but the best advice may be to "plan globally and implement locally." The first part of the formula is self-evident: develop a worldwide strategy that is commensurate with the company's long-term goals and then target appropriate foreign acquisitions or partners. Successful implementation of a global strategy requires equally careful attention to the second part of the formula: a strong individual focus on every operation in every country. In each case, it is vital to understand and be ready to deal with local customs and regulations, compensation practices, and labor markets as well as with the national and company cultures.

   A truly global company is one that can be at home in every part of the world. In a global merger of the chemicals subsidiaries of three large oil and gas companies, mapping the cultural differences and similarities produced a stunning example of what it means to be truly global. Each of the merger participants had operations around the globe and found that the attributes of their corporate cultures, regardless of location, were stronger than the attributes of their national cultures. In fact, the company affiliations of employees of each country could be identified by the profiles of their respective companies. So understanding corporate culture is an important element in melding workforces in mergers and acquisitions. ∎

APPENDIX B

Major Risks to Implementation

Jeffrey A. Schmidt

Our research for this book identified the 10 most significant risks in implementing mergers and acquisitions. These risks were highlighted in Chapter One and are more fully discussed below.

1. Inability to Sustain Financial Performance

Survey respondents say that sustaining the financial performance of the legacy companies' core businesses while going through a merger or acquisition is the major challenge to achieving success. Indeed, as many companies have learned the hard way, losing focus when integrating two businesses makes each of them especially vulnerable to competitors.

2. Loss of Productivity

Although this issue was rated second in importance in the Towers Perrin/SHRM Foundation survey, it is in many cases the first problem to surface. The days following the announcement of a merger or acquisition are a time of widespread uncertainty. Employees are anxiously searching for answers to many questions: Will I keep my job? Will I continue to like working here? Who will I report to? Will things be done differently around here in the future? This uncertainty will almost certainly cause productivity to falter. And those hoped-for synergies—such as an increase in productivity—will seem far less certain.

A merger or acquisition that gets off on the wrong foot may stumble into chaos and never regain its momentum. That's why it's so important to be prepared to address productivity issues before they arise. And productivity issues are largely people issues.

3. Incompatible Cultures

Excellent companies nurture high-performance work environments. However, a merger or acquisition of any magnitude can have a strong impact—either a positive or negative one—on the cultures of the affected organizations. That's why integrating culture in a thoughtful way is essential to the success of the newly formed company. As Jan Leschly, retired CEO of SmithKline Beecham, observed in a CEO Roundtable published in the *Harvard Business Review* ("Lessons from Master Acquirers: A CEO Roundtable on Making Mergers Succeed," May/June 2000), "In my experience, even if the rationale for a deal is terrific, the deal can still fall apart because of cultural differences."

Most mergers and acquisitions entail some degree of cultural melding as a necessity. As seasoned HR professionals know, successfully managing this aspect of integration requires good data and objective analysis of the cultures of the affected companies. Therefore, the first step in cultural melding is measurement. This can be done in a variety of ways, with tools and techniques suited to each situation. Armed with this information, management can decide where the two cultures are likely to be at odds, where there will be the greatest areas of compatibility, and—perhaps most important—where cultural differences might result in new thinking and new ways of doing things that will help the new company succeed.

Irrespective of which approach is selected to assess culture, it's critical to complete the assessment as early in the integration process as possible. In fact, one thing HR managers who have gone through unsuccessful mergers or acquisitions agree on is that next time around they'll do a culture assessment a lot sooner.

4. Loss of Key Talent

The success of a deal hinges on retaining the key talent in both organizations. Loss of key talent is problematic in every deal, but it can be catastrophic in some situations. For example, in high-technology acquisitions where the target company's core assets are people rather than physical or financial assets, an exodus of scientists and engineers can absolutely confound the deal's economic rationale. Similarly, an investment banking firm would be virtually worthless without the talented contributors who made it successful before a merger or acquisition.

Yet talent is always portable and marketable. And during that volatile period following an announcement of a merger or acquisition, competitors often respond to the threat they perceive from the new combination by recruiting the participating companies' key talent. Or, in the absence of well-designed change-in-control agreements, key people with vested stock options and attractive severance packages may simply decide to retire or to change careers or employers.

Retaining key talent must be treated as a top priority for leadership of the new company. As a senior vice president for human resources of a giant global corporation that had made several major cross-border acquisitions stated, "You always lose important knowledge and weaken your capabilities when talented and experienced people leave a company that's been acquired. But, you can't keep all of the best people. You can't even know for certain who they are. Moreover, what knowledge is lost when such people depart can't be predicted accurately in advance. It will take a year or more to really understand and count your losses. Worse yet, once you know, you inevitably discover that some of what's been lost cannot be replaced."

5. Clash of Management Styles

Conflicts between the two former chief executives usually result in the departure of one of them. In most cases, the survivor will be the CEO of the dominant company. Peter Bijur, the former CEO of Texaco, Inc., resigned before Chevron had secured the final regulatory approvals to proceed with its acquisition of his company. That said, in some instances, the chief executive of an acquired company can assume the top role.

Conflict resolution is emerging as a growing professional discipline, and skilled practitioners in this field have developed useful techniques for helping people understand the causes of their differences and learn how to work together effectively. At a number of companies, HR professionals trained in conflict resolution often work in tandem with outside specialists to ease the difficult but necessary task of resolving clashes of ego or personality so that the new company can move on.

6. Inability to Manage or Implement Change

It's important to recognize that most employees expect significant change following a merger or acquisition. In fact, many are ready and willing to start anew. This atmosphere offers ample opportunities to introduce new organization, management processes, culture, and human resource programs—or add new elements to those of the combining organizations.

Since a merger or acquisition will bring substantial changes for everyone in both organizations, a good plan for managing change and helping employees adjust will accelerate and smooth the transition process. As study after study confirms, change management is most effective when a company can provide each employee with a satisfactory answer to the question: "What's in it for me?"

As one vice president of communications put it, "Communication is critical. We need to do a better job of helping people understand, 'What about me? My desk? My colleagues? My work?' If you don't have a way to answer those [questions] quickly in a programmatic way, the silence will grind people to a halt."

7. Slow Decision-Making

Even if decision-making at both companies was relatively efficient before the merger or acquisition, there is a danger that the pace will decline after the deal is made—particularly during the integration period.

This happens because managers from one or both companies are operating under an unfamiliar corporate structure. They may be reporting to different managers. They may be obliged to use unfamiliar forms, techniques, and systems. And, more often than not, many of them may feel as if they're walking on eggs, afraid that if they make a mistake they will lose their jobs.

And yet, timely decision-making is crucial for the new company. As one senior vice president of HR puts it, "In today's business environment, companies can't afford the luxury of time. Rather, speed and responsiveness should be the hallmarks of an effective integration process."

8. Wrong People for Key Jobs

To help ensure that the right people are selected for key jobs, a careful evaluation of the top talent at both companies must be made before integration begins. Top managers need a coherent selection process and the data to make good choices.

Inevitably, there will be some bad appointments. Sometimes people making the appointments will ignore good advice, sometimes the individuals being appointed don't live up to the expectations detailed in their evaluations, and sometimes the evaluations are inaccurate.

9. Insufficient Communication

According to Tig Krekel, CEO of Hughes Space and Communications and CEO Roundtable participant, "You need constant communication to avoid paralysis and maintain morale." To which Allstate's Ed Lilly, a member of the same CEO Roundtable, adds, "… we communicate, communicate, communicate. We say the same thing over and over again to the acquired company, to ourselves, to Wall Street. That way, a common understanding of what we're trying to do can emerge."

During the early days of a merger or acquisition, the rumor mill will be operating at full throttle, and a considerable amount of inaccurate information will be making the rounds. If rumors are their only source of information, employees will tend to believe what they hear. That's one reason an effective communications program is so important—and why it should begin well before a deal closes. As one senior HR executive said, "From a high-level perspective, classic communication from the senior leader is critical to the success of the deal. In deals that have gone particularly well, that visible leadership and continuous reinforcement of the message was very helpful. You don't need spit and polish; you just need decent communications skills."

10. Inability to Define Direction or Implement New Business Model

Top executives must define the new business model for the combined organization and establish the direction in which they intend to lead it. The messages should be clear: "This is where we are going. This is how we intend to get there. This is how you can help."

Obviously, this effort can succeed only if the new company's senior leadership has a clear vision and business model in mind and is willing and able to lead the new organization in pursuing its corporate goals. ∎

APPENDIX C

More About Due Diligence

Andrew F. Giffin

The nature and scope of and approaches to the due diligence process were described in Chapter Four. This appendix elaborates on a central technique for helping to ensure the due diligence process is planned and managed in a comprehensive manner—namely, the use of due diligence checklists to identify the scope of issues to be covered. Typically, these lists are provided to the target to identify necessary documentation, key people to be interviewed, and other resources. They also provide a guide for the ad hoc due diligence team that usually includes acquirer staff and outside advisors.

Documentation and accompanying commentary provide the due diligence record and background for a summary report of results. These lists should reflect the key areas of investigation and the level of detail examined.

The due diligence team develops the lists for each acquisition. The team makes additions to the lists as it gains experience with each new acquisition. That said, good judgment must be applied to the development of these lists. The benefits of adding greater detail must be weighed against the time and resource constraints that invariably characterize the due diligence process.

The following sample lists are not meant to be exhaustive, but they illustrate the types of issues that should be considered. Terms such as "significant," "controlling," and others refer to threshold amounts that the acquirer must define. Following the lists are some interview suggestions.

Initial investigation in any of these areas can trigger requests for more detail. Moreover, each industry will have specialized lists that relate to the characteristics and risks of that business.

Remember that the goal is not to collect information for its own sake. Rather, it is to identify those key issues that have significant potential for challenging the merits of the deal or influencing the process of integration.

Due Diligence Lists

Verify Strategic Expectations

Note: The purpose of this material is to identify the target's existing and prospective corporate strategies and learn how these strategies fit with market demand and competitive constraints as well as corporate structures and ownership interests.

Business and Market Positioning
- Strategic plans, marketing studies, feasibility studies
- Company statements of strategic intent and marketing positions—mission and vision statements, advertisements, marketing materials
- Press releases and speeches by senior managers concerning company direction and policy
- References to the company in industry reports of investment bankers, accountants, financial analysts, trade press, etc.
- Descriptions of the markets the company operates in, including growth, geography, seasonality, business cycles, customer segments, suppliers, distributors, and competitors; identification of key industry trends and prospects for future performance
- Descriptions of major customer segments in terms of demand characteristics and geographic locations; identification of recurring customers and the relative strength of the customer relationship (e.g., number of customers with multiple product purchases, length of customer relationships)
- Lists of the company's largest customers with recent sales activity and current obligations
- Descriptions of products and services with recent and expected growth trends, basis for competitive position and profitability trends; identification of key competitors and relative competitive advantages
- Descriptions of distribution channels, including relationship with the company (e.g., employed, exclusive, independent), with cost structures, including sales compensation structures; identification of any major distributors that control a significant percentage of sales in any product or service line
- Description of advertising and promotion methods and costs
- Description of operating/manufacturing/administrative functions that are key to competitive success; comparison of cost and quality with major competitors
- Copies of reports of company performance compared with competitors using typical industry performance measures

Corporate Structure and Organization
- Copies of incorporation documentation with authorization to do business in good standing
- Lists of subsidiaries, affiliates, joint ventures, and partnerships, including ownership structure, other owners, and lines of business

- Copies of corporate by-laws, minutes, and documentation of actions of governing bodies within the organization (e.g., boards of directors, management committees)
- Lists of jurisdictions where business is conducted or facilities are located, with descriptions of business conducted and tax filing and payment requirements
- List of all government authorizations to operate, permits, licenses held or required to be held by the company
- Lists of agents and others with powers of attorney authorized to act on behalf of the company, with the nature and extent of their representation
- Lists of predecessor companies and prior company names
- Lists of principal officers and directors of separate corporations, including names, ages, compensation (all sources), stock ownership, and financial interests in related businesses

Securities
- Statement of outstanding and treasury shares of common and preferred stock and any other securities issued and authorized for each controlled corporate entity
- Lists of shareholders of 1 percent or more interest in any class of securities; lists of holders of options or rights to purchase or sell securities, with the terms of such rights; copies of any voting trust arrangements or other stockholder agreements
- Copies of stock transfer books and the status/location of stock certificates
- Description of any restrictions on rights of security transfer or exercise of ownership rights
- Copies of documents related to sale or repurchase of any company securities, including public sales and private placements
- History of dividend payments to security holders

Validate the Price

Note: The objective of due diligence is to identify evidence of value in assets and operating results, subject to liabilities and risks.

Financial Statements
- Five years of audited year-end and unaudited interim financial statements, both consolidated and consolidating for all controlled corporate entities
- History of auditor relationships, verification of independence and management letters issued, with related auditor correspondence
- Description of methods and procedures for establishing any special liability or equity reserves (this may include detailed inquiry where reserves are a significant part of the business—e.g., financial services)
- Description of significant changes in accounting procedures
- Suite of internal financial management reports
- Budgets, sales projections, and financial planning documents

- Capital management reports and projections
- Revenue and expense allocation and transfer pricing procedures
- Description of capital and other commitments
- Procedures for allocation of capital to new activities or major purchases, including criteria for selection and a history of recent allocations
- Descriptions of major loans, including mortgages, liens, pledges, or other security arrangements, and short-term and long-term debt instruments and financing agreements; documentation of the current status of these obligations, including any provision for waiver of default or other adjustments to terms
- Description of pricing policies and methods used to develop pricing assumptions, with copies of experience studies that back current pricing assumptions
- Description of acquisitions and divestitures in the past five years
- Documentation of joint venture, partnership, and merger or acquisition agreements
- Explanation of liabilities and contingencies not included in the financial statements
- Copies of major leases, service contracts, and other agreements that involve existing and future financial commitments
- List of major suppliers, with amount paid to each in the past three years
- Breakdown of revenues, expenses, and profit/loss by major product class and region
- Copies of SEC filings plus presentations to financial analysts, rating agencies, and creditors to secure financing or to report current financial conditions and prospects
- Evaluation of key trends in revenues, expenses, profit and loss, capital position, ROE, and other measures used in the relevant industries to measure competitive and financial performance
- Evaluation of asset valuation, the appropriateness of the asset mix compared with liabilities, liquidity, and other measures of financial strength

Property and Leases
- List of real estate owned and leased, including details of structures, equipment and use, with descriptions of restrictions on use, and appraised values (including methods used and appraisers)
- List of vehicles and equipment owned and leased; agreements for significant items
- List of premises where company assets are housed other than owned or leased property, with related agreements
- Commitments to maintain existing locations or property holdings (if any)

Investments
- Description of the portfolio of investments, including investment type, cost basis, current value, and method of valuation for each item; copies of external appraisals and references to published market valuations of assets

- Copies of agreements and sales documentation for the sale of significant assets in the past three years
- Copies of policies and procedures for cash management, investment, currency matching/hedging, and liquidity

Intellectual Property
- Schedule of registered and unregistered patents, trademarks, copyrights, and domain names with applicable terms (e.g., duration, jurisdictions, conditions); identification of maintenance requirements and history of maintenance
- Schedule of other inventions or trade-secret information considered to have significant value to the business, with valuation and efforts to protect this value
- Copies of contracts, licenses, or other agreements concerning the use of governmental funding or university and college facilities to develop computer programs or other intellectual property
- Copies of agreements that license or assign intellectual property rights to third parties
- Schedule of restrictions on the use of intellectual property rights (e.g., court orders)
- Procedures and appraisals supporting claimed value of intellectual property
- Procedures for protecting intellectual property
- Employment contracts that define employee rights to intellectual property created during employment
- Claims, or potential claims, against the company related to the use of intellectual property claimed by others

Valuations
- Copies of internal and external estimates of economic and appraised value of the overall business and component parts

Discover Significant Liabilities and Exposures

Note: See the previous section for items reported in financial statements and other liabilities and contingencies. This area includes both recorded and unrecorded or contingent risks. It includes efforts by the company to ensure or otherwise account for exposures.

Business Agreements
- Copies of standard forms for sales, distribution, transportation, warehousing, and purchase
- Copies of warranty agreements related to products and services
- Copies of significant nonstandard sales, distribution, transportation, warehousing, and purchase agreements
- Copies of advertising and public relations agreements
- Copies of agreements for the company(ies) acting as agent(s) for third parties
- Copies of agreements with major suppliers
- Copies of agreements with a party in which an officer, director, employee, or shareholder has a significant interest

- Assets used in the business in which an officer, director, employee, or shareholder has a significant interest
- Copies of technology licenses as licensor or licensee
- Copies of R&D agreements
- Copies of agreements to perform acts more than three months in the future
- Copies of government contracts, noting any clauses restricting ownership or business activity or imposing security requirements
- List of such contracts currently in negotiations or renegotiations
- List of any contractual arrangements subject to cancellation or claims for damages or loss

Employee Obligations

Note: See other references to pay and benefit plans, union contracts, intellectual property rights, and other relationships with employees that can arise, particularly with respect to employees who are retired, disabled, or acquired with prior company acquisitions. These are covered in the main body of this book, in other appendices, or both.

- Description of any complaints and claims for failure to meet civil and criminal laws and regulations concerning employment status (e.g., equal opportunity, exposure to hazards)

Tax Matters

Note: Are past, present, and future tax obligations accounted for and efficiently applied?

- Copies of all national, regional, local, and foreign income, VAT, property, and franchise tax returns filed by each company
- Copies of correspondence with tax authorities concerning questions and adjustments on filings
- List of tax audits conducted with determination letters or reports
- Schedule of annual tax filing requirements
- Copies of any agreements, consents, elections, or waivers filed or made with taxing authorities; copies of orders of taxing authorities or courts on tax matters
- Copies of tax allocation, indemnification, or other arrangements among affiliated companies
- Copies of legal or accounting tax opinions and advice received by the company related to tax reporting
- Schedule of tax credits and deferrals carried forward and any contingent tax obligations, past, present, or future (e.g., disputed past tax liability)
- Description of any prior open tax year issues

Insurance and Risk Management

Note: The overarching purpose of this topical area is to ensure that the company has a comprehensive understanding of and provision for enterprise risks.

- Risk management plans or other documents outlining risks and plans for managing risks
- Description of properties or activities that have potential for special risks (e.g., aircraft, marine vessels, marine terminals, railroads, fine arts, precious metals,

underground excavation, property in flood zones, distribution of alcoholic beverages)
- Copies of insurance policies and other risk management arrangements (captives; self insurance, including property coverage; workers compensation/employers liability; business interruption; directors and officers liability; general and products liability; professional liability; automobile liability; excess liability; pension trust liability; crime and surety bonds; etc.)
- Analysis of the ability of insurance vendors and other facilities to meet obligations under contracts and agreements
- Copies of agreements, arrangements, or other commitments to indemnification by the company to third parties
- Schedule of loss experience, insured or not, with descriptions of pending claims
- Copies of disaster recovery plans, including recent tests and updates
- Copies of policies and procedures related to loss control including physical (e.g., buildings, vehicle fleets), systems, records, product liability, etc.
- Description of loss control responsibility and staffing, including professional advisors and their roles
- Description of security policies and procedures, including access to facilities and detection and control systems
- Copies of policies and procedures related to product safety, including management safety leadership, requirements monitoring, engineering, industry support, customer incident/accident reporting, employee communication, customer communication, training, audits, etc.
- Product- and service-related incident/accident reports and investigative files
- Description of operating locations and facilities, including building age, condition, construction, building hazards, hazards from neighborhood
- Description of equipment used in business including age, condition, schedules for maintenance and replacement, and special hazards
- Comparison of exposures and coverages of entities to be combined

Litigation

Note: The key purpose of this inquiry is to discover what litigation is pending, threatened, or potential, and to determine the exposure.

- Description of each pending or threatened claim, lawsuit, arbitration, investigation, or request for injunction, for a claim or relief of $25,000 or more against the companies or its officers, directors, or employees (work-related)
- Description of each pending or threatened criminal, civil, or regulatory claim, litigation, or investigation alleging violation of laws or regulations applicable to the company
- Description of any outstanding judgments, decrees, injunctions, or orders against the company
- Most recent response to auditor's request for information about litigation and contingent liabilities

- Filings or other information provided to regulatory agencies
- Documentation of any disputes with suppliers, distributors, competitors, or customers for claims amounting to $25,000 or more

Environmental and Related Matters
- Copies of all internal reports concerning environmental matters at current or previously owned or leased properties
- Copies of applications, statements, or reports filed with government or quasi-governmental agencies concerning environmental, health, or safety issues
- Copies of notices, complaints, lawsuits, or similar documents received by the company concerning environmental, health, or safety issues
- Company reports concerning waste disposal matters (e.g., compliance with waste disposal regulations)
- Description of any premises currently or previously owned or operated by the company with known or suspected toxic or other hazardous materials
- Reports, manifests, or other documents relating to hazardous waste or material management
- Documents related to removal of asbestos
- Descriptions of any underground or other storage tanks or facilities used for potential environmental contaminants
- Environmental audits by public agents, through private contracts or done internally
- Description of any environmental impairment liability insurance purchased in the past five years

Confirm Leadership Commitment

Note: Examine press releases and speeches referenced in the first section of this checklist for public statements of intent. This topic will be addressed primarily through interviews and in the negotiating process.

Confirm Legal Ability to Combine

Note: See ownership structure indicated from corporate documents listed above. Legal advice will be included in this investigation.

Verify Expected Operational Capabilities

Note: The primary objective is to confirm that the strategic expectations for the combination can be implemented with the human and other resources available in the target.

Management Structure, Employment, Employee Relations
- Organizational chart showing principal units and managers, with employee counts and descriptions of major unit responsibilities
- Complete workforce profile including name, location, job title, function, pay grade, hire date, years of service, prior positions in the company, education, performance level, age, gender, ethnicity, PT/FT status, salary, incentives, bonuses,

vested and unvested stock, shift differentials and sales commissions, and comment on special value to the business for all employees for the current fiscal year
- Complete profiles of retired and disabled workers with continuing benefit rights
- Number of employees by function/operational area
- Copies of written employment agreements plus other oral and written commitments to employees
- Contractual arrangements with current or former employees concerning noncompetition, severance, change of control, rights to intellectual property, and other contingent obligations
- Copies of any union contracts and documentation of recent and current contract negotiations, complaints, disputes, and requests for information; identification of bargaining units, locations, unions, and employees covered in each agreement; description of the history of labor relations, including strikes, arbitration awards, unsuccessful organizing efforts, etc.
- Copies of agreements concerning confidentiality, nondisclosure, noncompetition
- Copies of agreements for temporary labor, consulting, outsourcing, and other forms of contracted services
- Copies of performance bonus and sales compensation plans
- Copies of deferred compensation plans with a schedule of accruals and continuing obligations
- Description of other special compensation arrangements (e.g., phantom stock)
- Description of procedures for classifying jobs and pay and benefit levels consistent with competitive market conditions
- Copies of joint venture or other contractual arrangements with other entities that may give employees of any of the parties special rights
- Identification of changes required in people-management practices as a result of the expected business combination, including transitional and long-term changes (i.e., anticipated integration requirements and related facts about current HR plans and practices of the target company)

Competitive Advantages Driven by Organizational/People Strengths
- Comparison of apparent strengths (from documentation and interviews) of key employees and units with opportunities for competitive advantage in the business
- Identification of key managers and other employees essential to maintaining competitive strength (for use in later integration activity)

Labor Availability/Catchment Areas
- Description of potential labor pools and ready availability of additional and replacement workers at primary locations

Confirm People Expectations—Retention, Cost, Cultural Fit
Payroll
Note: The underlying issue regards the status of full- and part-time employees.

- Payroll costs by major unit, by pay grade, and by employee category (e.g., managerial, technical, clerical)

Employee Benefit Plans

Note: In particular, an acquirer must understand the provisions for active, retired, and disabled employees. The reader should also review Appendix F: Benefits Alignment.

- Copies of retirement plans, including defined benefit plans, 401(k) plans, profit sharing plans, nonqualified retirement plans, employee stock purchase plans, and government-mandated contributions
- Copies of medical plans, including hospitalization, physician care, vision, hearing, dental, disability, and related plans
- Copies of life insurance plans, including group term, accidental death, and savings plans, as well as dependent coverage
- Copies of any plans for dependent care, legal assistance, wellness programs, mental illness, substance abuse, or similar programs
- Copies of policies for educational assistance
- Copies of time-off policies, including vacation, leaves of absence, sickness, maternity, and attendance to needs of family members
- Copies of severance and early retirement provisions
- Copies of policies concerning perquisites including company cars, club memberships, subsidized mortgages, etc.
- Copies of incentive pay and stock option plans
- Copies of employee handbooks and notices of personnel policies
- Copies of employee summary plan descriptions
- Copies of recent employee communications concerning pay and benefit programs
- Copies of special provisions applicable to change-in-control situations
- Comparison of plan provisions for units to be combined (to help anticipate opportunities and problems in combining programs)
- Impact of prospective staff adjustments (e.g., reductions, reassignments) on plan terms

Costs of Employee Benefit Programs

- Copies of internal reports on actual and estimated employee pay and benefit costs
- Copies of actuarial and other external estimates of employee pay and benefit costs
- Descriptions and reports (including required government labor and tax reports) of funding plans for employee retirement and other benefit plans, including contribution requirements for employers and employees
- Comparisons of company experience with competitors
- Copies of filings with government agencies (e.g., IRS, DOL, PBGC) concerning pay and benefit compliance, audits, investigations, reviews, or determinations (including compliance review and tax qualification)

- Description of any terminated pension plans or unfunded/underfunded pension liabilities with the current status of any outstanding obligation
- List of employees on leave of absence with obligations upon notice of return or termination
- List of employees to whom offers of employment have been made, with terms
- Description of the provision for workers compensation coverage, with lists of outstanding claims, copies of insurance policies, and estimates of future cost changes (see "Discover Significant Liabilities and Exposures")
- Copies of employee benefit vendor service agreements with evidence of vendors' ability to meet obligations (should be compared with plan requirements)
- Descriptions of outstanding and anticipated ("pipeline") employee claims under these provisions

Provisions for Needed Employee Support
- Copies of facilities management plans (current and prospective), including assignment of space for various activities and provision of equipment and other resources

Evaluate IT Position
- Description of computer and communication facilities, equipment, architecture, and operations
- Description of the role of key systems in business operations—for operations, sales, human resource management, finance, etc.
- Schedule of computer software, with ownership, licenses, and potential for claims on ownership other than by the company; provision of "roadmaps" of systems architecture; identification of significant variations for different locations and country operations
- Description of the role of systems in business processes, with emphasis on critical dependence on systems for maintaining operations
- Schedule of planned computer/communication system upgrades and known failures to match current and expected industry standards
- Procedures and manuals for system operation and maintenance
- Comparison of company computer and communications capabilities to those of key competitors
- Description of security and disaster recovery plans
- Analysis of expected impact on operations in the event of system failure and downtime

Understand Variations Among Company Units and Jurisdictions
Note: For all of the preceding topics, due diligence should determine the unique characteristics of each operating unit and separate jurisdiction.

Interviews

Interviews should be used to follow up on questions in each of the areas noted above. In addition, target company personnel should be encouraged to add commentary on operating philosophies and styles that will influence how the documentation should be evaluated (e.g., whether the organization sticks to, or ignores, published guidelines). Documentation cannot capture the organization's ability to adapt to changing conditions or employee reaction to the proposed transaction. Interviews can provide an impression of this capability and reactions.

In addition, some people outside the target organization should be interviewed, including outside counsel, suppliers, customers, accountants, insurance agents and companies, investment advisors, regulatory agencies, etc. These interviews provide invaluable perspectives and frequently raise issues not otherwise surfaced through other means. ∎

APPENDIX D

Executive Compensation Issues

John R. Ellerman and Richard N. Ericson

This appendix covers two key compensation matters in mergers and acquisitions: change-in-control programs and incentive compensation.

Change-in-Control Programs

Among the most visible, and often most controversial, aspects of implementing mergers and acquisitions (M&As) are the severance compensation and benefits paid to senior management who leave the new company. Journalists and institutional investors have frequently cited the large severance packages of terminating executives as excessive, egregious, and an unreasonable cost borne by shareholders.

Nonetheless, if carefully designed, a change-in-control (CIC) program can play an important role in the M&A process, helping to protect and even enhance shareholder value. A CIC program should place top executives in a position of neutrality regarding the deal and its implementation by removing concerns about their own job security, future pay, and benefits. A well-defined CIC program does not give the covered executives a compensation windfall for executing a deal but it does protect them from the negative impact an acquisition can have on their economic and job security.

Human resource managers should work closely with top management, the board's compensation committee, and various outside advisors in structuring such a program. This can be very challenging because it means rendering judgments about sensitive topics such as which executives should be covered, what level of severance benefits should be provided, whether tax "gross-ups" should be provided, and so forth.

The "Golden Parachute" Phenomenon

Early on, CIC agreements became popularly known as "golden parachutes." This label has endured for almost two decades. Even the Internal Revenue Code (IRC) refers to

Exhibit D.1 Prevalence of Companies in *Fortune* 1000/S&P 500 with Executive Golden Parachute Agreement

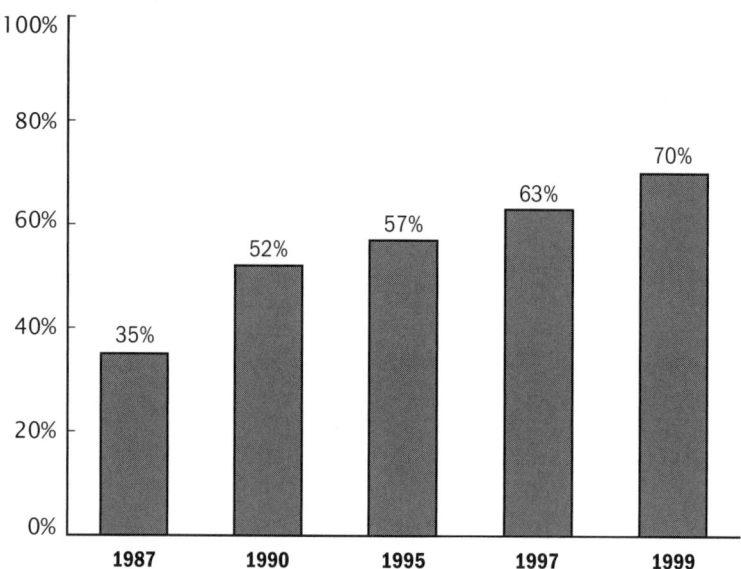

Source: ECAS, May 2000, database of 1,049 companies among Fortune 1000, S&P 500.

"excess parachute payments" for severance payments arising from CIC programs that exceed certain specified limits.

The first widely publicized use of CIC programs in a merger or acquisition occurred in mid-1982 during the attempted hostile takeover of Bendix Corporation by Martin Marietta Corporation. Bendix was eventually acquired by Allied Corporation, which emerged as the "white knight." The CEO of Bendix, William Agee, was slated to become CEO and number two executive of Allied-Bendix; however, his candidacy was over after only eight days with the newly combined company. It was later reported that Mr. Agee "pulled the ripcord on a 'golden parachute' deal written into the merger agreement." Mr. Agee's golden parachute was reported to be worth an estimated $4.1 million—the sum of his continued annual salary of $825,000 for five years after resignation.

The popularity of golden parachutes for top executives grew throughout the mid- and late-1980s, and by the mid-1990s had become a staple in the pay packages of top executives in *Fortune* 1000 companies. Although compensation/benefits can be protected through different vehicles (e.g., provisions in long-term incentive or benefit plans), the most common form is a CIC agreement (typically part of an employment contract or a stand-alone CIC severance agreement). A recent study published by the Executive Compensation Advisory Services reports that the use of golden parachutes is on the rise for top executives of large U.S. companies, as shown in *Exhibit D.1*.

The U.S. Congress validated the concept of golden parachutes with language defining reasonable or unreasonable severance compensation pursuant to CIC transactions with the passage of P.L. 98-369, the Deficit Reduction Act of 1984 (DEFRA). Under the umbrella of DEFRA, both a company and its executives are subject to harsh tax penalties if the size of golden parachute payments exceeds a designated level selected by the Internal Revenue Service (IRS). If a company provides an executive with "excess parachute payments" as defined by Section 280G of the IRC, the executive is subject to a 20 percent excise tax on the excess payments and the company loses its tax deduction for the excess amounts as well. Section 280G of the Code prevails today (though it exists as proposed legislation rather than ratified law), and companies have developed numerous approaches to minimizing the impact of such tax penalties on executives.

Design of CIC Programs

In most cases, design of a CIC program occurs before a company actually begins searching for an acquisition or merger partner, or is put in play as an acquisition target for another company. Alternatively, CIC agreements reached during a merger or acquisition may be tainted by proximity to the transaction. Moreover, some actions that may appear on the surface to have no visible connection to a golden parachute payment (e.g., granting of options, payment of incentive awards) may even be denied by the IRS.

Most CIC agreements fall into two broad categories: single-trigger and double-trigger arrangements. A single-trigger agreement provides for severance or other benefits following a change-in-control event (for example, closing or public announcement of intent to close) without necessarily requiring loss of employment. A typical single-trigger benefit is the immediate vesting of unvested stock options. About 80 percent of CIC programs, however, are double-trigger arrangements, according to a recent survey by Towers Perrin.

A double-trigger agreement requires two events to occur before the executives covered by the plan are entitled to severance payments: the first trigger is the change-in-control event; the second is the executive's involuntary termination anytime during a two- or three-year window following the first trigger. Many double-trigger plans also allow an executive to receive severance benefits after voluntary termination "for good cause" (a cut in the executive's pay, diminution of job duties, reduction in job title or status, etc.) or in some cases under a "no fault" walk-away provision that pays executives full severance benefits. The latter may require that the executive remain with the new company for a designated length of time.

The following paragraphs outline the provisions of a representative CIC program for a public company with revenues in the $5-billion to $10-billion range. This plan's design reflects contemporary practice; there are two or three tiers of participation, and each participant would have an individual written agreement setting forth the specific terms and provisions of coverage. The individual agreements vary by tier because the prospective average severance compensation varies by tier. The levels of severance compensation in the example below are representative of a company of this size.

Representative CIC Plan—Terms and Provisions

1. *Participation.* The CIC plan has three levels of participation or tiers.
   Tier I – CEO, COO, and CFO; possibly other executives
   Tier II – Executive VP and Senior VP positions (possibly 10 executives)
   Tier III – Other select officers (possibly 20–30 executives)
2. *Term of agreement.* Each participant's agreement has a three-year term and becomes operational only in the case of two triggering events: (1) a change in control and (2) involuntary or constructive termination of the employee. The individual agreements have an "evergreen provision" in that each agreement extends automatically for a new three-year term on the annual anniversary of the current agreement's inception. This provision ensures that each agreement will always have a three-year term going forward. During a 60-day period prior to the plan's anniversary date, the company may elect not to renew the agreement and prevent the automatic rollover from occurring. In that case, the executives covered by the plan have CIC protection for the remaining two-year period of the agreement's three-year term.
3. *Definition of change in control.* The following definition constitutes a "change in control," which will be the first trigger under the program (any one of the following):
   - Any person or persons acting together as an entity become beneficial owners of 25 percent or more of the company's voting shares.
   - A change in Board composition over any two-year period is substantial enough that the existing Board at the start of the period no longer constitutes a majority.
   - Shareholder approval of a merger or consolidation of the company in which the company's voting securities represent less than 60 percent of the surviving entity.
4. *Second triggering event.* In the event that the executive is a full-time employee at the time of the CIC event, he or she will be provided a 36-month period during which: (1) the executive is protected in the event of an involuntary termination by the company or its successor organization or (2) the executive determines that there are grounds for "constructive termination." The executive's termination under either of these two events results in severance compensation being provided pursuant to the terms of the program. "Constructive termination" is when the company, without the executive's written consent, requires of the executive any one of the following:
   - A reduction in base salary, target bonus, or long-term incentive opportunities
   - A diminution of job duties and responsibilities
   - A relocation of more than 75 miles from the executive's current office location
   - A failure to pay any previously deferred compensation
   - A failure to provide equivalent or reasonably equivalent benefits to those that were in place prior to the change in control
   - A failure by the company to honor all the terms and provisions of the executive's CIC agreement

Exhibit D.2 Prospective Severance Benefits to Representative CIC Plan

Compensation Elements	Tier I	Tier II	Tier III
1. Base salary and bonus	3.0 x Base salary + average bonus of past 2 years, payable in lump sum	2.0 x Base salary + average bonus of past 2 years, payable in lump sum	1.5 x Base salary + average bonus of past 2 years, payable in lump sum
2. Stock options and restricted stock	Accelerated vesting of all unvested options and restricted stock grants	Same as Tier I	Same as Tier I
3. Welfare benefits	Continuation of all life, disability, accident, and health insurance for 36 months following termination, or reasonably equivalent benefits	Continuation of all life, disability, accident, and health insurance for 24 months following termination, or reasonably equivalent benefits	Continuation of all life, disability, accident, and health insurance for 18 months following termination, or reasonably equivalent benefits
4. Retirement benefits	Credit equal to 36 months' continued service to a Supplemental Executive Retirement Plan (SERP) for existing retirement benefits (qualified and nonqualified plans, including both defined benefit [DB] and defined contribution [DC] plans) or equivalent cash lump sum payment	Credit equal to 24 months' continued service to a SERP for existing retirement benefits (qualified and nonqualified plans, including both DB and DC plans) or equivalent cash lump sum payment	Credit equal to 18 months' continued service to a SERP for existing retirement benefits (qualified and nonqualified plans, including both DB and DC plans) or equivalent cash lump sum payment
5. Tax gross-up, excise tax, and limitation on benefits	Gross-up provision to offset any excise taxes imposed by 280G	Severance compensation will be limited to 2.99 x the base year amount in order to protect the company and executive from the imposition of the 280(G) excise tax	Same as Tier II
6. Offsets	No requirements to mitigate any payout received as result of compensation from subsequent employer	Same as Tier I	Same as Tier I
7. Enforcement of agreement	All disputes regarding the agreement will be settled by formal arbitration	Same as Tier I	Same as Tier I

Source: Towers Perrin analysis.

5. *Termination due to discharge for cause, retirement, death, or voluntary termination (without constructive termination).* Under any of these events, the executive is not eligible to receive severance compensation or benefits pursuant to the CIC agreement. Terminations under these circumstances are subject to the company's nor-

Exhibit D.3 Hypothetical Example of Excise Taxes and Total Taxes Paid upon CIC

Executive:	John Doe
Current salary + bonus:	$250,000
Severance compensation in CIC:	$750,000 (3 times $250,000)
Executive's base W-2 amount:	$200,000 (Average of 5 years' W-2 earnings)
Executive's tax rate:	39.6% Marginal tax rate – federal
280G maximum benefit:	$599,999 (2.99 times $200,000)
Excise tax imposed (?):	Yes, $750,000 vs. $599,999
Excise tax amount:	$110,000 ([$750,000 – $200,000] times 20%)
Regular individual income tax:	$297,000 ($750,000 times 39.6%)
Total taxes paid:	$407,000 ($110,000 plus $297,000)
Severance compensation after tax:	$343,000 ($750,000 – $407,000)
Executive's effective tax rate:	54.3%
Company's compensation expense that is tax deductible:	$200,000 (executive's base amount)

Source: Towers Perrin analysis.

mal policies regarding such events and any compensation awards subject thereto.

6. *Severance compensation.* In the event that (1) the company experiences a change in control (first trigger) and (2) the executive's employment is involuntarily terminated within 36 months following the CIC or the executive terminates within 36 months following the CIC for constructive termination—either of which constitutes a second trigger—the executive receives the severance compensation set forth in *Exhibit D.2*.

Tax Penalties of IRC Section 280G

The 280G excise tax, which is added to the individual taxes incurred at the time of payment, is equal to 20 percent of the "excess parachute payments" that exceed one times the base compensation amount. The base compensation amount is equal to the five-year average W-2 earnings of the executive, and the permissible amount that can be paid without incurring the excise tax penalty is up to (but not including) three times the base compensation amount. In *Exhibit D.3*, we show an example of an executive subject to Section 280G and the tax penalty imposed.

As shown, the excise tax can be onerous for the individual executive. In addition, the excise tax disallows the company's tax deduction for any compensation above one times the base amount if the maximum allowed benefit under IRC 280G is exceeded.

The excise tax problem becomes even more complex when accelerated vesting of stock options, restricted shares, nonqualified deferred compensation payments, and the

Exhibit D.4 Hypothetical Example of an Internal Revenue Code Section 280G Change in Control Calculation and the Impact of Tax Penalties upon the Executive and the Company

The following example sets forth the calculations used to provide a tax gross-up payment to a hypothetical executive (let's call him John Doe) whose golden parachute payments are affected by the impact of the IRC Section 280G excise taxes. The following example assumes that the company elects to provide a tax gross-up payment to the executive for the excise tax. It should be noted that our example provides no consideration for the executive's state and local taxes, which also could directly affect the amount of the gross-up.

The following assumptions have been made with respect to John Doe and his prospective severance compensation:

- Current age 50, with 20 years' service
- SERP benefit vests at age 55 with 20 years of company service
- 5-year average W-2 amount equals $200,000
- Current base plus bonus amount equals $250,000
- Welfare benefits of $7,000 per year payable for 3 years following severance
- CIC severance multiple is 3 times base salary plus bonus
- 100,000 stock options were granted at $10 per share one year ago with a 4-year ratable vesting schedule (25% vest per full year of service)
- Total company tax rate assumed to be 40%
- Total executive tax rate assumed to be 39.6%

Based on the assumptions noted above, the proposed severance compensation exceeds the allowable Section 280G amount by approximately $1.7 million.

Executive	(A) Sec. 280G base amount (1)	(B) Sec. 280G limit	(C) Sec. 280G Total CIC severance amount	(D) Excess of total CIC payment over 280G Limit	Will the CIC payment be subject to excise tax?
John Doe	$200,000	[(3 × a) − 1] = b $599,999	$2,311,362	(c − b) = d $1,711,363	Yes

The above example results in John Doe having an excise tax liability of $422,272, and his gross-up payment becomes $1,045,229 in order to settle additional taxes incurred for the tax gross-up payment and additional excise tax payments thereon.

Executive	(A) Sec. 280G base amount (1)	(B) Sec. 280G limit	(C) Sec. 280G total CIC severance amount	(D) Excess of total CIC payment over 280G limit	(E) Sec. 280G total CIC payment above base amount	(F) 20% excise tax	(G) Gross-up payment amount	(H) Excise tax plus ordinary income tax	(I) After-tax total value of executive CIC benefit
John Doe	$200,000	[(3 × a) − 1] = b $598,000	$2,311,362	(c − b) = d $1,711,363	(c − a) = e $2,111,362	(20% × e) = f $422,272	f / (1 − .2 − .396) = g $1,045,229	$1,960,528	((c + g) − h) = I $1,396,063

The company forfeits its tax deduction for the amounts above one-times John Doe's base amount, with non-tax deductible CIC payments of $3,156,591. Assuming that the company's corporate tax rate is 40 percent, the cost of the lost deduction is $1,262,636, which has an after-tax cash cost to the company of $3,131,805.

Executive	Total cash severance	Value of stock option acceleration	Present value of additional welfare benefits	Present value of enhanced retirement benefits	Gross-up payment amount	Present value of total CIC payment	Non-tax deductible amount of CIC payments	Opportunity cost of lost tax deductions	Total implied company cost	Actual total after-tax company cash cost
John Doe	$750,000	$141,786	$19,576	$1,400,000	$1,045,229	$3,356,590	$3,156,591	$1,262,636	$4,397,441	$3,131,805

Appendix D—Executive Compensation Issues ▪ 263

like are involved. Section 280G requires that the value of accelerated vesting that is triggered pursuant to a CIC must be included in the parachute on a present-value basis.

One way companies can address the excise tax problem is to provide executives with a tax gross-up provision that offsets the executive's additional tax burden. A Towers Perrin survey (September 1999) of CIC practices of 119 U.S. companies found that 65 percent of these companies provide tax gross-ups of some sort for CEOs. The problem, however, is the high cost of gross-up payments to the company. In fact, the additional expense of the tax gross-up payment is sometimes 50 percent or more of the underlying cost of the parachute payments. For this reason, companies tend to provide tax gross-up payments to only the CEO and a very small number of senior executives. To illustrate the complexity and magnitude of the tax gross-up feature, *Exhibit D.4* describes a hypothetical example for an executive whose severance exceeds the statutory limits of Section 280G.

There are other ways companies can address the excise tax problem for the covered executive. One is to "cap" the payment at 2.99 times the statutory base amount, thereby limiting the severance to an amount within the safe harbor of Section 280G. Other ways include "conditional gross-up," "best net caps," or other kinds of cost/benefit trade-offs. *Exhibit D.5* discusses some of these approaches and their advantages in addressing the excise tax problem.

CIC Best Practices

Designing a fair and tax-effective CIC program can be a daunting task, but a company stands the best chance of success when it follows some basic tenets:

1. *Understand the objective.* The principal objective of a CIC program is to protect key members of senior management through the M&A process and thereby ensure their neutrality in acting on behalf of shareholder interests—all at a reasonable cost. Although there may be ancillary objectives associated with the program, this primary objective should remain the focus of the program's design.
2. *Develop the program proactively.* To preclude last-minute and hurried decision-making, the development and implementation of the CIC program should begin well before any M&A activity evolves. A well-designed program, developed in conjunction with the board of directors' compensation committee in advance of any M&A activity, constitutes sound corporate governance and dutifully respects shareholder interests.
3. *Adopt double-trigger agreements.* In consideration of the primary objective, the CIC program should be structured with double-trigger agreements. Top management should avoid the temptation of single-trigger, or a so-called "13th month free walk," provision that could reward executives simply for doing the deal.
4. *Evaluate prospective program costs.* Throughout the development process, the prospective costs of the program to the company and its shareholders must be carefully considered. Generally speaking, investors and deal-makers are comfortable with CIC program costs within the 2.5 to 3.5 percent range relative to the

Exhibit D.5 Addressing Tax Gross-Up Payments per IRC Section 280G

> The primary issue with gross-ups, of course, is their high cost to the company. That's because any payment that exceeds the legal limit (basically, a grant that is three times average five-year earnings) is subject to excise tax on all amounts over the *base amount*. In addition, the company loses its tax deduction. This makes exceeding the limit quite expensive—especially for parachutes that are only marginally above the 280G threshold. For this reason, it makes sense to make efficient trade-offs between the cost and the benefit of a gross-up provision.
>
> One approach is the use of a *conditional gross-up*. Here, a company caps CIC benefits if they exceed the three-times limit *by a small amount* (usually 10 percent to 20 percent) but provides full gross-ups on higher amounts.
>
> By way of example, consider the case of an executive with a $100,000 base amount and a parachute of $305,000. To keep this executive whole (with respect to excise and income taxes due on the parachute), the company has to provide a gross-up of over $100,000 (even in states with low ordinary income tax rates)—all to provide an extra $5,001 in benefits (the difference between this benefit and one capped at the $299,999 limit). And, in states with high marginal ordinary income tax rates, the gross-up could exceed $140,000. In addition, the company loses its tax deduction, worth around $70,000. Clearly, in such circumstances, a full gross-up is an expensive way to provide a small extra benefit to a participant.
>
> If, however, this company used a conditional gross-up, the situation would be quite different. The payment would have been capped at the 280G limit, ensuring that no gross-up is required. Only if the benefit exceeds the cap by a specified limit (generally 10 percent to 20 percent, as noted) would the gross-up be taxable. This ensures that a participant receives a benefit that limits the company's added financial exposure in instances where the additional value clearly does not justify the amount of the gross-up.
>
> The *best-net cap* is another strategy for companies that do not want to cap or gross-up benefits constantly. Here, a company would apply a cap if the individual were better off as a result. But if it were more advantageous for the individual to take the full amount of the CIC payment and pay all taxes due himself or herself, the cap would not apply.

Source: Towers Perrin analysis.

---

transaction price, although this is a general rule of thumb and not applicable in all situations. Prospective costs should be consistent with the underlying objective of the CIC program.

5. *Weigh carefully the incremental costs of tax gross-ups.* Consistent with Item 4 above, the cost/benefit relationship of tax gross-up payments should be carefully evaluated. Other approaches, such as conditional gross-ups, may be preferable in light of cost considerations.
6. *Evaluate participation carefully.* Boards of directors must exercise good judgment in determining who receives CIC protection. Numerous approaches, such as special retention incentive plans and broad-based severance plans, may be as effec-

tive, or even more effective, in providing CIC protection to selected executives. A company should consider which executives and other groups of employees are the most at risk pursuant to a CIC, and select the right mix of approaches to fit the nature of the risk.

Linking Executive Incentive Plans with M&A Performance Expectations

Company performance in the M&A arena has been rather mixed, and the structure of executive incentives may have a role in this area. Incentive plans should create explicit linkages between M&A performance expectations and actual results. Here's an example of an approach:

- A company has a target for pretax operating profit of $100 million for next year. Achieving this target drives its annual incentive plan. Future targets are expected to rise at a rate of about 10 percent per year, based on the current expectations the company holds about its business prospects.
- This company acquires another, paying a price of $200 million. The acquired company is expected to add operating profit of $40 million per year to the acquiring company's results, with subsequent profit levels rising about 10 percent per year. These profit expectations—coupled with the acquired company's capital requirements, risks, and cost of capital—are the basis for the board's approval of the acquisition.

In this simplified case, we would recommend the following:

- The new company's target for operating profit should be increased by $40 million to $140 million (in the coming year). Otherwise, the new company will target its performance below expectations and the deal will have underperformed in terms of shareholder value creation.
- Expected goals for the second year should be about $44 million higher than they would have been, due to the 10 percent annual growth expected from the acquired company's capital contribution.
- If the new company has capital requirements exceeding those forecast at the time of the deal, then goals for operating profit should be increased and vice versa. A pretax operating profit hurdle of 20 percent, for example, would mean that $10 million in unanticipated capital requirements increases the profit goal by $2 million.

This simplified example shows one way in which companies can adjust incentive targets so that management is encouraged to make good deals; however, many companies don't follow this obvious best practice. In fact, the typical process used to evaluate mergers and acquisitions tends to be connected only weakly to the process used to set incentive goals:

- Generally speaking, the merger evaluation process is mainly episodic while the setting of incentive goals follows an annual cycle.

- The former is usually limited in scope to the deal at hand or investment being reviewed, while the latter generally includes the overall company's operations and those of all of its distinct profit centers.
- The former typically involves a multiyear projection of financial results, while the latter is focused on the following year only (i.e., geared to the annual budget process used so commonly to set bonus goals).

As a result, most goal-based incentives ("operating incentives") attach rather weak accountabilities in M&A situations. These two processes should, however, be linked in a simple, tactical way. That's a best practice and an important ingredient in making and implementing successful deals.

Here's how that should work: Deals are typically based on expectations about the enhanced financial results of the new company (i.e., synergies) for three to five years. These expectations should be used as the explicit incentive targets for the acquired business for at least two years following deal completion. Arguments for goal "relief" for incentive plan purposes are thereby forced to surface at the time of the deal approval rather than later, when disappointing results may become apparent.

Using this approach, management will be accountable for getting the results promised from a merger. Moreover, the management system will be made to encourage consistently good deal selection, pricing, and implementation.

The foregoing exemplifies an "operating" incentive—that is, an incentive plan that links executive pay to business performance. Most bonus plans employ operating incentives, as do long-term incentive plans using performance shares or performance units. Simply put, in these cases, rewards depend on hitting performance targets.

Today, long-term incentive plans are largely equity-based, using stocks and options, rather than operating incentives. There are good reasons for this, such as the alignment with shareholder interests. Nevertheless, as a result of heavy equity granting, in many companies, managements tend to control a lot of stock—more than 7 percent, on average, for medium to large public companies in the United States.

One might assume that these stock holdings discourage management from employing value-destroying measures such as making bad acquisitions, but unfortunately this is not always the case. Poor deal selection, pricing, and implementation are sure means of destroying shareholder value. The rather dismal record of corporate success in this regard is a matter of public record.

Why are options and stocks not very effective in discouraging bad deals? The answer lies with the efficacy of stock-based incentives:

- Stock (and options) do not come with instructions on how to create value
- Stock prices often fluctuate for reasons beyond management's control or comprehension
- The stock market is a poor short-run feedback mechanism for many management decisions—both good and bad

These factors are compounded in a merger or acquisition, given the time lag between management decisions throughout the M&A process and shareholder value outcomes.

Accordingly, companies involved with M&As should use short- and long-term operating incentives. The example at the beginning of this section was based on an operating incentive structure; the incentive plan was based on an explicit goal for company financial performance, so that goal was adjusted to provide for the full expected results of the transaction. Such incentives can help to encourage decisions most likely to create the greatest shareholder value over the long run and to create real accountability for those results.

For example, in a joint venture within the energy industry, the chairman insisted that the next two years' incentive compensation for the senior management team depend in part on achieving the cost synergies that had been used to justify the deal to Wall Street. A new category of incentive was carved out between the annual bonus plan and the long-term incentive plan. This new category would be paid at the end of each of the first two years of the joint venture and would be dependent upon achieving the scheduled cost synergies. The total annual amount of the incentives available to the management team was not increased; but a portion of the incentives available was directly tied to the successful integration of the joint venture. ■

APPENDIX E

Functional Integration: Marketing and Sales

John D. Southwell

The purpose of this appendix is first to address the roles of the Marketing and Sales (M&S) functions in a merger or acquisition, and second to suggest how the Human Resources function can assist in ensuring that these two functions are properly engaged in all phases of integration activity. The general practice of ensuring in-depth involvement of marketing and sales only post-deal, when strategic goals and financial requirements are resolved, runs the risk of inadequate assessment of growth potential and downside risk—both during implementation and longer term.

To start, why do marketing and sales warrant any earlier involvement, or greater scrutiny, than any other function? After all, in pre-deal—and to a lesser extent during due diligence—generally a very small core of executives is involved, to ensure confidentiality and to move quickly. Indeed, from an internal perspective, all operating functions share the same departmental issues, concerns, and risks. In fact, if the primary justification for a merger or acquisition is cost savings (often focused on "duplicate" sales forces), the risks are significant that premature action will lead to counterproductive de-motivation and defections within the sales force.

However, mergers and acquisitions are increasingly justified by the "marketplace synergies" of the combined entity, rather than by just the cost savings potential from "downsizing." Because marketing and sales are the custodians of the organization's go-to-market strategies, and of the detailed consumer and customer fact base, their involvement is essential in accurately defining upside potential in the marketplace, and in assessing downside risk. Further, their advance preparation in properly planning, organizing, and staffing for growth is a prerequisite to capitalizing on these marketplace opportunities immediately as the deal "goes live," and for the critical first 100 days following.

Exhibit E.1   Integration Problem Areas and Symptoms

The Problem	The Symptoms
Strategy — strategy inadequate to deliver growth objectives	■ Detailed review of internal cost savings, but superficial, "top-down" analysis of marketplace opportunity ■ Growth forecasts underestimating competitive response and overestimating customer response
Organization — organization unprepared to meet "go live" timing	■ Lack of clear vision on new "way of working" prior to announcing senior Marketing and Sales structure ■ Delayed action, or no action, in integrating incompatible Marketing and Sales processes and systems ■ Defining detailed Marketing and Sales structure/headcount prior to resolution of cross-functional interaction
People — lack of critical resources and capabilities needed to implement marketplace growth strategy	■ Deferral of essential Marketing and Sales people upgrades for fear of interrupting business momentum during the implementation stage ■ Staffing decisions based only on internal availability, regardless of personal and functional capabilities defined for each Marketing and Sales role ■ Performance management and rewards systems incompatible with marketplace objectives

This appendix therefore outlines a role and checklist of activities for key M&S executives early in the pre-deal phase, with escalating participation during the due diligence and integration planning phases. Human Resources has an essential role in selecting the right people to participate, at the appropriate times, in the most effective manner (such as under the direction of a key senior executive, when direct participation in the pre-deal team may be inappropriate). Human Resources should also provide direction and quality control in the development of M&S business processes, organization resolution, and staffing—for companywide consistency.

In this sense, we view this appendix as a model for how HR can facilitate and support functional integration beyond the combination with its own functional counterpart.

Marketing and Sales Issues

Too often, there is an inadequate assessment of major M&S issues until the deal is closed. The pressure is to quickly plan integration details toward an announced implementation date. This tendency is so shortsighted that it can cause a merger or acquisition to fail outright, or at least result in significant shortfall of top-line performance versus objectives.

There are three general areas in which problems may occur:
■ *Strategy.* The defined top-down strategy proves inadequate to deliver the sales revenue growth objectives.

- *Organization.* The M&S functions are unprepared to meet the "go live" integration timing and therefore are unable to effectively develop and implement their launch plans.
- *People.* The M&S functions lack the critical resources and capabilities to implement the marketplace growth strategies.

Exhibit E.1 illustrates common symptoms of these three types of problems.

Successful Mergers and Acquisitions

The five critical roles for the M&S functions during the four phases of a merger are
- capture the value proposition;
- create the high-level M&S organization;
- resolve detailed business processes for marketplace management, and complete M&S structure and responsibilities;
- define the HR requirements within Marketing and Sales; and
- foster teamwork and build the desired culture within Marketing and Sales.

These roles are broadly sequential, although there is considerable overlap among them, and all have some degree of impact on all four stages of the M&A life cycle. Additionally, while leadership and participation should be drawn primarily from M&S ranks, the HR function has an essential role to play as well. HR should, in general, assume responsibility for
- ensuring that the right participants are selected in each stage,
- driving consistency of approach and methodology to that of other functions, and
- checking to ensure that implementation of the people plans for Marketing and Sales is consistent with the overall strategy and vision of the new company.

Let's look at each of these five roles in turn.

Capture the Value Proposition

During pre-deal, the potential of the new business is assessed, the broad company vision is defined, the goals are set, and the price of the deal is negotiated. Generally, these decisions should be based on a broad top-down assessment of market size, share potential, synergies in innovation or technology, and leverage of the new company against suppliers, channels, geographic markets, and customers (old and new). Usually, financial or corporate planning analysts perform this assessment under the direction of a few senior executives.

Unfortunately, this top-down marketplace assessment frequently overlooks the essential consumer and customer requirements for success. Projected synergies in product innovation may not mesh with known consumer attitudes and usage. Potential channel efficiencies may look only at the logistics of warehousing and distribution and overlook critical differences in customer segmentation. Leverage against large customers is frequently overestimated, as size of supplier is seldom a competitive advantage in the eyes of a customer unless significant shared benefits are defined.

Exhibit E.2 Capture the Value Proposition

Marketing and Sales Role	Human Resources Role
Strategy	Strategy
■ Potential of combined/new products and services ■ Resolve leverage against current/new channels, markets, and major customers ■ Assess marketplace resources, both people and spending, required to capitalize on potential and leverage	■ Ensure that future business direction is documented before function makes significant change to process or structure ■ Clarify/assess (1) degree of change involved; (2) organization's ability to sustain change

Cost savings often prove lower than projected, too, as targeted customer programs often resist anticipated combinations that water down their effectiveness.

In summary, participation by key M&S representatives is essential during this initial marketplace assessment, as well as in the setting of synergy goals consistent with bottom-up potential (by product, channel, geographic market, and key customer or customer segment). While some executives on the deal team may have a marketing or sales background, this may be insufficient if their ability to make a detailed analysis does not reflect sufficient current marketplace knowledge and judgment. *Exhibit E.2* shows the primary strategic roles that marketing, sales, and HR should play in this assessment and goal-setting process.

Create High-Level Organization

During pre-deal, an overall approach to the new organization must be defined—a vision of the principles guiding how it will be perceived, internally and externally; how it will operate; how it will be structured; and what capabilities it will possess to achieve competitive advantage. This broad vision must be followed quickly by a high-level definition of the cross-functional business processes for marketplace management, outlining how various functions will interact to deliver the consumer/customer proposition. The appointment of the most senior M&S executives, who will direct the detailed process, structure, and staffing decisions, should follow this outline.

The broad vision should be defined in pre-deal, before the potential merger develops too far and, most important, before the price of the deal is set. The high-level organization definition and appointment of senior functional managers should be completed during due diligence. While it is tempting to defer this to implementation planning, this seldom leaves sufficient time for effective M&S organization design (detailed) and staffing, let alone critical marketplace implementation planning. *Exhibit E.3* shows the roles that marketing and sales management should play and how HR can facilitate the process.

Exhibit E.3 Create "High-Level" Organization

Marketing and Sales Role	Human Resources Role
Processes and Organization	Processes and Organization
■ Resolve high-level, "go-to-market" processes and "way of working" ■ Determine centralized/decentralized authorities ■ Resolve senior Marketing and Sales management, structure, and responsibilities	■ Ensure that cross-functional processes are addressed, not just within each "functional silo" ■ Ensure consistency across business processes

Resolve Detailed Processes, Structure, and Responsibilities

As soon as the deal is announced (or no later than due diligence), a priority should be placed on assembling cross-functional teams at both companies, to define the detailed business processes in marketplace management (internal management processes as well—this is not just an M&S exercise). This is essential to design the specific roles, structure, and staffing for Marketing and Sales.

Typically, the roles and structure are defined, and staff selected, before processes are fully designed. The new organization is then charged with defining the business processes and role accountabilities after the launch. This cart-before-the-horse approach virtually guarantees that old approaches to organization structure and capabilities will be entrenched and that staffing will be based on existing appointments. In so doing, the one-time opportunity to create a new organization, with more effective ways of working and upgraded capabilities, will have been squandered—and the organization vision, so optimistically crafted earlier on, will be just empty bombast.

Proposed roles of Marketing and Sales, as well as HR, are listed in *Exhibit E.4*.

Define Human Resource Requirements

This role entails defining the general organizational capabilities and the specific functional competencies (by individual) required to deliver the organization defined above. The capability and competency definition should be conducted in parallel with business process design and role definition as a critical prerequisite to staff selection.

While the M&S functions should take ownership for design of the marketplace management processes and for specifying competencies for M&S positions, Human Resources must provide essential support throughout by

- ensuring that business process design for marketplace management is truly cross-functional, with consistent methodology and output to internal process design;
- defining organizational capabilities that properly reflect the new company's vision and drive significant change into structural design;

Exhibit E.4   Resolve Detailed Processes, Structure, and Responsibilities

Marketing and Sales Role	Human Resources Role
Detailed Design	Detailed Design
■ Define detailed processes for marketplace management, including 　■ Planning 　■ Implementation 　■ Monitoring and control ■ Resolve Marketing and Sales structure, staffing, and responsibilities ■ Develop performance management and rewards approach	■ Develop/assess capabilities required by position: 　■ Organizational capabilities 　■ Functional capabilities ■ Assist in defining structural evolution, consistent with people inventory

Exhibit E.5   Define Human Resource Requirements

Marketing and Sales Role	Human Resources Role
Resources	Resources
■ Determine required Marketing and Sales organizational capabilities ■ Resolve staff sourcing, internal and external, immediate and long term ■ Identify staff development requirements	■ Ensure consistent cross-functional implementation of recruiting, succession planning, and performance management processes ■ Lead/coordinate training and development: 　(1) Centralized for organization capabilities 　(2) Decentralized for functional capabilities

Exhibit E.6   Foster Teamwork and Build Desired Culture

Marketing and Sales Role	Human Resources Role
Culture	Culture
■ Define values and beliefs within Marketing and Sales ■ Share management attitudes and opinions ■ Influence behaviors and communicate	■ Sponsor/conduct culture assessment ■ Coordinate communication across all functions

- facilitating the process for making functional competency definitions (by individual/role) consistent across the new company;
- assessing and supporting staffing decisions; and
- helping to align sales incentive plans and performance management systems.

Exhibit E.5 shows the roles that Marketing and Sales and HR should play in determining the people needs for Marketing and Sales.

Foster Teamwork and Build Culture

Marketing and Sales requires the highest level of HR direction, coordination, and facilitation to help it build a culture and develop teamwork. In particular, it requires help with the items listed in *Exhibit E.6*.

Marketing and Sales Integration Process

This section provides a checklist of activities by stage for each of the areas previously defined (strategy, organization, and people). *Exhibit E.7* provides an overview and recommends specific activities.

Pre-Deal

During pre-deal, as soon as an initial analysis confirms the deal's potential and probability of success, a small core of senior M&S executives should be immediately engaged to conduct a sales and marketing due diligence. Human Resources should play a key role in selecting the group and in assisting throughout the "organization" and "people" deliberations (see *Exhibit E.8*, page 278).

These executives will have to operate as two separate groups—one for each company—until the due diligence stage. Each group should provide a detailed marketplace analysis for the new company, define the high-level organization approach for marketplace management, and assess the people implications of this approach.

Due Diligence

Once due diligence begins, the two teams should combine and possibly add some new members, including M&S managers and any other members of the marketplace management team. This is a good way to involve and motivate valuable employees, and it provides additional expert help for defining the M&S business processes and organization design. As the analysis becomes more detailed, the HR role becomes more critical as it helps identify participants, documents and coordinates approaches, and ensures consistency of output across all functions for both companies (see *Exhibit E.9*, page 279).

Integration Planning

By the time the deal has closed and integration planning starts, the M&S team has decided on a marketplace management approach, determined core business processes, mapped the organization structure, and made key appointments.

Exhibit E.7 Marketing and Sales Integration Process

	OVERALL	STRATEGY	ORGANIZATION	PEOPLE
	■ Coordination ■ Culture	■ Value proposition ■ Customer segmentation ■ Marketplace support	■ Business processes ■ Roles and structure ■ Technology	■ Capabilities ■ Staffing ■ Rewards

MERGER STAGES

Pre-Deal
- Small group of key Marketing and Sales executives
- Preliminary synergy assessment and quantification of costs for goal setting
- Human resources facilitation and support in organization and people assessments and implementations

Go-Live ▶

Due Diligence
- Larger group of Marketing and Sales managers mobilized
- Detailed assessment and quantification, based on shared data
- Executive-level Marketing and Sales appointments
- Human resources facilitation and support in organization and people assessments and implementations

Close Deal ▶

Integration
- Full cross-functional process design teams
  - Marketing and Sales lead "go-to-market" processes
  - Marketing and Sales participate in internal processes
- Resolution of "go-to-market" plans and full Marketing and Sales structure
- Human resources facilitation and support in organization and people assessment and implementation

Launch ▶

Implementation
- "Fast-track" implementation in marketplace
  - Products and services
  - Customers and channels
  - Competitive preemption
  - Communication plans
- Concerted effort to maintain business momentum
- Human resources facilitation and support in organization and people assessments and implementations

Integration planning can now concentrate on
- Full and complete process and structural design, down to the individual position level
- Marketing and Sales staff selection
- Development of marketplace launch plans, by product or service, and by channel, market, and key customer or customer segment

With the full complement of M&S talent from both companies now in place, there should be sufficient talent to quickly complete both exercises. The HR function plays an ever-expanding role in coordinating this effort and ensuring consistency of output and people selection across functions. Further, this must be aligned with the new company's goals, strategies, and vision. At this stage, time pressures and people problems can seem overwhelming, and HR must act as counsel on what is right, rather than what is expedient. *Exhibit E.10* (page 280) shows the complete list of M&S strategies to be accomplished during integration planning.

Implementation

At this stage, the new company is launched in the marketplace. Product and customer plans should now be in hand, and the right people ready to execute them. If these steps are not taken early, the M&S function will flounder and be vulnerable to competitive exploitation as it tries to staff the new organization, create tactical plans without a strategic foundation, and start a new organization with incomplete and poorly designed business processes.

Human Resources plays an essential role in implementation for Marketing and Sales, assisting with communications, process documentation, definition of accountabilities and capabilities by role, and staff selection (see *Exhibit E.11*, page 281).

Summary

Inevitably, as a merger or acquisition proceeds, it gathers its own momentum, and too often, carefully prepared plans get ignored. However, with a methodical approach to functional integration, sound planning, and step-by-step implementation to marketplace organization and program launches, there is greater likelihood of success. This approach results in faster evolution toward the desired organization vision and quickly gaining competitive advantage.

Exhibit E.8 Pre-Deal Stage

Overall Integration Process		Design Marketing and Sales Integration Process: Leadership, integration, teams, timing, resources, roles

Strategy

Market Value Proposition — Review market positioning versus competition by major product/service area → Identify upside potential of combined lineup and potential new offerings by major product/service area

Customer Segmentation — Review current and potential customer base, by channel, by market, by major customer → Review channel/customer priority, leverage, and access strategies

Marketplace Support — Evaluate resources required, both spending and customer management, to deliver the market value proposition against priority customer segments

Organization

Business Processes — Resolve high-level organization "way of working" for Marketing and Sales
- Centralization/decentralization
- Cross-functional interaction
- Desired behaviors and accountabilities

Roles and Structures — Develop high-level organization structure
- Business units and broad functional responsibilities
- Executive-level Marketing and Sales positions

Technology — Review critical information systems and technology required to support:
- Business processes
- Marketing and Sales accountabilities

People

Capabilities — Review organizational capabilities required to deliver "go to market" strategy

Staffing — Preliminary external assessment of Marketing and Sales talent
- Both acquirer and acquiree companies

Rewards — Review performance management and rewards programs for consistency
- Identify "red flags"

Preliminary quantification of incentive compensation, severance and retention options, costs

278 ■ MAKING MERGERS WORK

Exhibit E.9 Due Diligence Stage

▼ OFFER ACCEPTED   CLOSE DEAL ▼

Overall Integration Process

Plan detailed rollout to integration teams
- Staffing, time commitments, interaction
- Refine integration process and gain support

Strategy

Market Value Proposition

Refine positioning and upside potential by major product/service area
- Based on full data disclosure
- Risk/profitability assessment versus competition

Customer Segmentation

Resolution of size potential and access strategy:
- By target segment, channel, and major customer
- Risk assessment versus competition

Marketplace Support

Detailed assessment of cost, payout of marketplace spending, and staffing, based on full data disclosure

---

Organization

Business Processes

"Core" business process development
- Enlarged group of Marketing and Sales managers
- Core process mapping
- Macro-process linkages

Roles and Structures

Resolve "middle-management" roles and structure for Marketing and Sales
- Department roles and responsibilities
- Middle-management positions

Technology

Refine Marketing and Sales systems and technology requirements:
- Assess current platforms
- Define data needs and tool kit requirements

People

Capabilities

Resolve functional capabilities required to discharge key Marketing and Sales leadership positions

Staffing

Identify, tentatively select, and secure commitment of top Marketing and Sales leadership talent

Rewards

Resolve and quantify performance management approach and structure

Exhibit E.10 Integration Planning Stage

▼ CLOSE DEAL   GO LIVE ▼

Overall Integration Process	Develop and monitor detailed implementation plan critical path ■ Strategy, structure, people, culture
Strategy Market Value Proposition	Develop portfolio goals and strategies ■ Overall positioning by product/service offering ■ Financial and nonfinancial goals ■ Marketing strategies and sub-strategies
Customer Segmentation	Develop customer business plans, by customer/channel segment ■ Coverage ■ Business-building objectives ■ Negotiating strategies
Marketplace Support	Develop detailed launch programs ■ Advertising, pricing, and promotion ■ Customer/trade programs
Organization Business Processes	Detailed business process development ■ Cross-functional teams by process area ■ Full sub-process mapping ■ Responsibility by activity area ■ Micro-linkage, activity to activity
Roles and Structures	Resolve job descriptions by role ■ Reconciled with process activity responsibilities Resolve all Marketing and Sales positions ■ Structure ■ Staffing
Technology	Resolve technology/systems support to Marketing and Sales functions ■ Interim hardware, software, and database support ■ Data sourcing and communication
People Capabilities	Functional capabilities resolution by role Capabilities assessment by individual
Staffing	Full staffing of Marketing and Sales departments ■ Internal candidates ■ External recruits
Rewards	Resolution of performance management system Detailed rewards program resolved by position

Exhibit E.11 Implementation Stage

▼ LAUNCH

Overall Integration Process	Monitor and adjust implementation plan for "First 100 Days" ■ Strategy, structure, people, culture
Strategy Market Value Proposition	Launch in marketplace by product/service area
Customer Segmentation	Negotiate and close customer business plans by customer/channel segment
Marketplace Support	Launch in marketplace ■ By product/service area ■ By customer/channel segment
Organization Business Processes	Communication and training by process area by function
Roles and Structures	Ongoing supervision and dialogue to clarify and communicate roles and structure
Technology	Deploy interim technology support to Marketing and Sales
	Plan long-term migration to Marketing and Sales information systems
People Capabilities	Refine functional capabilities by role, ongoing
	Develop "three-year" orientation and training program, based on functional capabilities and individual assessment
Staffing	Ongoing staffing ■ Recruiting ■ Career development plans ■ Succession plans
Rewards	Implementation and refinement of performance management and rewards programs

Appendix E—Functional Integration ■ 281

APPENDIX F

Benefits Alignment

Samira A. Kaderali

Addressing employee benefits issues is a vital part of every merger or acquisition. The perspective of HR professionals should be brought to bear on these issues early in the deal-making process. Indeed, many related questions need to be addressed across strategic planning (pre-deal), due diligence, and integration planning stages. Answers to these questions may not be deal-breakers, but some may provide significant negotiation leverage. And, as the deal moves toward closure, the HR function must ensure that all important benefits issues are recognized and that explicit actions have been taken or are planned to address them.

Benefits alignment begins with a clear understanding of the new company's business strategies and any major cultural differences underpinning the designs of the legacy benefits plans and programs of the companies to be combined. Beyond such understanding, a wide range of pertinent business and people issues will continue to surface throughout the course of the deal, and HR must be prepared to respond before they become concerns.

HR's fundamental task is to articulate a rewards framework that can guide the design of an appropriate benefits plan—one that supports the new company's business objectives and fits with its desired values and implicit employment contract. The process for alignment is first to assess whether current plans meet the needs of the combined organization, then to reconcile and rationalize differences among them—building on the similarities and strengths of each. When reviewing the benefit plans in particular, HR should focus on how to achieve all available scale economies, retain key talent, maintain business momentum, and engage employees in the aspirations of the new company.

That's a tall order. The balance of this appendix outlines proven concepts and approaches that can help the skilled HR practitioner successfully negotiate the challenges of plan integration.

A Proven Alignment Process

The process, based on experience and results, is flexible and can be adapted to the degree of alignment or disconnect between the two companies' current benefits plans and objectives; current plans can be merged and fine-tuned, or an entirely new plan can be designed.

The alignment process for benefits encompasses four major steps:
- Assess and confirm plan objectives
- Evaluate the performance of current plans
- Design and evaluate plan alternatives
- Implement new plans (or supporting programs) and communicate with employees

This alignment process is straightforward. It assumes that benefits must support the new company's business objectives, including cost parameters, and help reinforce the desired culture. It also assumes that correct alignment must reflect the perceived value employees place on specific benefits. Benefits must be valued in the context of the other rewards programs. With this kind of understanding, the critical step is to determine the desired competitive positioning of benefits for the new company. The decision will determine what, if any, plan design changes should be made—either an entirely new plan or modification to one or both of the merging companies' plans.

Plan alignment will likely entail a transition. As a practical matter, each company's immediate needs must be accommodated while management moves them toward an integrated future. Beyond that, it is imperative that any new benefit plans and programs, and especially the business rationale behind them, be well understood and appreciated by both management and employees. If major changes are made, capitalizing on the similarities and strengths of the two companies' plans is an important way to minimize the disruption that may result.

Case Study: Health and Welfare (H&W) Plan Alignment for Major Bank Merger

The financial services industry has undergone major consolidation in recent years. Numerous mergers and acquisitions have significantly decreased the number of firms and have led to the formation of mammoth new organizations. National, and in some cases international, mergers and acquisitions have combined organizations with very diverse structures and cultures. What's more, these new entities are often faced with new external challenges such as new markets and unfamiliar governmental entities and regulations. These new companies must achieve all available efficiencies while retaining key talent, maintaining their competitiveness and business momentum, and engaging their employees and customers in the vision and promises of the new company.

In 1998, two major regional banks merged to form one national corporation. The goal for the merger of these two U.S. banks, Bank A and Bank B, was twofold: to create a nationwide firm with broad-based financial services for meeting customers' existing needs, and to expand into new geographic and product markets. The vision of the deal-makers was to create a bank with the scale and reach necessary to prosper in the highly competitive financial services industry and to deliver exceptional results through exceptional people.

The HR function was mobilized before the due diligence stage of the integration process. Because of philosophical differences in benefits approaches, the merger partners concluded that they should take an in-depth look at what they currently offered before deciding what the new bank's H&W programs should encompass. An extensive checklist was used to guide data collection. These data were then used to answer the important design questions that needed to be addressed. The data elements included the following:

- A complete list of current benefit plans
- Plan and trust documents (including all amendments)
- Insurance contracts (including all amendments)
- Administrative service and vendor contracts (including all amendments)
- Stop-loss policies
- Summary plan descriptions (active and retiree plans) and any material modification notices and pending changes
- Other communication materials describing benefits
- Administrative manuals
- Claim experience for each self-insured benefit plan (past three years)
- Premium experience for each fully insured benefit plan (past three years)
- IRS determination letters (retirement plans and 501(c)(9) VEBA trusts) and any pending determination letter application or ruling requests
- Audit history: both IRS and Department of Labor
- Forms 5500, including all schedules for past three years, if available
- Forms 990 (501(c)(9) VEBA trusts)
- Actuarial valuations—defined benefit pension plans, FAS 106, FAS 112 for past three years, if available
- Forms PBGC-1 (defined benefit plans)
- Information on any pending or threatened lawsuits or appeals for each plan
- Information on any multiemployer plans
- Collective bargaining agreements
- COBRA/HIPAA forms and disclosure materials
- Fidelity bond and fiduciary liability policy
- Investment management contracts and group annuity/GIC contracts for pension plans
- Audited financial statements (all self-insured benefits and qualified plans)

Once all the data elements were collected, a team systematically compared the two H&W programs. As the data were analyzed, many additional questions arose that required further research:

- Are there any nonnegotiable contractual benefits that we must continue to offer after moving forward?

- Are there any legal or contractual benefits obligations that were not recognized in the purchase offer price?
- Who are external advisors to the H&W plans (e.g., actuary, counsel)? How long have the parties served in that capacity?
- What is the relationship between each parent company and its subsidiaries with respect to administration, employee communication, etc.?
- What, if any, benefits are required to be maintained after closure (because of a formal or implicit commitment to employees)?
- If the deal closes in mid-year, how will employee cafeteria plan elections (IRC § 125) and flexible spending accounts (FSAs) be affected?
- Who is responsible for the internal administration of the health and welfare benefits? Payroll, HR, Finance, Data Processing?
- Are there any employees currently on medical or disability leave of absence? If so, how many? What benefits do they receive? How will these employees be handled moving forward? Who is responsible for the financial liability of these employees?
- What is the cost of recognizing past service in plans?
- For fully insured plans, are there any experience-related credits or losses that would have an unfavorable impact if the policy were canceled?
- Are there any benefits that are contingent on the sale of the company?
- How/where are benefit data maintained? How automated is the administration of plans?
- Will any of the existing health and welfare plans be maintained after closing?
- Who will be responsible for terminating discontinued plans? Notifying current vendors? Filing final 5500? Issuing COBRA/HIPAA notices and calculating severance benefits to employees who are laid off?
- Are there any pending or threatened lawsuits or outstanding appeals?

The specific questions that must be examined will vary from situation to situation. Having the responses to these questions, however, made it easier for Bank A to make intelligent decisions about how to proceed with the deal and with the integration of the two firms' benefit programs.

After completing due diligence, Bank A decided to move forward with the merger. Bank A and Bank B began the merger with very different benefits strategies, designs, and approaches. The first step for aligning the new bank's benefit plans was to articulate the rewards framework that management was trying to put in place. The next step was to evaluate the existing health and welfare programs in detail and assess the extent to which they met the needs of the combined organization. Individually, neither program adequately met the needs of the new organization. As a first step, HR itemized the differences between the plans, then began to build a unified plan based on the plans' similarities and strengths. Most of the data needed for design had been collected during due diligence, so the alignment effort moved from the plan comparisons to a blueprint for change. However, before the blueprint could be finalized, the design team needed a better understanding of what impact the changes in the new plan design would have on the new company's employees.

Since there were many different benefits features under the H&W plan umbrella, each benefit was evaluated and addressed individually to understand how changes would affect employees. This allowed Bank A to identify both the positive and negative changes that were going to occur from the perspectives of all the different groups of employees, including the following:

- Active salaried employees
- Hourly workers
- Various union groups
- Retiree groups—pre- and post-Medicare
- Grandfathered retiree groups
- Any other group of employees

In many mergers, employee relations problems arise after closing the deal, specifically because of the loss of employee health care benefits or an astronomical increase in the employee contributions. Because medical coverage tends to be the most visible and important H&W benefit for the vast majority of employees, Bank A spent a great amount of time reviewing both companies' health care strategies and options. Taken together, medical and dental benefits comprise a large portion of both the cost and the concerns raised during implementation. Fortunately, Banks A and B found that their medical coverage had many similarities in both design and philosophy. However, there were sharp differences in dental benefits, employee contribution levels, and benefit communication programs.

Many other questions had to be answered before final design changes could be made with confidence. These questions gave Bank A a deeper understanding of what was to be offered and a clearer understanding of the differences in view between the two companies. The two banks explored the following questions before developing their new health and welfare plan:

- What medical and dental plans are maintained today for employees? Retirees? Those on long-term disability (LTD)? Others (e.g., Board of Directors)? Are there separate prescription drug or mental health programs?
- What is the plan year?
- Who is eligible for coverage? Does coverage differ by location? Employment category? Line of business?
- What is the definition of a covered dependent?
- Who are the administrators/insurers?
- What is the delivery system (e.g., HMO, POS, PPO, and indemnity) and basic plan design?
- What is the basic design for each plan? (For retirees, are there different grandfather populations? COB? Pre-65 vs. Medicare-eligible?)
- What is the funding arrangement of each plan? 501(c)(9) VEBA trust (funded or unfunded)?

- Are there any claims reserves? What is the estimated volume of Incurred But Not Reported claims, and has it been recorded on the company's books?
- Are their any known high-cost claimants with ongoing claim activity?
- Will the stop-loss insurer pay any claims?
- Does the plan document or summary plan description (SPD) state that the company has the right to amend or terminate benefits?
- What are the premium-equivalent rates for each plan (or the COBRA rates)?
- What contributions are required by participants? (Necessitates a schedule of current contributions and comment on historical changes.) Active vs. retirees vs. LTD vs. leave of absence?
- Have all COBRA/HIPAA requirements been met?
- What is the FAS 106 liability?

Once these questions were answered during the integration planning stage, the detailed comparison of health care plans was completed and the similarities and differences became very apparent. Unfortunately, while the analysis gave Bank A a good basic understanding of the important design and funding issues associated with plan alignment, the underlying cultural and strategic issues involved did not surface until the implementation stage.

Life insurance is also a very visible and important H&W benefit to employees. Many of the same questions used to understand the medical and dental plans were also asked by Bank A regarding the Bank B life insurance plan, including the following:

- What types of life insurance plans are available? Basic? Supplemental? Accident, Death & Dismemberment? Business Travelers Accident Insurance? Dependent Life?
- What is the plan year?
- What is the plan design (volume, maximums, open enrollment rights, Evidence of Insurability requirements, waiver of premium, etc.)?
- Who is the insurer?

Here again, responses were analyzed and compared to what was currently being offered by Bank A.

Because employees do not see the value of STD/LTD until they need this benefit, it does not have as large an impact in a benefit plan integration/redesign as do some other H&W benefits. That said, the types of questions and concerns around disability programs alignment included the following:

- What is the plan design for disability/illness coverage?
- What is the plan year?
- What is the funding arrangement of each?
- Who is the administrator/insurer of each?
- Is there coordination with related programs (e.g., employee assistance program, mental health and workers' compensation)?

Redesign of this benefit was not as highly publicized as some of the other H&W benefits discussed earlier. Nonetheless, disability plan design and cost review should be an integral part of a complete alignment process.

Because workers' compensation is a benefit that is closely aligned with nonoccupational disability benefits, it is important to review both programs together. In fact, many economies can be achieved by purchasing integrated disability policies. Before doing so, however, it is important to uncover the following:

- Who is the workers' compensation carrier?
- What has the premium been for the most recent three years?

While workers' compensation insurance is another benefit that most employees do not perceive as having immediate value, it has many associated legal and regulatory compliance issues.

The last benefit to review is vacation, holiday, and paid time off. The review should take into account company policies and their cultural origins. Questions for review include the following:

- What are the vacation, holiday, and paid time-off policies? Do these policies differ by employment group?
- Is there any liability for banked/accrued vacation days?
- What other programs (e.g., sabbaticals) are in effect?

The vacation, holiday, and paid time-off programs are highly valued benefits and can be the trigger for negative employee reactions if drastic changes are made that employees consider a "take away."

After all the basic plans were reviewed, Bank A still needed to inquire about the other voluntary benefit options that Bank B offered to its employees, either as contributory or noncontributory programs:

- FSA
- Employee assistance program
- Vision
- Hearing
- Tuition reimbursement
- Charitable contribution match
- Employee recognition
- Long-term care
- Adoption assistance
- Dependent day care
- Other (e.g., parking, credit union, lunches)

Once all current plans for both companies were reviewed carefully, it was time to move on to designing and evaluating new plan alternatives.

HR and the H&W benefit team developed alternative plan designs and options for all the H&W benefits. Market strategies were determined for health care coverage to ensure that everyone would still have access to managed care options, and that plans that were inefficient, expensive, and had low employee enrollment were eliminated.

The team conducted extensive analysis to determine the impact of decisions on employees, including how much employees would be disrupted, who would lose their doctors, and who would need to change medical or dental plans. Because many employees would receive more health care options, including a new dental option, these options were emphasized in employee communications to send positive messages about the new H&W benefits program.

The team used two key considerations as guides when making benefit changes: minimal employee disruption and limited cost increases to both the company and employees. No plan option or benefit design change was made without these two critical factors being reviewed thoroughly and sensitively.

The next step in the design process was a review of the cost-sharing strategies. Because the two banks' policies differed, how employees would share in the costs of the new plan led to very sensitive discussions. A transition strategy was developed that over time moved all new bank employees onto the same cost-sharing platform.

Once alternatives had been considered and presented, management made the final decision on all plan elements, including plan options, delivery, design, pricing, and communication. Then the implementation began. (Depending on the complexity of a company's plan, the first step might involve selecting a new vendor, or it might be as simple as contacting the incumbent vendors and requesting renewal rates based on the increased employee population of the new company.)

At the new national corporation, the most important aspect of successfully aligning H&W plans then came to the fore—how to communicate the changes. Developing communications about the change was critical to helping employees understand why the new plan was being implemented and what it would mean to the new company's employees and their families. It was important, for example, for the employees from the legacy banks to understand from the beginning that because of the transition strategy, their employee contributions would be different for a year or two. If the information hadn't come from management, employees would have stumbled across it in casual conversation. Detailed, proactive communications helped management avoid many potential employee relations issues.

Implementing the new plan was the last step in the alignment process. This included communication, training, systems modifications, preparations for open enrollment, and ongoing management and coordination with vendors. HR had prepared an implementation plan and schedule that was communicated to all business units involved in the rollout.

The new national bank followed a successful approach to integrating the health and welfare benefit plan. Derived from an understanding of the new company's business objectives and rewards framework, the approach enabled the two companies to see the full range of steps that should be taken, and to find the right combination of plan elements that would best serve the new business and culture of the combined bank. ∎

ABOUT THE AUTHORS

John M. Burns
John M. Burns is a principal in Towers Perrin's Stamford, Connecticut, office, where he consults on retirement issues. Mr. Burns has more than 20 years of experience in the analysis, design, financing, and implementation of retirement and other benefit plans for large and small companies in a variety of industries. He has particular experience in human resource strategy and total rewards strategy.

Mary Cianni
Mary Cianni is a consultant in Towers Perrin's New York office. Dr. Cianni works with organizations undergoing transformation as a result of mergers or other organizational change. She has worked with pharmaceutical companies in the integration of their HR functions and their sales forces and has consulted with global companies on workforce diversity and on communication processes. She also assists clients with leadership development including managing during change and high-potential development.

Thomas O. Davenport
Tom Davenport is a principal in Towers Perrin's San Francisco office. He provides counsel on human capital strategy, change management, organization effectiveness, and business strategy to clients in the service, financial, retail, and manufacturing sectors, as well as to public sector organizations.

Mr. Davenport focuses much of his attention on helping clients improve the people-focused elements of business strategy implementation. He is the author of the book *Human Capital: What It Is and Why People Invest It*, published by the Jossey-Bass division of John Wiley & Sons in 1999.

John R. Ellerman
John R. Ellerman is a principal in Towers Perrin's Dallas office. Mr. Ellerman has more than 25 years of experience as an executive compensation consultant and regularly advises *Fortune* 500 companies on such matters as incentive plan design, alignment of compensation strategy with overall business strategy, selection of performance metrics that correlate with shareholder value creation, and related executive compensation issues.

Richard N. Ericson
Richard Ericson, a consultant based in Minneapolis, is one of Towers Perrin's leaders in the area of value-based incentive design. He has more than 18 years of experience consulting in the areas of shareholder value and compensation.

Mr. Ericson specializes in management and reward systems, emphasizing principles of shareholder value creation, an area known as value-based management. He is a frequent speaker to professional and industry audiences on the subjects of value-based systems for target setting, performance measurement, and rewards.

Louis R. Forbringer

Dr. Forbringer is president of O.E. Solutions. He brings over 18 years of corporate and consulting experience to his practice, working with organizations in the areas of leadership development, organization development, and strategic planning. His current research interests include executive development, organizational change and development, and mergers and acquisitions.

Dr. Forbringer is past president of the Society of Human Resources Management Foundation Board and is presently serving on the board of the Society's Certification Institute. He also serves as a director on the board of Allegiant Bank.

Andrew F. Giffin

Andrew Giffin is a principal of Tillinghast–Towers Perrin, the insurance management and actuarial consulting unit of Towers Perrin, located in New York. He is part of the Emerging Markets unit, assisting global financial services and local market clients in expanding and improving their operations in Latin America and Asia. He specializes in global insurance strategies, bancassurance and other integrated financial service strategies, M&A integration, financial services distribution, and competitive market analysis.

Samira A. Kaderali

Samira Kaderali is an associate in Towers Perrin's Chicago office. Ms. Kaderali specializes in health and welfare benefit issues and has a particular expertise in managed care.

François Lafaix

François Lafaix is a principal of Towers Perrin based in Washington, D.C. His experience includes conducting studies focused on market sizing and segmentation, growth strategy, relative cost positioning, market entry, and technology assessment. His most recent client engagements have focused on acquisition and divestiture support services, market penetration strategies, and competitive positioning.

Kenneth T. Ransby

Ken Ransby, a principal and manager of Towers Perrin's San Francisco office, specializes in the design and implementation of total compensation programs that are aligned with the business strategies of the client organization. He has also undertaken numerous assignments related to corporate mergers, acquisitions, and divestitures.

Mr. Ransby has made presentations to the Association of Canadian Pension Management, the Canadian Pension and Benefits Conference, and the Western Pension and Benefits Conference in the United States. He is the author of a chapter called

"Managing Total Compensation in Mergers and Acquisitions" in the book *Out of the Vortex: Finding Order in Merger and Acquisition Chaos*, published in 1999 by the American Compensation Association.

Brent L. Rice

Brent Rice is a former principal in Towers Perrin's Chicago office. He has more than 17 years of experience in management consulting and engineering line management, and has performed a number of organization effectiveness studies for service and manufacturing clients in North America.

Mr. Rice's organization effectiveness experience has involved implementation of shared services organizations, process re-engineering, merger integration, functional transformation, and organization restructuring. His strategy experience includes studies focused on mission formulation, strategy clarification, market and product assessments, strategic planning process, and manufacturing business strategy. The manufacturing studies required the use of manufacturing process mapping and competitive cost analysis.

Jeffrey A. Schmidt

Jeffrey A. Schmidt is currently the Managing Director for Innovation at Towers Perrin. He has nearly 25 years of consulting experience and has served as a member of Towers Perrin's Board of Directors, Management Committee, and Leadership Council.

In addition to implementing mergers, acquisitions, and joint ventures, Mr. Schmidt's consulting assignments have covered business and people strategy, organization design and capabilities, human resource effectiveness, cost reduction/profitability improvement, human capital measurement, and related management issues. He has published articles on a wide range of business performance issues and is frequently quoted in business and professional journals. Mr. Schmidt holds a B.S. in engineering with honors from the U.S. Military Academy and an M.B.A. from Harvard University.

John D. Southwell

John Southwell is a principal in Towers Perrin's Toronto office, where he is a member of the Sales and Marketing consulting practice. He brings both a functional and a general management perspective across a wide range of industries and project types.

In the strategic planning area, Mr. Southwell has in-depth expertise in the development of plans at various levels: corporate, division, department (especially, but not exclusively, in marketing and sales functions), category, and brand. He has been a leader in developing the firm's Organization Effectiveness practice, whereby strategic plans are driven into business process improvement, amended organization roles and structure, people development and training, systems upgrades, and cultural change.

Alfred J. Walker

Mr. Walker is a senior fellow with Towers Perrin located in the Parsippany, New Jersey, office. He is the global thought leader and leading technologist of the Human Resource Administration practice, which specializes in the application of technology to the human resource and management functions and examines new organizational models for more effective and efficient HR service delivery.

Mr. Walker is the author of three books on human resource information systems: *HRIS Development* (Van Nostrand Reinholdt, 1982); *Handbook of HRIS: Reshaping the HR Function With Technology* (McGraw Hill, 1992); and *Web-based HR* (McGraw Hill, 2001).

INDEX

A

AAdvantage program, 48
Acquisition targets
    attrition and retention practices of, 71
    business agreements of, 249–250
    CIC agreements and, 257–266
    data availability limitations by, 95–96
    employee obligations of, 250
    employees' expectations of, 253–255
    evaluating IT position of, 255
    insurance and risk management issues of, 250–251
    liabilities of, 81–82
    litigation issues of, 251–252
    negotiating the deal with, 62–64
    operational capabilities of, 252–253
    ownership structure issues of, 82–83
    preparing the offer to, 60–61
    reviewing environmental issues of, 252
    screening process for, 53–54, *59*
    selection process for, 56–58, 60
    signing letter of intent with, 64
    staffing model and, 69–70
    strategic expectations of, 78–79, 246–247
    tax matters of, 250
    uncovering capabilities of, 75–76
    understanding multiple units of, 85
Actuarial assumptions, 91
Administrative shared services, 165
Agilent Technologies, 223
Allied Corporation, 258
American Airlines, 48
Amoco Corporation, 38, 223
Anchors and road maps, 120
Antitrust requirement issues, 83
AOL-Time Warner, 25, 53, 83, 140
Apple Computers, 49
Application service providers (ASPs), 204

B

Back-room approach, 115
Bankers Trust, 223
Ben & Jerry's, 223
Bendix Corporation, 258
Benefit plans
    alignment process for, 283–284
    case study, 198
    communication issues and, 186–187
    cost savings issues and, 93
    evaluation of, 92, 93, 254–255
    health and welfare, 182–187
    retirement, 187–191
Berkshire Hathaway, 38, 60
BMW (auto maker), 50, 56, 220
Bonus plans, 267
British Telecom, 220

Broad-based stock option plans, 188
Buffet, Warren, 60
Business agreements, review of, 249–250
Business strategy, total rewards program and, 175
Business unit(s)
    alignment with company's strategy, 133
    communication issues and, 142
    HR organization transformation and, 159
    HR professionals and, 133–134
Business-to-business (B2B) e-commerce.
    See E-commerce

C

Call center technologies, 210
Capital markets, 26
Cascade approach for staffing, 115
Cash balance retirement plan, *190*
Cash compensation vs. staffing model, 69–70
Cash flow, 47
Center of Excellence program
    HR organization transformation and, 165
    integration planning and, 109
Change plan, 42–43
    creating team for, 120–121
    development of, 123–124
    HR organization transformation and, 161
    implementation of, 118
    integrated approach to, 118
    management of, 138–140, 243
    outline of, 124
    overview of, 117
    success factors for implementing, 140–146
    tailored to all levels of company, 119
    technology use in, 120
Change-in-control protection (CIC) agreements.
    See CIC agreements
Chase Manhattan, 52
CIC agreements, 70
    design of, 259
    excise taxes and, 262–264
    golden parachute concept of, 257–259
    issues to consider in, 195–196
    principles of, 264–266
    provisions of, 259–266
    severance benefits and, *261*
Cisco Systems, 26, 34, 72, 226
COBRA program, 186
Combined entity
    inability to define direction in, 244
    resolving business location issue of, 88
    screening process for selecting, 54
    total rewards program in, 177–180
Communication
    with all levels of company, 119
    benefits plan administration and, 186–187
    creating team for, 120–121

elements of, 16–17
with employees, 139–140, 148
in global M&As, 239
HR professionals' role in, 17–18
HR technology integration plan and, 211
implementation stage and, 142–143
importance of, 43–44
integrated approach to, 118
lack of, 244
measurement processes and, 148–149
overview of, 117
performance management system and, 193
retirement plan issues and, 191
staffing issues and, 135–136
success factors for, 118
technology use in, 120
Companies. *See* Organization(s)
Comparable transactions, 61
Competitive advantage, sources of, 48–50
Competitors, imitation by, 48
Component (COM) objects, 208
Conglomerate portfolio theory, 24–25
Consolidated Omnibus Budget Reconciliation Act (COBRA), 186
Contribution plans, 92–93
Core team
integration planning and, 108
project organization and, 105
Corporate culture. *See* Cultural issues
Cost savings, 33, 79
benefit plans, 93
health and welfare programs and, 185
retirement plan issues and, 191
Costs associated with terminations, 195
Crocker Bank, 39
Cultural issues
case study, 197
communication issues and, 117–118
cultural integration and, *10*, 86–87
defined, 8
due diligence process and, 79
in global M&As, 223–225, 238
HR professionals and, 14
implementation stage and, 132, 139
incompatibility in, 242
integration planning and, 113, 121–123
knowledge assets issues and, 229
leadership commitment and, 81
M&A failures and, 65
M&A screening process and, 55–56
performance management system and, 192

D

DaimlerChrysler, 29, *30*, 50
Data collection process
for benefits plan alignment, 285–286
in global M&As, 238
of HR organization, 162–163
Data room activity, 95–96
DB plans, 188, *190*, 191

DC plans, 188, 190, 191
Deal team, financial expectations issues and, 103
Deal-making process, 94–97
Deconglomeration, 24
Dedicated team model, 108
Deficit Reduction Act of 1984 (DEFRA), 259
Defined benefit (DB) plans, 188
vs. cash balance retirement plan, *190*
funding considerations for, 191
Defined contribution (DC) plans, 188
features of, 190
funding considerations for, 191
Demographic trends
mergers and acquisitions and, 26
shifting patterns in, 218–219
Deutsche Bank, 223
Deutsche Telekom (DT), 223, 224, 225
Developing countries, population growth in, 218–219
Due diligence stage, 5, 6
businesses with multiple units and, 85
cultural issues and, 86–87
discovering liabilities during, 81–82, 90–93, 249–252
employees' expectations during, 253–255
evaluating IT position during, 84–85, 255
external analysts' role during, 79
gearing up for, 64–65
in global M&As, 237–238
health plan liabilities issues and, 93
HR professionals' role in, 13–15, 70–72, 77, 88–90
identifying key talents during, 85–86
integration process and, 88
issues to consider in, 76
leadership commitment during, 81, 252
M&S functions during, 275, *279*
organizational capabilities issues and, 83–84, 252–253
overview of, 75, 245
ownership structure issues and, 82–83
people issues' analysis during, 84
preparing for, 70–72
resolving business location issue and, 88
termination benefits issues and, 93–94
time frames, *94*
validating price during, 80, 247–249
valuable activities during, *95*
verifying strategic expectations during, 78–79, 246–247
ways to navigate, 94–97
work environment issues and, 87–88

E

Earnings, 31, 34–35
E-commerce
innovation capability issues and, 227
technology impact on, 220
Employee liabilities
benefit plans, 93

health plan, 93
relocation issues, 88
retirement plan, 90–93
termination benefits, 93–94
Employee research
approaches to, 149–151
during integration planning, 123
retention issues and, 148
role in handling difficult issues, 147–148
on work/life programs, 194
Employee retention
HR professionals' role in, 156–157
total rewards model and, 84
Employee(s). *See also* Workforce evolution
benchmark comparisons for salaried, 179, 189
benefits plan issues of, 253–255
commitment during M&As, 130, 138
communication issues and, 142
cultural issues and, *122*
establishing connections with, 139–140
globalization issues and, 238
health and welfare programs for, 182–187
learning and career management for, 193–194
obligations review in M&As, 250
outplacement support for, 137–138
pay programs for, 180–182
perceptions about M&As, 146–147
performance management system for, 191–193
providing anchors and road maps to, 120
relations, status of, 87–88
response to change process, *119*
retention incentives for, 196–197
retirement plan issues of, 187–191
role in implementation stage, 143–146
role in staffing issues, 136–137
total rewards program and, 172–177
transition programs for, 113
work/life programs for, 194–195
Employment, growth in, 222
Enterprise resource planning (ERP) standards, 210
Environmental and related issues, 252
Environmental Protection Agency (EPA), 58
Equity-based rewards, 188
"Escalation of commitment" phenomenon, 63
European Monetary Union, 26, 83, 218
Excise tax, 262, 263
Executive compensation, 195–196
CIC agreements for, 257–266
in global M&As, 238
incentive plans and, 266–268
overview of, 257
Executive Compensation Advisory Services, 258
Executive recruiters, 67
External resources
for communication and change plan, 120–121
due diligence process and, 94–96
effective use of, *132*
employment costs issues and, 174–175
for handling key talents issues, 229
for implementation process, 130–131

F

Federal Communications Commission (FCC), 224
Financial performance, inability to sustain, 241
Financial services industries
benefits plan alignment for, 284–290
mergers and acquisitions in, 26
Financial statements
pro forma, 60
review during due diligence stage, 80, 247–248
Focus group data, 148
Foreign direct investment (FDI), 218
Foreign subsidiaries, 92–93
Function leadership teams, 133–134

G

Gartner Group, 220
GE Capital Services, 68, 72
GlaxoWellcome, 223
Global energy industries, 26–28
Global mergers and acquisitions
benefits integration for, 184
communication issues of, 239
cultural issues of, 223–224, 238
due diligence stage in, 237–238
formula for, 239
HR organization transformation and, 167–168
rise in, 28–29, 68
total rewards program in, 238
Global network model, 109
Globalization
economic expansion and, 222
growth of, 218
implications for M&As and, 222–223
overview of, 217
population growth impact on, 218–219
technology's role in, 219–220
Golden parachute agreements, 257–259

H

Health and welfare programs
administration of, 185–186
case study, 284–290
communication issues and, 186–187
cost comparison of, *184*
design and integration of, 182–184
evaluating liabilities of, 93
funding considerations for, 185
Health care industry, 222
High-price earnings (PE), 26
Hostile takeovers, 25, 63
HR leadership
mandate for, 141–142
role in globalization, 224–226
role in implementation stage, 145, 242
HR organization
administrative shared services and, 165
components of, 157–158
design process of, 160–165
implementation of, 168–169

line managers and, 165–166
outsourcing functions of, 160
program devised by, 158
transformation issues of, 159, 167–168
HR professionals, 6
  benefits plan administration and, 185–186, 283–284
  business units and, 133–134
  communication issues of, 16–18, 213
  employee retention issues of, 56
  important decisions by, 156–157
  innovation capability issues of, 227
  integration process issues of, *15*, 16, 41, 100–101, 110, 124–125, 156
  learning and career management issues of, 193–194
  pay program issues of, 182
  policies and reward program by, 101
  preparatory activities for, 66–68
  programs and plans, 88–89
  risk management perspective and, 39–40
  role in building new organization, 131–132, 134–138
  role in defining change program, 42–43
  role in due diligence stage, 13–15, 70–72, *77*, 79, 237–238
  role in establishing their credibility, 157
  role in handling knowledge assets, 228–230
  role in implementation stage, 16, 127, 140–141
  role in M&As, *12*, 36–39, 233–234
  role in M&S functions, 273–275
  role in people issues analysis, 84
  role in pre-deal stage, 13, 68–70
  role in screening process, 54–56
  skills needed by, 18–21
  technology issues of, 212–213
  uncertainties faced by, 155–156
HR service delivery
  architecture framework for, 208, *209*
  choosing platforms for, 209–210
  components of, 204
  model for, 203–204
  preferred methods of, 204–205
  selecting technologies for, 210–211
HR technology integration plan
  components of, 202–203
  development of, 201–202
  for employees, 166
  factors influencing, 200–201
  IT functions integration and, 212–213
  for managers, 167
  overview of, 199
  possible assumptions related to, 206–207
  principles for, 207–208
  process for, *210*
  purpose of, 199–200
  responsibilities for, 211–212
  scope of, 200
  systems solutions for, 205–206
  user role in implementation of, 211–212

vendors' contracts issues and, 211
web delivery environment for, 211
HTML Access, 210
Human resource professionals. *See* HR professionals
Hybrid approach for staffing, 115

I

Implementation stage, 5–6
  challenges of, 34
  commitment issues and, 138
  communication during, 142–143
  cultural issues and, 132, 139
  due diligence process and, 96–97
  employees' role during, 143–146
  factors for successful, *128*
  of HR organization, 168–169
  HR professionals' role during, 16, 156–157
  leadership's role during, 140–141
  M&S functions during, 277, *281*
  overview of, 127–128
  risks during, 241–244
  roadmap, 128–130
  staffing issues and, 135–136
  time frame, 128
Incentive plans, 266–268
Industrial Marketing Management, 49
Industries
  financial services, 26
  global energy, 26–28
  results of M&As in multiple, 32
  technology, 26
  value of M&A, 27
Information technology. *See also* HR technology integration
  during due diligence stage, 84–85, 255
  employment growth in, 222
  HR organization transformation and, 160
  HR technology integration plan and, 212–213
  impact on innovations, 226–227
  during integration planning, 114
  role in globalization, 219–220
  role in M&As, 25–26
Innovation capability
  impact on M&As, 222–223
  technology impact on, 226–227
Insurance and risk management issues, 250–251
Intangible assets, 49, 52, 68
Integration philosophies/process, 5, *15*, 37
  benefits plan administration and, 185–186
  challenges of, 32–33
  cultural issues and, 122–123
  due diligence process and, 75, 87, 88, 96–97
  elements of, 112–113, 123
  employee research during, 123
  for executive compensation, 195–196
  features of successful, 39–44
  financial expectations issues and, 103
  in global M&As, 239
  for health and welfare benefits, 182–187

HR design process and, 163–164
HR organization transformation and, 159
HR professionals' role in, 16, 100–101, 124–125, 156
influence on project organization, 103–105
for learning and career management, 193
M&As synergies and, 65
for M&S functions, 275–277, *280*
management of, 40–41
master schedule for, 42, 110
organizational capabilities issues and, 83–84
overview of, 99–100
for pay programs, 180–182
for performance management system, 191–193
for retention incentives, 196–197
for retirement plan benefits, 187–191
staffing issues and, 114–117
strategic framework for, 103
types of, 37–39
when to plan, 102
workforce evolution and, 232
for work/life programs, 194–195
Integration team
resourcing, 107–110
typical, *106*
Intellectual property, 249
Interactive voice response solution, 204
Internal rate of return (IRR), 53
Investment(s)
retirement plan issues and, 191
review during due diligence stage, 248–249
IRC section 280G, tax penalties of, 262, 263

J
Java Applets, 210
JDS Uniphase Corporation, 48, 62, 72

K
Key talent
cultural integration and, 86–87
evaluation of, 244
HR professionals' role in retaining, 56, 156–157, 231–232
identification of, 85–86
knowledge assets issues and, 229
loss of, 242–243
retention incentives for, 196–197
Knowledge assets/capital
challenges related to, 228
cultural issues and, 229
defined, 53
HR professionals' role in handling, 228–230
rising importance of, 220–221
Knowledge Earnings, defined, 52

L
Leadership
building new, 157
commitment issues, 81, 252

role in business units' alignment, 133
role in implementation stage, 140–141
teams, 133–134
Learning and career management
HR professionals' role in, 193–194
issues to consider in, 193–194
Letter of intent (LOI), signing, 64
Liabilities
employee, 90–93
evaluation of, 89–90, 249–252
health plan, 93
price-setting issues and, 81–82
Life cycle, mergers and acquisitions, 4–5
Lightweight Directory Access Protocol (LDAP), 210
Line managers, support for, 165–166
Litigation issues, 251–252
Local area network (LAN), 204, 208
Lucent Technologies, 226

M
Management
CIC agreements and, 70–72
coaching to deal with changes, 124
communication issues of, 16–18
cultural issues of, 83–84, 242–243
deal negotiations by, 62–64
employees' concerns about M&As and, 123
handling crisis situation by, 119
leadership commitment and, 81, 252
M&A strategy and, 50–51
overview of, 3
partnership with HR professionals, 37
role in handling employee research, 149–151
role in HR technology integration, 211
role in total rewards program and, 174–175
selection, 40
staffing issues of, 136–137
strategy clarification issues of, 41
termination issues of, 195
Marketing and sales functions
integration process for, 275–277
issues to consider in, 270–271
overview of, 269–270
roles for, 271–275
Martin Marietta Corporation, 258
Master schedule, development of, 110
Measurement processes
communication issues and, 148–149
employees' perceptions about M&As and, 146–147
financial measures and, 147
value of, 147–151
Mercer Management Consulting study, 31
Mergers and acquisitions. *See also* Global mergers and acquisitions; Leadership; Management
building new organization after, 131–132
business agreements review and, 249–250
challenges to successful implementation of, 33–34

Index ■ 299

CIC agreements in, 257–266
communication issues of, 244
cultural issues of, 242–243
downside risks in, 96–97
economics of, 34–36, 61–62
employee expectations issues of, 253–255
employee obligations issues of, 250
employees' role in, 130, 138, 143–146
environmental issues of, 252
executive incentive plans in, 266–268
external analysts' role in, 79
factors favoring, 29–30
in financial services, 26
future of, 217–218
in global energy, 26–28
history of, 23–26
inability to manage change in, 243
innovations impact on, 222–223
insurance and risk management issues of, 250–251
key talent loss in, 242–243
life cycle, 4–5
litigation issues of, 251–252
managing impact of, 21
marketing and sales functions in, 271–275
measurement processes in, 146–151
operational capabilities in, 252–253
overview of, 3–4
pre-deal stage as key element of, 73
preparing the offer for, 60–61
productivity loss in, 241
reasons for, 47–53
as a replicable process, 72–73
results of, 31–33
slow decision making issues of, 243–244
staffing opportunities in, 117
in technology industry, 28
technology issues of, 255
top ten pitfalls in, 33
total rewards program and, 175–176, 197–198
worldwide, 24
Mergers and acquisitions success
executive compensation issues for, 195–196
HR professionals' role in, 36–39
knowledge assets' importance to, 221
obstacles to achieving, 7–12
origins of, 65–73
resourcing models for, 107, 108–110
stakeholders' perceptions of, 102
work/life programs for, 194–195
Mergers and acquisitions synergies, 7–8
examples, 36
importance of, 51
integration process and, 65
performance incentives and, 44
screening process and, 56–57
total rewards program and, 175
Mobile assets. See Knowledge assets/capital
Mobilizing Invisible Assets, 49

Modern Portfolio Theory, 24
Multinational enterprises (MNEs), 218

N
National Association of Colleges and Employers, 230
National Semiconductor Corporation, 219
Net present value (NPV), 35, 37
Nondisclosure agreement (NDA), 62
Nortel Network, 226

O
Obstacles to achieving successful M&A, 7–12
Occupational Safety and Health Administration (OSHA), 58
Oligopolies, 24
Operational capabilities, verifying, 252–253
Operational data store (ODS), 212
Oracle, 206
Organic growth, 35, 50–51
Organizational capabilities
due diligence stage and, 83–84
globalization and, 222–223
HR design process and, 163–164
Organization(s)
architecture, 113–114
building new, 131–132
creating high-level, 272–273
cultural issues of, 9–10, 87, *122*
design, 134–135
executive compensation issues of, 195–196
factors affecting future business of, 217–218
health and welfare programs in, 182–187
HR organization transformation and, 167–168
HR professionals' role in, 65, 68–70
innovation capability issues of, 227
knowledge assets' importance in, 221
learning and career management in, 193–194
pay programs in, 180–182
performance management system in, 191–193
research methods used by, 149–151
retirement plan programs in, 187–191
review valuations of, 249
staffing implementation for, 135–136
total rewards program and, 177–180
work/life programs in, 194–195
Outplacement support, 137–138
Outside expertise. See External resources
Ownership structure issues, 82–83

P
Past service credits, 188
Pay programs
analysis of, 181–182
case study, 198
integration of, 180–181
inventory of, *181*
Pay-related issues, 89–90
People issues. See also Cultural issues

analysis by HR professionals, 68–70
analysis during due diligence stage, 84
assessment of, 112
PeopleSoft, 206, 208, 211
Performance expectations, 266–268
Performance management (PM) system
    goals of, 192
    issues to consider in, 192–193
    learning and career management and, 193–194
    overview of, 191–192
Performance measurement issues, 42
Pfizer, 230
Policies and reward program, 101
Population growth
    globalization and, 224
    shifting patterns in, 218–219
Positive returns in M&As, 31–32
Post-deal stage, 34–35
Postmortems after deal closure, 68
Potential partners. *See* Acquisition targets
Pre-deal stage, 4, 6
    growth requirements during, 34–35
    HR professionals' role in, 13, 66–70
    as key element for M&As, 73
    M&S functions during, 275, *278*
    serial acquirers and, 72–73
    steps in, 53–63
Price-setting issues
    due diligence process and, 80, 247–249
    liabilities and, 81–82
Productivity issues, 241
Profits, price-setting issues and, 80
Project managers, 108
Project organization/coordination
    approach to, 112
    elements of, 105
    integration planning influence on, 103–105
    project office and, 105–106
Property and leases, verifying, 248

Q
Quaker Oats Company, 29, 69

R
Regulatory requirement issues
    globalization and, 224
    ownership structure issues and, 82–83
Resourcing models, 107, 108–110
Retention issues
    employee research and, 148
    HR professionals' role in, 56, 156–157, 231–232
    incentives for key talent and, 196–197
    loss of key talent and, 242–243
    total rewards model and, 84
    workforce evolution and, 230
Retirement plan issues
    administration of, 191
    communication issues and, 191
    comparison of, *189*
    design and integration of, 187–188, 190
    evaluation of, 90–93
    funding considerations for, 191
Revenues, increasing shareholder value by growing, 47
Rewards program integration
    establishing, 171–172
    overview of, 171
Risk management perspective, 39–40

S
SDL Incorporated, 48, 62
Seagram Company, Ltd., The, 79
Securities and Exchange Commission, 58
Security firewalls, 210
Server hardware, 210
Severance compensation, 195, *261*, 262
Shareholder value
    CIC agreements and, 257
    competitive advantages and, 48–50
    defined, 47
    knowledge assets and, 221
    mergers and acquisitions and, 52, 61–62
    ways to increase, 47–48
SHRM Foundation
    survey of HR executives, 32
    survey on due diligence stage, 76
    survey on due diligence time frames, 94
    survey on HR programs, 89
    survey on integration philosophy, 40
    survey on staffing issues, 114
Slow decision making issues, 243–244
SmithKline Beecham, 223, 242
Software platforms, 210
Staffing model, 69–70
Staffing process
    approaches to, 114–116
    communication issues and, 136
    employees' role in, 136–137
    implementation of, 135–136
    managers' role in, 137
    opportunities, 117
    outplacement support for, 137–138
    selection process, 116
    training people involved in, 137
Stakeholder expectations
    communication issues and, 43–44
    performance measurement issues and, 42
Steering team, 105
Stock options, 188, 195–196
Stock-based incentives, 267
Strategic expectations, verifying, 78–79, 246–247
Strategic people management, 3, 6, 21, 165
Subject matter experts (SMEs), 108
Success, M&A, obstacles to achieving, 7–12
Successful companies
    capability level of, 20
    communication planning by, 18
SWAT team model, 108
Synergy Trap, The, 62

T

Tangible assets, 52
Tax gross-up payments, 264–265
Tax matters, review of, 250
Technology. *See* HR technology integration; Information technology
Termination(s)
    benefits, 93–94
    costs related to, 195
    of executives, 261–262
3Com, 226
Time constraints issues, due diligence process and, 94–95
Total rewards program
    allocation of dollars in, 177, *178*
    benchmark comparisons for, *179*
    case study, 197–198
    current vs. deferred, *178*
    development of, 176–177, 180
    employee retention issues and, 84
    executive compensation, 195–196
    framework, 172–175
    in global M&As, 238
    health and welfare programs, 182–187
    implementation stage and, 128, 132
    learning and career management, 193–194
    opportunity to make changes in, 175–176
    pay programs, 180–182
    performance management system, 191–193
    perspective on, 171
    quadrant chart, *172*
    retention incentives, 196–197
    retirement plans, 187–191
    revising, 175
    timetable for, 180
    work/life programs, 194–195
Towers Perrin
    survey of HR executives, 32
    survey on CIC agreements, 259, 264
    survey on due diligence stage, 76
    survey on due diligence time frames, 94
    survey on HR programs, 89
    survey on integration philosophy, 40
    survey on staffing issues, 114
Turnover issues, 148
280G excise tax, 262, 263

U

Universal Music, 79
Universal Pictures, 79
Unsuccessful companies, communication issues and, 18

V

Vivendi, 79
Vodafone Airtouch, 223
VoiceStream, 223, 225
Volkswagen AG, 50

W

Warner-Lambert, 230
Web-based communications, 160
Weighted average cost of capital (WACC), 53
Wells Fargo, 39
WinTel PC platform, 49
Work environment issues
    case study, 198
    consideration of, 87–88
Work sample test, 116
Workforce evolution
    economic expansion and, 221–222
    planning for, 230–232
Work/life programs
    determining types of, 194
    issues to consider in, 194–195